To Barbara

Thought you might like a copy to keep and re-read.
Your positive comments were appreciated
Paul

MY GENERATION:

HOW WE TRASHED OUR INHERITANCE

Paul Laxton

Authors online

An Authors OnLine Book

British Library Cataloguing Publication Data.
A catalogue record for this book is available from the British Library

ISBN 978-0-7552-1673-4

Authors OnLine Ltd
19 The Cinques
Gamlingay, Sandy
Bedfordshire SG19 3NU
England

This book is also available in e-book format, details of which are available at www.authorsonline.co.uk

ABOUT THE AUTHOR

Paul Laxton was born in Blackburn, Lancashire, in 1952. He was educated at St Mary's College, then a Roman Catholic direct grant Grammar School for boys in the town. In 1979 he obtained a Bachelor of Education (Upper Second Class Honours) in History and Education from the University of Keele. After teaching for five years in high schools in Kings Lynn and Newcastle-Under-Lyme he changed career and joined the prison service as a uniformed officer in 1984. The author served at nine different jails, rising to hold posts as Deputy Governor at Dover, Ford and Lewes prisons, along with stints in operational training and headquarters before retiring in 2010. An active trade unionist he served on the National Executive Committee of the Prison Governors Association from 2007 until his retirement. In 2013 he published his first book, "26 Years Behind Bars: The Recollections of a Prison Governor," which was crammed with fascinating anecdotes and penetrating insights into the English criminal justice system as well as exposing the suffocating nature of public sector bureaucracy.

In retirement he lives with his wife in West Yorkshire.

ACKNOWLEDGEMENTS

My good lady wife Lennie, (short for Leonore) for tolerating the endless hours I have been secluded in my study well away from my share of domestic chores.

My good friend Dave Robins for the time he spent reading and improving the first draft and for his good advice on some of the more controversial content.

My former colleagues in the Prison Governors Association who kept reminding me that I had promised to write this book once retired.

CONTENTS

CHAPTER 1

INTRODUCTION

This book does not claim to be a researched work of history, nor is it an autobiography or a memoir, although personal experience is invoked at intervals to illustrate the narrative from the perspective of a sometimes participant observer. It can be more accurately described as a rant or a polemic. If at times the language is vitriolic, I make no apology for that as I am genuinely angry as well as sad about how the educated elite of My Generation, the baby boomers, have transformed our country for the worse. I am sad given that mine was an optimistic generation and even more so because there was so much to do to unify our stratified society. We were a generation which grew up in an era of full employment and full stomachs. We were a generation that seized the personal and sexual freedoms that went hand in hand with economic freedom, scientific advance and the sort of opportunities via education, which were a distant dream for our parents. As a generation, we grew up under the spectre of nuclear annihilation and as such we sought to abolish war. As a generation we questioned everything and resented the fact that our country was run by a public school educated establishment that remained firmly in the saddle despite a cataclysmic world war, universal suffrage and death duties. My Generation preached its contempt for elitism. Our country was fusty and old fashioned; My Generation would make it modern and up to date, and to do so it would bring down class barriers. We saw organised religion as part of that establishment and adopted atheism or agnosticism. My Generation was not concerned only with Britain, it had an international perspective. My Generation railed against third world poverty and called for the redistribution of wealth. My Generation saw the EEC as a barrier to socialism. Colonialism and imperialism were to be replaced by the self determination of free peoples. As such it supported liberation movements. My Generation loved American Rock and Roll music, but loathed America for its militarism and its support for authoritarian regimes, whilst at the same time preaching freedom and democracy. My Generation stood for equality and stood against discrimination against ethnic minorities, women and homosexuals. My Generation hated apartheid in South Africa with an all consuming passion. Nearer home, My Generation regarded Unionist dominated Ulster as a near fascist state held together by brutal, partisan and unaccountable policing.

This book charts, from a personal perspective, what actually came to pass. My Generation abandoned organised religion and publicly professed faith, but forgot that a cohesive largely secular society needs an unambiguous moral code in which the concept of right and wrong is understood and conveyed and commands general respect, even amongst those who routinely breach it. Furthermore, that stricture must also apply to the elite. My Generation has actually redistributed wealth upwards to the greedy bankers and FTSE 100 executives. My Generation in power handed on to the coalition over 900,000 young people between the ages of 16-24 unemployed. My Generation in power restricted opportunity rather than expanded it. My Generation in power embraced feminism and the cult of the fatherless family as the way forward and still refuses to acknowledge the social catastrophe that ensued. My Generation, therefore, replaced the old class system and instead instituted a society that has a semi-permanent, ghetto dwelling, welfare supported underclass that serves only to reproduce itself and ensure that our prisons have a regular supply of customers. My Generation dropped its opposition to nuclear weapons, embraced American war aims, and invaded sovereign nations that only posed any threat at all to British citizens because of our slavish support of the USA. My Generation in power connived at torture by the American military machine and continued to lie about it when caught.

The sad truth is that My Generation reduced our collective freedoms rather than enhanced them. My Generation preached self-determination very selectively, and certainly not for our own country. My Generation in power not only embraced the EEC, it surrendered yet more sovereignty and the right to determine our own affairs to this bureaucratic Soviet style monster. My Generation abandoned control of our borders and imported the world's poor, but remained in denial when confronted with the consequences. Racial and communal strife were actually fuelled as people competed for scarce resources. My Generation in office enhanced the power of vocal and unrepresentative minorities at the expense of the majority, forgetting that positive discrimination equals reverse discrimination. My Generation bequeathed a police state with the full panoply of emergency powers, a developing DNA database, and a denunciation and surveillance culture that could have been imported from any country behind the Berlin Wall. My Generation appeared to have taken no cognisance of the huge political and historical significance of its demolition in 1989, the pent up yearning for freedom that was finally released. My Generation instead sought to introduce ID cards that would have effectively replicated the South African pass laws of the apartheid era and failed to appreciate the irony. Lastly, My Generation replaced the old establishment with itself as the new elite that conspires to suffocate democracy and ensure that its values dominate whatever the outcome of elections. Our political system now more resembles the corrupt and self-perpetuating circle of aristocrats that ruled our country in the 18th century, than it does any supposedly modern state.

It is fair to say that the educated elite of My Generation was mainly on the left of the political spectrum and therefore the average Daily Mail and Daily Telegraph reader will simply take the view that this book charts the failure of socialism. Built into that argument is an assumption that something that could be called socialism was actually pursued by My Generation in power. Chapter 8 will dispute that premise. However, this book is not an account of the sort of left to right journey undertaken by luminaries as diverse as Woodrow Wyatt, Paul Johnson or Rhodes Boyson, the last of whom was a known supporter of ID Cards. In fact, I don't believe that I have made the journey from left to right, insofar as the term has any real meaning in 2013. Like most of the educated members of My Generation in the early 1980s I was a suit and tie wearing professional making my way in the world. Long hair and flared jeans had been discarded and could be seen only on old photographs. At that time Labour in opposition was suffering from travails and splits that almost rent the party asunder. The convulsions that followed the electoral defeat of 1979 were far greater and more damaging to Labour as a potential party of government than those that followed the narrow defeat of 1951, an election in which Labour actually outpolled the Tories in total votes cast.

My personal position thirty years ago was broadly on the left of the party. I looked back fondly to the 1945-51 Labour government, but recognised that the world had changed and that there were new items on the agenda. I stood for the end of apartheid in South Africa and the eradication of racism at home. I supported the peaceful reunification of Ireland. I was opposed to the installation of Cruise Missiles, supported the plan for coal as a major plank of maintaining our country's energy needs, and believed that Britain should withdraw from the Common Market, as it was then called. I was a confirmed unilateralist, although I did not join CND. Indeed, I took what I believed to be the logical position in relation to nuclear weapons and supported withdrawal from NATO which was, and still is, dominated by the USA. I could see no logic in a moral position that said that Britain should give up nuclear weapons but at the same time shelter under the American nuclear umbrella. It is one of the great ironies of our post war history that we acquired our own nuclear weapons only because in 1962 President Kennedy overruled his advisors and agreed to sell Polaris to the government of Harold McMillan. Had McMillan been rebuffed, short of continuing to try and develop our own nuclear weapons at ruinous expense, this would have been our position. Of course one can only speculate about its potential effect on the subsequent history of Anglo-American relations. Perhaps also successive governments would have got the message that victory in World War II finished us as a great power rather than confirmed it. All weapons kill be they conventional, biological or nuclear. The issue is only one of scale. The difference was that the possession of nuclear weapons, combined with our role as the 51st state of the USA, made us an alternative target in the event of thermo-nuclear war. It is why the USA quickly changed its view about the value of the British deterrent. I stress I had no illusions about the authoritarian and militaristic nature of the USSR or any that it constituted a socialist paradise, but I did not accept the propaganda that we were fed that the Russians were coming and only the bomb stood between us and invasion. However I was not a pacifist. I supported credible defence and cheered alongside every other good citizen when the Falklands were swiftly liberated from Argentine tyranny.

With regard to the Labour party, I supported the demand for greater internal democracy, although again I had no illusions that there were parasitic groups such as the Militant Tendency for whom greater internal democracy was an opportunity to seize control of the most passive constituency parties, dominated as they were by unrepresentative cliques who had long since purged themselves of socialism. I cannot pretend that this did not come to pass in the most moribund local parties. I therefore supported Neil Kinnock in his quest to eradicate the cancer of Militant. I believe that most Labour voters and activists supported greater internal democracy for the right reasons, rather than to advance the cause of infiltrators. No doubt we would have been described as "useful idiots". With regard to the economy, I supported nationalisation of the commanding heights within a mixed economy where capitalism operated within a framework of reference, rather than determining the framework of reference. I saw my position as consistent with my reverence for the Attlee administration which achieved so much in facing the huge challenge of post war reconstruction. I grew to hate the "greed is good" society that burst open like a septic wound after the deregulation of the City in 1986. I was a committed trade unionist and a low key patriot, (perhaps too low key to be noticed) having no difficulty reconciling that position with my belief in British neutralism. Like most Labour supporters from working class backgrounds, I was less interested in environmentalism, feminism and gay rights. Despite not considering myself to be a Marxist, I took the classic Marxist position that these were issues subordinate to those of class and economic organisation. I was opposed to the death penalty, but did not believe that my moral sensibilities had the right to prevail over democracy in sovereign states. I retained my dislike of organised religion. The passing of time had not dimmed the memory of the tyranny of The Sisters of the Passion from which between the ages of five and eleven there had been no escape. Alastair Campbell's famous remark about the Blair government, uttered despite his political master's ostentatious religiosity, "We don't do God," would still resonate with me more than 30 years after I had left primary school. Thus, for the most part, I stood on the conventional left. I was further left on the issue of NATO, less to the left regarding affiliation to the Labour party, but in most respects easily recognisable to political friend and foe alike. Only my support for Israel, or more accurately my ability to see that the classic left position supporting the Palestinian Liberation Organisation in reality equalled the eradication of an Israeli state, would have attracted significantly adverse attention from those otherwise singing from the same hymn sheet.

Thirty years on I have inevitably changed and made some necessary accommodations with reality, but my core beliefs remain and with that a substantial part of the agenda. Going back over the previous two paragraphs, apartheid in South Africa and cruise missiles on our soil mercifully have gone. Ireland remains divided, but there is peace and the appetite for an armed solution is thankfully diminished. I still believe Ireland should be united, but see no reason to get animated given that the Republic has renounced its claim to the six counties. The coal industry is virtually dead, mortally wounded by Thatcherism with the coup de grace administered by environmentalists and climate change fanatics. The Russian bear is no longer a military threat to our legitimate interests (if indeed it ever was), but instead the USA embroils our country in Iraq, Afghanistan and potentially Iran exposing us to the worst excesses of Islamist terrorism. As a country we have been denied the peace dividend due to us from the fall of the Berlin Wall. My support for the existence of a viable state of Israel remains steadfast, but it is immoral to pretend that the Palestinians do not themselves have a claim to statehood. The question is where that state should be. In 1982 I became a home owner for the first time. Home ownership forces you to make accommodation with capitalism, not least because you are accumulating your own capital. The relationship between the acquisition of property and the retention of a left wing perspective is discussed in Chapter 14. Nevertheless, I don't believe it represents a quantum shift from the position I outlined in the previous paragraph. I am opposed to discrimination on the basis of race just as I was 30 years ago and am content that discrimination on the grounds of sexuality, gender and age, where demonstrably irrelevant, is wrong and has also been rendered unlawful. This is a position now accepted by most Conservatives. I have made no accommodation with my opposition to British membership of the EU and could only see myself moderating this position if the UK were to repudiate the federal nature of the EU, repatriate powers that are legitimately the prerogative of the nation state, and recover our fishing grounds, all this being confirmed via referendum. I do not intend to linger long gazing from my window in search of flying pigs.

The central thesis of this book is that My Generation when it attained power, some of which was attained whilst the Thatcher/Major administrations were in office, but principally after 1997, wasted and more than that, abused that power and thus the opportunity to make our country a better place for the majority of its citizens, and similarly abused and wasted the opportunity to make the UK a force for good in the world. The UK became less democratic and more authoritarian, its citizens as a whole much less free as basic liberties of innocence until guilt be proved, of speech and of association came under relentless fire. It is fair to say that for many years I was naive about the agenda of My Generation until the scales steadily fell from my eyes, and on that basis the elite have not merely wasted the opportunity to transform Britain for the better, but rather have deliberately transformed it in their own image, and therefore the abuses of power to which I refer in this book are not the product of reacting to newspaper headlines, a lack of understanding of our history, and a failure to have any coherent system of beliefs to replace the economic socialism of the parliamentary left that collapsed under the ascendancy of Thatcherism, but instead the product of an ideology that has its roots in Marxist-Leninism, which then abandoned the central tenet that revolution must come from the working class. The problem for those socialists who embraced Marx was that the working class, despite the opportunities provided by pre-first world war industrial unrest, the General Strike of 1926, and the Great Depression of the 1930s, only very fleetingly appeared revolutionary. The problem was replicated across the other industrialised countries, where governments either survived or lapsed into fascist dictatorship. Only Russia, which barely merited the description of industrialised, having a significant proletariat in only Moscow and Petrograd, its two largest cities, succumbed. Revolutionary socialists were faced with a conundrum – how does a revolution take place in the absence of revolutionary consciousness? The bridge to post Marxist thinkers was provided by Lenin who conceptualised the elite that would protect and expand revolutionary gains, and eliminate counter revolutionaries.

The answers to the conundrum were provided by under the radar thinkers like Gramsci and Marcuse. The former advocated the subversion of the principal institutions that underpinned the state; typically the universities, the main or established church, the state broadcaster, the police, the judiciary, and of course the political parties of the constitutional left. The latter stressed the importance of controlling language thus controlling the limits of acceptable discourse. One of the greatest ironies of our time is that the subversion of the Church of England accelerated under the most outwardly religious prime minister of my lifetime, and continued apace under his successor who was himself the son of a clergyman. On this basis New Labour is not a bland SDP lite, vaguely left of centre political party purged once and for all of socialism, but the principle vehicle of a revolutionary project. Lenin also spoke of "useful idiots" and Tony Blair, a man who carried almost no socialist ideological baggage, was the perfect front man. I am at a loss to fit Mr Blair's foreign policy adventures into this intellectual framework, but it is much less difficult with the politically correct domestic agenda.

Chapter 4 deals with the student movement of the late '60s and 1970s as I remember it. I cannot recall earnest discussions amongst the fractious and faction prone left about Gramsci and Marcuse largely because student revolutionaries had not yet abandoned the working class, yet it is the central strategy of these two thinkers that is the midwife of the politically correct society that is described in detail in this book. I am therefore unable to trace for the reader the precise points at which the future movers and shakers abandoned Marx, crossed the bridge provided by Lenin, and chose the route to a revolution carried out by an elite subverting institutions and appropriating language rather than a mass movement reaching the necessary state of consciousness, and then overthrowing the government using its industrial might. This was after all the period of stagflation and the high point of post war trade union militancy in defence of jobs and living standards, a militancy that would only end with the defeat of the miners' strike in 1985. It may be that the politically correct agenda, albeit for many a subsidiary one, which had become fashionable among student leaders, evolved over time as the former student revolutionaries sought to make their way in society, learning their lessons from failure in the industrial arena and being emboldened by success outside of it. It should be remembered that Mrs Thatcher's neo-Liberal economic revolutionaries also initially proceeded with caution and developed their agenda on experience as much as ideology. Either way, there is a seminal academic work out there waiting to be written on this subject. I lay claims only to have seen the student revolutionaries of My Generation at work in their environment, not to having predicted the unhappy future that came to pass.

If this book metaphorically pokes some readers with a stick to make them challenge their own assumptions and to evaluate for themselves the beliefs that have been foisted on their consciousness, then I will have succeeded. If this book challenges readers whose natural perspective is from the right of politics to abandon what I believe is essentially lazy thinking, either that socialism was abolished by Mr Blair or more likely that political correctness and liberal authoritarianism are simply updated versions of an old socialist creed that seeks to enslave us, then I will have succeeded. I would want those readers to consider more broadly what socialism as a progressive ideology should be about, rather than what luminaries such as the late C.A.R. Crosland or Harriet Harman say it is about and rather than what the perversions of post Marxist writers say it is about. Those readers might wish to go straight to Chapter 8. As for those readers who cannot be won over from their politically correct thought processes, unlike you I respect and unhesitatingly defend your right to disagree and to say so freely in open forum without fear of sanction. Finally, Chapter 20 aims to plot an idealistic and practical way forward that we may not live to see. It is one thing to offer a critique, but without a program it is simply a negative analysis. Unsurprisingly, the way forward is to re-energise our democracy and force parliament to share sovereignty with the people on a generous basis to counter the pretensions of the self-aggrandising political elite. Democracy is a journey rather than a destination.

PART ONE:

PROLOGUE TO POWER

CHAPTER 2

1 MAY 1997 – THE END OF A LONG DARK NIGHT

Probably the best account of that famous night is contained in the final chapter of John O'Farrell's book, "Things Can Only Get Better", subtitled "Eighteen Miserable Years in the Life of a Labour Supporter", in which O'Farrell gives his own highly individual take on the electoral wilderness years suffered by the party. "Things can only get better", was New Labour's campaign theme tune.

At the time I was living in Milton Keynes and voted in the South West constituency. The 1992 election in South West had seen the Tories victorious by 4,687 votes. The sitting MP was Barry Legg, a former member of Westminster Council, and a key ally of its former leader, Dame Shirley Porter. She was ordered to pay a massive surcharge as a result of being caught out by the District Auditor attempting to gerrymander council contests by selling off local authority housing to Tory supporters. After a prolonged legal battle, the House of Lords upheld the adjudication of the District Auditor. In 2003 Porter was stripped of her Dame-hood, awarded in 1991 for services to local government (!!!) and finally in the following year, 17 years after the scandal began, she negotiated a settlement of the surcharge at a figure of around £12 million. Unlike Labour's Phil Woolas in 2010, she was not cut adrift by her party when the scandal began. For all committed Labour supporters therefore, Barry Legg was deemed guilty by association and consequently Milton Keynes South West was seen as a key battleground against Tory sleaze.

The defeated Labour candidate in 1992 had been the Preston born Labour leader of the city council, Kevin Wilson. His replacement as candidate by Phyllis Starkey, as a consequence of an all women short list, was a matter of personal regret to me, as we had been friends more than 20 years previously when I was a fresher and he was President of the Students' Union at Madeley College of Education, a post which I would also be elected to, before embarking on a rather shorter teaching career. I met Phyllis Starkey once when given the task of escorting her around Woodhill prison. She had my vote without hesitation, but I can't help but feel that my fellow Lancastrian would have made a real mark. The subsequent achievements, or more accurately the lack of them, of the female members of the 1997 intake merely serves to underline the fact that undermining the meritocratic principle only results in mediocrity. 101 female Labour MPs were elected in 1997, compared to 13 Conservatives. 65 were new to the House, 35 of who benefited from all women shortlists. Of the three from the 1997 intake who made it to the cabinet, only Yvette Cooper can be considered a success. Indeed, she is the only one of the three who remains in the House of Commons. It is a pretty poor return for flagship social engineering.

Ever since 1970, when I was still just too young to vote, I had sat up on election night with both solid and liquid refreshment and enjoyed, or more usually endured the unfolding drama of election night on the BBC. No-one does it better. I remember the delight of February 1974, and the demise of Edward Heath, more so because it was unexpected and also because I could expect an end to the three day week. I also remember the despair of 1992. At the time I was living in Bedford, and assisted with "knocking up" of voters in a seat not won by Labour since 1966. It was a beautiful April day and, sadly, the nagging feeling that victory was ebbing away was confirmed by the early results. 1997 was always going to be different, but the scale of the victory was seismic. The first glimmers of the dawn had come in September 1992. On what is known as "Black Wednesday", the Tories undeserved reputation for economic competence was exploded. All they could now do was cling to office and hope that Labour would again falter with the winning line in sight. Instead it got worse for the government. The Conservatives ripped themselves to pieces over Europe and became the party of arrogance and sleaze. In 1995 "The Sun" deserted the Conservatives. Before then the Tory press had already started to give John Major personally, and his government, the sort of stick they normally saved for Labour. For me, and no doubt many other voters, it was almost refreshing to see the bile and vituperation directed elsewhere, even if it did not quite exorcise the ghost of the three previous elections, where it had clearly become impossible for Labour to get a fair hearing in the Tory press or the cowed BBC. The defection of "The Sun" did something to even up the odds. John Major limped on until the last permissible date for an election like Mr Micawber, hoping something would turn up, making his ill-fated government the only one since the passing of the Quinquennial Act in 1911, except when suspended due to the exigencies of war, to hold office for every single day of its term. The hapless Mr Major was never able to find a window of opportunity.

The opinion polls had predicted not only a Labour victory, but also the margin. After the embarrassments of the two previous elections, the BBC exit poll redeemed the corporation's reputation. Despite the fact the opinion polls had given Labour a huge lead continuously since "Black Wednesday", the party hierarchy were cautious. In 1966, the polls had predicted a Labour landslide. As it was, a majority of 96 was still a substantial achievement. In 1970, all bar one late poll had predicted a Labour victory. Only Edward Heath, the Conservative leader, truly believed that the Tories would win. In October 1974, the polls had predicted a working majority for Harold Wilson. Instead Labour had a majority of just 3. Fast forwarding to 1987, the BBC exit poll predicted an overall Conservative majority of just 26, a result Labour supporters would have died for. Instead Mrs Thatcher's majority was 102. In 1992, things were a little different, in that polls did show a slow drift back to the Conservative incumbents during the campaign. On the day a hung parliament was predicted, with the Tories as the largest single party. Instead Mr Major had a majority of 21, which on the basis of the share of the vote, should have been larger. Only Labour's better performance in key marginal seats, and perhaps the first evidence of tactical voting in England (but not Scotland at this election), propelled them to a position where Labour could believe that "one more heave" would see them return to power. A redistribution of seats gave Mr Major a notional majority of 50 to defend at the next election, but was little consolation as a series of by-election defeats and defections led to a minority government, forced to limp on until the inevitable General Election put it out of its misery.

Thus, there were valid historical reasons to be cautious and not underestimate innate conservatism amongst the electorate. The electorate had also changed. The cull of manufacturing had reduced the manual working class to just less than half the electorate, as opposed to around two thirds in 1970. The colour of your collar no longer necessarily defined your class. Labour could not be sure that its new found appeal to those who had been upwardly mobile during the Thatcher and Major years, would not evaporate when it came to marking the ballot paper. "Mondeo Man" and "Worcester Woman" could not be considered seduced until consummation was confirmed by the electoral equivalent of hanging a bloodied sheet out of the window. At roughly the same time as New Labour was repositioning itself towards the centre, Liberal Democrat leader Paddy Ashdown was abandoning the policy of equidistance, and moving his party towards Labour. Both parties had every reason to believe that a hung parliament could result from the next election, with a Lib-Lab coalition the only viable majority. For Paddy Ashdown, this was the result that might finally deliver the holy grail of proportional representation and seats at the cabinet table. For the new Labour leader, desperate to cast off any lingering hard left image and content to make his accommodation with social democracy, proportional representation was starting to look attractive, as perhaps the only means of keeping the Tories out of power and re-aligning the non-socialist left. Obviously much of this had to be whispered rather than spoken of out loud. As the campaign came to a close, Mr Blair himself is reputed to have felt that Labour would achieve a majority of 60.

No doubt the Conservatives would have settled for that as it would have left open the possibility of bouncing back at the next election. Looking back, the Tories seemed to be in complete denial about the bloodbath they were facing. They clung tenaciously to the proven tendency of the opinion polls to overestimate Labour support. It was apparent fairly quickly that nothing would save the Tories from defeat, only the margin was at issue. As I recall, the very earliest results in places like Sunderland were slightly misleading, because of lower turnouts. I think I became conscious that a landslide was really going to happen when Gisela Stuart captured Birmingham Edgbaston. This seat was once held by Neville Chamberlain, former Tory Prime Minister, and not even the opprobrium attached to his name by the policy of appeasement of Hitler would cost the Tories the seat in 1945. This was a seat never before won by Labour. In 1983, Labour had actually been third behind the Social Democrats. The swing of around 10% was in line with the national average. It was not the most sensational swing of the night, but it was the moment Labour dared to dream the impossible dream. The Conservatives now knew what was happening. Edwina Currie, interviewed on the BBC made no secret of her expectations in her Derbyshire South constituency. Admitting that the game was up, Mrs Currie told the interviewer that she expected to lose by 10,000. In the end the margin was 13,967.

Edwina Currie had no hope of successfully defending a majority of four and a half thousand. However, a 10,000 majority was no guarantee of a return to the house either. Labour's first and second most unexpected victories came in Harrow West and Hastings and Rye respectively with swings in excess of 16%. The most public Tory humiliation of the night came in Enfield Southgate, the supposedly safe seat of Michael Portillo, the third least likely of Labour's 1997 victories. Back in the 1990s Mr Portillo symbolised almost all that was loathed about the Tories. He was perceived as a man of overweening ambition, topped only by hubris. At this time he was an advocate of further privatisation and a devotee of market economics. He was the tallest of tall poppies and all those who stayed awake long enough for his declaration savoured the moment like no other. If the feeling was not orgasmic, it was certainly the climax of the night. Defeat changed him for the better and he would be back. Although Michael Portillo's opponent, Stephen Twigg, was not the only openly gay candidate standing, his wholly unexpected election marked a new maturity in the electorate towards sexual orientation, something which, in government, New Labour failed to take on board. During the night eight cabinet ministers would fall. There was something deeply pleasurable about watching the smug arrogance wiped from Tory faces. The electorate was showing them the same contempt that the Tories had developed for opponents who they believed were permanent losers. Former Headmaster and editor of "The Black Papers in Education", Sir Rhodes Boyson, received six of the best from the electorate in Brent North where there was a swing of over 13%. 23 years of incumbency counted for nothing. Even Sir Edward Heath found his majority of over 18,000 slashed to one of 3,569, a swing of 14%. Perhaps the most sensational result of all was in the new constituency of Castle Point, which contained the second highest percentage of owner occupiers in the land. New Labour had not merely come into an unexpected windfall, it had helped itself to the Tories' electoral capital as well.

As the night wore on, the carnage continued. Like many other voters active and passive, I kept looking at the screen in disbelief. Labour took both seats in Blackpool for the first time ever. Chester and Worcester also got their first Labour MPs. Both Luton seats were won, which sent another bête noir, John Carlisle, into obscurity. In the same part of the world, even St Albans was captured. On the south coast, Labour added all three Brighton and Hove seats to its remarkable results in the once "true blue" south. Peter Bruinvels failed to capture The Wrekin, a seat that could have been drawn for the Tories. As MP for Leicester East (1983-87), he once boasted of being the House of Commons most right wing MP. The other moment of unbridled delight came with the declaration in Tatton, where the independent Martin Bell unseated Neil Hamilton, another Tory MP who had found himself mired in very public sleaze. As one of the three MPs named as part of "Maggie's Militant tendency" in the ill-fated 1987 BBC documentary, his electoral downfall was one of the more pleasurable. The demise of Jonathan Aitken in Thanet South, yet another Tory MP mired in sleaze, on an above average swing of around 12%, was yet another compelling message sent by the voters. At this stage, Aitken's conviction for perjury was still in the future, but it is hard to believe that at least some of the voters who transferred their allegiance in his constituency were not of the view that there was no smoke without fire. It was party night for the Liberals also, doubling their numbers from 23 to 46 and scoring their own quota of sensational victories. Liberal Democrats could enjoy the unique (to them) feeling of a night of triumph without having to assume the responsibility of office. As I recall it was a very short night's sleep, but not to the detriment of its refreshing character.

Like the aftermath of an earthquake the damage was apparent in the cold (or rather warm) light of day. Just like an earthquake, it had altered the contours irrevocably. Labour had broken through in middle Britain in a way that would have been inconceivable only a few years earlier. The Conservatives, having embraced the market and in doing so accelerated the demise of class and deference as we knew it, paid the price of social change and their assault on traditional loyalties. Arrogance, sleaze and splits, laced with more than a touch of social Darwinism, earned them the soubriquet of the "nasty party" from one of their more perceptive survivors, future cabinet minister Theresa May. One thing the Conservative hierarchy had more contempt for than their opponents, was each other. The voters took their cue and expressed their contempt for the Tories

The Conservative party in the wilderness is not the subject of this book.

It is My Generation in power. In truth My Generation had steadily, and not always unobtrusively, been moving into positions of power in local government, the media, the law including the police, the social services, and all levels of the education system. Local government was a particular power base effectively abandoned by the Conservatives. The 1992 local elections held just a month after the General Election would be their last electoral success of the decade. The savage cull of Tory councillors in the years that followed presaged the 1997 triumph when the citadel was finally entered. My Generation now had its hands on national political power, the levers of government and the all-important gift of patronage.

So with the Tories banished to the outer darkness for the foreseeable future why was I uneasy? After all, knee jerk Labour support was part of my DNA. Back in 1979 I watched the election in company with among others, a Conservative voting friend whose father was the headmaster of Winchester College, the nation's finest academic establishment. In the same way, as I waited eagerly for the demise of pantomime villains in 1997, he was eager to see the demise of Dr David Owen. As it turned out Dr Owen survived, defected as one of the "gang of four", and played his part in keeping Labour in the electoral wilderness. For many years I would rue cheering his victory. After the painful debacle of 1983, Neil Kinnock, the new Leader, asked the party faithful to remember how they felt on the morning after the 1983 election, and to ensure that it never happened again. After Jim Callaghan's retirement as leader in 1980, none of the next three leaders would get the keys to Number 10, although it was death that terminated John Smith's ambitions rather than the voters. The 1983 manifesto was famously described by Labour MP Gerald Kaufman (now Sir Gerald) as the "longest suicide note in history". Over the next dozen years what would follow would be described by some Tories as the retreat from Moscow. I joined the party in 1984, but after a move of home into a new constituency, let my membership lapse in 1989. After moving to Milton Keynes in 1995, I was very tempted to re-join, but I could never quite persuade myself to do so. At the back of my mind was this nagging feeling that the SDP (Social Democrat Party), had re-emerged as New Labour. Dr Owen may have gone, but his legacy had not. This was not my only reservation.

Never having been a Marxist, and always having been a believer in the parliamentary road, the purge of the cancer of the Militant Tendency was welcomed by me. Neither did the Labour Party miss the likes of Arthur Scargill when he left the party. I welcomed the promise to compensate former GCHQ workers, who had been sacked when Mrs Thatcher deemed their union membership to be incompatible with national security. I also accepted, without too much difficulty, that we could not return to 1970s style industrial relations, particularly in the public sector, the socialised part of the economy. I saw the value of promoting the individual rights of workers rather than creating new collective rights. As a democrat, it was only right that secret ballots for industrial action should stay. If nothing else, it protected New Labour from the toxic effects of the type of strike called by Arthur Scargill in 1984, which destroyed his own trade union, and damaged the credibility of the Labour Party in seeking to represent the interests of working people in a very hostile political environment. I very much welcomed promises of genuine partnership and remember it being proclaimed by Jack Straw at our annual conference in 1998, although sadly disillusion was not far round the corner. Industrial peace was an essential concomitant of credible Labour government. I was delighted with a commitment to full employment, but realistic about what it would mean and what the timescale would be.

Part of the unease came with New Labour's embrace of wealthy men. It is one thing to accept, as I did, that there could be no going back to the tax regime of the '70s, which actively damaged the economy, but New Labour actively sought party funding from the kind of overpaid, self-aggrandising plutocrats it once affected to despise. Electoral credibility was not dependent on sucking up to the mega rich. No doubt those who had prospered so much in the Thatcher years wanted to pick the winning side, but there is no such thing as a free lunch. I'm not an economic illiterate, and understand the "Laffer curve" which demonstrates that an excessively high direct tax regime can and does reduce revenue, but New Labour seemed to be dealing with people who would happily stump up donations in return for a blind eye being turned to loopholes and tax havens. It is not unreasonable to ask capitalists to be patriotic. America does not hesitate to do so.

As a public sector worker, privatisation was a huge issue for me. Labour was surrounding itself with people who had made fortunes from privatisation, and had a vested interest in the letting of further contracts. Given that New Labour was committed to the spending plans of the outgoing Tory government, it was obvious to any halfwit that there would be no buying out of the contracts let to private security companies to run prisons. It is one thing to concede the economic argument to your opponents, it is quite another to embrace them. New Labour was actively getting into bed with tax dodgers. At the time of writing this chapter (March 2011), it is estimated that 10% of tax is evaded, which in round figures is £42 billion per annum. Ordinary citizens whose tax is deducted at source have no choice but to pay. Tax avoidance is the province of the wealthy and of large multi-national companies. This sort of money would wipe out the nation's enormous budget deficit in a little over three years. Mr Blair had also expressed his admiration for the New Zealand Labour Party, which to my eyes had reinvented itself as a Thatcherite party that positively embraced privatisation. My detailed views on privatisation are expressed elsewhere in this tome. I was uncomfortable also with Gordon Brown's seemingly unconditional admiration of American dynamism. It is undeniable that under President Clinton (1993-2001), the American economy revived and huge numbers of jobs were created, but it is important to recognise that it was low paid "mac jobs" that predominated. However, I was certainly encouraged by the promise of a national minimum wage, which doesn't exist in the USA, but found the proposed figure lacking in ambition and not cognisant of the cost of living in London. Nevertheless, I had no inkling that New Labour planned to abandon the working class and solidify the underclass created by eighteen years of Tory rule. New Labour had promised to "think the unthinkable" about welfare. Given a healthy economy and unemployment at its lowest since Labour was last in office, the timing seemed propitious. It is probably true that a withdrawal from the EEC position would have been an electoral albatross as it was in 1983. However, much had changed in the interim and federalism was on the march. New Labour found a policy around which it could easily unite and resonate with the electorate by undertaking not to join the Euro until conditions were right, which on the basis of Gordon Brown's five tests, could be put off forever were it politically expedient. New Labour had learned the lesson of Black Wednesday, when the country was forced out of the European Monetary System (EMS). However, I did feel that New Labour could afford a more assertive stance and steal a few Euro-sceptic clothes without damaging its electoral prospects. However, one must remember that patriotism had not been a significant reason to oppose EEC membership back in the early '80s amongst New Labour's elite when it was party policy, adherence to which was compulsory if you wanted a career.

Even more so than with Europe, continuing with the policy of unilateral nuclear disarmament would have let the Tories off the hook and made a majority Labour government impossible. There is no getting away from it, the British love their bomb. With the fall of the Berlin Wall, the collapse of the Soviet state, and the end of the Cold War, mutually assured destruction was no longer perceived as a threat, and Neil Kinnock was able to re-position the party without too much difficulty. Quite why we needed a deterrent when there was no-one to deter was not explained. In due course, Mr Blair would fill that void by identifying Iran and North Korea to replace the Russian bear. However, like many who had experienced Labour's darkest days, the issue of the bomb had ceased to resonate. I can't claim it as a valid reason for not re-joining and readily accept that any referendum held on keeping nuclear weapons would only go one way.

If New Labour had made accommodation with the now defunct SDP over Europe and nuclear weapons and with the Tories over the economy, it made no concessions over its authoritarian politically correct agenda. It did not need to do so as the electorate was simply not interested. The 1997 election was no more than a plebiscite on the Major years. New Labour had re-positioned itself on the issues that the broad electorate cared about and newspaper stories about "loony left" councils were the equivalent of howling at the moon. Promises to incorporate the Human Rights Act into British law or a promise to update Race Relations legislation, or to strike down the infamous "Clause 28" which forbade the promotion of homosexuality in schools and reduce the age of gay consent to 16, had no influence on my decision not to re-join, any more than they influenced the election. How these issues played out, and my views on them, are discussed elsewhere in this book. If I am honest, I would have to admit from a partisan perspective deriving considerable pleasure from the succession of defeats suffered by the outgoing Conservative Home Secretary, Michael Howard, in the courts even before the Human Rights Act was enacted. The prison service, which I had joined in 1984, was not a comfortable working environment for managers in the mid '90s. The high profile Category "A" escapes from Whitemoor and Parkhurst prisons had not unreasonably eroded public confidence, but at the time many of us felt that we laboured in a micro-managed blame culture and that the Home Secretary refused to accept any political responsibility. At the time I did not appreciate the kind of precedents that were being set by this outbreak of judicial activism. I did not then make the link with proposed Human Rights legislation. Jack Straw would later claim that the credibility of the Human Rights Act was prejudiced by judicial interpretation, rather than its intrinsic propensities. Mr Straw may not genuinely have known what forces were being unleashed, but I have no doubt that other influential members of My Generation in and out of Parliament, understood the project very well, but were keeping quiet about it. What we have since learned about immigration policy demonstrated this amply.

The part of the politically correct agenda which most influenced my decision not to rejoin was that espoused by the sisterhood. Feminism as a creed is a child of resentment and as such is more driven by emotion than reason. Put simply all women shortlists did not give women equality with their male counterparts, it gave them a privileged position. If you dispense with merit as a criterion, then you enfranchise mediocrity. It is noticeable that virtually all of Labour's high achieving women in the last twenty years made it on merit in competition with men. Margaret Beckett had to find a second seat after her defeat in 1979. Her performance as temporary leader after John Smith's death was faultless. Betty Boothroyd became a distinguished Speaker of the House of Commons. Harriet Harman became Deputy Leader of the party and Patricia Hewitt reached the Cabinet. I have rather less time for the last two aforementioned, but that is not the point. They made it on their merits. As it turned out all women shortlists were ruled unlawful under the Sex Discrimination Act (1975) in December 1995. However, the 38 selections already made were not overturned, and 35 were elected in 1997, all of them whom, as Diane Abbott pointed out, were white. The point is obvious. If all women shortlists were to be party policy, how could it resist all Asian shortlists in Bradford, Blackburn or Leicester, all black shortlists in Brent, and all gay shortlists in Brighton and Hove. New Labour would re-legalise all women shortlists in 2002. After all women shortlists were ruled unlawful, New Labour resorted to overriding local party democracy by parachuting in preferred candidates. Yvette Cooper would be a beneficiary. The real casualty would be internal party democracy, which for me was a major issue.

I remember reading somewhere that in the USA, 60% of heterosexual male white Anglo-Saxon protestant voters were default Republicans. In terms of winning the presidency and other major offices, this gives the

Democrats a mountain to climb. The answer was the construction of a "rainbow coalition" of women, organised labour (spelt without the "U" in America) and ethnic, sexual and religious minorities. The working assumption is that a coalition of disadvantaged minorities can take power by virtue of this bloc voting. As a theory it has obvious flaws. Firstly, women are not a minority and there is little to suggest that women's issues here or in the USA have influence to the extent that major elections are actually decided as a consequence. Secondly, it assumes that these voters have a common identity in terms of class interest, and of course in the USA that class is an issue at all in voting. The USA does not have an equivalent of a nationally competitive Labour party. Nevertheless, in a Labour party that had moved close to the American Democrats under Bill Clinton's presidency, this was an attractive concept. New Labour already had the ethnic minority vote largely in its pocket. However, the rainbow coalition only delivers when sufficient white middle class votes move over into the Labour (in the USA the Democrat) column. Thus New Labour could appear to be abandoning doctrinaire socialism to broaden its appeal and win over middle England, but at the same time adopt the Post-Marxist heresy of espousing victimised minorities to drive through an agenda of revolutionary social change, but without the need for violent revolution. This theory is perfectly suited to an environment where the working class is non-revolutionary and socially conservative, and where the tradition of participatory democracy has atrophied. New Labour would pull this trick successfully at three consecutive general elections and force the Conservatives to opt into political correctness. The Liberal Democrats were already on board.

CHAPTER 3

THE BABY BOOMERS' INHERITANCE – CLASS AND DEFERENCE

Baby boomer is a generic term given to those born after the end of World War II, until around the mid-sixties, when the post war birth rate finally fell. However, the definition excludes cultural and political parameters. Those born in the 1960s are recognisably a different generation. For myself, I prefer to place the end of the birth of My Generation in the early summer of 1957. The reasoning behind this is that anyone born after 5 June 1957 would not have been eligible to vote in the referendum on the re-negotiated terms of entry into the Common Market , which was held on 5 June 1975, and the results declared the following day, by coincidence the anniversary of D Day 1944. General Eisenhower had originally planned the invasion for 5 June, but was thwarted by the weather. Thus, there is a genuine division between those whose first experience of national electoral participation pre-dates Mrs Thatcher coming to power, and those for whom it coincides. It is also the case that most baby boomers defined in this way would have completed their Higher Education before the world changed under Mrs Thatcher. I offer my apologies to those born on 6 June 1957, but hope they can see that my arbitrary choice of date is both logical and ironic. As I write the first male baby boomers have recently joined their female peers in collecting the old age pension.

This chapter, when read with Chapters 4 and 5, is not intended to be a history of childhood and adolescence in the post war era. Neither is it intended to be a social history of the period, which in any case would be impossible without writing a wholly different book, which would be very much at odds with its stated purpose. It is therefore a very personal account, which seeks to put into context the failings of My Generation when we came into our inheritance and made our way into positions of power and influence. It paves the way for subsequent chapters and I hope explains some of my anger and frustration at the way in which the movers and shakers of My Generation have squandered our inheritance but unlike the prodigal son, are defiantly unrepentant. However, this is not a chapter that will eulogise about warm beer, village green cricket and cycling spinsters. It is not a chapter that will wallow in nostalgia for a lost world that never existed outside of Enid Blyton stories. A big part of My Generation's inheritance was what needed to be done to make our country and our world a better place when the torch was handed on. Maintaining the harmony of continuity and change is the challenge facing every new generation. Those who fail to understand that are a liability in positions of power and influence.

It is no good pretending that as a generation we have not been dealt a hand of cards unavailable to previous or future generations. Those of us able to take advantage of grammar schools and grants for Higher Education have had an unrivalled all too brief window of opportunity. As a generation we have not had to make any blood sacrifices for our freedom. With the end of conscription in 1960, armed service and the associated risks were for volunteers only. As a generation, we were the first to have our own culture and more to the point, the means to pay for it. In 1955, 4 million singles were purchased by record buyers. In 1965, fuelled by the money in teenagers' pockets, that total peaked at 65 million, only rising above that figure again in more recent years with the advent of cheap digital downloading. It only fell because the Beatles transformed the album market, much to the delight of the record companies who now had a fast growing market for more expensive long players. With economic freedom comes personal freedom, and with personal freedom comes sexual freedom, although this was not granted anything other than grudgingly. Our parents' generation probably had the best deal from the labour market, coming closest to jobs for life. The price was paid in advance during World War II. My Generation's expectations would come under fire in the 1980s. Nevertheless, those of us who got through that painful era of economic adjustment without suffering unemployment have done very well and became the most prosperous older working generation ever. As a generalisation, it comes with some caveats. It helps not to have been divorced and not have a second family. It helps if your children have left home and your parents are dead, or at least not suffering from Alzheimer's disease. The typical family is much harder to locate in 2011 than it was in 1961. The divorce rate at that time was a mere 7%. The only boys I can recall without fathers had mothers who were widows.

No chapter in a book of this nature would be complete without reference to social class. I would imagine many readers, whether or not they are from My Generation, will be familiar with that memorable sketch on social class from the satirical programme, "The Frost Report", which featured John Cleese, Ronnie Barker and Ronnie Corbett, as the upper class, middle class and working class males respectively. Memorably, Corbett says at the end, "And I know my place". Indeed many did. I am also reminded of an A level British Constitution question from the late '60s. "Homogeneity, Consensus and Deference - Discuss the extent to which these are still major characteristics of British Society." I can't remember the exact words, but that is pretty close. Class mattered. Therefore, so did challenging class barriers.

Although Britain underwent major change as a consequence of World War II and the Labour Government that followed, it could fairly be argued that nothing was more resistant to change than class. As something that occupied people's minds, it was the equivalent of the modern obsession with property prices. Where you were in the social pecking order mattered, and it was particularly important to identify those immediately above and below. In its crudest terms, it was about who addressed you as "Mr", and who was not required to. Class was more subtle than simply upper, middle and lower. Within the upper class, there were those who were aristocratic and those who were not. Harold McMillan, Prime Minister 1957-63, married into the Devonshire family and was described by his future father-in-law, the then Duke Of Devonshire, as "trade". McMillan was a scion of the publishing firm that still bears the name. He had also to suffer his wife's persistent adultery in silence. The upper classes did not accept bourgeoisie sexual mores, nor did they accept resort to the divorce courts. To break this unwritten code would exclude the individual from every aristocratic dinner party in the land. McMillan was also noted for the extremely aristocratic nature of his Cabinet, which at one point contained 11 Old Etonians, including his successor as prime minister, Lord Home, who renounced his title and became Sir Alec Douglas-Home. The influence of Eton would reach its peak just at the point at which the Beatles were taking youth culture and popular culture into the mainstream of British life. Sir Alec's seven predecessors, dating back to 1935, were all public school educated. Those born to rule usually did. After Sir Alec, there would not be a public school educated prime minister until Tony Blair in 1997. It would be 2010 before another Old Etonian entered 10 Downing Street as prime minister.

Monarchy and government was simply the visible apex of the dominance of the nation's upper classes. 19th century Victorian entrepreneurs had not hesitated to send their sons to public school and move up the social ladder. Birmingham screw manufacturer Joseph Chamberlain was one such example. His sons, Austen and Neville would attend Rugby. Both would lead the Conservative party and Neville would become prime minister. Their father had done his best to wreck it. Below parliament, the leading firms in industry, commerce and the City of London, the Civil and Diplomatic Services, the traditional professions of the Law, Medicine and the Clergy, and the Armed Forces were dominated at their apexes by the products of schools that educated only one child in twenty. The number of domestic servants may have fallen dramatically from their inter war peak, but the power and influence of the upper class appeared largely unaffected. Harold Wilson's accession to the premiership was symbolic and a triumph for social mobility for an earlier generation. The election of Edward Heath to the leadership of the Conservative Party in 1965 was probably more significant in that the Tories had got the message that they must change, and not rely on the deference vote to get working class support. Just as significant about Heath's election was the fact that the Tories engaged in a transparent democratic process to choose a new leader, which was unprecedented for the party. Harold Wilson was successfully getting across the message that the class system stood in the way of social progress and caused industrial strife. He preached modernisation in an era when upper class certainty was undermined by the Profumo affair in 1963. Wilson was in his prime from 1963 to 1966, and always caught the tide. Rather like Tony Blair a generation later, he had a "teflon" period, where it appeared he could do no wrong, followed by a swift and dramatic reputational collapse. The great tragedy is that the engine of social mobility would first stall and then go into reverse under the Labour governments of Tony Blair and Gordon Brown.

The class system relied for its maintenance on subtle barriers to entry, and on its secret weapon, deference. A working class student might well be bright enough to attend Sandhurst, but he would not have the financial wherewithal to purchase the dress uniform or to sustain the cost of life in the officer's mess. In the legal profession, pupil barristers were often not paid, rather like interns today. Requirements such as having to dine daily in the Inns of Court only added to insurmountable financial burdens. The professions would get the message that these barriers were unsustainable, but, sadly, change has not always proved to be permanent, as the rise of the intern, another dreadful American import, demonstrates.

Unlike the barriers given as examples above, deference is not necessarily incompatible with social mobility. Where it presents as politeness, reserve or respect, I would like to see it come back into fashion. The land of the universal first name is not necessarily a happier one. There is a piece of black and white film in existence, dating from March 1964, in which the Beatles are receiving a presentation from Harold Wilson, then Leader of the Opposition. I can't recall the nature of the presentation, but two things are striking. Firstly, the fact that the future prime minister was in the company of mere pop stars, but more strikingly that John Lennon (but not Paul McCartney) referred to Wilson as "Harold", rather than as Mr Wilson. This was a very public declaration that deference was breaking down, but the pace would be uneven. Who was entitled to be addressed formally and who would expect to be addressed by an unadorned surname would have seemed hideously complex to fictional Martians observing our primitive people. On receiving their MBEs from the Queen in 1965, the Beatles would have been addressed as "Mr Lennon, Mr McCartney, Mr Harrison and Mr Starr" (though whether their former headmasters would have extended the same courtesy is open to doubt). This formal address would have put them on a par with Ministers of the Crown. Royal servants would have still been addressed by surname, although this would change to first names by the end of the 1970s. Ministers of the Crown and their spouses would still be addressed formally to denote their higher status, and the fact that they were emphatically not servants. It is this point that Cherie Blair failed to grasp when she unsuccessfully asked the Princess Royal to call her "Cherie".

The use of surnames without titles was still common in the 1960s, although it is interesting to note that as early in the post war era as 1956, "The Daily Telegraph" was trying to decide whether a clerk should be referred to as "Mr". They decided not. In our Post Modern era, "The Guardian" does not distinguish between who gets an appellation and who does not. Regardless of status, surnames only are used. Presumably "The Guardian" believes that what was once a symbol of a deferential and unequal society is now a symbol of one that is democratic and equality orientated. Thus Ministers of the Crown are referred to in the same way as serving prisoners. Once again, Orwell has been vindicated. I have had to decide myself the extent to which unadorned surnames are used in this book. I have opted for what I believe is largely conventional. The dead are referred to by surname as are sportsmen, authors and artists in the broadest sense. With reference to the living, current and former ministers of the crown are referred to either formally or by using the full name. A surname only is used in context, i.e. The Blair government. The reader will note that I follow an earlier convention in that women are not referred to by surname alone, except for crooks. The list of institutions where subordinate people could expect to be addressed by surname in the mid '60s was still very long. It included schools, the Civil and Diplomatic Services, Royal and Domestic service, the Police, the Armed Forces and the Universities. In Her Majesty's Prisons, it was actually a disciplinary offence for a member of staff to address a prisoner other than by surname. We are now close to a point following a recent legal judgement, where the reverse will apply. That now means that convicted prisoners are treated with more respect than private soldiers who fight for their country. At Oxford and Cambridge universities, College servants or "scouts" as they were known, were addressed by surname by teenage students who until the voting age was reduced to 18 in 1968 were not regarded as adults.

In the world of sport, its rulers fought to keep mere professionals in their place. Sir Stanley Matthews recalls in his autobiography how a letter inviting him to represent his country would begin, "Dear Matthews,". Looking back it seems appallingly disrespectful of the greatest footballer of his era. This was replicated at club level, where the local butcher or gentleman's outfitter on the club board presumed to address international footballers as though they were schoolboys. In lawn tennis, the practice of Wimbledon umpires addressing male tennis players by surname only ceased when Ilie Nastase objected to it in 1972. In Horse Racing, change came as late as 1981 after considerable public disquiet was expressed following a programme showing amateur stewards at a major meeting addressing leading professional jockeys by surname. Racing stewards were predominantly upper class and/or aristocratic. Where professional sport encountered the upper classes, a tinge of snobbery was added to the mix. Old school amateurs like Gubby Allan, former England cricket captain, thought it was absolutely fine to address Fred Trueman, then England's premier fast bowler, by surname in front of schoolchildren. Elevation to the peak of one's profession in management did not necessarily change the way a man was perceived by his social betters. Sir Harold Thompson, a key figure in the Football Association in the 1960s and 1970s, still addressed Sir Alf Ramsey by surname, even after he was knighted. The notoriously chippy Don Revie, who became England soccer manager in 1974, did get the better of one verbal joust. On introducing himself to Revie, Thompson said, "When I get to know you better, Revie, I may call you Don". Revie's response was, "When I get to know you better, Thompson, I may call you Sir Harold". Needless to say, no working relationship developed. Even amateur Rugby Union players were no better treated. Welsh internationals travelled second class by train to London for the biennial meeting with England at Twickenham and were patronised by club officials who would never have smelt an international cap, but who saw it as their due to travel first class. If the players had to stand... well that was simply tough.

To Marxists, the existence of the monarchy legitimises the class system and the privilege that goes with it. What it symbolises vastly outweighs the little residual political power it retains. The monarchy holds together the system. It was described by Bagehot in "The English Constitution (1867) as "the buckle that fastens... the hinge that binds". He also described the monarchy as "the dignified rather than the efficient part of the constitution". The monarchy is resolutely un-meritocratic. Status and station are endowed by accident of birth, not by talent. However, it must be said that the palace has not obviously been occupied by any more turkeys than the White House. Talent or the lack of it is not the exclusive preserve of the elected any more than it is of the dynastic. What was noticeable, and it only slowly began to break down in the 1970s, was that the attitude of the media towards the monarchy was not simply deferential, it was positively reverential. The lifestyle of the Queen's late sister, Princess Margaret, we now know was particularly racy. She had inexhaustible stamina for late nights, a considerable capacity for alcohol, and a blissful disregard for the conservative sexual mores of the time. Her list of lovers cannot be accurately catalogued, since the press did not pry and a gentleman never told. Nevertheless, as she moved into middle age, her behaviour began to attract criticism from other than just Willie Hamilton MP. It has to be said that Princess Margaret's hypocrisy, when criticising the Duchess of York's affairs, was simply breathtaking.

The Prince of Wales was another member of the Royal Family who would benefit from press reticence in the 1970s, as he cut a sexual swathe through the daughters of the aristocracy. Since those heady days, Prince Charles has been more bruised by the decline of deference and respect over just a generation than any other member of the Royal Family. Bagehot also expressed the view that the monarchy were associated with giving a moral lead to the nation, which is fine until what you say in your marriage vows and what you actually do are not merely at odds, but in the public domain. It is reputed that some members of the Royal Family believe that the 1969 documentary, "The Royal Family", started the rot because it let light in on the magic. As such, they ceased to be a quasi deity, and it paved the way for the havoc that was wreaked on the institution by the late Princess of Wales. I will return to the monarchy in the chapter on celebrity.

As has been indicated, class mattered throughout the system. Pinning down the middle class as it was fifty years ago, is easier than it is now, although less easy than when describing the inter war period. Probably the easiest way for an external observer to distinguish between the upper and middle classes was the retinue of servants led by a butler. However, amongst the upper echelons, the upper middle classes had not arrived until they could speak the private language and fall in with the customs of the upper class without error. What was "U" and "Non-U" as it was amusingly described in the '60s, betrayed your origins. If you said toilet instead of lavatory, and used a serviette as opposed to a napkin, then you had failed the upper class entry examination. Amongst the "middling Middle Classes", the presence of servants was a badge of status. They would certainly not have a butler, but would have at least a parlour maid and a cook. After war broke out, the solid middle classes could no longer afford such luxuries, as much higher taxes were needed to pay for the war effort. Taxes would never return to the levels that would sustain servants for what were almost always single income households as married middle class women typically did not work. In any event, men were needed to fight and women to take their places in factories, on the land, and also in administrative support roles. After the war, as we entered a generation in which full employment was the norm, there was no appetite to return to service. The middle classes had to content themselves with free grammar school places for their sons and daughters in lieu of the servants their incomes no longer supported.

Solidly middle class people wore suits for work and did not necessarily remove their ties on arriving home. Middle class people did not earn their living by manual labour, even if their wives now had to do their own washing. Senior civil servants wore bowler hats and carried umbrellas on the commute to work. Their daughters wore boaters to school. One only has to look at archive footage of the '50s and '60s to see how much of this was true. Hats were actually very important. Cloth caps were worn by working class people. I can remember to this day my own father collecting me from my first grammar school swimming gala in October 1964. He turned up wearing a trilby for this brief encounter with Blackburn's middle classes. Perceiving a need to hide one's origins in certain situations was not abnormal in aspirational families. Girls' grammar schools were for young ladies and the eating of chips in the street, or riding pillion on motor cycles was "common". What was considered "common" was as much a badge of class as "U and Non-U" at the intersection of the upper and upper middle classes. Meals were another badge of class. Middle class people had breakfast, lunch and dinner, although further up the scale supper was the normal third meal as dinner described set piece occasions. Working class families had breakfast, dinner and tea, and the final meal could be as early as half past four.

Marriage was another minefield. It was very important that their daughter's suitors had prospects. A police officer would only be a good catch if he had the potential to reach Inspector, at which point they could breathe easily as this was middle class. Unless marriage was undertaken early, daughters would have to earn a living and this could be a tricky area. I am reminded of Ken Livingstone's recollection of his brief sojourn with teacher training in which he described the female student body as being made up of vicars' daughters. He no doubt exaggerated for effect, but his observations contained more than a grain of truth. Some 10 years after his experience, I too attended a College of Education, as they had become known, and was struck by the number of not very academic middle class girls for whom teaching was the only obvious alternative to being secretaries (apart from marriage to a wealthy man not typically found in your average College of Education), with the drop in status that implied. On a sliding scale, teaching infants was more genteel than teaching juniors, and in Secondary Education, teaching in a girls' only school carried higher status than one that was mixed. Such was the wonderful concoction of class and snobbery. As far as male offspring were concerned, parents were concerned to keep them away from working class girls, who were perceived to have looser morals, with the obvious risk that entailed. Looking back on my student days, my recollection is that in general, the more sexually liberated women were found further up the social scale. Sadly, I did not work that out at the time.

Further down the social scale was another tricky area, the cusp between the middle and working classes. On the face of it, the distinction was straightforward. If the head of the household did manual work, he and his family were working class. This was still the case with the self-employed, even if they were also employers. On this basis Edward Heath whose father was a self-employed carpenter, was of upper working class origin. His great rival, Harold Wilson, whose father was a chemist, was therefore lower middle class. Lower middle class people had never had servants. Clerical and junior managerial jobs did not provide the income levels to enjoy the segregated housing of their social betters. The acquisition of a bathroom and central heating would have to wait until they could be afforded before those creature comforts were installed, unless they occupied a council house built as they were to Parker-Morris standards. It is hard to believe that once of a time references were needed before a council property could be occupied. So the lower middle classes lived cheek by jowl with the working classes. Here, deference ran at a lower level and was often absent. The local bobby, the classroom teacher and the parish curate could still expect formal address, but it was not necessarily an indicator of their social superiority. Christian names were reserved for family, friends and workmates. The habit of close friends addressing each other by surname alone was a practice that only pertained further up the social scale.

The class conflict at this level of society was superbly captured in a long forgotten TV sitcom, "Beggar My Neighbour", which ran from 1966 to 1968, starring the late Reg Varney and Peter Jones. Varney's character was a fitter who earned significantly more than this next door neighbour, who was an assistant manager at the firm. Just to complicate matters Varney's character was married to his neighbour's wife's sister. Television sitcoms of this era specialised in class, as it both touched all our lives and provided seemingly endless opportunities for observant and witty writers to hit the mark and the funny bone at the same time. Staff status, as it was then called, may have come with the benefits of an office, a separate canteen and sick pay, but it did not come with overtime and production bonuses, the benefits that trade union membership conferred in an era of full employment. At this end of the spectrum, income could defy rather than define class. Varney's neighbours in the sitcom stoically endured genteel poverty deferring a gratification that always seemed out of reach. They were doomed to be socially immobile, in that the suburban detached was on ice until seniority finally delivered promotion. In the north of England, where I grew up, there was a tradition of working people buying their own modest terraced properties, which were rather more affordable than they have since become. The working classes were also paid weekly. This would only change under Mrs Thatcher, when employers finally felt able to remove the burden of administering weekly cash pay packets. In 2011, 75% of workers are now paid monthly.

Gradations were just as important among the working classes themselves. Home ownership ranked above renting, but renting a council house ranked above renting privately. The poorest housing, inevitably, was in the privately rented sector. Post war slum clearance would take a generation and sadly create new slums from high rise flats. Perhaps the most obvious gradation recognised within the working class, was the distinction between skilled, semi-skilled, and unskilled labour, which was rigorously policed by the Trade Unions. Here class and income mirrored each other. Spousal earnings were a bonus and women were frequently paid significantly less than men for the same work. It would take until the 1975 Equal Pay Act for that to become unlawful. My father was a train driver, which was considered skilled employment. However, our place in the social structure was adversely affected by my mother's Roman Catholic faith (we were therefore brought up as Catholics), and her Irish origins. Black and Asian immigrants ranked below those of Irish extraction, but Poles ranked above the Irish, despite their shared Catholicism. Irish Protestantism only cut any ice among the Irish themselves. Above all, respectability mattered. Criminality, unemployment, and unmarried motherhood in the family plummeted people down the social scale. Given the Methodist tradition, being teetotal added value to one's respectability score. For those who did drink, suits were worn on Sunday and the lower middle classes used the lounge, whilst their working class neighbours used the slightly cheaper public bar. One room vertical drinking monstrosities were for the future. Finally, when returning home from the pub, it was not respectable to urinate in the back yard because another member of the family was occupying the lavatory. The use of course language outside of the work place and particularly in front of women, was not remotely respectable. The notion that women would "eff and blind" as a matter of course, in the way they do today, would have been incomprehensible as a vision of the future. Respectability was THE working class virtue.

The workplace was the public cockpit of class warfare. Unlike after the cessation of hostilities in 1918, there was no going back for the working classes after 1945. Attlee's government promptly repealed the 1927 Trades Disputes Act and full employment saw a continued increase in union membership and an ever growing confidence in dealing with their employers. Trade Union membership would only finally peak in 1979 at over 13 million. It has fallen back steadily to around 7 million, which was the pre-war level. The Conservatives accepted, for the most part, that there was no going back and that organised labour would not merely have to be accommodated, it would have to be invited to the top table. For a generation, anything else was perceived to be electoral suicide. The arithmetic of class was straightforward. The Tories had to hang on to their approximately one-third share of working class votes to remain electorally competitive, what was known as the deference vote. The demise of the Liberal party to an electoral sideshow completed the political re-alignment which had been taking place between the wars, and had almost for that entire period benefited the Conservative Party, as Labour sought to replace the Liberals as a party of Government.

Strike action was made unlawful during the war. It was to remain unlawful for almost the full duration of the 1945-51 Labour government, as reconstruction was put first. Part of the explanation for the Tory victory of 1951 (in seats but not votes), was its promise to "set the people free". The Trade Unions would take advantage of that freedom. Churchill appointed the emollient Walter Monckton as his Minister of Labour, and though from time to time governments sought pay pauses, pay freezes, or just pay restraint, full employment ensured that wages were bid upwards, well ahead of prices, and if we are honest, sometimes at the cost of industrial competitiveness. As well as pay, Trade Unions policed job boundaries zealously. Demarcation disputes were a source of great frustration to employers, as organised labour sought to protect jobs by ensuring that there was a clear divide between the tasks of tradesmen. The same applied to less skilled labour in the docks. There, dockworkers fought bitterly against containerisation, which was the private sector's revolt against the dockers' monopoly. Without going into details, workers who "stuffed" the containers (to use the expression current at the time) were paid less than dockers and therefore were undercutting them. The docks were a traditional theatre of class conflict. Only recently emancipated from the thrall of the casual system, the dockers were determined to hold on to their new found power and newly fattened reliable pay packets. Sadly, their affluence would last less than a generation. The traditional docks in many areas are now theme parks, industrial estates (with, in truth, very little industry), and worst of all, up market housing developments for yuppies.

Other theatres of war were printing, motor manufacture and the railways, which was the field that impacted most on the public. Workers in nationalised industries such as the railways and mines expected the state to set the gold standard for terms and conditions. Union leaders made no distinction between private and state capitalism. Socialism in Britain was very much what was on the agenda of the Trade Union movement. Conflict sharpened in the late '60s and early '70s as first Labour floated then ducked Trade Union reform, and then the Conservatives passed the Industrial Relations Act, which was bitterly resisted by the TUC. At the same time, there were definite signs that post war full employment was under threat as British industry became gradually less competitive. During the '50s and '60s, economists considered that 300,000 or less people on the unemployed register constituted full employment as this figure was composed only of those between jobs, the sick and the absolutely unemployable. In practice, the figure was often below this level, and immigration filled the gap. By the late '60s, unemployment had crept above the half million mark. In 1972, the symbolic figure of one million was passed for the first time since the Arctic winter of 1947. The Heath government embarked on a dash for growth that had short term success, but added considerably to inflationary pressures, which in turn applied upward pressure to pay. By 1975, unemployment rose again above the totemic million, a figure that it has never since fallen below. Industrial militancy typically peaks during an economic downturn, and both major parties would pay an electoral price. To add to Tory woes, the miners emerged from a long hibernation from the fields of conflict and struck successfully in 1972 and 1974.

However, it should be remembered that even at its zenith, trade unions could recruit little more than half the workforce into membership. Of those in trade unions, the vast majority of members never went on strike. It would also be unfair to condemn all employers. There were many good firms out there, large and small, some with active trade unions and others none at all. In the high days of full employment, workers could and did take their labour elsewhere. On the other hand, British workers were remarkably loyal, and many stayed with the same employer for many years, sometimes for an entire working life, national service excepted. British workers were very often content with paternalism and happy to defer to their social betters, in return for job security and a guaranteed weekly pay packet. Deference and militancy were both part of the contrasting industrial picture.

I am of the view that politicians and management, for the most part, get the trade unions they deserve. There is little that can be done to reason with the ideologically motivated, but the average trade union leader, and the average member of a trade union, does not see the trade union as a vehicle of red revolution. Trade unions exist to negotiate pay and conditions collectively, maintain and expand employment rights, and generally act as a barrier to poor behaviour by employers. In a capitalist world, trade unions police a moral frontier that would otherwise be ignored. There is no shortage of modern examples of where no sort of social contract or sense of social responsibility exists amongst those who manage capitalism. Banking is the obvious example. By the end of the 1970s, Britain was dubbed "the sick man of Europe". The class barriers maintained by employers were symbolised by separate dining and toilet facilities, and satirised in films such as "I'm All Right, Jack", and TV sitcoms such as "The Rag Trade", and the aforementioned "Beggar My Neighbour". Amusing though it seems looking back, this was not simple British eccentricity. This was about a society where working people were constantly reminded that they were second class citizens, who existed only to ensure that their social betters could be kept to the standard to which they were accustomed. A "them and us" society does not encourage innovation, transparency, and openness to change. We were out of kilter with what was happening in successful economies such as Japan, Germany and the more abrasive USA. None of these economies were prepared to allow rigid and outdated notions of class and deference to obstruct economic success.

This was our world and it is one of the great ironies of history that class and deference as we knew it, was abolished by Mrs Thatcher. The price that would be paid was the creation of an underclass that defers to no-one.

CHAPTER 4

GROWING UP

There is a huge amount of literature about life in post war Britain and I don't expect that this chapter will add anything significant to the sum of human knowledge. In one sense, post war Britain is still with us. Mercifully, there has not been another world outbreak of hostilities and the aging survivors of the last conflict are still around. Indeed, as I began this book, there was still one surviving combatant from World War I. In another sense, post war Britain ended in 1979 when Mrs Thatcher drew a line under the post war consensus. Looking back, World War II was the dominant feature of childhood, largely because it was the dominant influence on our parents, who either had fought in it or contributed to it in some other way, and had survived. The war ruled the lives of two generations long after VJ day. Children's comics continued to have heroic characters such as Captain Hurricane some 25 years after the cessation of hostilities, who was never less than brave, never wounded, never vanquished, and if captured, always escaped. The Film Industry dined out on the conflict for a similar length of time.

Its most obvious manifestation was in the home. Most fathers had served in the war. They were used to discipline, order and obedience, the last of these without question. My grandmother was shrewd enough to get my father and his younger brother on to the railway when they were 17. She took advantage of the fact that her late husband had been a driver. Indeed, working on the railway was part of a family tradition at the time. In this way my father and my uncle discovered that they were in reserved occupations and would not be called up. However, given that the home front had also operated on military lines, it made no difference to the style of parenting. Fathers simply expected to be obeyed and be deferred to by all as head of the household. As I recall, it was no different in the houses of my friends. Even though the father may never have climbed above the rank of private soldier in the war, at home he ruled the roost, he gave the orders, had his own chair nearest the fire, and a meal on the table when he returned home from work. A man's home, however modest, was his castle, and within that confined space he was a king, and the rest of the family were his subjects. Children were to be seen and not heard, especially if your father had been working nights. You did not have a conversation with your parents, you received a series of commands; "No," "Wait," "Get to bed," "Get up," "Shut up," "Don't argue with your elders," "Eat your greens," were typical examples of the limited vocabulary. If they asked for anything that cost money, children were told, "money doesn't grow on trees," and "we can't afford it". It was all pretty easy to learn.

The attitude to food was another example of the influence of the war. Although rationing actually improved the diet of many working class families, it was still a precious commodity. We were expected to eat whatever was put in front of us. My father would intone solemnly, "Waste not want not, sayeth the Lord." The kitchen table was not a place for conversation. We were told to "let your meat stop your mouth." These aphorisms came direct from my paternal grandmother, for whom thrift was the cardinal virtue. My father would wipe his plate with a slice of bread. If we were hungry, we were directed to the bread bin, and not to the biscuit barrel as we would have preferred, not that there was anything in it after Friday. Thursday was pay day. My father's diet included pigs' trotters, tripe and onions, and a broth made from a sheep's head, from which he also ate the brains, to the envy of the family cat. Mercifully he did not inflict this part of his diet on the rest of his family. Not until the early '80s did the last of these "delicacies" disappear from his diet. Offal was a staple for working class families. Thus we often had lamb's liver, kidneys and ox tongue. The menu, if one could call it that, was almost unchanging from week to week.

When I was at primary school I lived near enough to the school to come home for dinner (not lunch). This was a hot meal, usually stew with mincemeat, shepherd's pie with cabbage, sprouts or carrots, or home made potato pie which had a crust. If it was not pie, it was mashed potatoes with vegetables and one scrawny lamb cutlet or similar piece of meat. Roast potatoes were Saturdays only, except at Christmas. This was with stewed beef and carrots. Mercifully, new potatoes took over from mash in the summer. As an adult, I will not have mash on my plate, so much did I grow to loathe it. Puddings were semolina, tapioca and rice. Rhubarb and custard were regulars as we had free rhubarb from the garden. Living in a farm cottage had that major advantage over terraced homes, which simply had yards. Apple pie appeared on a Wednesday, which was baking day. My mother would make ginger cake, which helped eke out the meagre biscuit ration. When all else failed, there was a bowl of custard. Tea was not an important meal and if a hot meal was served at all it was sausage and beans, fish fingers and peas, or pancakes and even potato cakes. However, I do recall that for a spell we did have fish and chips, with my mother preparing her own batter once a week in the evening. Fish and chips fresh from the chip shop was a treat only on the Saturdays we visited my maternal grandmother. As I recall, three portions of chips had to be split between four people, five if my father was there. If we complained about the paucity of chips, he would tell us that too many chips gave you a square arse. Years later I would enjoy the moment in his old age when he complained of insufficient chips being cooked by my mother whose rule was one potato per person, regardless of the size of the said tuber. When I went to grammar school, my mother decided that my sister would also take school dinners and she switched the main meal to the evening. This was a real bonus as we also had a hot meal at school, and they served chips twice a week. Clearly they were not worried about the shape of our backsides, so long as they could get a strap across them.

We lived in a rented farm cottage, so there was no central heating until 1973. Typically, only one room was heated by a coal fire, although the other downstairs room and the bedrooms all had fireplaces. I was allowed to light a paraffin heater in winter to do my homework, and also to burn it all night when it was very cold. The windows froze up in winter, and as the toilet was outside, we used chamber pots if caught short during the night. Complaints about the bitter winter of 1963 garnered no sympathy. We were told firmly that 1947 was much worse and not to be so soft. Naturally, your parents had the armchairs closest to the fire and male children were expected to go out and bring in coal at intervals. We lived on top of each other and there was no privacy. Only very lucky children had their own bedroom, and luckier still were those who had one in a centrally heated home.

In many respects, manliness was defined by fatherhood and heading your own household. Fathers were not gentle people. In working class households where I grew up, fathers did not want their boys to grow up as cissies. Mums were not allowed to be too protective and an excess of sympathy shown after a minor cut or injury was sustained was frowned upon. Pain had to be born stoically and harshness was considered character building. Life was unfair, so get used to it. Tears were also forbidden for boys. Only girls cried. The same rules applied at school. If you could manage a look of defiance walking back to your seat after being caned or strapped at school, so much the better. The better you could handle corporal punishment at school, the higher your place in the pecking order. Being seen as soft was perceived as a symptom of latent homosexuality.

Working men were paid weekly in cash. More women worked than ever before, but were routinely paid less than men. Possibly the biggest difference between our world as children and our world as parents, is that a man's wage was expected to support a family in its own right. We have now moved to a position where only the very well off can live off one salary. No-one now seriously expects a man to support a family on his own. During my childhood a man who could not was not a man at all. Although women were no longer expected to resign from certain roles such as teaching on marriage, work was incompatible with bringing up small children. There was no maternity leave, no maternity pay, and no flexible working. It should also be remembered that family allowance was paid to the father via the tax system. Not until 1975 was child benefit paid directly to the mother. Part time working was an option when all children were at school and there was the benefit of the extended family. Grandparents, if still alive or not at work themselves, usually lived close by and could provide help with childcare in school holidays. Where parents worked opposite shifts in the mills (6 to 2 and 2 to 10), this provided round the clock care in the home and the benefit of two wages, but the cotton trade did not pay well by comparison to other available work. However, the essential point is that it was the male wage that mattered, particularly as, as has been said, women normally received less pay for the same work. For married women, work fitted around the family, rather than the family around their work. My own mother did not work from 1952, when I was born, until 1960, when my sister joined me at primary school. Her job was part time, mornings only. She ceased work shortly before my brother was born in the October of

1961, and did not work again for another 15 years. Any notions of a swift return to work were rudely shattered by the birth of another child. My family experience was by no means untypical.

It may seem incredible that as late as the 1960s there were still husbands who banned their wives from working altogether, so great would have been the assault on their masculinity. In my father's circles it was also considered unmanly to hand over your wage packet unopened, although I am sure many did, but without admitting it in the pub in front of their friends. My father was happy to tell my mother what he had brought home when there was no overtime, but much more reticent when there was spare money to go drinking. He was one of a breed of men who would give their wives housekeeping, rather than hand it over and be given back spending money. Whichever pattern prevailed, tobacco would be treated as an essential, given up only when unemployed, which was a non issue when the baby boomers were children.

However, although I have painted a picture of working class life as a patriarchy ruled by tyrannical men, working class women should not be seen as a species of doormats, liable to beatings from drunken husbands. Andy Capp certainly existed, but he was not the dominant species of working class male. Working class women were incredible money managers. It was instilled into them by their own mothers who had experienced the hungry '30s. Wives no longer needed the pawnbroker, but folk memories were long. My grandmother's generation also carried another folk memory; that of husbands drinking away their wages at the pub on payday, eventually arriving home intoxicated with empty pockets. I do not know how prevalent this sort of behaviour was, but I do recall my own grandmother, who was born in 1900, telling me that her father went straight home from work on payday, wage packet intact, unlike some of her friends' fathers. I also recall reading somewhere about Lloyd George excoriating the practice of treating, i.e. buying beer in rounds. Not unexpectedly, this increases both consumption and expense. Pubs were open all day during my grandmother's childhood, and this would only cease when Lloyd George restricted licensing hours in 1915, when working class drinking habits were adversely affecting the war effort in the munitions factories. Whether these folk memories helped create the stereotypical British "battle-axe" complete with curlers, rolling pin and withering put downs of male inadequacy, I do not know. What I do know is that patriarchy could be, and was, restricted by strong women whose humble homes were never less than immaculate. The men may have thought they were in charge, but in the home the reality could be very different. A man's role was to earn and provide. A woman's role was to run home and family. A husband might preside, but his wife would rule the domestic roost. However, whatever the relative of power and influence between individual couples, the family was most certainly not a democracy. In matters of discipline, children swiftly discovered that there was not the width of a cigarette paper between their parents, and between their parents and the neighbours.

The family was the first place you learned about pecking order. Finding and knowing your place was part of life. Aspiration was good, but getting above yourself was not. Everything material had to be earned. One thing that an adult did not have to earn was respect from children; it had to be given. The biggest single difference between the classroom of my youth and the classroom of today, was the teacher began with respect and could only lose it, whereas the modern teacher starts with no respect and has to earn it. Of course, our teachers could always resort to the stick to enforce respect whereas modern teachers are almost bereft of effective sanctions. Children did not address adults by their first name. Close friends of your parents that you saw frequently, were addressed as Uncle Fred and Aunty Ethel (or whatever their names were), despite not being related. This was as close as familiarity got. All other adults were addressed formally. The idea that children merited respect, if considered at all, would have been seen as complete nonsense. Not until you brought home a wage were you worthy of a modicum of respect. Even then, parents were perfectly clear that you were a child until you were 21, when you were entitled to a door key of your own. Despite the lowering of the age of majority in 1968, my parents treated my 18th birthday two years later as being no different to those that had gone before. However, I did graduate to a door key early.

Starting work was a major rite of passage for working class boys, as it brought enhanced status in the home and elevated the new worker above his siblings, as he now brought something in rather than took it out. It brought an end to running errands and conferred the privilege of smoking in the house, the habit being the norm in working class households by one or often both parents. However, in the world of work the new boy or girl was clear from day one where they stood in the pecking order – at the bottom. You moved up one when the next apprentice or office junior arrived. Seniority was everything in the workplace. Working men had no compunction about giving a cheeky young boy a clip round the ear or a dig in the ribs. It was a salutary reminder about the immutable laws of the pecking order. Working girls were not quite as well placed domestically if there were no younger siblings, as unfortunately the evening's washing up fell outside of routine working hours. Teenage workers, unlike their fathers, were expected to hand over their wages and be given spending money. Such arrangements would now be unlawful as well as inconceivable. Only at the age of 21 could this arrangement be terminated as of right and the young worker pay board, if still living at home. In practice, boarding usually began earlier.

The rising standard of living in the 1950s brought labour saving gadgets, televisions and telephones steadily into working class homes as these items came into the reach of workers' budgets. Car ownership also grew incrementally. The television and the motor car would change society irrevocably as they ushered in the ability of people to put up barriers between themselves and their neighbours. Viewing and travel became private experiences. By 1961, television ownership had grown from a privileged few a decade ago, to 75% of households. Ten years later, it had reached 91%, and colour TV's were replacing black and white sets. In 1947, the mangle was a staple item in almost every home for wringing out the washing before it was hung on the line. In that year, it appeared in the first "shopping basket" that the government prepared and published for monitoring price changes and inflation. By 1962, automatic washing machines were so widespread that the mangle was removed from the index. I can just about remember my mother using one on the traditional Monday wash. Labour saving gadgets, such as washing machines and vacuum cleaners, significantly improved the lot of housewives in a very short space of time, and growing car and television ownership transformed leisure. The Clean Air Act, which came into force in 1960, was also a boon to washing lines. Those whose homes were closest to the factories lived cheek by jowl with smoke belching chimneys, which again I can remember from my childhood. However, as I also recall smokeless zones were subjected to some low level sabotage. My father was not alone in burning coal at night, rather than the more expensive coke. It was a shame to waste coal liberated from the railway. We got our toilet rolls from the same source.

The advent of television and the motor car also affected attendances at soccer, rugby league and cricket matches. Attendances at professional sport boomed massively just after the war, but from the mid '50s onwards dropped significantly and would not rise again until England won the World Cup in 1966. After a brief hiatus, the decline resumed. Competition for the worker's disposable income was taking its toll. For those who kept up the football watching habit, there were two other significant changes. Until the 1960s, supporting the home town team was virtually unquestioned. The maximum wage and the "retain and transfer" system ensured player loyalty without paying for it. Travel to away games was limited to major cup games and local derbies at grounds that could still be reached after Saturday morning at work. It was not uncommon for fans to watch matches at the grounds of local rivals when their own club was playing away, as it offered a second opportunity to see the stars of the day such as Stanley Matthews and Tom Finney. Football was not tribal, but this changed significantly from about 1965 when outbreaks of hooliganism began to break out at grounds. By the end of the decade, helped by the popularity of the skinhead movement amongst working class youth, every professional club had its own "firm", whose key aim was to take the home supporters' end. Fans no longer automatically supported the home town team. A combination of rising disposable income, willingness and ability to travel, and the desire to see teams made fashionable by Match of the Day and its ITV counterpart were contributory factors. The big city clubs were the winners. In 1960, Lancashire had five town clubs in Division One. By 1971, all had been relegated and in the case of Blackburn and Bolton were beginning life in Division Three for the 1971-72 campaign. It would get much worse. By 1987 Blackpool, Bolton, Preston and Burnley had all experienced the league's lowest tier, Division Four. Burnley came desperately close to losing league status altogether in that same year. Young fans wanted to be associated with winners and the stardust and romance that accompanied Manchester United's recovery from the Munich Air Crash made them the most attractive club of all for the new breed of non-native supporter. It is also worth noting that following larger clubs improved the chances of some "aggro" on the terraces and outside grounds. In my year at Grammar School when I started in 1964, boys supported either Blackburn Rovers or Burnley. The number of boys coming to school from Accrington and the Rossendale Valley accounted for the Burnley fans. By 1968, a number of my 15 year old peers were travelling to watch Manchester United, Manchester City, Everton,

Liverpool and Leeds. Rovers and Burnley were for losers. Fortunately, many of us kept the faith.

The picture I have painted is one where on the face of it, there is little to complain about. Full stomachs, full employment and fat wage packets gave plenty of grounds for contentment. The older generation could spend their new found wealth on labour saving appliances, TV's, fridges and motor cars. The younger generation had a consumer economy all of their own; records, clothes, magazines, and, for those at work, motor scooters or motor cycles. Crime was low, slums were being cleared and social mobility was on the rise. The last conscripts received their call up papers in 1960, completing the transition to a peace time economy. Prime Minister Harold McMillan told the country in 1957 that most of us "had never had it so good". In the material sense it was true, and that also went for the rest of the western world. However, in another respect there was ferment and not just in the first world. Millions of words have been devoted by eminent historians to that period when the old order and its certainties were challenged by intellectuals, broadcasters, and young people with unprecedented economic power. Its causes, its social impact, and its time parameters have been debated, debunked, and by some, very much disparaged. For men like Lord Tebbit, this period carries a convenient if not totally accurate label of "the sixties", uttered with disdain and distaste about a time when society lost its moral compass, found again only when Mrs Thatcher came to power. For some, the times really were changing and noticeably. Bob Dylan in his song "The Times they are a Changing" written in 1964, reminded parents forcefully of the new order with his line "Your sons and your daughters are beyond your command". For others, the "sixties" passed them by and were essentially a London metropolitan phenomenon, a party to which they were not invited. I am reminded of part of Philip Larkin's little rhyme in response to the Profumo Scandal:

> "Sexual intercourse began in 1963, rather late for me, between the end of the Chatterley trial and the Beatles first LP."

The notion that it was a private party to which most of us were not invited is closer to my own experience. And where "Swinging London" threatened to impinge on our lives, our parents and teachers mounted their own barricades. When long hair became fashionable, we had inspections at school. A whole year would be made to remain behind and the Discipline Master walked behind every boy. A tap on the shoulder indicated your hair was too long and you would have to stand out at the front and await six of the best. It took more than a year, and a new headmaster, for that to change and for corporal punishment to no longer be a weapon against non-conformist hair length. I take the view that if the older generation found something to resist in provincial Blackburn, then something must have been happening, and the debate is about the speed at which it permeated all levels of society. The time parameter is difficult, because the failed Hungarian revolution, the exploding of the H Bomb, and the advent of Rock and Roll and the beginnings of youth culture, occurred when most baby boomers were children, some not born, yet their influence on the next decade is undeniable. Arthur Marwick dates the period of ferment as circa 1958 to 1974. All of these phenomena are children of World War II.

So what was there to fight against? In everyday life it was the stifling requirement to conform. There was the class system described elsewhere. There was the threat of annihilation. There was capitalism and imperialism. Fascism was dormant but there were racial and other forms of prejudice that were endemic. Economic liberation came to young people with full employment, rising social mobility and the grant aided expansion of higher education. With it came the confidence to push at boundaries. Social reformers who tried in vain during the previous decade to legalise male homosexuality, abolish the death penalty, and make abortion available on the NHS as opposed to from back street quacks, found that they were pushing at a door that was at least partially open. The first Race Relations Acts were passed in the 1960s, but it should be noted that they had been preceded by restrictions on immigration, which in the 1960s unequivocally equalled what was called "coloured immigration".

It is now fashionable to criticise the "nanny state", with its Health and Safety culture, the wrapping of children in cotton wool, and its endless lectures and injunctions to lead a healthy lifestyle. These criticisms are entirely justified. However, I do not share the view that the desire to regulate, the desire to control, the desire to restrict freedom unnecessarily is the prerogative of the left in politics. We need to stop, think and recall how it was behind the rosy glow of street corner football, grazed knees, and conkers baked hard in the oven. Take Sundays. As a child I wished someone would. The atmosphere was sullen, brooding and joyless, even on a bright summer day. No organised sport was played, as it was unlawful to charge entrance fees on Sundays. In Lancashire, local cricket leagues began to get round this by charging spectators for programmes purchased outside the ground. Only the three day working week in 1973-74 signalled the beginning of the end of 10 years of this nonsense, but even then professional soccer clubs who switched to Sundays so that the workers, whose three days were Thursday to Saturday could attend matches, still had to go through the absurdity of compulsory programme purchase before the law was eventually changed. Municipal children's playgrounds would be locked. Near where I grew up, church-owned sports field carried a notice that said, "No games on Sundays". We ignored it and when the women came out of Sunday afternoon service, they would see us off, only for us to return 5 minutes later when they had left. Also on Sundays your local grocer (no supermarkets then) was not allowed to sell tinned or packaged food. It was fresh food only although in truth the Shops Act was observed only in breach. At least for us Catholics there was only one service. The Church of England children followed theirs with Sunday school. The Methodists had three services to attend. For the adults the pubs opened only from 12-2PM and then again from 7 - 10.30PM. Off licences were similarly restricted. As I recall, some cinemas were open, but again programmes had to be purchased. Sunday was the "Lord's day" and pleasure was forbidden. However the veneer of godliness merely concealed the hypocrisy. Church attendance may have been higher, but people still fornicated, beat their wives and got roaring drunk. Public respectability concealed private vice. Compulsory religion had no impact on narrow minds, rank ignorance and wilful prejudice.

My Generation will also remember the restrictions on listening, viewing and reading, where our moral guardians were determined to impose their own values. In terms of what you could read, the Obscene Publications Act (1959) defined obscenity as material likely to deprave or corrupt, a pretty subjective test. The Act was swiftly tested when Penguin Books published D.H.Lawrence's long banned novel, "Lady Chatterley's Lover". The prosecution of Penguin failed, in a large measure due to the prosecuting barrister, Eton, Oxford and the Guards, asking the jury if it was a book they would want their servants to read. In a country where frustration with the class system was simmering, this was too much. Personally I could do without the coarsening of language over the last 50 years, but if novelists are not free to explore the mixture of class, human emotion and sexual desire, then we are not a free society. Prosecutions would continue sporadically until the early '70s, with the "OZ" trial of 1971 the most famous. By appearing to aim "The Little Red School Book" at adolescents, they probably invited prosecution and imprisonment, although the authors were swiftly freed on appeal. Ancient blasphemy laws were revived in 1976 by clean-up campaigner, Mary Whitehouse, against the publishers of "Gay News".

Until 1968, The Lord Chamberlain could censor plays prior to them going on stage. As regards the cinema, local watch committees viewed films with adult themes before deciding whether or not they could be shown to the local populace. The fact that the British Board of Film Censors had awarded an "X" certificate cut no ice with the local moral guardians. The sheer absurdity of local councillors shuffling along in their raincoats and mufflers to a private showing looking every inch the stereotypical dirty old men, did not occur to them. Naturally, if a film was passed as suitable, it would garner an audience out of all proportion to its cinematic merit. It is worth remembering that as late as 1979 local worthies in some areas prevented the screening of "The Life of Brian". We had to be protected from sex and nudity, although oddly enough, the Trojan horse of naturist films proved relatively uncontroversial with the censors, perhaps because they were explicitly asexual. However, what could be shown in the cinema was liberalised before television. This was probably because of the classification system, and in the pre-video age it was much easier to prevent minors from seeing films that had adult themes.

At the end of World War II, very few people had television. There was one channel, BBC, run by the high minded Lord Reith, for whom the mission of television was to educate. A second channel, ITV, arrived in 1955. Unlike the BBC, it would be funded by advertising revenue, rather than a licence fee. The opposition Labour Party opposed the second channel, as much as anything on the grounds of commercial vulgarity. The new channel did not hesitate to aim for the newly affluent working classes with its mixture of game shows, American imports and an emerging genre, the soap opera. The masses did not want televised Radio 4 (or the Home Service to use its proper title until 1967), and the viewing figures reflected that. The regional franchises became a licence to print money for the shareholders. This was popular capitalism at work. However, it is important to remember that television was still strictly rationed.

There were no morning programmes on weekdays, and only "Watch with Mother" on BBC in the early afternoon. Apart from this and Welsh language programmes which were screened at about 4.30PM, television did not begin until 5.00PM with children's programmes. By 11.00PM it was all over. Saturday had children's programmes in the morning and sport in the afternoon. Sunday had religious services in the morning and old films in the afternoon, usually westerns or war films, both of which enjoyed their heyday in the 1950s and 1960s. The epilogue closed transmission every night. Nothing was on the screen more than the test card. Programmes that were screened were watched like a hawk by Mary Whitehouse and her associates for the slightest sign of moral degeneration, which would be signified by any sexual content that even faintly contradicted her moral code of sex being a private matter for married people only. Anything that smacked of loose morals was taboo. She also declared war on the word "bloody". At this stage (1965) only Kenneth Tynan had used the word "fuck" on television. The word "cunt" was heard on our screens five years later, again on a live broadcast. Not until 1979 was it used in a scripted pre-recorded program. Under Hugh Carleton-Green, who was Director General in the mid '60s, the BBC forged ahead with its ground breaking Wednesday Plays, and cutting edge comedy such as "Steptoe and Son" and "Till Death Us Do Part". Mrs Whitehouse did not discriminate between Harold Pinter and Alf Garnett as she vented her fury at Greene. He refused to see her and also gave her no platform for her views. Unless you lived through those times, it is difficult to appreciate that the fight for freedom of the screens was a real one, and one that was bitterly contested.

What was happening on our screens in terms of sexual expression reflected the breakdown of traditional sexual mores. The argument of "clean up" campaigners that televised sexual licentiousness caused or accelerated the rejection of a traditional code of sexual morality, is far too simplistic. It also ignores the social impact of what is still the most important single breakthrough in terms of a woman's control of her fertility; the contraceptive pill. Its impact cannot be understated. Originally, it was prescribed only for married women in 1964, but in 1968, to the consternation of moral campaigners, prescription was extended to single women. Reliable contraception freed women from inconvenient pregnancy, and freed single women from the stigma of producing a bastard child. In theory, assuming that "the pill" caused them no other medical problems, women had total control of their own fertility and of their sex lives, though whether they have exercised those controls effectively and in their own best interests is a different argument, not considered at the time. In practice, it took a few years before single young women adapted to the new regime and had the confidence to go to the doctor for a prescription. It is interesting to note that as late as 1971, around a quarter of young men and a third of young women were virgins on their wedding day. On the one hand from a modern vantage point, it seems remarkably high, but on the other hand it illustrates the extent to which the bourgeois proscription of pre-marital intercourse was being ignored, not least by their offspring.

Outside of the new metropolitan elite of the famous and the fashionable, the "swinging sixties" arrived slowly, if at all. Students were perhaps best placed to claim sexual freedom. The possession of one's own single room away from the parental home obviated the need to use the back seat of a car or manufacture a "baby sitting" opportunity. Universities and colleges had done their best to segregate the sexes and prevent sexual liaisons, on the basis that they acted in loco parentis. Rules at one time did not only bar what was euphemistically referred to as "overnight visiting", but also insisted that room doors were open during the day, if a member of the opposite sex was present. The breakdown of these rules was accelerated by the lowering of the age of majority to 18 in 1968, which if my memory serves me well, was when Britain was scandalised by Keele University students sunbathing naked. The authorities retreated fairly swiftly from regulating student's private lives to a position of neutrality. Dons who felt it demeaning to act as sex snoopers, were now able to withdraw from their secondary role as policemen of sexual morality. However, the battle for a private personal life was not won without casualties. As late as 1972, Lord Denning, the "visitor" at a Yorkshire College of Education, confirmed the expulsion of a female student caught entertaining her boyfriend overnight. His explosion of sexually repressed condemnation was on a par with Lord Hailsham's famous television tirade about John Profumo's liaison with Christine Keeler. The Colleges of Education, better known by their earlier name of Teacher Training Colleges, were more traditional and paternalistic, and this tradition only disappeared with the institutions themselves as they were absorbed into Universities and Polytechnics.

As I have indicated, the real agenda for most young people was not to "swing", but to enjoy a private life. I recall entering the doctor's waiting room at a College of Education early in my first term in October 1974, and finding it packed with female freshers. I later learned that the queue was for prescriptions for the pill. It would be quite wrong to see this as a prescription for promiscuity. Most young women simply wanted to enjoy risk free steady relationships. Living away from home avoided questions from parents about the reasons for visiting a doctor. Thus, going on the pill was part of the culture of respectability and a rite of passage to adulthood. Unmarried motherhood was losing its stigma, but in 1974 was not compatible with being a student teacher. Pregnancy no longer resulted in expulsion, but there was almost no flexibility in course provision and certainly no crèches. There were only two choices; quitting the course or obtaining a termination. It should also be remembered that for most baby boomers their higher education came between the advent of the pill, and the herpes and HIV scares that would bedevil a later generation. Young men could reject the condom with impunity. Contraception was a woman's job and they had to get used to it.

Returning to the media, particularly in terms of what we could listen to, we not only had moral guardians, but also cultural ones. Radio did not have an equivalent of ITV. It was a BBC monopoly. We also had the dead hand of the Musicians' Union, which restricted "needle time", with the consequences that more often than not if you heard your favourite disc, it was being played by an orchestra or brass band employed by the BBC. Until 1964, the only source of continuous pop music was Radio Luxembourg which had a very poor signal that faded in and out, and only broadcast from 7PM to midnight, not much use to schoolboys sent to bed at nine o'clock, unless you could smuggle your transistor radio upstairs. The advent of pirate radio in 1964 was sheer bliss. It smashed the establishment's cultural monopoly of radio. Young people now had their own channel and could hear the music they loved. Although there could be no going back, "Auntie" BBC would not lift her skirts until 1967. Junior Choice, on Saturday mornings, continued to close with a classical piece and children were to feel grateful when their names were read out and a request played. The problem was that most children did not get the request of their choice. In August 1967, Anthony Wedgwood Benn (as he was then known) succeeded in driving the pirates from the airwaves when the Marine Offences Act became law. BBC filled the gap with Radio One at the end of September. It was not the same and it lacked spontaneity. Producers controlled the play lists, rather than the disc jockeys, but at least we had our own radio channel that would develop, diversify and ultimately become a dinosaur. The advent of Radio One put an end to the restrictive practices of the Musicians' Union, but it did not put an end to censorship. "Auntie" still banned explicit sexual content, most notably "Je t'aime... moi non plus", the October 1969 Number One single that "Top of the Pops" could not feature, with its French lyrics and heavy breathing. However, the self-appointed censors could be fooled. In 1973, Lou Reed's "Walk on the Wild Side" received endless air play despite a reference to "giving head". Clearly "Auntie" did not know that this was American slang for fellatio.

For all that television opened up our world, social attitudes lagged behind legislation. A survey conducted at around the time homosexuality was legalised in 1967 revealed that only 12% of respondents felt tolerant towards gay sex, although that term was not then in use. A 2004 Gallup poll found 54% of respondents favouring gay marriage. A poll taken by the Times in 2009 found the figure even higher at 61%. This is more than change over 40 years, it is a quantum leap. However, it should not be assumed that tolerance equalled immediate acceptance. That came only with time. The "buggers' charter", as it was labelled by opponents, legitimised what was considered to be deviant rather than normal for those who were gay. A read through House of Commons speeches in the debates readily confirms that at this stage many legislators were driven by pity rather than by any notion of equal validity. Gay men were no longer subject to blackmail, but the closet remained the safest place for another two decades. It was normal in TV programmes for gays to be referred to as puffs and queers. In everyday conversation, language was more colourful. My own father's preferred expression was "brown hatters". It took me a little while to work out the allusion. Nevertheless, homosexual law reform, however timid it may seem in retrospect, was the beginning sine qua non.

Attitudes to race were very similar. Words such as "Wog, nigger, Paki and chink", were in common parlance and transcended the class system. At public school, any boy whose parents lived in the colonies was nicknamed wog or nigger despite the whiteness of his skin. The popular BBC comedy, "Till Death Us Do Part", which first hit the screens in 1965, was intended to expose the awfulness of racism by creating the ranting monster that was Alf Garnett. The downside was that the words coon, nig-nog and sambo were added to the racist vocabulary. Black comedian

Lenny Henry recalled that the programme seemed to produce at regular intervals, new insults for his schoolmates to hurl at him. The creator, Johnny Speight, should not have his motives impugned. His anti-racist credentials were on open display. He could not have anticipated the law of unintended consequences. Racism was not entirely black and white. Black youths were welcome in skinhead gangs, where they were known as "spades". One of the favourite sports of skinhead gangs was "Paki bashing". Pakistanis were a complete mystery, and popular folk lore in Blackburn had it that they ate cat food. It seems unbelievable that this occurred within our lifetime. It's hard to blame that kind of ignorance on the legacy of empire. Anti-Jewish prejudice also remained very strong in the 1960s. As I shall discuss elsewhere in this book, the intelligentsia were probably the worst of all. Anti-Semitism has become the officially licensed prejudice. Working class boys contented themselves with Jew jokes, usually set in a concentration camp with the teller doing a less than passable impression of a Nazi officer.

The biggest issue for educated young people in the late 1950s was nuclear weapons. The Campaign for Nuclear Disarmament had a simple slogan, "ban the bomb". The issue would cause ferment in the Labour Party as well as the universities. The party adopted unilateral nuclear disarmament in 1960, but this was reversed at the 1961 conference. Opponents of unilateralism accused CND of being communists or at least Soviet sympathisers and stooges. The standard of political debate on the subject would hit new lows when CND revived in the early '80s. Nuclear disarmament would give way to Vietnam as the big issue from 1965 onwards, culminating in massive demonstrations outside the American embassy in 1968. Closer to home, "The Troubles" erupted in Northern Ireland as the septic boil of the Orange State finally burst and, within four years, Edward Heath's government was forced to introduce Direct Rule in the province and put an end to 50 years of elected dictatorship. Catholics in Ulster had suffered levels of discrimination which bordered on that suffered by negroes in the southern states of America. Like America's racial struggle, Ireland was played out on live television. No-one could fail to be shocked by the partisanship and violence of the police. If Wilson's government received some credit for its handling of Northern Ireland, it got none for supporting the USA in Vietnam in return for their help in the propping up of our economy, but at least Wilson refused to commit troops. Educated young people were massively disillusioned with Labour, and Vietnam was the catalyst for the growth of explicitly Marxist political groupings in the universities. Students were also desperately unhappy at the Wilson government's failure to dislodge the illegal white minority regime in the British colony of Rhodesia, and also excoriated Labour for selling arms to the apartheid regime in South Africa. These issues would resonate even more than Vietnam. Ireland remained a running sore but as the tragedy of Vietnam reached its denouement, Palestine took its place as the next cause for the nation's educated elite – of which more anon.

CHAPTER 5

EDUCATING MY GENERATION

Remembering my earliest days in Primary School involves trawling back to the furthest recesses of the memory. One thing that is common across generations is the sheer bewildering disorientation a child feels on that first day in school. For many children it is the first forcible separation from your mother. This is a little mitigated if you are not the eldest, as there is the comfort of a sibling as you are left in the school yard. In more modern times, exposure to pre-school nurseries is probably more substantial mitigation. However, back in August 1957, no concessions were made. I still have a very clear memory of the first day when, along with 40 or so other equally bewildered children, some in tears, we were herded into a large classroom and made to form lines between rows of desks. Further to one side, there were two other lines of children. I discovered that these infants were a year older than us and knew what to do. For this was assembly and after silence was decreed prayers began. Like many new children, I did not know the words but would swiftly learn them, and in the meantime would copy the older infants by putting my hands together. Our teacher was Mrs Sumner, who had two sons further up the school. I don't remember that much about the first year, but I do remember the teaching of reading by phonic methods, the daily stories about Jesus, Mary and Joseph, and being allowed to play with plasticine two or three times a week. In this first year, our only exposure to regimentation was the lining up to go back into class, which was very structured and disciplined. I can remember one male teacher, a Mr Bradley I think, who would actually stand at the front, cane in hand, as he supervised the lines of children.

Life became a good deal less comfortable in the older infants class, which was taught by the Deputy Head teacher. Miss Eccles was a ferocious disciplinarian who used the strap on a daily basis. Not only were we subject to corporal punishment at the age of 5-6, we also had formal examinations before Christmas and in the summer term. After these examinations we were placed in rank order. This was done publicly by the headmistress, a truly terrifying nun of Irish extraction, Sister Paul of the Cross. At the end of this procedure, there would be a crocodile of each year group in the assembly hall. Unlike the Bible, the first were first, and the last most definitely last. At least we still got to play on a Friday afternoon and still got to go home at 15.45. I also went home for dinner, as did many other children.

On moving into junior school religion loomed much larger. At seven we were deemed to have reached the age of reason. Therefore, we could now commit sin and go to hell. The biggest sin of all was missing Mass. Our class teacher kept a register. Very swiftly you learned not to tell the truth if you had not attended Mass on Sunday or a Holy Day, as it invited public humiliation. In this year, we were also introduced to the delights of First Holy Communion, before which we had to make the first confession of sins. Mrs Slater also kept a register of sacramental participation. The second biggest sin was to take Holy Communion without having sought absolution for missing Mass. I vividly remember one girl being hauled out of class to the parish priest to make a confession. Our teacher was convinced, and indeed sought to convince us, that this poor seven year old child would face eternal damnation, if she died before making a confession of this grave sin. We were hit really hard with religion at this stage. I used to hate the annual May procession and the weekly hymn practice. Although not a Jesuit foundation, they really did believe in the mantra, "give me the boy at the age of seven and I will give you the man". I think they were blissfully unaware of the law of unintended consequences.

Hymn practice and the May procession were survivable by keeping your hands together and miming or mumbling, St Joseph's Penny was not. This annual levy lasted from Ash Wednesday to Maundy Thursday, a period of almost six weeks during which we were encouraged, browbeaten and humiliated into handing over as much money as we could beg, borrow or otherwise acquire to this charity. Every St Joseph's Penny Card had twelve squares. For every penny handed over, you were allowed to "prick" a square. Records of donations were kept and posted publicly. This was nature's way of reminding you who was poor, not that this was any excuse. I still remember being hauled in front of my younger sister's class to be asked how much I had given and how much pocket money I received. My abiding memories of St Edward's RC primary school, Darwen, are of a discipline that sought to humiliate and intimidate. It was not particularly the issue of physical punishment. None of them had strong strapping or caning arms and you grew to accept it as part of the diet, albeit a large part. It was the fact that the atmosphere was always heavy, brooding and oppressive. It wasn't just the predictable cycle of St Joseph's Penny collection, Priest's inspection and the Monday morning ritual interrogation of Mass and sacramental attendance, which were bad enough in their own right, but the random way in which individually or collectively you could arouse the ire of the Sisters of the Passion. They believed you were put on earth to suffer, and were delighted to demonstrate that to you practically at regular intervals. John Lennon wrote in his song Working Class Hero, "They hate you if you're clever and despise a fool". It encapsulates perfectly my experience of primary school. If you were bright, then you were singled out for punishment as the nuns feared you would get above yourself. If you were dull, then ignorance could equally be cured by the strap. Either way, you lost. Getting out of that environment in the summer of 1964 was something I looked forward to, even more than the family holiday. Only then would "terror by penguin" come to an end.

It is pretty clear from reading the accounts of those of My Generation and indeed my parent's generation who have gone into print, that my experiences are little different from everyone else who enjoyed or more accurately endured a Catholic education. In fairness, I have to say that secondary school was much better. There were a couple of sadists in cassocks that I recall, and some beatings that I witnessed or heard about that went beyond what was acceptable, even to believers in physical punishment. However, this was rare. The Marist Fathers did not seek to emulate the reputation of the Irish Christian Brothers who were famously labelled as "too stupid to be teachers and too brutal to be priests". We had to be socialised into the school and discipline was at its strictest in the first half term. Thereafter, things settled into a predictable rhythm. It is also fair to say, on the oral evidence of my contemporaries, that discipline in non-religious foundations was every bit as uncompromising. At least in the public sector it was the masters who ruled. Prefects had only the power to report, whereas in many of our well known public schools they had the right to beat and use younger boys as servants or "fags", as they were commonly known. As most pupils were boarders there was no escape. Fagging and beating by prefects had largely disappeared by the mid-'70s, but private education below the level of the leading public schools was of variable quality and concealed abuses, including sexual abuse, which are still coming to light. Small foundations owner run by private individuals, rather than boards or trusts, were the most scandal prone. At the other end of the spectrum, the most disadvantaged, who had fallen into criminality or were in danger of it, could find themselves in Approved Schools. These were well below the public radar and were often a by-word for brutality. The Court Lees affair of 1967, which among other things discovered the use of non-regulation thicker canes, not dissimilar to those used to flog criminals in Singapore, signalled the demise of the Approved School System. In 1972 they were renamed Community Homes and the ethos changed.

At this point it is only fair to declare openly that I was a grammar school boy. My primary school class contained 42 children. As I recall, 6 boys passed that year and oddly enough I can recall their names without hesitation. Five of us went to St Mary's College, which was the direct grant Grammar School for Catholic boys in Blackburn. It was founded by the Marist order. The sixth boy, Chris Watson, was sent by his parents to Stoneyhurst College, an independent Jesuit foundation. I do not recall with the same clarity the names of all the girls who passed, but I believe the number was broadly similar, making a pass rate of 30%. Equally, I cannot recall, nor do I have access to the information, regarding the percentage of places available to the Catholic population of Blackburn and the surrounding small towns. What I can say is that for my Primary School it was an all consuming passion for the nuns to get as many boys into St Mary's College and as many girls into Notre Dame (known colloquially as "the convent")as they possibly could. Thus, the last two years of primary schooling were composed of an exceptionally narrow curriculum, which concentrated almost exclusively on what was needed to pass this critical examination, Arithmetic, English and what these days we call non-verbal reasoning, then simply known as Intelligence. The Blackburn 11-plus was in two parts, with the non-verbal reasoning first part acting as a qualifying hurdle. For the most part our education was deadly dull. No History, no Geography, no Science were taught until after the examination in March. Only Religious Instruction intruded on the 11-plus factory. The only time the 11-plus took a back seat was when the parish priest's annual inspection was imminent.

The obvious plus of being schooled in an environment dominated by the 11-plus was that we were taught to read and write. It seems incredible that 50 years on from my own Primary School days standards of numeracy and literacy have actually fallen. The educational elite and the methods they have propagated must take the blame. The abandonment of phonics, in favour of inferior methods, and the baleful influence of progressive educational theorists, has turned learning into an accidental by-product of what else goes on in classrooms. There must be no pressure, no punishment and no pecking order.

Readers of my generation will recall that there were two ways in which Grammar Schools were funded, when as a consequence of the 1944 Act, Grammar School education was available free of fees to all those who received that piece of paper that confirmed you had passed the 11-plus. Schools were either maintained by the local authority in their entirety, or were funded by a combination of a "direct grant", local authority purchase of free places, and fees paid by parents who could afford it, for those who had not passed the 11-plus and/or the entrance examination. These schools were known as Direct Grant schools and contained some of the most prestigious day schools in the land such as Manchester and Bradford Grammar Schools. Entrance to this group of schools, unlike LEA maintain Grammar Schools, was not guaranteed by 11-plus success. A further hurdle of a highly competitive entrance examination and/or an interview had to be surmounted for the leading schools. A third of places on the governing body were allocated to local education authority representatives. In financial terms, the higher the number of fee paying pupils (maximum 50%), the greater the independence. One quarter of funding came direct from central government (hence the terminology), and a minimum of 25% from the LEA. In practice the proportion of LEA funding was higher, particularly in Roman Catholic foundations.

In my own home town of Blackburn, there were three Direct Grant schools; the two Catholic schools previously mentioned and the historic Queen Elizabeth's Grammar School, known locally by its initials, QEGS. Grammar school provision was supplemented by Blackburn Girls High School, and Blackburn Technical and Grammar School. As I cannot find the Girls High School, founded in 1883, in the list of Direct Grant schools, I have assumed that it became part of the maintained sector. Only the "Tech", as it was known, was not single sex. It is pointless to pretend that grammar schools were not dominated by the offspring of the middle classes, despite the fact that intelligence is distributed randomly across social classes, rather than having a proportional relationship with social class origin. Nevertheless, it cannot be denied that the radically increased free provision of Grammar School places (pre-1944 Act it was 25% of a smaller grammar school base), provided far greater opportunities for the children of working class backgrounds and contributed to heightened social mobility. In my own grammar school, the children of the middle classes were much less preponderant, which reflected the social make-up of Blackburn and the surrounding towns. The cotton belt had attracted Irish immigrants in numbers, and after 1945, there was a significant Polish population. Typically, the most recent immigrants took their place at the bottom of the social heap. As the Irish and the Poles were predominantly Roman Catholic, that was reflected in the form registers at my school.

Teaching methods were largely didactic. The master's job was to teach; ours was to listen and learn. We had a speaking part only when invited. However it would be wrong to view grammar school education as Japanese-lite. In English lessons we read plays out loud and periodically debated major issues. My first English teacher, Mr Rose, who died in 2007 at the venerable age of 93, was truly inspirational and I remember him to this day. In the sixth form in particular, we were encouraged to question and challenge the orthodoxy of the authors and historians we read. Although I was not one of my school's most distinguished alumni, it was here that I developed the mantra that sustains this book; when something becomes the prevailing orthodoxy it must be challenged. The constant pushing of the frontiers of knowledge and intellectual boundaries stems from that tenet. Organisationally, there was a homework timetable in addition to the timetable of lessons. We were expected to stand when any teacher entered the room. You were expected to give of your best at all times. The school prize night, and the musical recital that followed it, was the highlight of the year, as it put St Mary's College firmly in the public eye and the headmaster and guest speaker's speeches were given full coverage in the local paper. My school was proud of its role in contributing to the social mobility of working class boys. We were expected to realise our potential; indeed not to do so was almost a sin, which may explain partially why I need to write this book in retirement. We were also exhorted on our final day in school to go out in to the world and "Be good Christian men". Our education, therefore, had a wider social purpose. Whether there is any correlation between that philosophy and the numbers who entered the public sector professions can only be speculated upon. If there is a correlation, then the laws of unanticipated consequences have struck again.

Sport was also very important, which reflected the influence of the muscular Christianity associated with Dr Arnold. We were a Soccer school rather than a Rugby school, although a Rugby team was formed in 1968. Monday morning assembly finished with a mini-version of the classified check as Saturday's football results were read out; first eleven first and the under 12s last. I recall one occasion when the under 13s were hammered 9-0 after being only one down at half time. The Headmaster demanded that the captain report to his study directly after assembly. The irony is that the skipper of that team, John Waddington, was that rare breed of schoolboy footballer who went on to enjoy a professional career, and won a Third Division Championship medal with Blackburn Rovers in 1975. Alas, the year team he captained was simply weak by the usual standard. The expected standards of behaviour when representing the school were very high. The captain of my own year was ordered from the pitch by a master for daring to argue with the referee. There was no waiting for the referee to send him off, and no substitute was sent on. Part of me feels like I am describing an alien world in enunciating grammar school values as the rejection of them within the comprehensive world seems so complete. However, one little oddity worth noting is that on reaching the sixth form, which I did in 1969, we were permitted to smoke in the sixth form common room, whereas below that level it was a beating offence. By this time the link between cigarette smoking and cancer was very much in the public domain. Looking back it seems very much at odds with the sporting ethos, although it has to be said that smoking was not that much less common amongst professional sportsmen, outside of the dressing room. Mercifully I gave up the habit in 1980. The non-smoking orthodoxy is one I am certainly not minded to challenge.

I left school in 1971, having flunked all bar one of my A levels. I would add a second one three years later when I got the message that spending my life on a factory floor, with only the next pay day to look forward to, was not the way to optimise my potential. In retrospect, not entering Higher Education until I was mature enough to benefit from it, having tasted the alternative, was the key to success. I have no doubt that I would never have coped with the distractions at 18 and would have probably spent a lifetime answering the question "What happened to the boy most likely to succeed?" rather than three years. So, in October 1974, I formally enrolled as a student at Madeley College of Education and would eventually emerge with an Upper Second Class Honours in History and Education from the University of Keele. However, although members of the university, B.Ed students were second class citizens and, largely, we stayed on our own campus amongst our own kind. My exposure to the educated elite would not come through seminars and tutorials at Keele; it would come through attendance at National Union of Students (NUS) Conferences. National Conferences took place twice a year, but there were also sectoral conferences such as Teacher Education and a residential training event for new Student Union officers. If public school Army Cadet Forces were seen as the initial training ground for future military officers, then NUS was the training ground for the elite of My Generation. I contend that it was significantly more important than the Oxford or Cambridge Union Presidencies in terms of the influence on our national life, particularly since 1997. Jack Straw is probably the best known former NUS President. During my time as a student, the presidency was held successively by Charles Clarke, who would later rise to Home Secretary, Sue Slipman, first female President, who for many years was the Chief Executive of the National Council for One Parent Families, and Trevor Phillips, who was the first black President and who now heads up the Commission for Equality and Human Rights, which is arguably the most influential and powerful non-elected office in the land. Vice President in 1974-5 was Alistair Stewart, the ITN newsreader who was then known as Al Stewart, not to be confused with the singer of the "Year of the Cat". These are simply the names I remember. I did not know them and they did not know me. College of Education students were strictly second class. Whereas delegates from the neglected Further Education Colleges were adopted and patronised as a cause, Colleges of Education were seen as Philistine institutions whose culture was dominated by the Rugby Club and were irredeemably sexist. There was probably more than a grain of truth in the stereotype.

It never occurred to me at the time that the politics of the Junior Common Room and NUS Conference would be the prototype of how we are now ruled and governed. How naïve and unworldly can you be. It would be fair to say that student politics were as unrepresentative of students in much the same way as the governing elite is unrepresentative of the public at large. Not that we cared. The dominant political group in that era was known as the Broad Left, a loose alliance of Labour, Liberal and Communist students who held all the main elected offices. This alliance was well to the left of the then governing Labour party. Further to the left were the various revolutionary and openly Marxist/ Trotskyist groups, such as the IMG (International Marxist Group) and the student offshoot of the Socialist Workers Party. These ultra left groups tended to be more fractious, less disciplined and more inclined to argue arcane doctrinal interpretations of Marx and Engels, and of Mao and Lenin. They were also notably posh. My memory is of a public school wannabe proletariat. Prominent alumni of the revolutionary left of that era include Labour MP, Fiona MacTaggart, herself well born, and Hugh Lanning, subsequently Deputy General Secretary of the PCS trade union. To the right was the Federation of Conservative Students (FCS), in their pre-Thatcherite incarnation. At this stage they did not chant "Hang Mandela" or expose themselves in conference venue bars. Elections were by proportional representation, which allowed both FCS and ultra left groups to be represented on the National Executive Committee, but without holding any major offices. Occasionally, Cambridge footlights style student humour would intrude, such as the year a slate of candidates styling themselves as Epicureans stood for election. The pursuit of pleasure was perhaps more typical of students as a whole. Plus ca change... plus ca meme chose.

Student conferences were intense affairs. Even though NUS had the Winter Gardens booked until midnight on all but the final day, the agenda was never completed. This was usually because of disruptive behaviour that made life extremely hard for the conference Chair. I will give just two examples. On the last day one year, conference was disrupted by a demonstration of delegates, mainly from revolutionary left groups, protesting about the failure to debate gay rights. The fact that this agenda item had not been reached was the fault of the constant disruptive behaviour of this same group of students and this did not occur to them. Needless to say, there was no debate. On another occasion, conference was interrupted by a speaker who I believe may have been the aforementioned Hugh Lanning, wishing to raise an urgent matter, i.e. an incident in the bar of the Park House Hotel where a barman had referred to a female delegate as a "chick". You will get a pretty good idea of the main concerns of student activists from these vignettes. You will also get a picture of a future that has come to pass. Indeed, I wrote the first draft of this chapter just two days after question time on 27 April 2011, when the Prime Minister, David Cameron, said to Labour's Angela Eagle, "Calm down, dear". Cue splenetic outbursts, outraged dignity and total lack of proportion. Sound familiar? Sadly, the elite of the next generation have taken the political correctness of my generation to heart uncritically. As for the Park House, well some of us were not going to miss out on their then excellent Boddington's bitter. There was also the problem of finding another venue open until four o'clock in the morning. Pleasures of the flesh were an unmissable part of NUS conference, and it should not be thought that the political elite were teetotal or virginal. NUS Conference was both a genuine test of stamina and allergy to penicillin. Including drinking time, it could be a twenty hour day. As I recall the Winter Gardens in Blackpool, in those days the normal venue, sold beer in two pint mugs to thirsty students of a strong constitution.

It will not surprise anyone to learn that students of my era were obsessed with race. It has to be said that there was plenty to be obsessed about. Britain was a significantly more racist society than it is now. It must also be remembered that both South Africa and Zimbabwe (then still commonly known as Rhodesia) had oppressive white minority governments, the latter led by Ian Smith. South Africa was ruthless in dealing with dissent and deaths in police custody were common. Steve Biko is simply the best known. Both countries executed insurgents and saboteurs. At the time, it was possible to envisage the downfall of the Smith regime, as the white minority was very small and guerrillas were making headway. In South Africa, majority rule was just a dream. No-one was more welcome at the rostrum than black South African students invited to speak about the horrors of apartheid. However, the anti-racism of delegates came with a twist. One of the great causes of the time for students, and indeed still is, was Palestine. For many delegates, the state of Israel was not merely oppressive, but an illegitimate occupying power. Israeli nationalism, often referred to as Zionism, was labelled as racist. One of the loudest and most emotional proponents of Palestinian Rights was a student named Tony Greenstein, himself a Jew, and more than 35 years on he is still active in the same cause in the Brighton area. I have never encountered a man who excoriated his own origins so much. The last Jew to take on the sins of the Israelites to this extent was crucified. The rights and wrongs of the Middle East powder keg are discussed in the chapter on foreign affairs. The significant point here is that one can trace the gestation of the policy of pinning the racist label on those who disagreed in order to shut down debate. After all, isn't everyone bar the BNP and similar groups opposed to racism? This weapon of shutting down debate has been used very effectively with regard to immigration. People who disagree are stripped of honour by being designated as a moral defective, rather than someone with a different point of view. Routinely at NUS conference, delegates approved the hearing of a speaker from the Palestinian equivalent of NUS, but refused to grant speaking rights to anyone representing Israel. This was the policy of "no platform" for racists in action. I have to confess that I did once subscribe to the "No platform" approach. I would change my mind pretty swiftly on two grounds: it cannot be enforced without violence and it allows racism to be defined by a clique in any way they wish. Here you can see the gestation of Diversity training, which in its own way has become the equivalent of re-education as it was practiced in China and other totalitarian states. Control of the language of debate is a powerful weapon in the hands of those with totalitarian inclinations and access to power, a lethal combination. Given that NUS was a mainly atheist gathering, it is ironic that it most resembled a theocracy.

The feminists as a group were best avoided, as they were the least tolerant, and frequently the most aggressive and at the same time absurd debaters. There were no ladies and girls, only women. Whole student constitutions were rewritten to purge them of gender specific references, such as Chairman, which became Chairperson, and then Chair. These individuals would demand wages for housework and curfews for men. The irony of the sheer violence of their tone and language did not occur to them. I can recall one speaker waxing lyrical about problems with oglers and wolf whistling builders. This point always seems to be made by the least attractive women. Presumably blondes need to be sent for re-education. However, again it presaged the future. No building firm can get a council contract without a company policy on harassment and draconian penalties for transgressors. Feminists have killed the harmless wolf whistle. God help the Geordie who uses the term "pet" or "hinny" in a council workplace in Newcastle-upon-Tyne. Possibly the most outrageous contribution from a female delegate was to state openly from the rostrum that most men in the room had raped a woman at some point in their lives. Presumably only those celibate or gay were excluded from this extraordinary tirade. Nevertheless, this was another speech that predicted the future, where men are condemned as feckless, intrinsically violent, and as such render the institution of fatherhood unnecessary, except of course as a walking wallet. We have long since reached the point where the burden of proof in rape cases and other allegations of a sexual nature has been reversed. I will return to this point in the chapter on Feminism.

As far as democracy was concerned, the preferred model was that of a self-styled "People's Democracy" controlled by an elite group that it took its cue from Lenin. After all, how can the revolution survive and prosper without comrades who keep it on the right track, punishing heresy and hunting down counter revolutionaries. Only those who speak the language of closed debate can join the party.

At NUS conferences I witnessed the birth of the future even if I did not predict it.

CHAPTER 6

MRS THATCHER IN POWER - SURVIVING THE LONG DARK NIGHT

Although Mrs Thatcher was forced from office in November 1990, the John Major premiership is treated in this book as a continuation of the Thatcher era, rather than a break with it. The long dark night began as the first results came in on election night, 3 May 1979. After Labour was re-elected narrowly in October 1974, it was obvious to observers, although not to the man himself, that Edward Heath's days as Conservative leader were numbered. The problem for the Conservatives was that there was not an obvious successor, given the reluctance of any of Heath's supporters to break ranks, and those on the right of the party had seen their hopes dashed when an ill-judged speech by Sir Keith Joseph in the summer of that year about working class breeding habits, ruled him out of contention as a potential successor. So when Heath was forced to call a leadership election, he believed that he could survive, as did many political commentators. The challenger, Margaret Thatcher, was told curtly by Heath, on doing him the courtesy of informing him that she was to stand in the election, "You'll lose". Mrs Thatcher was known to the public as "Thatcher the milk snatcher", after school milk was withdrawn from older children during her term as Education Secretary, the only cabinet post she had held. Other than that short lived bout of controversy, Mrs Thatcher's ministerial career was unremarkable. She was competent, swift to master briefs, and ferociously hard working. There had been no hints of disloyalty, no straying from her brief, and no hints of ambition beyond cabinet status. Mrs Thatcher had herself said, when the question was put to her, that she did not expect there to be a woman Prime Minister in her lifetime.

Mrs Thatcher's elevation to the cabinet can partly be attributed to James Prior, one of the foremost of Heath's lieutenants. The new Prime Minister consulted James (now Lord) Prior about the token woman in cabinet, which had become something of a post war tradition. Female emancipation had progressed to the extent that Prime Ministers had to have one woman in the cabinet. Heath was advised that it should be Mrs Thatcher as she was the most able. Apart from the crude sexism, the other thing that is remarkable is that Heath had no idea as to her ability. Heath followed Churchill's precedent by giving her the Education portfolio. She remained in that office throughout the 1970-74 Parliament, untouched by frequent ministerial reshuffles. When the Tory party went to its leadership poll in January 1975, the task was seen by many to render Heath's position untenable and pave the way for Heath to retire and be succeeded by William Whitelaw, who was hugely popular within the party. He was a clubbable and convivial man, at home in any company, unlike Heath who had a complete absence of social graces and was tolerated, rather than loved, by his party. The trick therefore, was to ensure that Heath topped the poll on the first ballot, but with the kind of majority that would be seen as well short of an endorsement. The writing would be on the wall for Heath, and Whitelaw could then step forward as the unity candidate, without having to play the role of Brutus. Unfortunately, the Tory grandees got their sums wrong and underestimated the visceral dislike of Heath within the party and the desire for a change of direction. Mrs Thatcher was ahead on the first ballot, which created an unstoppable momentum. On the second ballot, Mrs Thatcher polled 146 votes to Whitelaw's 79. History had been made and this was only the start.

The Labour Party no doubt believed that their opponents had taken leave of their senses. She was patronised in the house by the vastly experienced Labour Prime Ministers, Harold Wilson and his successor James Callaghan, the latter rather more politely. Prime Minister's questions came to radio in the mid-seventies. On listening to Callaghan, he almost seemed to be patting the opposition leader on the head in reply. Mrs Thatcher was not at her best in set piece Commons occasions either. She lacked the flair and panache shown by Harold Wilson and, more recently, by Tony Blair and David Cameron in leading the opposition. Lloyd George once remarked that Neville Chamberlain looked at world affairs through the wrong end of a municipal drainpipe. Although Mrs Thatcher's anti-Soviet tirades played well with the Tory faithful, and earned her the soubriquet of the "Iron Lady" from the Russians, her simplistic view of foreign affairs was a definite weakness. In this she mirrored Ronald Reagan across the water in the USA. In British terms, Mrs Thatcher was dismissed as suburban and provincial by colleagues and opponents alike, with all that those put downs implied in terms of social and intellectual status. The Tories were stuck with her and she would only get one shot. However, it should not be suggested that the Tory party as a whole was aghast at what it had done. It should be remembered that for members of the 1970 Tory intake such as Norman Tebbit and Cecil Parkinson, who were true believers in the readily abandoned 1970 election manifesto, Mrs Thatcher was a beacon of hope for those who wanted to break with consensus economics. Mrs Thatcher was also warmly endorsed by the traditional right, who loathed Heath's liberalism on issues such as the death penalty and immigration.

After Labour lost its overall majority in 1976, the Tories swiftly rediscovered their ancient secret weapon of loyalty, on permanent alert for the day Jim Callaghan's government toppled, for the election they craved. There was only one point during Mrs Thatcher's tenure as opposition leader when it seemed just possible that Labour could be re-elected. This was in October 1978, but James Callaghan took the view that neck and neck in the polls was not a risk worth taking. However, the winter of discontent, as it will always be known to posterity, shattered Callaghan's calculations that industrial peace would hold thus driving down inflation further, and creating a favourable wind for his party in 1979. The inability to manage the trade unions had been the Tories' Achilles heel. It was the one thing, all else being equal, that could cost them the election. Labour had seemed so sure footed in handling the unions, to the howling frustration of the Tory press, which loathed their influence with a passion. Jack Jones, Leader of the Transport and General Workers Union (now known as Unite), sued the Daily Mail successfully for libel after an article which labelled him "Emperor Jones". Jones, a Spanish Civil War veteran, was probably the most powerful Trade Union leader in history between 1974 and his retirement in 1978. It may be significant that his retirement preceded "The Winter of Discontent", an event that would not be equalled in domestic political significance until Black Wednesday in September 1992 train wrecked the Tories' reputation for economic competence. In an act of unparalleled fratricide, the unions had wrecked the electoral prospects of the party that they had created and invited retribution from an incoming Tory government.

There was real anger about unburied bodies and heaps of uncollected festering rubbish. The socialised sector of the economy was a dreadful advert for Labour rule. For those of us who were committed Labour supporters, the twilight that preceded the long dark night started here. The result was inevitable. The phenomenon of Tory posters in student windows gave some major clues about the views of first time voters. The only issue was the margin. The swing to the Conservatives was a little over 5%, the highest since 1945. The Tory majority of 43 was a long way from a landslide, yet one could discern a break with the past and that this was not business as usual. As for Labour, it went off to lick its wounds, engage in the in-fighting that historically follows loss of office, and make its own unique contribution to the length of the long dark night.

Looking back with the passage of time and the mellowing of age, the Tory manifesto of 1979 does not look too frightening. Indeed, the Conservatives, despite the winter of discontent, were careful about the extent to which they might frighten the trade union horses. The future Employment Secretary, James Prior, along with other "Heath men" acted as a restraining influence on Mrs Thatcher until 1981, when he was despatched to Northern Ireland and the Prime Minister finally broke the shackles of post war consensus in her own party and remodelled her cabinet to suit her free market tastes. The manifesto is a short document long on aspiration, but the few specifics set the tone for a Prime Minister quietly determined to break with the past. The confidence that comes with success that eventually turned to arrogance and hubris would come later. There were few promises, but what promises there were presaged the future.

The Tories set out five tasks. Firstly to restore economic health and re-balance trade union rights. Economic policy would be very different to Labour. Inflation would not be controlled by incomes policies and pay norms. It would be done by controlling the money supply. The policy became known as monetarism and, in simple terms, was seen as the polar opposite of Keynesian demand management and pump priming. It should be said that the Labour Chancellor, Denis Healey, had already begun to use monetarist techniques, not that Labour was advertising the fact, given the general unpopularity of Healey's economic policy in Labour's own ranks. Borrowing would be reduced as would the Government share of GDP. There would be economies and a war on waste. Public sector pay would be based on affordability. Government departments would have cash limited budgets. The Tories would look to the private sector to rebalance the economy in favour of wealth creation. The National Enterprise Board would therefore be marginalized and the private sector left to get on with it. At this stage, the proposals for trade unions were moderate calling for reviews of the closed shop and picketing, and the potential use of secret ballots, although no-one could have been in doubt about the direction of travel. However, the Conservatives intended to ban the closed shop in the non-industrial civil service and stop social security being paid to strikers' families. All of this and more came to pass. However, the effect on the economic health of the patient is much debated. There were two periods of runaway inflation, Black Wednesday in 1992, and parts of the country where the decline of economic health was accelerated rather than assuaged, points to which I shall return.

The Conservatives second task was to restore incentives, reward success and thus create new jobs, not by direct act of government, but by emancipating the private sector. Bettering yourself was to be encouraged not punished. A major plank of the program was to switch the emphasis from direct to indirect taxation. The manifesto made no specific mention of VAT, but it was virtually doubled from 8% to 15% by the budget of 1981. The Tories would reduce income tax (and did substantially, particularly the top rate which had fallen from 83% to 40% by 1988) and this would be a priority over the reform of domestic rates, a pet project of Mrs Thatcher's that ultimately brought about her downfall. There would certainly be no wealth tax as promised by Labour. Also in this manifesto were the first tentative prods at privatisation, a word not then in general use. The Tories promised no further nationalisation (obviously) and to sell back to the private sector aerospace and shipping, with shares available to the public, whereas Labour had promised further nationalisations with building land, insurance, banking, pharmaceuticals and road haulage all on the shopping list. The bus transport market would be opened up. The Employment Protection Act would be amended in favour of employers, the activities of the British National Oil Corporation would be reviewed, and Britain would demand radical changes to the Common Agricultural Policy and demand British fish for British fishermen. Apart from the EEC, where Mrs Thatcher settled for a rebate instead, this radical agenda came to pass.

The third task was upholding the rule of law and parliamentary democracy. There would be a free vote on the restoration of capital punishment, as unlike her three predecessors, Mrs Thatcher was a supporter of the death penalty. Devolution for Scotland was not on the agenda and neither was a repeal of the 1949 Government of Ireland Act, which basically guaranteed that the six counties remained part of the UK until the day catholics stopped emigrating and concentrated on out-breeding their protestant fellow countrymen. House of Lords reform was most definitely out. There were hints at the disastrous unit fines policy, which was eventually instituted and swiftly abandoned under John Major. Finally, and significantly, the Tories outbid Labour decisively for the support of the police, promising to implement in full immediately rather than stage the recommendations of Lord Edmund-Davies into police pay. The significance of this promise would not become apparent until 1984.

The fourth task was to support the family and home ownership. Here the Tories struck gold. The promise to sell council homes to tenants at discount prices resonated with the public and challenged Labour directly for the working class vote. They also promised to introduce shorthold tenancies to unblock the private rental market. The Tories had shaken off their fear of being tarred with Rachmanism. The Tories also planned to eliminate the poverty trap that discouraged the transition from benefits to work. In that they failed and as I write, another Conservative minister, Ian Duncan-Smith is trying to crack the conundrum. They also intended to tax benefits, but in fairness this was also part of Labour's plans. Like his predecessors, Mr Duncan-Smith is hampered by the absence of employment for claimants to make the transition to, although unlike his predecessors, he cannot be blamed for its absence. The party also promised to repeal the requirement for LEAs to adopt the comprehensive school model, and to introduce the assisted places scheme. However, there was to be no return of direct grant schools. There was nothing radical about an education policy that shut the grammar school stable door after the horse had bolted.

The final task was to strengthen defences and work with allies. Mrs Thatcher was much more of a cross Atlantic supporter than Edward Heath. She would welcome the election of Ronald Reagan as US President in 1980 and he would play a critical role in her place in history. Mrs Thatcher was an implacable and strident foe of communism, but essentially there was nothing radical in this policy. It was more a noisy reaffirmation that would serve the Tories well, as Labour turned its back on what in reality had been a fairly bi-partisan approach to friends and foes when in government. Where there was a significant difference was Rhodesia, soon to be known officially as Zimbabwe. Mrs Thatcher had been inclined to accept the legitimacy of Bishop Muzorewa's majority rule government. Labour simply saw the Bishop as a fig leaf for the continued rule of Ian Smith. Mrs Thatcher would come to accept that Robert Mugabe and Joshua Nkomo who led the liberation movements, were more representative of the black majority and in due course brought about the end of UDI. Sadly, Robert Mugabe would waste his chance to inscribe his name in history as something better than just another syphilitic dictator of the type all too familiar to the long suffering inhabitants of Africa. Zimbabwe would become yet another corruptly ruled African country.

On the face of it, there is nothing exceptionable about this right of centre agenda in the sense that much of it is now part of our national fabric. New Labour largely conceded the economic argument to the disciples of Hayek and Freedman, firstly in order to get elected, and then for the first four years in office at the very least. As regards Trade Unions, Tory legislation remains virtually intact. It is now almost the least controversial part of the Thatcher agenda. The unions have had no difficulty in adapting to the loss of the closed shop, the end of mass picketing, and compulsory secret ballots. Only those who see trade unions as vehicles of red revolution seek to put the clock back. Let's be honest. The closed shop is not compatible with individual freedom to join or not join an organisation, mass picketing is the refuge of those who lack confidence in their cause, and only a secret ballot can give a true picture of whether members genuinely desire to take industrial action. After all, there have been secret ballots for parliamentary elections since 1832. One should also acknowledge that secret balloting is paid for out of public funds.

It is a complete myth that Tory legislation neutered the unions. What slashed trade union membership and with it the power of the unions, was the remaking of the industrial landscape and the re-balancing of the economy. It would be silly to pretend that manufacturing was not already in slow decline. Both Tory and Labour governments had sought to manage that decline and limit the consequences. Mrs Thatcher's government did neither of these things. Sir Geoffrey Howe's savage deflationary budget of 1981 accelerated the decline of manufacturing. Within a few short years the traditional heavy industries of coal, steel and shipbuilding were decimated. The remaining textile mills in Lancashire and Yorkshire faced the same fate. The mills that were not demolished eventually became blocks of flats. On a personal level, I was struck most of all by the impact on the once prosperous metal bashing belt of the West Midlands. I moved to Stoke-on-Trent from King's Lynn in the autumn of 1983 and joined the Labour party early the following year. A train journey from Stoke-on-Trent to Birmingham was an illustrated lesson in Thatcherism for those fortunate enough to have avoided unemployment. The last part of the trip from Wolverhampton through Dudley and into Birmingham was like passing through a giant scrapyard. All hope ended here. For those in traditional industrial areas it was a long dark night of enforced idleness, their own future stolen and that of their children given over to the drug dealers.

The coal industry was the key domestic set piece industrial battle of the Thatcher era. The Tories had no more intention of keeping open uneconomic pits than they had of maintaining uneconomic steel plants. The first major strike during the premiership of Mrs Thatcher actually occurred in the steel industry. The pay dispute was fought to a standstill with no real winner. However, it left the Iron and Steel Trades Confederation in no fit state to fight off the rundown, and then privatisation, of the industry. As far as the miners were concerned, Mrs Thatcher actually sidestepped the battle in 1981, when she discovered to her horror that coal stocks were nowhere near great enough to withstand a strike. At this point the miners were still led by Joe Gormley, a traditional trade union leader who did not see his members as the vanguard of revolution. However, he retired the following year and was replaced by Arthur Scargill, an implacable revolutionary socialist with roots in pre First World War syndicalism. Mr Scargill was denied his strike in 1982 when a 9.3% pay rise was accepted but his moment came over further pit closures in 1984. The Coal Board's chairman was now Ian McGregor, an American industrialist with a very American approach to cost cutting and trade unions that obstructed management prerogatives. The appointment could not have been more deliberately confrontational. Whether you love or loathe the man and what he stood for, Mr Scargill was nothing if not brave and principled. However, he was a lousy tactician and up against a foe that would not, indeed could not allow him to win.

This time the government was ready. Coal stocks were high, the police were prepared for mass picketing and more than willing to arrest fundraisers, and the magistracy were eager to redefine the word "scab" as a criminal offence and grant bail to arrested pickets only on terms that kept them away from the picket line. After the 1972 strike, which was the high point of mass picketing when Saltley coking depot was successfully shut down, and the miners won their wage demands hands down, many miners called the extra pound notes "Arthur Scargills", for it was he who personally led the mass picket. In 1984-5, police rank and file got its own "Arthur Scargills", in the way of unlimited overtime. The most disquieting feature of this dispute is that the police and magistracy became associated with the interests of party government, rather than the state. Louis X1V of France declared that he was the state, which as an absolute hereditary monarch in 17th century France, should not surprise us. An elected government in a democracy should understand that it is merely the temporary custodian. Whatever one's feelings about Arthur Scargill, describing him as "the enemy within" smacks of a government unable to accept that democracy exists outside a parliamentary majority. The trade unions, along with the Monarchy, the House of Lords, the media, local government, the churches and the universities are part of the fabric of our nation, or to use an earlier term, estates of the realm.

Arthur Scargill's biggest weakness was his failure to gain authorisation for a national strike via the ballot box. Constitutionally, it may have been within the rules to allow regional committees to authorise strike action, although the courts would rule otherwise, but it de-legitimised the strike in the eyes of the public. Nottinghamshire miners were better paid and the pits were not at risk of closure in 1984. Without a national ballot, Mr Scargill had no loyalty card to play with the Nottinghamshire coalfield. They refused to strike, in due course seceded from the NUM, and effectively invited the pickets into their coalfield. The split was a gift to Ian McGregor, the Tories and the police. Arthur Scargill was an easily identifiable pantomime villain, except that this was for real and a fight to the finish. Ultimately, many miners would have their convictions overturned and compensation paid by the police, but these were facts relegated to the small print by the Tory dominated media. Nor did it get sacked miners redundancy payments and certainly not their jobs back, assuming those jobs still existed. The NUM leader appeared to have one opportunity to settle on something resembling advantageous terms when NACODS, the National Association of Colliery Overmen,

Deputies, and Shotfirers gained a mandate from their members in the autumn of 1984 to join the strike, if negotiations with the Coal Board over pit closures failed. This was the only moment in the entire dispute when the government and the NCB were in danger of defeat. The strike bound pits were at risk of not being re-opened if the safety men withdrew their labour or refused to cross picket lines. NACODS had a weapon that could force the employer to the table, as the country had to have sufficient economic working pits. However, it was also a weapon that could backfire if their bluff was called and NACODS closed the door on their own jobs. Arthur Scargill was reviled as a fantasist for claiming that 70 pits were to close. In the end, it was more than double that as the shocking price of a failed strike was paid. The NUM and NACODS had taken a position to ACAS that pits should only close due to safety reasons or exhaustion. Had the NCB been forced to accept these terms, then the NUM could have claimed victory. For reasons still not clearly understood, NACODS moved position unilaterally to one of merely seeking an independent element into the existing review system for pits perceived by management to be superfluous. Arthur Scargill could not accept this position and from that point on it was a question only of when the strike would be abandoned, rather than if. He himself is convinced that Mrs Thatcher deliberately sabotaged negotiations at points at which breakthrough seemed likely, and that M15 agents were at work. This is the kind of thing unlikely to be officially revealed in the lifetime of any veterans of this dispute.

The defeat of the miners marked the high point of Mrs Thatcher's supremacy. When added to the Falklands triumph and the 1983 election landslide, it painted a picture of life under the ultimate conviction politician at her zenith. Two years earlier, Mrs Thatcher's re-election was far from guaranteed. In that year Mrs Thatcher moved to secure her own position in the cabinet by remodelling it in a more congenial image. In doing so, she would stand or fall by the deflationary policy that was intended to banish inflation, which in fairness was part of her inheritance as the Callaghan government failed to make the 5% policy stick. For electoral reasons Mrs Thatcher had no choice but agree to abide by the results of independent pay reviews for key professionals set in motion by her predecessor. By 1981, the Labour party was being convulsed by the Social Democrat secession. The "gang of four" as they were known, Roy Jenkins, Shirley Williams, David Owen and William Rogers announced the formation of a new party. More than a score of

Labour MPs joined them, but only one Tory. However, the SDP failed to attract senior serving Labour party figures such as Denis Healey and Roy Hattersley, neither of whom would consider leaving the party they loved. Apart from David Owen, there were not enough front bench defections to lend enough credibility or start a stampede. At the time Jenkins and Mrs (now Baroness) Williams were no longer in Parliament. The former had left of his own volition in 1977 for a stint as President of the European Commission, and the latter had lost her seat in 1979. Both would return in by-elections and as the popularity of the Tories waned in the wake of their economic policy, there was a tantalising vision of British politics being completely remodelled. David Steel, the Liberal leader, seized the opportunity for the two parties to co-operate and create a viable third force. The SDP, as it styled itself, appealed to professionals and to people who had never participated in politics before. It made more limited headway amongst working class voters for whom Jenkins was more posh than Mrs Thatcher. To committed Labour supporters he was simply a traitor.

The drift of the professional classes away from the Tories began almost imperceptibly in that era, its real impact not felt until 1997. Between Mrs Thatcher's two landslides, the government began to seriously alienate public sector professionals who still voted Conservative in significant numbers. The nurses were cheated twice; once when a pay rise was not backdated and then again in a grading review. Even the Tory papers were unimpressed. Home Secretary Douglas Hurd rejected a recommendation regarding an increase in police widows' pensions. Given that police officers die in the line of duty, this was crass. This was the first step on the road to the notorious Sheehy report, commissioned by the government reporting in 1994 in which it appeared that Mr Major's government had declared war on the workers who had helped them win the miners' strike. The decision not to implement the bulk of the report did not undo the damage. The Prison Officers' Association, the majority of whose members were ex-servicemen, at the time probably had a greater percentage of Tory voters than any other trade union bar the Police Federation. As with the police small attacks on prison officers would grow into large ones, with privatisation the most deadly. The electoral impact was concealed by the crossover of aspirant working class voters (the C2s), who had lost patience with trade unions, particularly in the public sector, and those working class voters who found Labour unpatriotic and were prepared to vote against their natural class interest. The SDP's "gang of four" were figures of the past for these voters.

Despite all its problems Labour remained competitive in 1981. Opinion polls showed the three parties almost neck and neck on occasions. The Liberals and the SDP carved up the constituencies with relatively little local dissension. Sensible Liberals understood at this time that they could not breakthrough on their own. In 1979, Mr Steel had spoken of 50 key seats. In fact they were reduced to 10 MPs, mostly on the Celtic fringes. In 1981 he would be telling candidates "go back to your constituencies and prepare for government". However, by 1983, that was as unrealistic as the 50 key seats target had been four years earlier. The Falklands war changed everything. Mrs Thatcher herself could not have survived the loss of the islands to Argentina. Indeed such was the shock of the invasion that the Foreign Secretary resigned as did the Defence Secretary, although his resignation was refused. Where Jim Callaghan had sent a gunboat, the Conservatives had somehow inadvertently given the impression, via a defence review (euphemism for cuts) that 1500 sheep farmers were an expensive luxury. Without wishing to demean in any way the sheer brilliance that marked the planning and execution that expelled the invaders, Mrs Thatcher was also fortunate that the American President, Ronald Reagan, ultimately gave the work of the task force his blessing. His Secretary of State, Al Haig, quite clearly stood for a negotiated settlement, which could only favour Argentina. The Tories also knew from either bitter experience or folk memory that previous American presidents, notably Franklin Roosevelt and Dwight Eisenhower, had taken a dim view of British imperial pretensions in the past. The victory heralded a surge of patriotic pride throughout the nation. Labour on the other hand, led by the confirmed unilateralist Michael Foot since December 1980, now appeared both unpatriotic and as a party of appeasement. The unfairness of this, given Foot's coruscating criticism of Chamberlain's appeasement of the Axis powers in the 1930s, culminating in the brilliant polemic "Guilty Men", cut no ice with voters. Foot was old and had not fought in the war as his eyesight was simply not good enough. Mrs Thatcher had gone to Oxford rather than join the Women's Services, but it simply did not register with voters.

The Prime Minister went to the polls in June 1983, almost a year before it was constitutionally necessary. Although there was a swing from

Labour to Conservative of 4.0%, the Conservative vote actually dropped from 43.9% to 42.4%, demonstrating that although Mrs Thatcher was at the height of her popularity, she was also a deeply divisive figure. It was the split on the left that delivered the landslide majority of 144. Labour polled 27.6% of the vote, their lowest since replacing the Liberals as challengers to the Conservatives, and the SDP/Liberal Alliance polled 25.4% of votes cast. For the Alliance it was deeply disappointing. There was no breakthrough, not even the consolation of second place. Moreover the even spread of Alliance support delivered them only 23 seats compared to Labour's 209. There was no tactical voting in this election. Shirley Williams lost her seat and William Rogers did not come close to being elected. Jenkins resigned as SDP leader to be replaced by David Owen, a divisive figure who would eventually join the Tories. At the next election, voters would continue to prefer the real thing. Dr Owen's relationship with David Steel was uneasy, made worse by the former's ready assumption that he was the senior partner. Four years later, the dream was over and David Steel would have his revenge by forcing a merger and effectively ending David Owen's career. The Tories had defied all conventional wisdom and won an election with three million people unemployed. So much for the 1979 campaign slogan, "Labour isn't working". The Falklands factor had delivered victory and confirmed that we now lived in an era of one party rule. For Labour, the painful process of re-grouping began. Labour was forced to accept the unpalatable truth that something approaching half of trade unionists voted Tory. Neil Kinnock and Roy Hattersley became Leader and Deputy Leader respectively. Tony Benn's defeat at the 1983 election ensured that there would be no challenge from further left than Neil Kinnock.

1984 only served to confirm Mrs Thatcher's Teflon image as she survived an attempt by the IRA to blow herself and her party to smithereens in their conference hotel at Brighton. That same year there was a significant Orwellian moment when the government banned trade union membership at GCHQ, the implication being that trade unionism and national security were incompatible. The workers who were sacked for refusing to give up trade union membership had to wait 13 years for justice. This was Mrs Thatcher's government at its most shameful. In the early 1980s, Cold War paranoia on both sides was at a new height. The Russian gerontocracy that ruled the USSR was seriously alarmed by the rhetoric of President Reagan, who had also survived an assassination attempt, and Mrs Thatcher. When cruise missiles were sited in England, the Campaign for Nuclear Disarmament gained a new lease of life. For the Tories and their press, anti-nuclear campaigners were not simply mistaken or people they disagreed with, they were moral defectives, fellow travellers and traitors. To say that the language of debate was distasteful is an understatement. These were febrile times and the world probably came closer to nuclear oblivion than at any time since the Cuba crisis in 1962. No-one would have predicted in 1984 that five years later the Berlin Wall would have fallen and the Cold War would be over. The Warsaw Pact disintegrated thereafter and states old and new found their way on to the map of Europe, all this without any twitchy fingers near the nuclear buttons. The real praise for this state of affairs belongs to Mikhail Gorbachev, who succeeded Chernenko in 1985, and his own successor, the frequently inebriated Boris Yeltsin, not the first functioning alcoholic to achieve hero status in 20th century history.

For Mrs Thatcher's admirers, the defining theme of her premiership is national renewal. Depending on the political point of view, the costs of that renewal were either unacceptable or unavoidable. I am angry about the damage to communities, but don't labour under any illusion that the alternative of a siege economy would have delivered anything other than prolonged misery for the people Labour claimed to represent. This does not mean that the Tories do not have a case to answer. The re-balancing of the economy from manufacturing to services, from north to south, from public to private is a far from unvarnished triumph. As a consequence, we have few goods to sell, an overpopulated south east of the country, and control of our fuel and power supplies in foreign hands. Some of this, I suspect, is the law of unanticipated consequences. Nevertheless, Mrs Thatcher's economic policy paved the way for the victory of people almost beyond the reach of democracy, the unaccountable, trans-national and corporate elite. We know it best by its shorthand name: globalisation. Revolutions tend to have dynamics of their own. However, what was clear and deliberate at the time, and wholly damaging to the health of our body politic, was the contempt for opposition. This was the most poisonous bequest to New Labour and sadly one they inherited with enthusiasm.

After the defeat of the miners' strike, the re-balancing of the economy accelerated. Trade unions could not establish themselves in the new businesses that replaced the old, and where they survived in the private sector, were up against employers who used de-recognition as a weapon. Labour party funding was badly hit by the decline in trade union numbers, as it reduced the value of the political levy, that part of the union subscription that was transferred automatically to the Labour Party unless the member opted out. Sadly, Labour would respond by courting tax dodging big business in the same way as the Conservatives. There was a downside to driving down pay as a means of pricing workers back into work. The Tories made a god of the free market, and indeed Mrs Thatcher's most devoted followers were more ardent worshippers than the lady herself. The problem is that the free market drives down wages for significant numbers of workers below subsistence levels. Thus the new market rents had to be subsidised by housing benefits, now not just the preserve of the army of unemployed. Enoch Powell pointed out quite correctly in parliament that this revived the system of outdoor relief for the poor that pre-dated the 1834 Poor Law Amendment Act which established the workhouse. However, to paraphrase the Tories own totem, there was no alternative. Having let the free market beast loose, the government had no choice but to subsidise the working casualties as well as the unemployed ones. As has been said, the demise of the smokestack industries and the switch to high finance as the driver of the country's prosperity made the economy even more London centric. The south east was prosperous and growing in population. The re-distribution of seats before the 1983 election already reflected this trend and the next re-distribution before the 1997 election would more fully reflect the Thatcherite revolution as more depopulated urban constituencies that were historic Labour strongholds, disappeared from the electoral map.

The other major plank of economic restructuring was the privatisation of state owned industries. Nationalisation of key sectors of the economy defined the Labour party and delineated it from its political opponents until Tony Blair became leader, when the historic clause four, which committed the Labour party to secure for workers by hand and by brain the fruits of their labour, was finally junked in favour of something more anodyne. Although the old clause four says nothing whatsoever about nationalisation, it rapidly became the interpretation associated with the party. For Labour stalwarts of the inter war years it was the solution to a mismanaged and misfiring economy. The coal industry was talismanic in that sense. In 1914, the industry employed a million men. The coal owners were ruthless and exploitative employers, their mines were inefficient, uncompetitive and lacking investment. The coal industry in the inter war years symbolised what was a very difficult period in which capitalism failed to deliver on the dreams of those who survived the Great War. Socialisation in the form of nationalisation was the cure. The planned economy would reach the parts that capitalism could not. It is important to remember that nationalisation was seen as a logical and progressive solution, as well as an article of faith. The Great Depression and its role in the genesis of World War Two had very much shaken the almost unchallengeable intellectual supremacy of classical economics. The point is that by 1945 nationalisation was an idea whose time had come. Thus fuel, power and transport were nationalised. Labour also nationalised the Bank of England, and created its most enduring legacy, the National Health Service. The only nationalisation seriously contested by the Tories was Iron and Steel. It was the only industry de-nationalised by the Churchill government, and it would be re-nationalised by Harold Wilson's first government. Thus state owned industry became part of the fabric of our lives. When one adds in local government, the state workforce at its peak exceeded seven million. Even Mr Brown's wholesale expansion of the public sector could not get it back up to that figure.

Edward Heath's Conservatives in 1970 had promised some fringe denationalisation, which they called "hiving off". In the end, only the state owned public houses in Carlisle were returned to the private sector. In fact, the Heath government was forced into further nationalisations of Rolls Royce and Upper Clyde Shipbuilders to avoid the collapse of these companies and the economic and electoral collateral that entailed. As far as Mrs Thatcher's acolytes were concerned, they should have been allowed to go bust. If there was no longer a market for their goods, then they had no future. As governments struggled to cope with "stagflation" as it was called in the 1970s, the new right of neo-liberal thinkers were emboldened to move into the intellectual territory that Keynesians were now unable to defend as economies failed to respond to their medicine. Thus, there was a theoretical underpinning of a general dissatisfaction with sclerotic nationalised industries that had become the new dinosaurs, were perceived to work in favour of those employed in them rather than the citizen, and despite the lack of investment in vital infrastructure such as the railways, were perceived as bottomless pits. As the Tories cautiously developed their critique, Labour clung ever more fiercely to nationalisation, and promised more of it still. The nationalised industries were over manned as was local government and the civil service. Workers understood the safety and security of the public sector, the size of which disguised the true level of unemployment. Under Mrs Thatcher, a large part of the disguise would be stripped away.

As far as the public message was concerned, privatisation was on one hand about value for money and reducing costs and on the other hand another strand of popular capitalism that would see share ownership become part of our national fabric, just as it was in the USA. Thus, we were encouraged to buy shares in newly privatised gas, electric, telecommunications and water companies, although it was not intended that private monopolies replace public ones as there would be competition from new private players. In local government services such as refuse collection would be put out to tender. The biggest losers were trade unions who lost their industrial and organisational base. All the privatised industries would contract, none more so than the mines which would sink to less than 10,000 workers based mainly in Nottinghamshire and South Yorkshire, as entire coalfields were closed. For the Tories privatisation was the happy coincidence of an economic mantra that rejuvenated their party and decimated the class enemy. The Tories had promised no more beer and sandwiches at Number 10 for trade union leaders. Their economic revolution made the days of Jack Jones and Hugh Scanlon dictating terms to Labour and Tory prime ministers alike seem like a relic of a distant and almost forgotten past. All privatisations have been contested, but the problem for those advocating nationalisation was that the intellectual ground had shifted from under their feet. Given that the monolithic Communist state of China has adopted a version of capitalism that would readily have been recognised by Dickens, it is difficult to see how and when a fractured left now more interested in equality, liberal interventionism and environmental issues is going to produce an influential critique of the British experience of privatisation. Only the shameful opening of private prisons has generated anything resembling an intellectual ferment about the state contracting out its obligations to those who now have a vested economic interest in penal policy. The crucial difference is that the privatisation of a shrunken coal industry is a matter of economic organisation, not a test of the morality of the government.

An honest audit of privatisation would paint a very patchy picture. Firstly the Conservatives sold off state industry at give away prices. Secondly, and one of the best examples, is prison privatisation, (the NHS is another) where new projects were carried out under the terms of the Private Finance Initiative (PFI), effectively a very expensive mortgage taken out by the state using taxpayers' money. Thus the contractor incurs no risk for the life of the mortgage. Someone tell me – what kind of capitalism is this where there is a complete absence of entrepreneurship? The Tories took no steps to prevent our water, power and ports from falling into the hands of foreign companies. I shall say more about New Labour's shameful record in a later chapter. As one would expect, competition created winners and losers. Public bus transport is a classic example of how privatisation shook out. Bus routes are now controlled by a small number of companies who have created an oligopoly in the industry as a whole, and local monopolies where a particular company is dominant. Low fares are as much a myth on the buses, as low cost electricity and gas where the regulators appear powerless to strike any sort of balance between the interests of consumers and shareholders. The privatisation of the power industries has been nothing short of a disaster for consumers, and an ongoing gravy train for the profiteers who own and run these outfits. The price of rail travel is truly terrifying. Fuel, power and the railways are further examples of oligopolies that act against the public interest. It is gratifying that a telephone line can be connected much quicker than in the bad old days of nationalisation, but it hardly makes the case for privatisation. One of the boasts of the privatisation lobby was that the customer would be king. Well I know of no monarch who would have to spend forever on the phone waiting to get through to a call centre in Mumbai to report a power cut.

Indeed, contempt for the consumer is a profound underlying theme of the Thatcher years, even if it was an unintended consequence. The de-mutualisation of many building societies created monsters that abandoned localism and the ready intimacy with borrowers and savers. Instead they became vast profit making machines. Mrs Thatcher's government encouraged private pension provision by individuals. Again, it is easy to understand the thinking. Firstly it is about promoting personal responsibility which eases the burden on the taxpayer and releases the individual from the grip of a company pension scheme which might not best suit their circumstances. The mis-selling of pensions would be the enduring scandal of 18 years of Tory rule. Banks now existed to promote financial services, and the majority of us, who were not remotely interested in their latest wheeze, would be forced to mutter in the queue as some low paid cashier attempted to hit her target by buttonholing a random customer at the counter. For the winners, often referred to as "yuppies", brilliantly satirised by Harry Enfield's character, "Loadsamoney", the late '80s were the golden years after the stock market was de-regulated. The well born and the well educated thrived as they always did, but they were joined at the apex by a moneyed class infinitely more vulgar than the rock and roll aristocracy that had moved up the social scale two decades earlier. Class became a much more complex animal than I had known when growing up. Indeed Mrs Thatcher abolished class as we knew it, but at the same time made her own contribution to the decline of social mobility as opportunities migrated south, an option open only to a minority of inhabitants of the de-industrialised wastelands. Again, we have the law of unintended consequences at work. The sale of council houses and market rents in the private sector acted to reduce the mobility of labour. Moving was an option mainly for the single and the very single minded. Mrs Thatcher never answered the question as to how one was to be expected to save a month's rent in advance, and a deposit of similar from the meagre proceeds of unemployment benefit.

At times, it seemed like the government was on permanent war footing; a mindset that is intolerant of opposition. The BBC was heavily criticised for its Falklands War coverage, and was forced to apologise humiliatingly for its program about three prominent Tory right wingers, "Maggie's Militant Tendency". Norman Tebbit was the usual attack dog deployed. The Conservatives have complained bitterly and indeed quite reasonably about BBC bias since 1997. Unfortunately, they do not stop to consider their own role in alienating the national broadcaster. The press was almost entirely Tory, so there was no plurality of messages. Mrs Thatcher also went to war on local government, using rate capping as a device to cut spending and more brutally disposing of an entire tier of local government, which included the Greater London Council. There is a fair argument for these measures and it is based on the fact that the bulk of the cost of local government is paid for out of national taxation. No government dare transfer the burden. However, it was just too much of a coincidence that the councils ceasing to exist were all Labour controlled. I concede readily that some of these councils were run by truly dreadful people who perverted the cause of socialism. Nevertheless, shutting down democracy is a totalitarian action not justified by the temporary popularity of a few fruit cakes. In the end,

Mrs Thatcher would deliver on her promise to reform the domestic rates and introduce an individual payment by also resident adults, universally known as the poll tax. Although it can be argued that a tax of this nature better makes the link between the cost of services and the consumer, it was a highly regressive tax which bore down most on the poorest. The lowest wage earners and particularly young workers still living with their parents were hit hardest of all.

Mrs Thatcher's ministers also had an unhappy knack of demonising the unemployed. I think most of us despise terminally lazy work-shy scroungers, and none more so than decent working people, but a party that puts two million people on the dole in its first term is not in occupation of the moral high ground. The vast majority of the army of unemployed wished to work. They did not want to live on the dole, they did not want to have sons who never acquired the work habit, nor did they want to have daughters who got pregnant in order to get a council house and associated benefits. I will not insult the intelligence of the reader by the lazy quoting of Norman "On your bike" Tebbit out of context. Far worse than this were Peter Lilley's attacks on the unemployed at Tory Party conference, where he would sing his own lyrics to Gilbert and Sullivan operettas to the delight of the faithful. It demeaned an essentially urbane and intelligent politician. It was as though Mrs Thatcher's government had declared war on those who were not her supporters. This was the logical consequence of the Falklands which relieved Mrs Thatcher of the burden of keeping the voting population in work. Its mirror image was the failure of the British left to offer a united coherent alternative at general elections. Arrogance, sleaze and hubris would eventually be as much a hallmark of this government as its remaking of the economic landscape. Mrs Thatcher and her acolytes forgot about the importance of nurturing democracy. My Generation in power would repeat that mistake.

PART TWO:

ACHIEVING, ABUSING AND WASTING POWER

CHAPTER 7

LONG TO REIGN OVER US: THE POLITICAL CLASS

I am indebted to Peter Oborne's seminal work "The Triumph of the Political Class",, published by Simon and Schuster in 2007. His book provided me with necessary building blocks for developing the ideas inside my head about the new establishment that now dominates our political life and seems to have successfully reproduced itself in the next generation. Whether Mr Oborne approves of the direction in which I have taken his ideas is another matter. In part two of the book the reader will see that I have argued that the leading lights of the political elite not only transcend party, but also that they are intensely ideological drawing on the works of Gramsci and Marcuse for their inspiration and intellectual underpinning. The political elite do not pay public homage to their ideological mentors partly because the word "Marx" in post Marxist thinking has a nasty habit of frightening the horses, but also because the new orthodoxy has been imbibed almost sub- consciously without deep thought and if it has been debated at all, it has been debated via intellectual tramlines that are at the same time very broad and very narrow. The political elite rarely talk openly about subverting institutions (Gramsci) or control of language (Marcuse), instead they talk about fairness, equality and respecting diversity. On the face of it these are not revolutionary concepts, at least not within our lifetimes. Ask the average citizen whether they believe society should be fairer, more equal and more tolerant and the average citizen will respond in the affirmative. It seems so obvious and non-contentious that it would appear to transcend ideology and create a new consensus to which all can subscribe. One doesn't need to go to university where these ideas are taught. Even true Conservatives can get in on the act ferociously criticising greedy bankers and calling for ethical capitalism in language not much different to that used by Labour leader Ed Miliband. It has been a Conservative newspaper that has led the campaign to get the killers of Stephen Lawrence behind bars.

My view that the ideology of the political elite is imbibed in part subconsciously and sometimes even subliminally takes my thinking further than Peter Oborne. He estimates the political class to be around 5,000 strong. According to him the political class comprises most MPs, MEPs, MSPs and their Welsh equivalents plus the lobbyists, quangocrats, researchers and special advisers. However, politics needs to be defined more broadly as the affairs of the citizen. As Mr Oborne himself argues, the political class does not operate solely in conventional political spheres. He cites lobbying and business as examples with the obvious potential for corruption. My strong contention is that the political elite and its candidate members operate very effectively in or against the institutions of the nation that previously acted as bulwarks against the aggrandisement of power by governments unable to distinguish themselves from the state. These institutions are well known to us; the Crown, the House of Lords, the Church of England, the Roman Catholic Church, the Universities, the BBC, the Newspapers, the Trade Unions, Local Government and Charitable organisations.

To this list can be added the coercive arm of the state which comprises the Police, the National Offender Management Service itself composed of the Prison and Probation Services, the Courts and the Armed Forces. Traditionally each of these organisations in its own way has been distanced from government. Apart from the Metropolitan Police where the Commissioner is appointed by the Home Secretary, Chief Constables are appointed locally for each of the 43 regional forces. Historically they have enjoyed considerable independence constrained only by their local Police Committee, although this may change with the advent of elected Police Commissioners to replace police committees in 2013. Even the Met had had the Metropolitan Police Authority as a buffer between it and the Home Secretary. As late as 1984, police chiefs resisted an attempt by Mrs Thatcher to attend a strategy meeting during the Miners' strike of 1984-85. The independence of the courts from the state was established by statute with the Habeas Corpus Act of 1679 which buried the spectre of extra judicial imprisonment. Although prison governors have been civil servants since 1877 when local authority prisons were brought under central control alongside what were then known as convict prisons, until the last two decades they enjoyed considerable independence together with a prestige significantly higher than more senior civil servants. They had considerable authority at local level to develop policy in dealing with incarcerated offenders. The Armed Forces quite obviously do not enjoy the same independence, but as professionals they were trusted and could be relied upon not to interfere in civil matters. Indeed, politicians largely maintained their side of the bargain and with the exception of Northern Ireland, kept troops off the streets in all but brief and genuine emergencies. Although troops were deployed during the Tonypandy riot of 1910 and again during the General Strike of 1926, no British citizens were killed by British troops in what were bitterly contested industrial disputes. Only in Northern Ireland have civilians died at the hands of troops, which is more a reflection of the venality of politicians than endemic indiscipline amongst soldiers.

It is my contention that the political elite have either infiltrated or seized power from all of these even including the Roman Catholic Church. The more coercive the power of the institution, the more significant is the progress of revolutionary political correctness. The wholesale corruption of the police and prison services by the movers and shakers of My Generation are dealt with in detail in Chapters 14 and 15 respectively. So who are the elite, where do its members come from and how do they operate? Peter Oborne argues that university is the recruiting ground. This mirrors my own experience described in Chapter Five, "Educating My Generation". So many movers and shakers from My Generation were student activists and were almost exclusively on the left of the political spectrum. Jack Straw (born 1947) was NUS President, Gordon Brown (born 1951) was sensationally elected Rector of Edinburgh University as a student, and Charles Clarke (born 1950) was the second New Labour Home Secretary to have served as NUS President. Others have made their way leading single issue organisations, in journalism or in heading up important and very powerful quangos. Respectively, examples are Sue Slipman (born 1949) former head of the National Council for One Parent Families, defender of the discredited Child Support Agency and a former Director of Camelot, the lottery quango which redistributes money from the poor to politically correct causes; David Aaronovitch (born 1954) influential journalist at The Independent and now The Times; and perhaps the best known of all outside the House of Commons, Trevor Phillips (born 1953), head of the Commission for Equality and Human Rights. All three were elected to the NUS Presidency between 1977 and 1980 after serving in more junior offices on the National Executive Committee. All were well into their twenties when taking on the role and were effectively professional politicians before the term came into the political lexicon. Student activism was not a pre-condition of joining the elite, as the rise of Tony Blair demonstrates. What matters is the network. In theory, entry to this class is open to all. The university experience at the hands of post-modernist academics, initially from an earlier generation but now from mine, trumps social background and renders redundant the old school tie. Indeed those who attended independent schools play it down, and those who attended comprehensives play it up for all that it is worth. This is a very different establishment to that described by Anthony Sampson in his seminal work, "The Anatomy of Britain" (1962). Fitting in is what matters, having a common intellectual perspective, and common political goals after university. Life after university rarely involves business unless it is lobbying. The most common form of private sector employment is the law, but it is not likely to be commercial law. Typically the elite will be involved in Health and Safety cases, claims against the Police, Prison Service and Health Service, and claims on behalf of illegal immigrants. These law firms are private sector in name only as almost their entire income comes from the public purse via legal aid. The new establishment operates in the most fertile areas for its political agenda.

Returning to my examples, Sue Slipman was from a working class background in Brixton, as was Trevor Phillips in Wood Green. David Aaronovitch was from an academic background like the Miliband brothers. Gordon Brown and Tony Blair were from professional backgrounds, in Mr Blair's case one comfortable enough to afford elite independent schooling. Ironically both Sue Slipman and David Aaronovitch are from Jewish backgrounds, not a comfortable place to be heading an organisation containing a determined group of activists whose Anti-Semitism was visible at every conference. The new establishment transcends traditional class, race and sexuality barriers. Differences over the conflict between Arab and Jew, although fought with real venom, do not significantly diminish the homogeneity of approach, outlook and modus operandi of the elite.

As has been said and indeed cannot be emphasised enough, the overtly politically correct are not found just among parliamentarians, their advisors and the legally aided law profession. The new establishment can be found at the head of Police forces, major departments of the Civil Service, and regional Fire Services. With good reason Sir Ian Blair (born 1953), Metropolitan Police Commissioner 2005-08 and prior to that Deputy Commissioner, was known as Britain's most politically correct policeman. The Prison Service was headed by another member of the new establishment, Martin (since 1 January 2013 Sir Martin) Narey, born in Middlesbrough in 1955. From 1998 to 2005 he was successively Director General of the Prison Service, Chief Executive of NOMS and Commissioner for Correctional Services within the Home Office, rising to the highest Civil Service rank of Permanent Secretary. Back in 2006, a group of Catholic Glasgow fire fighters were disciplined for refusing to hand out leaflets at a Gay Pride march in which participants dressed as priests and nuns lampooned their church. Not until 2009 were the disciplinary awards removed as a consequence of the fire fighters taking their case to an employment tribunal. Brian Sweeney, Head of Glasgow's Fire Service from 2004 to 2011 was allowed to retire early from the service in July of that year, and then be reinstated a month later. This is a classic example of how the elite play the system and look after each other. The new establishment is well entrenched in local government, as both councillors and senior executives.

Quangos are a particularly important source of power. Trevor Phillips has already been mentioned, but two other names worthy of note are Dame Suzi Leather (born 1956), Chair of the Charity Commission 2006-12 and a professional quangocrat since 2000. Her salary at the Charity Commission was revealed as in excess of 104k per annum in 2010 for a three day week. Dame Suzi is a fervent radical feminist who denies the need for a father in children's lives. She became best known for using her position to pressurise independent schools to provide more bursaries on pain of loss of charitable status. Needless to say her own background is privileged. In 2012, Professor Les Ebdon (born 1947), Vice Chancellor of the University of Bedfordshire, was confirmed as the government's new University Fair Access tsar by a Conservative minister. Professor Ebdon is famed for his championing of "mickey mouse" degrees such as Spa Management and Media Studies. Luton is about as far as it gets from dreaming spires and is a shining example of the drive to the dumbed down comprehensive university in the name of combating elitism. Control of the Education system is crucial to the revolutionary project and this was the first of its triumphs, victory being completed rather than started by My Generation. The triumph is all the more notable given that Mrs Thatcher was not only Prime Minister 1979-90, but also Education Secretary 1970-74. It is one of the supreme ironies of our time that more approvals for local authority plans to introduce comprehensive schooling were signed by Mrs Thatcher than any other Education Secretary between 1965 and 1979. Even today, the issue of Grammar Schools is too toxic for serious Conservative reformers like the current Education Secretary, Michael Gove.

The behaviour of our governing elite in the courts and immigration tribunals has probably attracted the most public opprobrium. Even new establishment politicians such as Jack Straw have been moved to attack their judgements. A variety of foreign criminals have successfully claimed that their human rights would be breached if deported to their country of origin. These include convicted hijackers and terrorists and those who incite terrorism such as Abu Qatada whose human rights trump those of innocent citizens (including Muslims) not to be blown to pieces by Islamist fanatics. Criminals have avoided deportation to Jamaica by pretending to be gay, and in one notorious case a man gained the support of an Immigration Tribunal to stay in Britain on the basis that he owned a cat. This particular piece of nonsense was overturned further up the system, but is another chilling insight into the contempt held for the ordinary hard pressed taxpaying citizen by the political elite.

The House of Lords is stuffed to the gunwales with political placemen and women put there by the Blair government in order to create a New Labour majority in the Upper House. A number of peers have proved unreliable and ungrateful by rebelling, as appointees need not fear the whips or the electorate. The House of Lords, with its accompanying flummery and ceremony, is in many ways a perverse institution. It is easy to argue that, along with the Crown, it is a prime example of a lack of democratic accountability and therefore lacks legitimacy. It is unfortunate that our elite do not have the same view of European super state institutions, which are accountable to no-one and lack any form of democratic legitimacy, apart from the toothless European parliament. Unlike European institutions, the House of Lords has very limited powers. It can amend bills, but amendments are not binding on the House of Commons. It can delay bills, but only for up to a year, but it cannot delay money bills, so unlike the political crisis that pertained just over 100 years ago it cannot refuse supply. The very absurdity of being appointed and still in part hereditary allows it to exercise independence of judgement, should it choose to do so. This is why hereditary peers were targeted for abolition and this is why the political class are now changing their thinking to supporting an elected upper house whose members will be constrained by political patronage and personal ambition.

Amongst our other great institutions, the citadel of the Church of England has been breached and that of the BBC completely conquered. The Church of England has been for more than two decades paralysed by ongoing internal wrangling over female ordination and gay rights. The result has been that as a public we know far more about those debates within the church than we do about the role of the Anglican faith in our society. The disputes which have often been conducted in an atmosphere of real intolerance have driven some members into the Roman Catholic Church and far more into no church at all. I am not a religious person and am a stern critic of theocracy, but what is occurring here is the classic subversion of an institution from within. Only John Sentamu, Archbishop of York, stands convincingly against the next assault on the citadel, gay marriage in church. This issue is covered in detail in Chapter 17.

As for the BBC, it is a completely hopeless case. The organisation has recently gone to considerable expense to conceal an internal report which concluded that its coverage of the Middle East was biased against Israel. Its coverage of so called climate change is nothing short of propaganda. Its coverage of the row between Home Secretary Teresa May and Justice Secretary Ken Clarke about what is known as "Catgate" (the case of the illegal migrant initially granted leave to stay in the UK because he owned a cat), was embarrassing as the BBC simply refused to acknowledge that Mrs May had exposed the truth about the matter. More recently, its coverage of the tragic death of Whitney Houston was out of all proportion to the merits of a faded, has been drug addict singer who, in reality, merits no more than a footnote in the history of music in the rock and roll era. The politically correct would have us believe that she was a victim and that her ex-husband was responsible for the addictions that killed her. Thus, the addled diva is elevated to the status of a feminist icon. Feminism is dealt with in detail in Chapter 17 and the cult of celebrity in Chapter 18.

Two pillars of our establishment that might once have seemed immune to the blandishments of political correctness have also suffered some serious, although not terminal, blows. The Crown and the Roman Catholic Church are by the very nature of exclusivity of birth and vocation respectively, almost impossible to infiltrate. Unlike the Church of England, Roman Catholic clergy are expected to believe in God. They are also expected to preach the gospel and regard the Bible as revealed truth. The new establishment has had to find other methods of attack. The church has made a rod for its own back by its failure over a long period to deal with the problem of paedophilia amongst a clergy that vows celibacy. The abused have found their voices and exposure has hit the credibility of the church hard. As such, it was in a weakened state to fight a crucial battle with the government for the independence of Catholic adoption societies from new rules making consideration of gay couples as adoptive parents mandatory. The Catholic Church elected to wind down its adoption societies, with the outcome that national adoption figures fell even further. The new establishment is perfectly content for the most vulnerable of children to be collateral damage.

The Crown has suffered in a number of ways. Most recently, the Coalition government announced that the rules of succession will change after Prince William becomes king. The first born or eldest surviving will become monarch regardless of gender, replacing a thousand years of primogeniture. This has been done in the name of equality and modernisation, with no understanding of the historical context. The whole purpose of succession passing down the male line was to prevent the Crown falling into foreign hands. It is why Elizabeth I never married and why Victoria and our current monarch were careful to marry beneath themselves. As chance would have it, the birth of Prince George has put the matter on ice for another generation. More recently, with the passing of the Fixed Term Parliaments Act, the prerogative of the Crown to dissolve parliament has been virtually abolished. Neither of the measures featured in the Conservative manifesto and the electorate has not been remotely consulted about what are major constitutional changes. They are a perfect example of the arrogance of the political class which has successfully reproduced itself in the next generation. Like the Roman Catholic Church, the Crown had already been weakened, first by the divorce and then by the death of Princess Diana, an event which allowed Mr Blair to dictate terms to the monarchy in a manner not seen since the 17th century. The death of Diana and its place in politically correct history is discussed in Chapter 18.

I have previously mentioned the Charity Commission, headed from 2006 to 2012 by Dame Suzi Leather. Organisations with charitable status have a long and honourable history of promoting social reform as opposed to social revolution. Historically, this has been based around single issues and should not be seen as the sole province of those considered left of centre. The cause of civil liberties is a particular example and one of the most principled campaigners is former Conservative leadership contender, David Davis. Nevertheless, charitable status attracts tax concessions, which means they are subsidised by you and I. Liberty, the organisation that exists to campaign for our freedoms is headed by Shami Chakrabarti, who is not a member of My Generation, but is a fully paid up member of the political elite, being a believer in intrinsic human rights and prominent supporter of UK subordination to the European Court of Human Rights. Indeed, the organisation gives annual Human Rights awards. Just recently this stance has come back to bite Liberty which supported retired businessman Christopher Tappin (65) who was extradited to the USA on 24 February 2012 under the one sided extradition treaty with the USA. The Home Secretary was left with no choice but to sign the order after ECHR ruled that Mr Tappin's human rights had not been breached. Mr Tappin is, of course, not a member of any protected minority group. Technically, Liberty itself is not a charity but it is funded by a charity, the Civil Liberties Trust, which is simply an organisation under the Liberty umbrella. Its Chief Executive, Ms Chakrabarti, is normally a gifted communicator, but she revealed her true colours when arguing that strengthening the legal protection enjoyed by householders to use force against intruders amounted to the right to execute burglars. She went on to make herself ridiculous by arguing that family members rolling home late at night could also be at risk.

Liberty was once known as the NCCL, the National Council for Civil Liberties. Prominent members of My Generation cut their teeth in the organisation. Patricia Hewitt, future New Labour Cabinet Minister, was its chief officer from 1974 to 1983 and for part of that period the young Harriet Harman was its legal officer. It is not widely known that during the tenure of these future New Labour luminaries, (the NCCL was founded as a cross party organisation in 1934 to campaign for fundamental freedoms), the NCCL was in bed with the Paedophile Information Exchange, headed at the time by Tom O'Carroll who has accumulated serial convictions for child pornography offences. P.I.E. was affiliated to the NCCL until 1983, and its members attended NCCL meetings seeking, and getting its support for, the decriminalisation of child pornography where there was no evidence of harm being caused to the child photographed (!!!).A similar organisation, Paedophile Action for Liberation (P.A.L.), an offshoot of South London Gay Liberation, was also affiliated to the NCCL and later assimilated into P.I.E. This was a tawdry period in the history of an organisation that most hold in high regard. The fact that some Gay Rights organisations supported P.I.E. and their connection with the upcoming elite of My Generation, does much to explain the gay social worker scandal in Islington in the 1980s when the council, headed by future New Labour Children's Minister (!!!), Margaret Hodge, under the banner of Equal Opportunities actively recruited gay social workers, a number of whom turned out to be active paedophiles posing as homosexuals. Radical homosexuals operate under the cover of challenging and eradicating homophobia, when the real agenda is to capture the hearts, minds and crucially the sexuality of the young. Gay men and women, wishing only to live their lives in peace, find themselves, by default, represented by organisations like Stonewall arguing that same sex mutual masturbation and oral sex should be taught in schools, I presume without practical demonstrations. I have laboured the point to demonstrate how but also where the political elite operate. The political elite have deeply penetrated not only conventional politics defined at its broadest, but have also politicised the private and personal. It is important to remember that the family is a theatre of revolutionary war. Chapter 17, which deals with Sexuality, Feminism and the Family, explores this revolutionary agenda in detail.

I will mention one other charity, NACRO, formerly the National Association for The Care and Resettlement of Offenders, headed by former Prison Governor, Paul McDowell, in order to illustrate another disturbing development. I know Paul McDowell personally and have nothing but admiration for his unstinting commitment to reducing re-offending, which ultimately protects the wider community. Nevertheless, the manner in which organisations such as NACRO have become part of the machinery of government is grounds for grave concern. Third sector organisations like NACRO not only bid for contracts in the same way as public sector bodies such as the Prison and Probation Services and private companies such as G4S who are major players in the contracted out sector of the Prison Service, but also engage in joint bids with public or private sector bidders. It needs to be remembered that the shareholders of private companies involved in the custody of prisoners on behalf of the state, have a vested interest in incarceration. This is the crucial moral objection to private sector prisons. Mr McDowell runs his organisation as a business and in 2010 it was forced to make 100 redundancies, owing to loss of contracts. What concerns me is that the political class has succeeded in not merely nationalising but absorbing charitable organisations into the machinery of government. This is not their purpose and in its own way it is as damaging to their independence as overt identification with the nation's governing elite. Like anyone else, NACRO will inevitably be judged by the company it keeps.

Having contended that the overt political class is larger and has more tentacles than that described by Peter Oborne, I now propose to take the argument further. The political class has a layered substratum on which it depends to maintain its penetration of public sector organisations and to maintain the culture of denunciation that is essential to keep the working classes in order. What differentiates this substratum is the mute acceptance of the politically correct agenda. These are the led, not the leaders, the foot soldiers of political correctness. These members may not even recognise themselves as members of the political class, albeit as the lower orders. University graduates will predominate at senior levels and a number of these will have received their education at the expense of the employer. In organisations like the police and the prison service where a degree is not necessary at entry level, typical members will be fast track recruits, the vast majority of which will be graduates. Amongst this group, politically correct attitudes such as support for multiculturalism (the Diversity agenda), the anti-discrimination agenda (euphemism for positive discrimination), the Stonewall agenda, opposition to the nation state (apart from Palestine) and a belief in intrinsic human rights will be de rigueur. The feminist agenda will be particularly towards the fore, as the public sector is increasingly the career of choice for educated young women. Two thirds of NHS managers are female and the prison service fast track schemes have been attracting women in disproportionate numbers for some years. The values I have described will largely be received in this group. Despite the fact that the top layer of this group will largely be composed of those of above average intelligence, the set of values will largely be unquestioned. If members of this group had habits of intellectual rumination, they will have been discarded, and if not discarded entirely certainly not applied. This group of people will be career minded and largely loyal to their organisation. There will be those who are not true believers, those who harbour doubt and those who are inwardly sceptical. However, it would be wrong to assume that this last group will assume the role of loyal opposition. Firstly, the politically correct do not accept the validity of the term. Secondly, this group have careers and pensions to consider, mortgages to pay and families to feed in the same way as their unthinking peers. The lower layers of this group will be rather less well educated and in organisations like the prison service will operate as staff trainers, low level complaints investigators and compilers of statistics. They will not be trusted by peers and often appear isolated as a team that is workforce as far as management is concerned, and management as far as the workforce is concerned.

The UK does not have a secret police (although it does have secret family courts). Instead, the political elite have created Diversity directorates in public sector organisations to ensure that their values are transmitted, and the canteen culture counteracted. They exist to facilitate denunciation and dismissal. They also exercise regulation on private sector contractors, whose personnel are forbidden to wolf whistle, and influence licensing powers, for instance forbidding taxi drivers to display miniature St George flags during major international football competitions. These departments are sources of employment and career preferment. The Metropolitan Police has a 36 strong Diversity Directorate headed by a fully paid up member of the nation's ruling elite with a cadre of foot soldiers. This is the body that polices the police on behalf of the elite. They can advise as to whom is the right type, or more accurately "right sort" of person for sought after opportunities. In this way, they can lock in some of the key members of the lower layer of this substratum, the largely uneducated police officers, prison officers, fire fighters and clerks who not unreasonably also want a career and in many cases are every bit as capable of being successful managers as their university educated colleagues. Amongst this group are people still capable of thinking for themselves. Amongst this group are people known by their bosses not to have the prescribed attitudes, but shrewd enough not to break prescribed behavioural codes, and not caring about promotion and thus immune to the disease of political correctness. Those for whom it is sufficient to be a constable, a fire fighter or a main grade prison officer will recognise themselves from the description. This is why new establishment figures advocate that the police and prison service should become graduate professions, as over time it will ensure that every entrant is programmed into the agenda. The fact that it will cost the equivalent of a small mortgage to join the police or prison service will deter those intelligent but not particularly educated members of the working classes, who have traditionally seen these branches of the criminal justice system as careers. The political class preaches social inclusion but in reality practices social exclusion.

Our political elite claim to be believers in both equality and equality of opportunity. The meaning of these terms and the necessary conflict between them is discussed in detail in Chapter 8. Essentially, if you believe in competitive opportunity you accept unequal outcomes. If you believe in equality of opportunity then you believe in an equal right to unequal outcomes. This is a key part of what the politically correct claim to mean by equality. On the face of it, that sounds something like the principles employed by the handicapper in horse racing, where theoretically in a handicap the weights are framed so that all the horses dead heat. In practice that never happens as outcomes are influenced by the ground, by jockeyship and the general wellbeing of the competitors. However, the real difference between horse racing and life under the elite is that in racing horses are handicapped to provide a competitive spectacle, but in life under the elite it is to produce desired outcomes, the most important of which is to maintain the hegemony of the political class. Thus, at the macro political level, political parties constrain local autonomy by insisting on all women shortlists, operating pre-selection procedures to weed out undesirables and, in extremis, parachute in preferred candidates over the heads of the local party. Similar procedures operate wherever the elite influence or control public policy. My former employer, HM Prison Service, now part of the National Offender Management Service (NOMS), operates in a very similar way, and I make detailed reference to it to illustrate the point and have little doubt that readers who have worked in other large public sector organisations will recognise familiar patterns. The prison system is dealt with in depth in Chapter 15 and includes further observations on its organisation, management and politicisation in addition to those contained in the remainder of this chapter.

The prison service that I joined in 1984 mirrored the armed forces with its two modes of entry. Graduates were recruited as assistant governors and those who had left school at 16 (15 before 1972) with few or no qualifications were recruited as prison officers. There were therefore two schemes of promotion; for prison officers the summit was Chief Officer, roughly the equivalent of the Regimental Sergeant Major in the Army or Chief Petty Officer in the Navy, and for Assistant Governors to in-charge Governor. The assistant governors were the effective equivalent of the commissioned ranks in the Armed Forces. In the same way that army officers went to Sandhurst, assistant governors attended the staff college in the rather less attractive surroundings of Wakefield, sandwiched between the railway and Wakefield Prison, itself a stronghold of the Prison Officers Association. The divide was perceived to be social as well as educational and the annual internal competition for prison officers seeking to become assistant governors was described as "The Country House Test". It was one that few passed. In practice, as employment opportunities constricted from the mid 1970s onwards, an increasing number of grammar school boys and a sprinkling of graduates found their way into the lower ranks. In my own training section of 25 recruits in 1984, there were three graduates, including myself. This archaic class based system was swept away in 1987 and the unified service created. From that point it became possible to progress via a common route of promotion from prison officer to in-charge governor, and from 1992 to the Senior Civil Service when area managers were created. The Assistant Governor Scheme was replaced by an Accelerated Promotion Scheme (APS), whose first recruits began their course in the autumn of 1990. Of the original sixteen, only two were specifically graduate recruits. Of the remaining fourteen, thirteen were recruited from the uniformed ranks, three of whom were graduates. The fourteenth individual was a female clerk. There was only one other woman on the course, a graduate but a serving prison officer rather than a graduate recruit. The scheme has been modified over the years, but essentially all recruits must serve a year as a prison officer and after that a year as a uniformed manager before being eligible to compete for a junior governor grade post that marks the first real step on the ladder. The real change has been in the composition of the membership of the scheme. It is now almost exclusively graduate entry with a pronounced female majority. Like its predecessor, NOMS uses a process that mirrors entry to what used to be known as the Administrative Class of the Civil Service, a three day residential assessment consisting of written assignments, non-verbal IQ and Mathematical tests, and oral assessments. In seeking to broaden its management recruitment, the service has engaged in what are known as Cross Hierarchical moves from across the Civil Service structure and more recently from outside industry direct to senior manager level in a bid to bring in business skills and bridge what NOMS calls a "talent gap". The military model of recruitment for a civilian occupation, abolished in 1987, had long been an anachronism. A system based on merit and a common learning and training experience for all managers on the operational front line had much to commend it. What has actually happened apart from a short lived burst of Spring, is that the principle of merit and the principle of a unified service have been eroded. As a consequence the gap between senior managers and the ground floor is greater than ever. The virtual apartheid of the pre 1987 era has been restored.

It will not be widely known that respect for Diversity, as it is termed, is a key part of recruitment and promotion procedures. In the Job Simulation Assessment Centre (JSAC – the prison service loves acronyms) scenarios, respect for Diversity actually carries the highest weighting. Again, on the face of it, this can seem unremarkable and no more than a necessary precaution against promoting those with prejudices against women, gays and ethnic minorities, and those with no empathy with the disabled. In an organisation where by definition there is an enormous power gap between the staff and those who they incarcerate, it makes obvious sense to weed out those with irrational prejudices against their fellow human beings. The prison service is a very hierarchical organisation so again it makes sense to avoid empowering those likely to abuse the power that comes with responsibility. It needs to be sure that its future managers will not tolerate unlawful discrimination against staff or prisoners. For supervisory and more senior posts, there will also be an interview and it is at this stage that a significant departure from a process that would command the assent of most reasonable people takes place. Tell an interviewer that you are colour or gender blind and regard a person's sexuality as a private matter and you will not be selected. Tell the assessors that money would be better spent on the intensive teaching of English to foreign nationals, rather than spending a fortune on translating documents, and you will not be appointed. Tell the panel you believe that Seasonal Affective Disorder (SAD) is simply being too idle to get out of bed on a cold winter's morning, and likewise you will not be appointed. These are not acceptable answers. You have forgotten, or more likely never learned that colour blindness fails to recognise identity, that sexuality is a public not a private matter, and that that failure to support the translation of documents into numerous foreign languages indicates a lack of commitment to multiculturalism. As for SAD equating to laziness, you have failed to recognise disability and act on it appropriately. The interview is crucial part of the selection process, as senior management is unable to interfere with the assessment centres and therefore this is their opportunity to weed out the ideologically impure.

Ideological assessment is not foolproof. People can be trained to mouth the appropriate responses and slip through the net. It has also failed to eliminate bullying merely transferring it from being a problem principally for those further down the food chain as it was when I joined, to one now very much a problem within management teams. Other forces are also at work. Internally NOMS is deeply wedded to a new public managerial cult and its attendant target culture, with all the pressures that imposes. There are external pressures from politicians to find scapegoats when things go pear shaped and the media gets excited. It is important not to be holding the shit parcel marked "blame" when the music stops. Bullying is the logical consequence of these pressures and it should be no surprise that staff appropriate anti-discrimination procedures for their own purposes. However, navigating the process successfully does not guarantee promotion. It is important to remember that in the prison service you compete for patronage rather than promotion. In 1992 the post of area manager, now known as Deputy Director of Custody, line managing on a geographical basis around a dozen in-charge governors, was created and gradually replaced the grade management system previously administered by HQ. In short, what has happened in that period is a massive power grab. Unless you have the support of one of these all powerful feudal barons, you will never achieve an in-charge post, regardless of your marks at an assessment centre. You will get interviews, but will never be selected. You will always be told that there was a better candidate. The process has since been refined further. HQ now has a list within a list, an elite group of people recognised by their area managers as people of exceptional potential. This process stops qualified candidates from chalking up endless rejections and after a period they are automatically removed from the list. Could you imagine having your qualifications annulled by your employer in any other walk of life? Well this is what happens in the prison service. I qualified as a teacher in 1977, and have not taught since 1984, but my qualification can never be annulled. Returning to the elite group, its members will not always be that bright, but they will always be the right sort. The prison service boasts of being an equal opportunity employer, a true meritocracy. The truth is that under the heel of the new establishment, merit is no longer objectively defined. The new establishment ruthlessly controls entry and success in professions that were once conduits for social mobility and as such were able to constantly refresh themselves intellectually. Public sector professions and organisations are now the chief conduits for the ideological totalitarianism of modern political correctness, an observation I am sure will resonate with the oppressed who take the time to read this book.

CHAPTER 8

FREEDOM, EQUALITY AND HUMAN RIGHTS: THE SEARCH FOR THE HOLY GRAIL

Before commencing this chapter, I found myself remembering the bewilderment I felt in the sixth form at school when confronted with an essay title, "Was Bismarck a Conservative or a Reactionary?" Some years later, as a teacher, I used this to illustrate a particular message to my own sixth form students; define your terms. Do our politicians, judges and opinion formers ever stop to think coherently about the terminology they are using? Somehow I doubt it when it is so much easier to use these terms as buzzwords and sound bites. So what is freedom? Well, it is not something that exists in a fixed objective state such as death, the Russian winter or Pythagoras's theorem. It is a concept that can be expressed both positively and negatively in terms of "freedom to" and "freedom from". It is about personal autonomy in everyday life, the ability to choose one's friends, pursue one's own interests, and to be left undisturbed to do so. The boundary of freedom was defined by J.S. Mill as the point at which the exercise of personal autonomy does harm to others. Freedom can also be expressed as "freedom of", as in freedom of speech and freedom of association. These freedoms are usually expressed as "freedom under the law" and are therefore subject to legal constraints which can and do change. There is therefore a synthesis of authority and freedom which must be kept in careful balance by skilled governance. It should also be emphasised that in our country the citizen has traditionally been free to do whatever is not forbidden by law, as opposed to seeking permission. Thus autonomy is part of the DNA of our common law.

Freedom can also be found buttressed by an adjective, examples of which are economic and sexual freedom, again constrained by law or moral code. To set free means to liberate or turn loose. It has positive connotations because, historically, freedom has had to be fought for, nurtured and protected. The freedoms that existed were the prerogative of the powerful few, and even then far from guaranteed whether they existed in the Ancient Greece of Socrates and Plato or the Plantagenet England of King John. Thus Magna Carta is a hugely significant historical occurrence, even though its immediate social effect was limited to a few hundred magnates who had united to circumscribe the royal prerogative and the divine right of kings. Magna Carta enshrined the right of those covered by it to Habeas Corpus, trial by one's peers, and freedom from the arbitrary confiscation of property. Over the centuries, serfs and then slaves would be freed and men would be free to become wealthy other than by royal patronage. In the 20th century colonies would seek freedom from their imperial masters and new nations would emerge as a consequence. It is not difficult to see why freedom is attractive and why sections of the population not previously covered by the freedom that the owners of property had achieved, aspired to greater freedom for themselves. Organisations such as trade unions, women's groups and civil rights groups in the USA and closer to home in Northern Ireland developed and flourished in order to gain their share of that precious commodity; freedom. Thus, freedom developed an explicit communal dimension. However, liberation became not just a demand for the powerful to share their freedom, it became a moral imperative. Men such as Martin Luther King, a Baptist Minister, invested freedom with religious and moral significance which can be seen as ironic, given the role of organised religion in suppressing freedom over the centuries, a role for which it still has considerable enthusiasm.

Freedom therefore is part of the history of human conflict. Those who would argue that freedom is God given need to study the record of the faiths and the churches which exist to worship him. Where organised religion acknowledges freedom it does so with strict boundaries, mainly regarding sexual behaviour, the breaching of which is described as licence. Here, Christianity attempts to fill a void not covered by the law, the very area where personal autonomy is maximised. It does not occur to them that freedom without licence may not be freedom worth having. In Islamic countries Sharia law ensures that the religion and society are one, thus constricting that area of personal autonomy.

Religious freedom is therefore an oxymoron. Radical Muslims explicitly reject freedom as anti-Islamic. In practice, in the western world and also the Communist world, organised religion, Christian, Muslim and Jewish have been forced to make their accommodation with secular forces. The faithful satisfy themselves with being free to restrict their own freedom, accepting with good or ill grace the democratic limitations on proscribing the freedoms of others. In return, organised religion benefits from secular legal protection, which radical Islam exploits and abuses.

Freedom does not only conflict with faith, it conflicts with itself across the political spectrum. On the political spectrum there is a rough divide between those who stress individual freedom and those who stress communal freedom which is not adequately explained by crude left and right labelling. Thus, in the UK, economic conservatives who espouse the free market are frequently a very different creature from American conservatives who are even more devoted to the free market and individual self-sufficiency. British neo liberals, who in party political terms are Conservatives, tend to be socially liberal on abortion and homosexuality and regard pre-marital chastity as a quaint historical custom. They are not especially religious. American "neo cons", however, are almost to a man and woman socially conservative, opposed to socialised healthcare, abortion, gay rights and sexual relations outside marriage, although their personal lives do not always reach the standards to which they claim to aspire. None of this will prevent them from telling you that they live in the freest country in the world. The right to bear arms, enshrined in the US Constitution (as they interpret it), is a key symbol of rugged individualism and the ultimate protector of the freedom of the individual. Unlike their British counterparts, public profession of Christianity will be an integral part of their lives. An emphasis on communal rights is more typical of the Socialist left. Nevertheless, an emphasis on communal rights, such as the freedom from tyranny, is not the sole property of the political left. In Ulster for instance Protestant Unionists who are often both socially conservative and economically neo liberal, will be found citing their ancient liberties, their opposition to the religious totalitarianism of Roman Catholicism and their right of self-determination, in this case the right to remain as part of the UK. Mrs Thatcher herself was an enthusiastic supporter of Lech Walesa, the formidable leader of Solidarity, the pro-democracy trade union movement in Communist Poland in the early '80s, who eventually became the democratically elected president of the country.

Support for peoples seeking to be free was part of the mantra of 19th century liberals who believed that peoples should have autonomy as well as individuals. They campaigned for the abolition of slavery and self-determination for those trapped under the Turkish yoke, as well as for freedom of expression, expanded suffrage and equality before the law. Socialists have also espoused national self-determination as part of their opposition to colonialism and imperialism, but have not tended to count the Soviet Union and China as imperialist powers.

For those on the left, the 19th century Liberal program for freedom is not necessarily sufficient and indeed individual freedom may run counter to the greater freedom needed by the community. In this respect Socialism is a true descendant of Jeremy Bentham, who formulated the test of that which produced the greatest happiness. The Russian and Chinese peasantries may have begged to differ. Nevertheless, possession of the franchise is no guarantee of social change, particularly if the political system conspires to frustrate the will of the electorate, as we know to our cost regarding the EU. Similarly, the abolition of slavery produced an incomplete freedom where it was replaced only by a 72 hour working week, poverty pay and squalid housing. Equally, freedom of expression had no meaning for the illiterate masses excluded from meaningful participation in society. Equality under the law is no guarantee of access to justice, as many African Americans still find today in the United States. Thus for those on the left of politics, capitalism, the great economic engine of the modern world liberates only the few and merely transfers power from an agrarian elite to an industrial elite. The right to sell your labour to any employer you choose is meaningless if the imbalance of power makes it impossible to bid up your wages and living standards. Capitalism spawned trade unions and co-operatives, which emphasised the communitarian over the individual. The Labour party was heir to this communitarian tradition. It was formed so that working people had a party that genuinely represented their legitimate interests and aspirations, to change and re-balance society to further the freedom of the excluded working class: those on whose toil and sweat the wealth of the nation was built; those whose lives would be most forfeit in the defence of the realm. This was Labour's moral purpose. I write as someone steeped in the communitarian tradition. If we truly believe that freedom is a good thing, and I do, then My Generation in power and New Labour in particular must be judged by its success or failure in enhancing the overall freedom of the community. One of the key themes of this book is that New Labour gave away our communal sovereignty and abandoned its historic mission, enhancing the freedoms only of the most anti-social elements, the fat cat bankers at one end, the feral underclass at the other, and a host of special interest groups in between, whose own pleadings were largely devoid of any genuine communitarian instincts.

Equality, human rights and fairness are perhaps the three most used expressions in the political lexicon in the UK. In the USA far more is heard about freedom, virtually nothing about equality and fairness is determined by the functioning of the market. Americans are passionate about democracy and their constitutional rights. For Americans breaches of human rights therefore occur only in countries that do not have functioning democratic institutions. Deputy Prime Minister Nick Clegg, in the seminal General Election debates of 2010, used the word "fairness" so frequently I lost count. The Prime Minister, David Cameron, and his Chancellor, George Osborne, also have a fondness for the word. Fairness is defined by our politicians according to the issue and finding a coherent philosophy amongst its protagonists is like herding cats. Insofar as the jelly can be nailed to the wall, the call for fairness from the political class is a cocktail of guilt ridden philanthropy at home and abroad, dreamy "one world" universalism, and primary school yard notions of justice. I doubt they have looked at the English Dictionary, which defines "fair" as that which is just, impartial or according to the rules. Thus in soccer or rugby an impartial referee interprets the rules. He may be a poor referee, but by definition he is fair, unless there is evidence of corruption. Once we leave the sports field, things become more complicated. Governments are ideological by definition. They have a critique, an ideal, and a program. Fairness is therefore something more than a set of rules to facilitate sport and popular entertainment. The word "just" is more instructive. It is defined as that which is right, deserved or fitting, which gives it moral purpose and buttresses freedom.

The concept of fairness, in terms of justice, has been around as long as communities have had systems of government and social organisation. Henry II (1154-1189) took seriously his duties as feudal overlord by touring the country and establishing the principle that the king's courts delivered justice. He also substituted jury trial for trial by ordeal. Whilst it can be argued that Henry's reforms were part of a plan to put the barons back in their box after nearly two decades of civil war and re-establish royal authority, Henry had clearly grasped that even in an autocracy such as medieval feudalism, a system of justice in which those high and low had confidence legitimised the monarchy. Henry would never have conceded that a royal personage needed consent to rule, but he would have understood the contractual nature of feudalism. When that implied contract broke down, monarchs found their thrones imperilled. King John was lucky enough to die before he was overthrown, having been brought to heel by the barons at Runnymede and forced to sign Magna Carta in 1215. Edward II (1307-1327), Richard II (1377-1399) and Charles I (1625-1649) would all lose their thrones, and indeed their lives, when the contract with the most influential subjects broke down. The invocation of the divine right of kings would not save them when they ceased to be perceived as just rulers. The moral base for determining what was just was the will of God as expressed through his church. In medieval times and until fairly recently, the prevailing social hierarchy was perceived as divinely willed. Even non churchgoers will be familiar with the hymn "All Things Bright and Beautiful" lyrics written by Mrs Alexander in 1848, still sung in school assemblies to this day, which contains the immortal lines:

> "The rich man in his castle, the poor man at his gate, God made them high or lowly, ordered in estate."

Until the Reformation, the Papacy perceived itself as having jurisdiction over kings in both religious and secular matters. Thus, kingship was an arm of God. In England the Reformation reversed the position and made the Church of England an arm of the monarch. This in due course was challenged by Protestant dissenters whose power reached its zenith during the English Civil War. Nevertheless, whether Roman Catholic, established Church Of England, or Protestant Dissenter, organised religion via its priests and biblical texts prescribed the moral code. The Commandments proscribed adultery as well as murder and theft. The Bible regulated sexual boundaries proscribing sodomy and bestiality, and prescribing death as the penalty. Thus, laws against homosexuality were perceived to be just. The system of justice therefore reflected the prevailing power structure and the parts of the moral code that were codified in law as opposed to being left to divine judgement on death. It would take philosophers like Locke and John Stuart Mill to embed the concept of individual freedom limited only by the doing of harm to others into this framework, where it has not always co-existed easily.

Progressively, over the last half century, the religious basis for our moral code has been eroded and replaced by a secular code prescribed by our ruling elite, which sadly owes very little to Mill. New Labour, unlike its Old Labour predecessors, is no longer three parts Methodism to one part Marx. The new God is secular political correctness derived from Gramsci and Greer delivered by a propaganda machine that would have been envied by Goebbels, which has contempt for democracy, the only force which has the moral and popular strength to defeat feudal, religious and secular autocracy and thus enhance individual and collective freedom. I shall return to this theme in the final chapter of this book.

Labour politicians prefer to talk about equality and also equality of opportunity, sometimes in the same breath, both of which they equate with fairness. It was a Labour Government that passed the 2009 Equality Act, of which Liberal Democrats are fully supportive. Conservatives talk about Equality of Opportunity on a regular basis, less frequently about equality, unless it is about equality before the law. The Human Rights Act was passed by Labour in office in 1998. Although it did not need Liberal Democrat votes, they were and remain enthusiastic supporters. The Conservative leadership tells us that it believes in intrinsic Human Rights, but not how they are interpreted in Strasbourg, preferring instead a British Bill of Rights, although there is little sign of this policy being pursued seriously. They will resolve their semi-contradictory position only by going back to Bentham. For their opponents, the self evident nature and universality of Human Rights is all, and overrides both sovereignty and democracy, forgetting that it is sovereignty and democracy that create and expand rights at the expense of political elites who believe they are our betters and seek to remain our masters.

The political lexicon is a combination of loose talk and beguiling theory. As a recently active trade unionist up against an employer that uses expressions like institutional reform and workforce modernisation, I know from experience that the appropriation of these terms is actually part of a sinister strategy to steal the high ground. The political elite are thus disciples of Marcuse as well as Gramsci both of whom reinterpreted Marxist Leninism for western societies in which the working classes eschew revolution. Therefore, to oppose the proposals is not just to be labelled a Luddite or a dinosaur, it is also to be labelled as some kind of moral defective. It is like being denounced as a counter revolutionary in Soviet Russia, but without the trip to the Lubyanka jail. Your disagreement is therefore without honour. Very much the same applies if you oppose that for which its proponents claim the promotion of equality, fairness and human rights, often all three together. As has been said this is deliberate and often conceals a decided lack of intellectual rigour. Where some measure of intellectual rigour has been applied, this too will often be concealed. Very few politicians on the left now claim openly to be influenced by Marx and certainly not by Marcuse and Gramsci. Similarly on the right, senior Conservative politicians do not admit to the influence of Friedman or Hayek. However, it is a mistake to believe that somehow unpopular ideology has been removed from politics. It is still very much present, but much more skilfully packaged. As a consequence the electorate has become infantilised. We have discovered to our cost, under the premiership of Mr Blair, what happens when style triumphs over substance.

So what do we mean by equality? Without greater precision, it is like trying to plait fog, never mind find the Holy Grail. In Mathematics, equality is absolute, so it does what it says on the tin. In an equilateral triangle, all three sides are equal and all the angles are 60 degrees. If the sides are not equal, the angles are not equal, and it is not an equilateral triangle. In a right angled triangle, the square of the hypotenuse is equal to the square of the other two sides combined. If that is not so, then it is not a right angled triangle. This is absolute equality. Mathematical notions of equality do not apply to human beings. Although recognisably human, we are not equally endowed in terms of physical characteristics. Some men grow taller than others, some men are more heavily built, and some men have larger penises. Women are generally shorter and lighter than men, but have a higher pain threshold. Like men there are natural variations in height and build, and other visible physical features. None of this may matter, but it is also the case that human beings are endowed with different mental capacities. Only a tiny minority are capable of an IQ score that entitles them to membership of Mensa. These are obvious inequalities about which nothing can be done. We console ourselves with believing that we are all equal in the sight of God, and are intrinsically of equal worth by virtue of our humanity. Those who are not religious are not deterred from using the intrinsic argument for equality. In one sense it is a curious concept. We have no means of verifying that God, if indeed he exists, created us as equal in his sight. It is a matter of faith. For those who do not have faith, it leaves open the question; how DO we know that human beings are intrinsically of equal worth? We do not and cannot. Indeed it has been argued that there are many human beings of less or no worth that as a society and as a world we would be better off keeping from sight, using to carry tasks suitable only for inferior creatures, or getting rid of them all together. The ultimate conclusions of such an argument are leper colonies, slave labour and genocide, all of which we have seen in the lifetime of the baby boomer generation. Nevertheless, this does not prevent us from having maximum security prisons to contain the most dangerous and predatory, so quite properly this philosophy has a pragmatic face. Cataclysmic events such as the Second World War have reinforced the necessity to self-endow the human race with the concept of its members having equal worth as an essential barrier to lapses into barbarism. Thus Germany and Japan, whose citizens in uniform carried out unspeakable atrocities in that conflict, have long been integrated back into the family of nations. How well that barrier against barbarism works is a matter for argument, particularly amongst the failed states of Africa. Equal worth is also not accepted by militant Islam, which advocates murder or at the very least forced conversion of unbelievers. The concept of universal equal worth by its very nature implies freedom. We need to be free from the threat of casual murder, slavery and banishment if a common humanity is to have any meaning. However, liberty is not just freedom from, it is also freedom to. This is where the conflict with equality begins.

So what do politicians, and more pertinently, politicians of My Generation and their unquestioning heirs mean when they talk about equality? The answer is a combination of inequalities that need to be rectified. They talk about inequalities between men and women in terms of pay and power, inequalities between the majority white British community and citizens of ethnic minorities, inequalities between gay and straight, able bodied and disabled, and broad inequalities between those who enjoy social advantage, as compared to those who are socially disadvantaged i.e. inequalities of access. The whole purpose of the 2009 Equality Act is to force all public bodies, including government, to consider that there is equality of treatment for those considered to be in minority groups who are perceived as the victims of less equal treatment, of inequalities of access, and lack of equality of opportunity. It is important to remember that equality is a journey, not a destination. This is a double edged sword, which allows for the concept of greater equality and its pursuit, but also ensures that the argument for greater equality never ends. Thus, its campaigners are on a permanent war footing. Taxpayer funded bodies, such as the Commission for Equality and Human Rights, therefore have the justification to be a permanent part of our landscape as the ever vigilant watchdog of equality. So far this is relatively easy to understand. The problem lies in the underlying assumptions that underpin what on the face of it is entirely reasonable.

Firstly, the politically correct assume that all designated minority groups are the victims of unfair discrimination, and more pertinently, that this is ongoing. Few would deny that ethnic minorities have in the past suffered from racial discrimination, that women suffered social and financial disadvantage, and that the treatment of gay men went beyond discrimination and extended into legalised persecution. However, as a society, we have moved on and moved on profoundly. 40 years ago racial discrimination was part of the national DNA and as such there was a real battle to be won. 40 years on discrimination on the grounds of skin colour alone is now the province of fringe groups such as the BNP and Combat 18. Yet, sadly, the political elite refuses to challenge the cultural issues in West Indian families that contribute so much to the fact that black boys are the lowest achieving group in our schools, other than the children of travellers. The prevailing myth is that racial discrimination is at the heart of failure. The truth is that black boys lack appropriate role models, because of endemic fatherlessness in the Caribbean community. Weak school discipline, far removed from that which prevails in the former colonies, reinforces behavioural problems. In addition, Caribbean culture despises homosexuality and working hard at school is perceived to be gay. Yet our egalitarians believe that challenging the failings of minority cultures is discriminatory practice in itself, since it is tantamount to saying that those cultural values are inferior or wrong. Influenced by post modernism, My Generation in power does not believe in the concept of objective truth. A similar situation pertains with Travellers where near total illiteracy is still prevalent. Their lifestyle is a cultural expression that cannot be challenged. So for minority groups, failure, disadvantage and social exclusion are prices they must continue to pay for cultural equality.

For women of Asian origin and in particular Muslim faith, the situation is even worse. The ruling class taboo against challenge to minority cultural norms exposes women to domestic violence, forced matrimony, genital mutilation and even death, if they are perceived to have dishonoured the family. Sexual equality is but a chimera for these women. Our ruling elite are content to ignore the plight of women from ethnic minorities and the same applies to their children. Unless a child is killed, social workers will ignore children having the devil beaten out of them by African parents, the use of curtain wire to beat their children by West Indian mothers and bullying and physical chastisement in Islamic Madrassas, the numbers of which are growing exponentially.

The politically correct reinforce their proscription on challenges to the cultural norms of minorities with an additional weapon to close down debate and that is the circumscription of free speech. Gays have full legal and social equality, apart from the right of religious marriage. As a precursor to this right being granted, the political elite are clamping down on criticism from Christians. In a case reported in the press on Sunday 23 October 2011, Adrian Smith a 54 year old Housing Manager for the Trafford Trust has been demoted at work from a £35k per year job to a £21k per year job, which assuming he retires at 65, equates to a pre tax fine of £150k. His crime; to suggest on his private face book page that gay marriage took equality too far. Readers will have gathered that I am no great lover of organised religion, but if Travellers can have an adverse view about homosexuality, and Muslims can express adverse views about homosexuality without sanction, then common equality demands that Christianity can do the same. Here again, we have this cultural hypocrisy in action. If it can be debated in parliament and by the press, then it can be debated by Adrian Smith and there are no rational or justifiable grounds for persecuting him for alleged homophobia. Even Stonewall accepts that criticism is legitimate if it is temperate, in other words within a democratic tradition where we accept that our views cannot always prevail, and when they do there is no triumphalism. Peter Tatchell, Britain's most prominent gay rights campaigner, has also defended Mr Smith's right to freedom of expression.

Marriage is a religious custom, the union of one man and one woman, ostensibly for life excluding all others, and it exists as an institution to bring up the next generation in a stable and loving environment. Where and when there was one universal church, it had the monopoly on marriage although not until 1566, at the Council of Trent, when the Roman Catholic Church was faced with the challenge of reformation throughout Western Europe, did it insist that a marriage was only valid if carried out by a catholic priest in the presence of witnesses. To this day the Catholic Church does not recognise civil marriages and therefore divorcees from civil marriages can marry in a catholic church. In 1753 Protestant England passed a law that recognised marriages only if these were conducted in a religious setting, which had serious consequences for heirs in non-recognised unions. In 1836, this was amended to permit registrars to conduct civil ceremonies. This is the origin of our dual system. Elsewhere in Europe, the law developed differently. In 1792, three years after the French revolutionary ferment commenced, the government decided that only civil marriage would be recognised. Religious marriage would not be recognised as valid on its own. This position was formalised under the Napoleonic Code and remains the law to this day. In post unification Germany, the same position was formalised. Religious marriage is an "add on" for the devout. The opposite pertains in Muslim countries, where no distinction is drawn between the secular and the religious, and therefore civil marriage is a concept that would simply not be contemplated. Similarly in Israel, where the distinction is intellectually understood, religious marriage remains the only option, as indeed it was in biblical times.

In 2004 in Britain, same sex civil partnerships were recognised by law for the first time. Ceremonies were required by law to be devoid of religious content. However, the Equality Act of 2010 permitted religious content, though religious bodies such as the Church of England were not compelled to offer facilities for civil partnerships. Under pressure from Stonewall, consultation began about the provision of same sex marriage. Success was rapid and civil gay marriage was legislated for in 2013. The Church of England, which is in an interesting position given its status as the established church in England (but not elsewhere in the UK), has said it will not conduct gay marriages. Indeed, it is not permitted to under the terms of the legislation. Similarly in Scotland the SNP Deputy First Minister has said that churches will not be required to offer gay marriage. However, it remains to be seen if churches can retain their exemption and the experience of gay adoptions, whereby the Roman Catholic Church felt obliged to close down its successful adoption societies, is not encouraging. A recent judgement by the European Court of Human Rights indicates the direction of travel. Perhaps unexpectedly the court has ruled that there is no human right for gays to marry, as opposed to entering into a civil partnership. However, ECHR also ruled that where gay marriage was permitted by law, gay men and women should have access to a religious marriage.

The Coalition legislated on gay marriage in full knowledge of this judgement. In due course, it could lead to the disestablishment of the Church of England should it choose to stand its ground on the status quo. This would be a huge constitutional upheaval. Thus, there is an ongoing debate that will continue in subsequent parliaments as the inevitable legal challenge wends its way to ECHR.

Faith is not logical so the logical position is to hand back religious marriage to the faithful. There is nothing worse than the hypocrisy played out every Saturday in the nation's Christian churches, where the faithless get the blessing of a cleric for their union and a nice background for their wedding photographs. At this juncture, I will confess to having participated in such a charade. My point is this; non believer couples should unite in civil partnerships in the same way as gay couples. This is true equality as it excludes all those who cannot abide by the rules of the club. It is no different than excluding Conservatives from the Labour Party. There is no arguable loss of freedom. Furthermore, divorce would not be available to those married in religious ceremonies, except where provided for by the faith or denomination in question. Thus, Roman Catholics would need to have an additional civil ceremony in order to anticipate the use of the civil facility of divorce. Of course this is too neat a solution for our bogus equality campaigners. They prefer to offer the privileged position of immunity from scrutiny and criticism to minority groups even when members of those groups suffer grievously. It should also be said that this solution would extricate the Church of England from its self-inflicted predicament, although I suspect that it would prove too religious a solution for its taste as faith does not always seem to be a pre-condition of membership. African Anglicans, known for their traditional beliefs as regards marriage and sexual matters, would probably be delighted.

As has been said, the iniquity of discrimination and the identity of those who indulge in it are built in assumptions. Thus, only white people can be racist and only men can be sexist. Quite how this explains Idi Amin or genocide in Rwanda is beyond their intellectual capacity. How the columns of feminist writers which appear even in papers like the Daily Mail, which demean and demonise men on a regular basis, are not considered sexist can only be explained by one-eyed hypocrisy. If male journalists wrote articles about female shopping habits, pre-menstrual tension and intimate grooming all hell would be let loose. Bernard

Manning would have been resurrected. We are back to the special treatment.

However, ending the argument at this juncture neglects what is actually a very important question – is Socialism simply about equality? Equality campaigners by their acceptance of the validity of equality of opportunity implicitly accept the contradiction. Peter Mandelson was merely the most vocal of the New Labour reformers when he asked the party to lose its inhibitions about those who had become wealthy via their own efforts. Essentially, equality of opportunity as a concept legitimises merit, however imperfect the systems are for recognising merit. Also, whichever way you dress it up, equality of opportunity is about the right to be unequal, albeit an equal right to become unequal. Equality of opportunity allowed working class children like me to become professional people, to acquire status, property and eventually the dubious privilege of being a higher rate taxpayer. I went to grammar school in 1964, but it is doubtful whether I could have gone 30 years earlier, even had a free place actually been available. Working class families, for the most part, could not afford the uniform, the sports kit and other accoutrements required. The means tested benefits of the 1930s did not extend to such things. Equally, I could not have gone to university until 1962 when student grants first became widely available. Although these were means tested, only the most prosperous working class families were required to contribute.

Modern egalitarians understandably seek to underpin equality of opportunity with equality of access, but do so in a deeply flawed way. As has been said earlier in this chapter, the unwillingness to challenge unhealthy cultures amongst ethnic minorities will always hamper the educational life chances of Afro-Caribbean boys and Muslim girls. As has been discussed in detail in Chapter 15, white working class boys are denied access to success in the education system, as much by the feminisation of education as by any other factor. And even if you resolve this problem, there remain barriers to success in terms of "bog standard" comprehensives that limit aspiration, the failure to get a grip on the drug culture, and family breakdown on sink estates. As such carping about the sharp elbowed middle classes commandeering the best school places, demanding the best for their children in those schools, and the willingness of those families to make sacrifices, is unbecoming of serious politicians, particularly as there is plenty of evidence that these self same politicians behave in exactly the same way. The behaviour of Tony Blair and Harriet Harman in securing prized school places for their children received detailed press coverage. Less column inches were devoted to Diane Abbot, at the time unique as a black female Labour MP, who diverted her son away from the local comprehensive on the basis of avoiding contamination with the gang culture. Some local authorities have decided to solve the equality of access problem to good schools by holding ballots. In doing so, they have replaced the lottery of the post code with the lottery of the ballot. They have implicitly accepted defeat in the fight to provide a good education for all our children. It is why, with a heavy heart, I have changed my mind about the local authority monopoly on the provision of public compulsory education and am now willing to espouse academies, although I draw the line at free schools, which have already shown their capacity to be abused by radical Islamists. Our children have been let down by an unholy alliance of Local Authorities and "progressive" educational professionals. Equality that is based on dumbing down to the lowest common denominator is not equality worth having. If Socialism is about equality of misery, then it has abandoned its historic moral purpose to transform the condition of the people. Social mobility has actually declined from where we were 40 years ago, which is a stunning indictment of our education system and those who have wielded power within it. The chapter on Education and Higher Education deals with this anti-meritocratic culture in detail.

I take the view that socialism is not exclusively about equality, although reducing avoidable and damaging inequalities must always be on the agenda. Socialism is also about justice, economic organisation and wider communal considerations. As I have said earlier, a philosophy for socialism should also be committed to freedom and democracy, which go hand in hand and should use the criteria set by Bentham and Mill, rather than Marx and Trotsky to audit success.

Essentially justice is about what is deserved and equally pertinently the community sees that the anti-social get their just deserts, usually courtesy of the newspaper as few people actually use the public gallery in the courts. This is the concept of open justice in action. If one accepts that justice is about getting what is deserved, then by its very nature one accepts that there are groups and individuals who will deserve less on the basis that that is just. This does not weaken the notion of equal worth as a human being, as one is being treated in a just way. Some simple examples will suffice. Thus, a professional club may include in its disciplinary code a fine for players sent off by the referee for violent conduct or repeated dissent. This happens because a player has let his team mates down by being ordered off, and therefore forcing his colleagues to finish the game a man short. The same player will also be banned by the FA. Thus, it is just that his monthly pay packet is lighter than that of colleagues because, by his own stupidity, he is not available for work. He is undeserving of equal pay. On the other hand, a player whose leg is broken will be paid. It would be unjust to deprive him of his remuneration in paid employment where accidental injury is an occupational hazard which is difficult to mitigate. Thus, the concept of justice also establishes the concept of discrimination on legitimate grounds. The criminal justice system, working properly, does what it says on the tin and provides justice, which is necessary to protect the community from the dangerous and the predatory, to facilitate restitution and to facilitate rehabilitation for all bar the small minority for whom it is impossible. If we look at the trials of war criminals after 1945, these principles can be seen in action. The trials were of course powerless to prevent genocide and other war crimes, but the establishment and legitimisation of such tribunals puts dictators and warlords in Europe on notice that justice will catch up with them in the end as Serbian war criminals have found out. Although I am personally opposed to the death penalty, the execution of Hitler's principal lieutenants and the imposition of long prison terms on other senior Nazis, occurred only after hard evidence was obtained and tested by cross examination in court. The families of the victims got justice. The perpetrators made restitution with their lives or with their time given over to custody. Germany (or West Germany as it became) paid financial reparations and, in due course, was rehabilitated into the family of nations.

Until the arrival of Tony Blair, the Labour Party believed passionately in the reorganisation of the economy on socialist lines, which not unexpectedly caused internal divisions as to what those lines should be. As has been said, nationalisation of key industries was the main way in which this was ideologically demonstrated, and this was the reason why Crosland was so vilified after the publication of "The Future of Socialism" in 1956. Chapter 19 deals with New Labour's economic record in detail. One can only speculate what Crosland would have made of the synthesis of his thinking on equality with the subversive revolutionary doctrines of Marcuse and Gramsci in action, had he lived.

In short, New Labour accepted the economic settlement bequeathed to it by the Tories. It embraced extreme wealth and casino capitalism, accepted and then embraced privatisation, furthered the decline of manufacturing, and acquiesced in globalism. Equality did not extend to the spoils of capitalism, as indeed it does not in Communist China. New Labour economic policy was purged not only of any socialist content, but also of any meaningful regulation of the worst excesses of capitalism, something for which succeeding generations are paying dearly. The party would also make the mistake of confusing high public spending with equality and with socialism. I am clear that intelligent, targeted public spending can further progressive aims and greater equality, but not where it creates impenetrable bureaucracies which corrupt the body politic, conspire against the public, and serve only the members of the political class and their adherents. One of Bill Clinton's best remembered campaign slogans from 1992 was, "It's the economy, stupid". Ultimately, New Labour's failure to remember that, would cost them office in 2010, leaving the party ideologically stranded with nothing meaningful to contribute in the face of a global economic crisis.

Whether the Labour party was ever a socialist party at all is much debated by left of centre thinkers. If indeed it was, it had certainly ceased to be one by the time it lost office in May 2010. It failed the tests of justice and economic management as well as its self imposed test of equality. As a people we have become less rather than more free, as New Labour also failed the communitarian test. My Generation in office empowered minorities at the expense of the majority, empowered the anti- social at the expense of the pro-social, and empowered the dishonest at the expense of the honest in creating a parasitic culture. When the Human Rights Act received the royal assent in 1998 and the Convention was incorporated into British law, Pandora's Box burst open. Arguing against the Human Rights Act and the assumptions that lie behind it is to invite the guns of bile, vitriol, and the lowest level of pseudo intellectual invective to be trained upon the author. The Human Rights Act relies on the premise that as human beings we have natural, intrinsic and self evident rights on the simple basis of being human. As Bentham said of Locke's assertion of natural rights, this is "Nonsense on stilts". There is no demonstrable evidence for this any more than there is evidence for the existence of God. It is a matter of faith. Thus the Human Rights Act has been foisted upon us by a theocracy hiding under the skirts of democracy. Animal Rights activists use exactly the same theocratic argument to justify the notion of animal rights. Quite how they synthesise the roles of carnivore and herbivore in the animal kingdom is an enduring mystery to me. As ever, some have rights like racehorses, foxes and any creature being experimented upon, but others like chickens decimated by foxes and cattle infected with TB by badgers do not. The same problem applies in human affairs, except that a great deal more harm is caused. An obvious example is the right of terrorists to rely on Article Eight of the Convention on Human Rights, the right to a family life, to avoid deportation and thus trump the rights of a community not to be bombed. This highlights the second key intellectual weakness of the natural rights position, in that it elevates the interests of individuals and special interest groups above that of the wider community.

The reality is that the rights we possess as individuals and as a community derive from the laws that have been made to regulate human affairs. Laws, therefore, reflect the values of a community, or at least its ruling classes, at a given point in time. Animal rights derive from the same human source. We may be one species, but we are divided by history and the spoils of war, by race, religion and culture, by language and the environment in which we work and seek to raise the next generation. History tells that rights have not merely had to be campaigned for, but also fought and died for, where notions of tolerance and democratic debate did not and still do not exist. Communities have had to fight for the right to determine their own future, sometimes running up against communities equally determined to carve out their own future in disputed territory as the conflict between Jew and Arab so amply demonstrates. It is noticeable that human rights campaigners rapidly abandon their abstract self evident principles in the Middle East and side unequivocally with the Palestinian Arabs. Emotional partisanship thus trumps reason. The Universal Declaration of Human Rights and subsequently the European Convention on Human Rights arose out of the emotional vulnerability of the leaders of the victors of World War II, and later of the new leaders of the vanquished, who were profoundly affected by the genocide, the gargantuan scale of slaughter and the sheer disregard for human life that characterised the conflict, which was made worse by the fact that modern nations, not feudal baronies, waged aggressive war. An estimated 60 million people died over the six years of war, 60% of these being civilians. The Soviet Union suffered around 26 million deaths at German hands, the highest of any belligerent. This represented about 13% of the total population of that unfortunate country. Like nationalisation of industry, internationalism was an idea for which time had come.

In discussing the European Convention on Human Rights, I am deeply indebted to the intellectual and historical framework provided by Dominic Raab, MP for Esher and Walton, in his book "The Assault on Liberty", which has allowed me to develop my own thinking on the subject, in what I believe is a coherent way. Where I differ with Mr Raab is in my belief that the UK should withdraw from the Convention as a natural consequence of the way forward that I propound in the final chapter. I don't believe that there is a compromise position that will not be subverted by the political elite, particularly amongst the judiciary. Moreover, a written constitution with its own guarantees within a sovereign state has no need of an international court to interfere and impose its own morality or interpretation. As I have already argued, I do not accept the validity of natural rights, and do not accept the validity of international law, except that established by treaty among sovereign states, capable only of being amended by those same sovereign states. On this basis, an international court operating independently of sovereign states has no legitimacy.

Britain played a leading role in setting up the European Convention on Human Rights. Indeed much of the wording was devised by the British negotiating team. However, Sir Eric Beckett, the Foreign and Commonwealth Office legal advisor, presciently warned that a supra national court would be a claimant's paradise. Attlee's advisors also warned against this and predicted the subversion of the convention in support of spurious claims: "To allow Governments to become the object of such potentially vague charges by individuals is to invite Communists, crooks and cranks of every type to bring actions." Lord Jowett, the Lord Chancellor, further briefed the cabinet as follows: "The real vice of the document therefore consists in its lack of precision... It completely passes the wit of man to guess what results would be arrived at by a tribunal composed of elected persons who need not even be lawyers, drawn from various European states possessing completely different systems of law, and whose deliberations take place behind closed doors... the whole document reeks of compromise." Attlee's government used its brains. It made a great show of being the first country to sign up to the Convention, but opted out of the jurisdiction of Strasbourg, where the court sat. This remained the position until 1966 when Harold Wilson's government decided to submit to its jurisdiction.

Inevitably, the court began to take on a life of its own. It moved from being a body that protected a core set of defined and circumscribed rights to one which described itself as a "living instrument". Thus, Strasbourg was no longer in the business of interpreting and applying the text of the Convention, it was in the business of expanding and making the law. The Strasbourg court was therefore appropriating for itself the power of judicial legislation, a clear breach of the separation of powers that is an integral part of our political and legal system. Nowhere in the Convention is there any power to make new law. In fact, just the opposite is true. The very first article of the Convention makes it clear that it is the job of the court to apply the list of rights as defined in section one. Thus we have judicial usurpation. Sir Gerald Fitzmaurice, British judge at Strasbourg in the 1970s made the point that it is "for the states upon whose consent the Convention rests, and from which consent alone it derives its obligatory force, to close the gap or put right the defect by an amendment - not for a judicial tribunal to substitute itself for the Convention makers, to do their work for them."

The European Court of Human Rights remained below the radar for the British public until 1978, when it ruled that birching in the Isle of Man breached Article 3 of the Convention: "No one shall be subjected to torture or to inhuman or degrading treatment or punishment." In 1985 it made a similar ruling regarding corporal punishment without parental consent in schools. The government duly legislated to outlaw corporal punishment in the state sector in 1986 and in independent schools in 1989. These were the belated consequences of Harold Wilson's decision to accept the jurisdiction of the court. Corporal punishment of children by adults is an emotive subject. For those of My Generation, it was virtually impossible to avoid the cane, strap or slipper – and often all three in the same school, and sometimes on the same day. Indeed for anyone over the age of 40, it was at the very least a live threat and a significant deterrent. However, it is not the business of a foreign court exceeding its legitimate authority to make the law in this or any other country that is a signatory to the Convention. Perhaps a better example is the recent furore over the Strasbourg ruling that the British government must give the vote to serving prisoners. There is no argument here that this usurpation not interpretation. The Convention makes no mention of the suffrage, indeed it was specifically excluded at the request of the French. The ruling can and should be ignored on this basis. In exceeding its authority, the Court loses any claim to democratic legitimacy.

Bizarrely, Strasbourg does not make case law in the way that we would understand it, by building on precedent, the basis for our common law. The failure to apply precedent inevitably means that judgements are arbitrary, inconsistent and even contradictory. This means that British judges, if they are so minded, can ignore precedent, ignore the intention of parliament when it passed a particular law, and embark on almost untrammelled judicial activism. The Chinese walls that governed the separation of powers have been broken down. However, it must be remembered that British courts were not compelled by the Act to adopt Strasbourg case law, although they were expected to take it into account. There was nothing new in being expected to deliver judgements that were compatible with our responsibilities as signatories to the Convention. They were free to interpret the Convention to suit local circumstances. They have chosen not to do so. Theoretically, the Human Rights Act did no more than allow British citizens to use the domestic courts to enforce the Convention rather than have the expense and delay of going to Strasbourg. No new rights were conferred. The Convention does not require national courts to treat Strasbourg as a Further Court of Appeal. Its job is supervisory and it has no role, unless the domestic system for protecting human rights breaks down. It is a subsidiary court, not a superior one. There was no expectation when the Convention was promulgated in 1950 that member states would surrender sovereignty, without which we cease to be a free people. My Generation, which dominates the ranks of the judiciary, took a different view and actively chose to submit and surrender. They chose to interpret the Act in a way that did the most damage to the power of parliament and our already weak democracy. My Generation in power hates our country and our way of life so much that they chose to interpret the Act in the most unpatriotic way, possibly threatening the security of our borders and putting our citizens at increased risk of terrorism. They have come out openly as members of the political elite that have seized power in this country. The disciples of Gramsci have seized control of yet another institution and suborned it to the political correctness of our new masters.

The Human Rights Act, which came into force in October 2000, has made us much less free as a nation. It has made justice arbitrary and capricious. It has enfranchised the criminal and the corrupt and fostered a culture of entitlement amongst the undeserving, who look upon the British taxpayer with the same relish as a leech looks upon bare flesh. The aforementioned culture of entitlement works directly against the communitarian principles that used to underpin the thinking of the mainstream British left. As such, the Human Rights Act does not advance the cause of socialism. It is a convenient vehicle of the elite whose agenda is to drive through permanent revolutionary change against the wishes of the ordinary citizen. Our political masters are more than content to ignore the Convention when it conflicts with their agenda. Elsewhere in this book, the examples are readily available. Article 10, the Right of Free Expression, is limited to politically correct points of view. Article 8, the Right to a Private and Family Life so beloved of the lawyers trying to prevent the deportation of terrorists and criminals, offers no protection against the right of entry to your home by numerous obscure officials and social workers, no protection from the state and its officials snooping on your Emails, and offers nothing to children desperately needing adoptive parents. Article 9, Freedom of Thought, Conscience and Religion does not apply to Christians. The huge gaps in Article 5, the Right to Liberty, offers no protection from a state determined to arrest as many people as possible in order to collect their DNA. It also offers no protection against the European Arrest Warrant or the one sided extradition treaty with the USA. Article 6, the Right to a Fair Trial, offers no protection to individuals dismissed from their work after, in the employer's view unsatisfactory vetting, because the unsubstantiated view of a Detective Constable about an individual who has had contact with the police, but never been charged with an offence, is used against them.

Subsequent chapters will set out in detail how My Generation in power has betrayed the people of this country by handing over sovereignty to Europe, creating a quasi police state, and subverting our institutions and democracy at every turn.

CHAPTER 9

RACE RELATIONS, IMMIGRATION AND ANTI-SEMITISM

Racism is simply defined as a belief that one racial group is inherently superior to others. On that basis, supposedly inferior groups may suffer disadvantages such as relative economic and social exclusion at one end to persecution and/or slavery at the other. Racism requires real or perceived identifiable racial characteristics that differentiate the groups concerned. Skin colour is the most obvious and has been the most potent form of racial discrimination in the lifetime of the baby boomers and at other points in our history. Racism has a long and dishonourable history and is frequently presented as a white on black or white on brown phenomenon, because of the slave trade and its consequences and also because of the European imperial legacy that would result in Apartheid in South Africa and migration by people of a different colour from the Caribbean and the Asian sub-continent to this and other European countries. However, despite the unedifying aspects of our history, it is a complete myth that racism is practiced only by white people against those of different skin colours. Labour MP Diane Abbot, the first black female member of the House of Commons, has claimed that Britain invented racism. It is sad that an otherwise intelligent woman, who should be a role model for her community, peddles this garbage. Brown skinned Asians have suffered vicious discrimination in the West Indies and East Africa from their black skinned fellow human beings. The Japanese treated the Chinese people with total contempt and vicious brutality during their invasion of China in the 1930s. Within Africa, different ethnic groups have not hesitated to prey on minorities they regard as inferior and unclean. The massacres in Rwanda are a classic example. It should also be remembered that it was Africans who sold their conquered fellow Africans to European slave traders, and that they had been selling them to Arab traders for hundreds of years previously.

However, there is no argument that racism was a huge issue when My Generation were young and that it became almost the defining cause of educated baby boomers, more so even than feminism and gay rights. When the first Race Relations Act was passed in 1965, there was no denying that the UK was largely a racist country. During the childhood and youth of My Generation, the UK was fast divesting itself of its imperial commitments. Colonisation had a religious genesis. The Plantation of Ulster began privately in 1606 and was taken up as Crown policy by James I in 1609. Two years earlier, the first British colony in America was established in Jamestown, Virginia. In 1620 the Pilgrim Fathers landed. All these colonists were Protestant. Some settlers in Ireland were Anglicans but the Scots were Presbyterians, the local brand of puritan. Early American colonists were exclusively puritan in search of religious freedom. In Ireland, the traditional Catholic chieftains had their lands expropriated. England sought to colonise rebellion out of the Irish psyche. 50 years later, after the unsuccessful rebellion against Cromwell, the plantation was extended as part of a brutal reprisal policy. From these small acorns sprang British imperial might. It should also be remembered that in these times of deep loyalty to the monarchy, colonists were also doing the King's work. The colonies were places to get rich, places to which convicts were transported and places in which younger sons without inheritances could prosper. The native populations, where they existed, were subject peoples regarded as inferior by colonists. They practiced alien religions, held cows as sacred, and burned their widows amongst other things. The heart of Africa was not opened up until the latter part of the 19th century, so relationships had developed differently. There, the coastal tribes were partners in what was known as the "Slave Triangle", which began with British goods being traded for slaves brought to the African ports, the said slaves were then exported and sold to new masters in the American and West Indian colonies and the goods they produced, most importantly cotton and sugar cane, sold in Gt. Britain. In the new world (America and the West Indies) there was gross under population. Heavy manual labour in hot conditions was considered unsuitable for white Europeans. Black slaves, used to the heat of tropical Africa, were considered eminently suitable and eminently disposable. Thus, imperial vanity and commercial imperatives, overlaid with a religious veneer in parts of the world where the population was a different skin colour, gave birth to the racism that was already entrenched when the first non-white immigrants began arriving from the commonwealth in the 1950s. Britain was in many ways conditioned to make them unwelcome.

At my primary school in particular, but also at my grammar school, we had text books that were a generation out of date. Atlases still showed the full extent of the empire as it was at its zenith after World War I. As a near contemporary, Diane Abbot would no doubt have seen these atlases in the schools she attended. The school budget did not run to catching up with independent countries, some in the commonwealth and some not. When I undertook teaching practice in the mid '70s, I still came across these text books. The natives were depicted as uncivilised, unchristian and as practising cannibalism. According to these text books, our mission had been to civilise these peoples and bring them to God. Great political leaders such as Winston Churchill and hugely intelligent people like Enoch Powell were so immersed in the mystique of Empire that they could not conceive of coloured races (this was the kind of language used at the time) becoming self governing. Imperial rule was the antidote to a predilection for barbarism.

It is undeniable that Britain has disreputable skeletons in its Imperial cupboard. Britain traded slaves, tied people to cannons and blasted them to smithereens as a form of execution, and deliberately introduced smallpox to the indigenous population of North America, which had no immunity to this deadly disease. However, Britain does compare favourably to other imperial nations and the USA. In 1772 slavery was declared unlawful in England. Four years later the American colonies declared their independence from Great Britain, but it would take until 1865 for slaves to finally be freed in the Southern states. Slave owners in what became known as the Confederacy, defied bans on importation by using breeding programs from existing stock. In 1807 Britain abolished slave trading and in 1833 banned the institution in the British colonies. Among the Imperialist countries, Britain took the lead in breaking the slave trade. In terms of colonial rule, British rule by comparison to countries such as Belgium, France and the Netherlands was relatively enlightened and tolerant and rather less exploitative. The Congo was brutally ruled and systematically exploited by Belgium. The descendants of Dutch colonists in South Africa invented the pernicious doctrine of apartheid and backed it up with brute force and ignorance. The closing years of French rule in Algeria were peppered with atrocities, both within the colony and on the streets of Paris. No one would deny that this country has a history with slave trading, but for Tony Blair to make a grovelling apology without any acknowledgement of the work of people such as William Wilberforce and Thomas Clarkson to bring about abolition, and the determination shown by British governments to police the ban on the high seas, stank of both political correctness and the trademark elitist refusal to say anything praiseworthy about our history. Why anyone should wish to apologise for something not their responsibility is a complete mystery to me. With breathtaking hypocrisy, Mr Blair apologised for the slave trade and the Irish potato famine, but uttered not a word of contrition about the invasion of Iraq in 2003 under pretexts that he knew not only to have no merit, but to be false.

Returning to the racist inheritance, my parents' generation grew up with Empire and the perceived notions of superiority in their school text books and the newspapers. The barbarity of the Japanese in World War II reinforced such notions. It was my parents' and grandparents' generation who, when renting out rooms, put up notices that said "No coloureds, No Irish and No dogs", which until 1965 was perfectly legal. There is an episode from "Steptoe and Son", a comedy on which I was reared, where Albert Steptoe, the father and World War I veteran drafts an advert to go in the local newsagents advertising a room. At the end of the advert it said simply "No wogs". It must be noted that Galton and Simpson's script, like those of Johnny Speight who introduced the monstrous Alf Garnett to our screens at around the same time, sought to expose the petty indignities and the ridiculousness of racism (or more accurately racialism as it was then termed) in that episode. Race was not a recurring theme in Steptoe and Son, but it was the dominant theme in Speight's scripts for "Till Death Do Us Part". Perhaps ironically, the role of Alf Garnett was played by a Jewish actor, Warren Mitchell. Two other comedies, "Curry and Chips" written by Speight which ran for one series in 1969 and "Love Thy Neighbour" written by Vince Powell and Harry Driver which ran from 1972 to 1976, were rather less successful in conveying an anti- racist message. In Curry and Chips, Spike Milligan "blacked up" and played the part of an Irish Pakistani who was nicknamed Paki Paddy. Despite Speight's protestations, the ITV governors forced the show off the screen after just one series. I would never challenge Speight's anti racist credentials, but a "blacked up character" was just not a credible vehicle for a serious message. Milligan blacked up again in 1975 for a BBC series called "The Melting Pot" which was pulled after just one of its scheduled six episode run. There was an element of one step forward one step back with television in this era as "The Black and White Minstrel Show", in which "blacked up" entertainers made up most of the cast and which engaged in pretty blatant racial stereotyping, ran until 1978, having first been screened in 1958. The stage show actually ran until 1987.

However, if ground breaking TV programmes sought to expose racism, boys' comics persisted with the stereotypes. In "The Valiant" which I took, and had often to wait for my father to finish reading before I could have it, Germans were Krauts, Japanese were Nips and Italians were Eyeties. African natives had bones through their noses and captured white explorers were boiled alive in cooking pots, whilst the tribesman danced and whooped in celebration. They were portrayed as simple to the point of retarded and spoke pigeon English. Native Americans got the same treatment. In the "Beano", there was a cartoon character known as Little Plum, full name Little Plum Stealing Varmint. He was a member of the "Smelly feet" tribe and Hole in Um Head was one of his friends. Anything large was "heap big". No doubt you get the picture. The character was a weekly regular until as late as 1986. Little Plum has been reintroduced, but now conforms to modern political correctness. The pigeon English has gone. American cartoons also carried the stereotype. Popeye the sailor man escaped from an Indian (Native American) cooking pot only because he could get at his spinach. Belgium had Herge and his eponymous cartoon hero Tintin, who likewise took a dim view of the cranial capacity of the black man.

This was our world and into it came a new wave of immigrants from the New (i.e. non white) Commonwealth. In 1948 the British Nationality Act created citizens of the UK and the colonies, all of whom formally gained the right to settle in the UK. Even prior to this legislation, there was no restriction on British subjects (as they were then called) of the Empire settling in another part of the Empire. At the time, these rights were uncontroversial as migration was largely the other way with Britons seeking to make their fortunes in the vast expanses of the Empire. Nevertheless, a taste of the future arrived the same year when the vessel "The Windrush" docked in the UK with 493 migrants from Jamaica to the alarm of some MPs. By 1962, when the first Act restricting

Commonwealth immigration (most countries of the former Empire were either independent or proceeding rapidly towards independence by this point) was passed, substantial communities from the West Indies and the Asian sub-continent had established themselves in the UK. Further immigration acts would follow.

Critics of those who call for a clamp down on immigration often cite the fact that immigration is not new. What is new, particularly since 1997, is the sheer scale. After the revocation of The Edict of Nantes by Louis XIV of France in 1685, around 50,000 Protestant Huguenots found their way to Britain before the end of the century, around 20% of these joining the plantation of Ireland. Huguenots and their immediate descendants came to represent around 1% of the population. In the 19th century, after the Irish potato famine, there was significant and continued migration to England and Scotland, so much so that it is estimated that at least one sixth of the population have an Irish grandparent. Another significant influx of immigrants came when the Russian Tsar resumed anti -Jewish pogroms in 1881. Between 1881 and 1914 the Jewish population in Britain grew from 65,000 to 300,000 and the influx was concentrated in major cities, which was not welcomed by the working classes and their trade unions as Britain's industrial hegemony was coming under increasing challenge from Germany and the USA. An Aliens Act was passed in 1905, giving the government power to refuse entry to those deemed undesirable. The complaints about the influx of foreign Jews would be familiar to modern ears, Russian Jews struggling to integrate and competing for jobs and housing, thus driving down wages and driving up rents.

I am obliged to Migration Watch for its illuminating statistics about New Commonwealth immigration. According to Migration Watch some 472,000 migrants arrived between 1955 and 1962 which equates to a little under 70,000 per year. A series of Immigration Acts 1962, 1968 and 1971 were passed and these were intended to bring to a close primary immigration, i.e. the migration of male heads of families to find work. Future migration, in theory, would be restricted to dependants. In the end it is numbers that count and the numbers settling actually rose before they fell. In the 1970s settlement figures were around 72,000 a year and in the 1980s and early 1990s the figure was around 54,000 per year. However, there was huge growth in the early years of New Labour in office which the 1999 net migration figure of 97,000 illustrates perfectly. In 1971 the New Commonwealth population of the UK was around 1 million. It is now about 4 million or 7% of the population. This population will continue to grow as a proportion of total population as a result of both natural reproduction and continued immigration. Births to all mothers born outside the EU accounted for 14% of the total in 1999. By the end of 2013 that had increased to 26.5%. Until 1983 the number of immigrants was at least counterbalanced by the number of emigrants. Since that year, net inflow has grown exponentially and has now reached a rate equivalent to 1.5 million people per decade and this is projected to continue. This is an average figure of 150,000 per annum, i.e. more than twice the average that alarmed the politicians of the 1960s, and almost three times the immigration rate of the 1980s, which unlike those figures has no counterbalance. As ever, averages are misleading. Net migration was 215,000 in 2010 (official figures). This was not a peak figure. In 2004 the figure actually exceeded 250,000 compared to (only!) 97,000 in 1999. Thus by 1999 New Labour first virtually doubled immigration, and then within five years multiplied it a further two and a half times. The Conservatives, in their election manifesto of 2010, promised to reduce immigration to the levels of 20 years ago, in their words tens of thousands rather than hundreds of thousands. In government, there has been compromise with Liberal Democrat partners over skilled workers and Conservative spokesmen have talked of getting the figure down to 90,000 by 2015, which is rather less ambitious. However, the Institute for Public Policy Research has concluded that government plans will have no impact and that net immigration would still be around 200,000 in 2011. It was, in fact, lower than that at 153,000 but in the year ending December 2012 had climbed back up to 175,000. There was an even more steepling rise in 2013 when net immigration climbed to 212,000. Permanent emigration by British citizens was expected to be as low as 30,000 in 2011 according to an IPPR report published in 2010. The conclusion is obvious, that without further measures net immigration will not fall significantly below current levels. Labour's Alan Johnson calculated that the Coalition measures would impact on 1 in potential 7 migrants, a slightly more generous estimate than the IPPR, but one that would still leave a net immigration figure of over 170,000 non EU migrants per annum ad infinitum. In 2010 some 121,000 migrants were from the Indian sub-continent, which demonstrates the total ineffectiveness of various Immigration Acts. I emphasise that the figures in this paragraph exclude migration to and from the EU, over which we have no control.

The Polish population grew from 75,000 in 2003 to over 500,000 by 2011. It should also be added that non EU immigration is no longer restricted to the New Commonwealth. There is significant migration from the Middle East and from African countries that were not British colonies. It is fair to assume that the bulk of these people will settle permanently, as there is every incentive to bring the family.

In permitting immigration on such a terrifying scale, New Labour has betrayed the class from which it sprang. However, not only has it betrayed the white working class it has also betrayed the black and Asian working classes which took root in this country and have produced a new generation, and, in the case of the earliest migrants, another two generations. The original migrants arrived in a time of plenty. Unemployment in the 1950s routinely stood at around 300,000 people "signing on" at any one time. Fifty plus years later, the numbers claiming Job Seekers Allowance, which is paid only for six months, is more than five times that figure. Over 2.5 million people are registered as unemployed. Those figures are terrifying enough, but the true extent of unemployment is disguised by the numbers on incapacity benefit and early retirees, who will never again be part of the workforce. The true number of economically inactive adults below the age at which state pensions can be claimed is around 5 million. Even at it's lowest in the New Labour era (1997-2010) that figure will rarely have fallen below four million. That figure was inherited from their Tory predecessors who used a number of statistical devices one of which was paying no benefits to under 18s thus keeping them off the official unemployment figures. It is also down to the Tories for beginning the exponential rise in Incapacity Benefit (now renamed Employment Support Allowance) claimants. The key point is that this is the background against which My Generation in power permitted immigration on an unprecedented scale and engaged in a social experiment, the consequences of which would be felt for a century even if all immigration ceased today. Most shockingly of all, there was no democratic mandate for demographic change. Indeed, evidence has emerged thanks to the Freedom of Information Act that it was a deliberate but unspoken plan to change the face of Britain and "dish the right" for good.

For the more vigilant, Robin Cook's speech to the Social Market Foundation in 2001 is extremely revealing. The new elite simply decided what was good for us. Immigration now had a social rather than economic purpose, i.e. to remake British society in its own multicultural image. Regardless of the social consequences, "immigration would be celebrated for its lack of attachment to, and origins in British culture," (quoted in Spiked Online, Brendan O'Neil, 2010 Election – Question Everything). In the speech Cook outlined his hostility to traditional notions of being "British". He said, "The British are not a race, but a countless gathering of different races and communities... (their) pluralism is not a burden we must accept. It is an immense asset that contributes to the cultural and economic vitality of our nation." Cook further argued, "The diversity of modern Britain expressed through devolution and multiculturalism is more consistent with the historical experience of our islands." This speech is remarkable, not only for its candour, but for its historical illiteracy. Presumably, Cook believed that a society stratified into Normans and Saxons was an example of multiculturalism. In due course the conquerors became anglicised and English replaced French as the language of court. As for devolution, an essentially modern term, I can't see that a medieval Welsh prince doing homage for his land really counts. In its own way Cook's speech is the New Labour equivalent of Mrs Thatcher's notorious pronunciation that "There is no such thing as society."

I have stated earlier that immigration is not new and made reference to significant migrations by Huguenots, Irish and Jews. However, the notion that we are a nation of immigrants is as mythical as being a nation of shopkeepers. From the Norman Conquest to the arrival of the Huguenots in 1685, there was virtually no immigration. The protestant Huguenots were easily absorbed in a Protestant state. The Jewish population, at around 300,000, is virtually unchanged from 1914, representing 0.05% of the total population of the UK. Irish immigration has been very significant, as mentioned in the previous paragraph, but other than increasing the Roman Catholic population it has had little cultural impact. Cook's claim that cultural diversity was the historical norm is simply ludicrous and ill befits an intelligent man who showed some honour before his death. However, in the last fifty years, the New Commonwealth immigrant population defined as settlers and their offspring born in Britain has grown from around 1% of the population to around 7% of the population. The number of migrants and their descendants in the UK is of course higher than that at any one time, because of migration from both the EU and non Commonwealth countries.

So what are the issues about immigration? Well, it would be disingenuous to try and argue that the original issue regarding immigrants was not race. They were black or they were brown. They were fine when they came over to play cricket, but that was about all. All the imperial myths and comic book caricatures were deployed. Black men were lazy, dirty and oversexed. The word "nigger" was rapidly re-imported from the USA. Asians stank of garlic brought upon by an unvarying curry diet, kept cows sacred and burned their widows. Asian Doctors said "goodness gracious me" in a funny accent. These are just examples, there are many more. Migrants from the West Indies at least had the advantage of being Christian, whereas Asian immigrants followed religions virtually unknown in the UK. The original settlers may have come to an unwelcoming land as regards their new neighbours, but they were more welcome with employers. In the 1950s unemployment hit historic lows. There were large scale vacancies in the NHS and for unskilled labour in the private sector. The Immigration Acts of the 1960s and 1970s were aimed mainly at New Commonwealth i.e. black and brown immigrants. As this is undeniably true, it has been seized on by the politically correct as incontrovertible evidence that Britain was, and remains, racist as long as it restricts immigration. To borrow from Bentham again, this is nonsense on stilts. As I have argued before, there is no such thing as natural rights or human rights derived innately from our common humanity. Our rights come from laws that have been passed and customs that have developed in self regulating communities that differ from their neighbours in ways that are obvious such colour, language and religion to name but a few. There is certainly no right to migrate to a place of one's choosing, natural or otherwise as the "No Borders" fruitcakes would have us believe.

The British post war boom and the unprecedentedly low unemployment disguised the country's underlying economic problems. By the time Harold MacMillan, who a few years earlier had told the country that "most people had never had it so good" (and in fairness he was right), resigned in 1963, unemployment was on the rise and inevitably was impacting on the older industrial areas the worst. Compared to the unemployment we have suffered since, it was small beer but to a generation of workers who had been either children or young people in the 1930s it was alarming. The Conservative Party, which had been badly beaten at the 1945 election despite the leadership of the massively and deservedly popular Winston Churchill, was acutely nervous about the level of unemployment which for them signalled potential electoral doom. Thus an immigrant population not wanted for straightforward xenophobic reasons, had to be restricted because of its impact on the employment prospects of the indigenous population. Two of the Immigration Acts were passed by Conservative governments, the other in 1968 by a Labour government. It was Labour that passed the first Race Relations Act (1965), a weak measure that did not extend to housing and employment. This was rectified by a further Act three years later, but race relations nevertheless remained under the ambit of civil rather than criminal law. Labour did not find it difficult in this era to embrace both social reform and their working class base simultaneously. In 1966, in an acclaimed speech Roy Jenkins, that most passionate of social reformers and Home Secretary from December 1965 to November 1967, defined integration which he supported, "not as flattening process of assimilation but as equal opportunity accompanied by cultural diversity in an atmosphere of mutual tolerance." Edward Heath, the Conservative opposition leader, had no hesitation in dismissing Enoch Powell, the most high profile of old school imperialists from his shadow cabinet in 1968 after his notorious "Rivers of Blood" speech. There is simply no evidence to support a charge of racism against men such as Jenkins and Heath. They understood that numbers were part of the equation if there was to be social cohesion, and if we were to reach the integrated society visualised by Jenkins. Social cohesion is always at risk if there is competition for work, for housing, and for healthcare. The majority of immigrants enter the economic food chain close to the bottom. It is ludicrous to expect the indigenous community not to resent a policy which increases the economic disadvantages they already suffer when unemployment is creeping up. Those who live at the margins are always at greatest risk of being marginalised. The next generation also suffers if schools are not resourced to meet the demands of non- English speaking children, with the obvious impact that has on class teaching. In short, immigration controls brought in by the Wilson and Callaghan governments were classic Labour communitarian responses.

There is a plethora of sometimes confusing statistics regarding the effect of immigration on the social and economic wellbeing of the nation. A culture of spin and stifling of debate has made it difficult to get the issues on the table without New Labour apologists screaming racism at every turn. A report from the Organisation for Economic Co-operation and Development (OECD) shows that this small island is the second most popular destination for migrants, second only to the USA which has a four times larger population and a massively better record for job creation. Intriguingly, the report shows that the UK is one of a minority of countries where immigrants are more likely to be in work. In the first decade of the 21st century the number of British born workers fell by 140,000, but the number of foreign workers rose by 1.77 million. In the first year after 2004, the year our borders were opened to workers from the new members of the EU, unemployment rocketed by 100,000. It tells us the obvious i.e. that the indigenous population has lost out because of uncontrolled immigration but it is a fascinating statistic for other reasons. It tells us, firstly, that Britain's employers have little interest in ethnicity and much more in suitability, contrary to what the Race Relations industry contends on a daily basis, but also one that tells us plenty about our benefit system and the dreadful state of our Education system. It tells us also that the nation's employers are not particularly patriotic, but then My Generation in power has amply demonstrated its loathing for patriotism, so it is no wonder that employers have taken their cue from government. As far as pay is concerned, the effect on the already misleading statistic of average pay has been negligible, but according to the Migration Advisory Committee (MAC), set up ironically by the last Labour government, while higher wages have got higher, lower wages have got lower. The minimum wage has become a ceiling rather than a floor. Will someone tell me how it is the business of a Labour government to drive down the pay of lower income groups? It is a shaming inversion of the principles of the party's founding fathers.

The MAC report provides a further interesting insight. It found that between 2005 and 2010 the number of migrants of working age in employment grew by 700,000 and the number of British born workers in employment fell by 160,000. Put another way, for every 100 jobs taken by working age migrants, 23 British born workers lose theirs. Most casual readers would be surprised only that the figure is not higher but there are explanations. The most enterprising entrepreneurial migrants actually increase economic activity and create jobs, thus increasing gross domestic product (GDP). Others fill jobs that British workers will not do, which tells us something about our benefits system. Others fill jobs that British workers cannot do, which tells us something about the skills gap, our crap education system and extended dumbed down schooling which replaced the apprenticeship system. Youth unemployment has grown by 450,000 since 2004. The majority of these young people have never held a permanent full time job. Finally, as shown above, another group physically displaces British born workers who were in employment.

Those who support high levels of immigration often cite the increased gross domestic product as evidence that the migrants taken as a whole put more in than they take out, and other than playing the race card, this is their principal intellectual challenge to those who point out the effect of immigration on pay and infrastructure. However, this does not tell the full story. The same members of the political class follow this up with selective use of statistics which purport to show that immigrants taken as a whole contribute more in taxes than they take out in benefits. According to a study based on data from the Office of National Statistics, in the period 2001-2011, immigrants from the European Economic Area (EU plus Iceland, Liechtenstein and Norway) paid 34% more in taxes than they took out in benefits and healthcare, a net gain of £22 billion to the exchequer. However for the period 1995-2011 the figure was a much more modest 4%, generating about £8.8 billion in that period. However, the other headline statistic ignored by the BBC, the Liberal Democrats and the rest of the political class was the fact that non-EU migrants contribute only 86% of what they receive back in benefits and healthcare, (the native population of the UK paid 93% of what it got back over the same period) amounting to around £108 billion over the 16 year period of the survey. This demonstrates beyond all reasonable doubt that we are a magnet for the world's poor. It therefore remains to be seen whether the impact of EU migration will remain positive once calculations are available regarding Bulgarian and Romanian citizens who got full access to our labour market and benefit system in January 2014.

It is readily conceded that most immigrants genuinely come to work but it needs to be remembered that 80% of benefits are paid to people in work. According to HMRC migrant workers receive £5 billion per annum in tax credits, 17% of the total paid out. The baleful legacy of Mrs Thatcher and Mr Blair of a high rent, low wage economy has made the UK particularly attractive to hard working but low skilled people. Bringing over the family therefore becomes a particularly attractive option. Once a family is here they are far more likely to settle permanently. It has to be remembered that once a community is settled it becomes attractive to join. This is part of the "chain" or more accurately, ratchet effect of immigration.

Among other abuses there is a small but growing problem with polygamous marriages and the multiple families on welfare this generates. Health tourism from Africa is a significant issue. There was a scandalous story in 2011 of a Nigerian mother coming to the UK to give birth to quintuplets at a cost to the NHS of £250,000. If this lady and her family stay in the UK, and live on benefits for the next 18 years, they stand to collect almost double that amount, before inflation, even with the proposed benefits cap. Naturally, I wish this lady and her children good health but it will be many years, if ever, that the country gets a return on its investment in the form of a meaningful economic contribution. Migrants of this type, who have no intention of working, apply pressure not just to the benefits system but also to our social infrastructure of housing, hospitals and schools. The larger the family the greater the largesse distributed. Part of the problem ministers have got with driving down the Housing Benefit bill for London is the upward pressure on rents caused by London being a magnet for immigrants. The housing market simply cannot cope and landlords simply cash in. There is also the issue of criminality. The population of Wisbech (circa 20,000) is only two thirds British born. One third of the population is from the Baltic States and Russia. Many are hard working but there are serious issues with drink related crime, gang violence and an intimidating "wild west" atmosphere in a once quiet market town. There are similar issues in Boston. In Peterborough, a much larger conurbation in the same part of the world, there is tent city on the riverbank. In London and other big cities, Roma gangs are active in pick pocketing and child trafficking. Eastern European criminals have muscled in on the sex trade, something on which New Labour's crack down on kerb crawlers will have no impact. Thus, as well as those who do contribute and raise economic activity, we import the needy and the greedy, the desperate and the despicable, all at the expense of the taxpayer. In addition to this, we have a major problem with illegal immigration. Not only is our country attractive because of its generosity, we have a legal system courtesy of Human Rights legislation which makes it exceptionally difficult to deport these parasites. Thus, we are lumbered with rapists, terrorists and other members of the criminal classes who only need to own a cat or sire a bastard for our political elite sitting on Immigration Tribunals or in the courts to give them leave to stay.

None of these issues are remotely about the colour of a man's skin. While there are no doubt still a small minority of people who object to immigration on racial grounds alone, views confined to adherents of groups like the BNP and Combat 18, the vast bulk of objections to mass immigration are legitimately based on social and economic grounds. In any event, many immigrants are not distinguishable until they open their mouths to speak their own language. Indeed racism can be more of an issue where ethnic minorities are absent and there is no challenge to stereotypes. Uncontrolled immigration can breed racism when the frustration endured by inability to access decent housing, employment and school places for children becomes channelled against ethnic minority groups. This type of racism, where it exists, is the fault of our ruling political elite who don't seem to grasp that controlled immigration is actually a useful weapon in dealing with racism. Controlled immigration refreshes the community by opening it up to new cultural influences that the host community grows to appreciate and assimilate. The propensity to see those who are different negatively diminishes. Legislation has a necessary place in proscribing unacceptable behaviour against minorities, but the greatest weapon is time. Familiarity does not breed contempt, it breeds tolerance.

Our race relations industry would have it that we are a deeply racist society. The Macpherson report into the investigation of the dreadful murder of Stephen Lawrence in 1993, published in 2000, had the downside of giving a massive impetus to the race relations industry. Macpherson coined the phrase "institutionally racist" to describe the Metropolitan Police, and a host of public bodies, including my own then employer, the Prison Service, rushed to the public confessional to admit their own catalogue of sin which must be seen in the context of the terrible and preventable murder of Zaid Mubarak by his racist cellmate the night before his release. There have also been some dreadful cases in the police, where BME officers have been stitched up with criminal offences sometimes resulting in imprisonment and in a notorious case in Cleveland, it took twelve years for the wrong to be put right and the officer reinstated. There was also the shocking victimisation of Sikh officer, Sergeant Gurpal Virdi, by bosses in the Metropolitan Police, a campaign that has continued after his retirement. On the other hand after two trials, we now know that former Metropolitan Police Commander and former Chairman of the Black Police Association, Ali Dizaei, was rightly prosecuted and not a long term victim of racism within the Met. Mike Fuller, former Chief Constable of Kent, became the first black Chief Officer of Police, smashing through what had seemed one of the most impenetrable glass ceilings.

The term "institutional racism" was defined by Macpherson as follows: "The collective failure of an organisation to provide an appropriate and professional service to people because of their colour, culture and ethnic origin." In other words racism is integral, part of the DNA, and often unspoken. Ordinary policeman and subsequently prison officers were outraged at being dubbed racists. No one would pretend that these organisations did not have a minority of bigots. Possibly the worst example I have come across was the notorious "coon run" in the Metropolitan Police in the 1970s. Basically each constable on shift would put a sum of money into the pot and the first to bring back a black prisoner scooped the pool. As well as alienating staff, this definition is pointless in that it does not identify individual perpetrators. No one is to blame, yet everyone is to blame. Its existence in an organisation cannot be demonstrated empirically and therefore, logically, it cannot be demonstrated to have been eradicated. As such it is a recipe for continuing grievance and continuing bureaucratic meddling. In the public sector this means more processes, more forms to fill in and more managerial monitoring of so called performance indicators.

It is a serious weakness of this all too prevalent style of public sector management that it focuses on outputs rather than outcomes. Stephen Lawrence's parents know that the murder of their son could not have been prevented. Their subsequent lives would have been much more tolerable had the police investigation not been shot through with incompetence and professional neglect, and that from over promoted and poorly motivated officers. It tells us a great deal more about the absence of performance management, adequate supervision and recruitment into CID than it does about racism. Time and a further inquiry may eventually show that it tells us something about corruption. Recent revelations about the shredding of documents and the withholding of evidence to the Macpherson enquiry point in that direction. The fact that no one was disciplined or demoted only reinforced the sense of grievance the Lawrence family must have felt. They will not thank me for saying this, but there is no evidence that the murder of a working class white youth would have been investigated any more competently by this clapped out team of detectives. It is a quantum leap to ascribe professional ineptitude and/or corruption to unconscious racism. After the murder of Zaid Mubarak in HMYOI Feltham, again no individuals were held accountable, but a whole institution was labelled racist on the basis of one preventable outrage. What has followed has been the predictable public sector orgy of form filling and arse covering, the very antithesis of the leadership that is needed, and is actually available from very capable men and women in both organisations who need to be given the freedom to make a difference, not bound with red tape and over-prescription from above. When that happens, grieving Lawrence and Mubarak families and others like them, will have real rather than paper assurance that their sacrifice has not been in vain, and they will also be free from the tentacles of professional anti-racists who have a vested interest in maintaining a picture of a racist society.

In that climate, the culture of denunciation flourishes and is officially encouraged. Quite properly it should be possible for people to report racist incidents without fear and be treated as having acted in good faith, unless and until that is demonstrated to the contrary. The problem stemming from Macpherson is that a racial incident is defined as such by the perception of the individual. The race relations industry simply assumes the accuracy of the perception. Thus, we have the nonsensical situation occurring whereby a seven year old boy is logged as a racist by his school for innocently asking a classmate why his skin was a different colour. Quite rightly his outraged parents refused to sign their agreement that a racist incident had taken place. Even worse was the experience of a fourteen year old British schoolgirl who found herself being arrested (yes arrested!) for objecting to being placed in a classroom work group where she was the only one speaking English. What happened to inclusivity? It is all the more terrifying that supposedly intelligent and educated people such as teachers have willingly signed up for membership of the British version of the Stasi. I note with approval the completely different approach of Arsene Wenger, the Frenchman who manages Arsenal F.C., who presides over a multi ethnic and multi lingual dressing room. He respects the fact that he works in England by insisting that English is the language of the dressing room.

The acceptance of minorities takes time. How much time will depend on numbers and the economic effect, and also on the perception that minorities give to themselves. Jewish and Irish migrants in the 19th century were accepted over time and integrated successfully. It is always difficult to discuss racism with an ethnic minority colleague. I readily concede that as a member of the majority ethnic community, I have no experience of racial discrimination. I do, however, have experience of discrimination on the grounds of age and trade union activity by my former employer, although it would not necessarily be the most useful point to make in discussion. It is a mistake to assume that the experiences of individual members of minority communities are the same. Equally individuals deal with it differently. I have served with a number of ethnic minority colleagues, some of whom have found racism lurking in every jar, and others who have been embarrassed by the organisation's clumsy attempts to enlist them for the latest anti-racist initiative in career development. Being singled out as different has been the last thing they have wanted. Being recognised as advanced on merit by colleagues rather than advanced on the basis of favouritism is what they desire most of all. The politics of identity are not for them. What they want is a colour blind society. To the Race Relations industry, this is false consciousness, which is simply the polite way of calling them "Uncle Toms".

It must irk the hell out of the modern zealots that the most effective campaigners for justice for Stephen Lawrence have been Associated Newspapers who publish the Daily Mail, seen by its "right on" critics as the most right wing paper your newsagent will put on open display. The point here is that legislation, and the Race Relations Acts of 1965, 1968 and 1976 were very necessary, and the activities of bodies such as the Commission for Racial Equality do not of themselves deliver racial equality and freedom from discrimination. Newspapers play a huge role in reflecting public outrage. Papers such as the Daily Mail which aims at Middle England, and the Sun which has a mainly white working class readership are much more effective than The Guardian which preaches only to the converted. It gives a lie to the view that anti-racism is the sole prerogative of the left in politics. The Mail could have been bankrupted and its editor jailed after it named Stephen Lawrence's murderers. The papers were also very effective in challenging racism in the army. Another bête noir of the post Marxist elite, Prince Charles, lent his weight to stamping out the disgraceful racism which was keeping black recruits out of elite Guards' regiments. Well beneath the radar, racism has been tackled on an everyday basis by decent men and women who simply will not stand for it. Decent people have not sat idle and let evil flourish.

The truth is that as a society we have moved on and racism is now a marginal activity. Black footballers no longer face wall to wall crude racist abuse from hostile crowds, nor do they have bananas thrown at them. This sort of behaviour is now the province of the odd idiot and football clubs deal with them very firmly. Football grounds are no longer the intimidating hell holes that they were in the 1980s. Black and mixed race comedians have made their way in the entertainment world. The brilliant comedy "Goodness Gracious Me", featuring Indian actors satirising both themselves and the British, could never have been screened a generation earlier. British born ethnic minority athletes and other sportsmen are cheered and cherished in the same way as their white compatriots. There is a growing black and Asian middle class. It is true that ethnic minorities are over represented in prison, and underrepresented in the professions. For the political elite this is hard evidence of racism. It concerns me that 18% of the prison population is from ethnic minorities, proportionally more than double the BME population. As ever, explanations other than racism are ignored. The sad truth is cultural factors are at work. The obvious example is the Afro Caribbean community where endemic fatherlessness is a huge factor in criminality, under achievement, and the failure to engage with society. Racism becomes an excuse for failure rather than a valid reason. In 1981 there were major riots in Brixton and it would be difficult to deny that the racial prejudice of a significant number of police officers was not an issue. This was the era of the aforementioned "coon run". The same cannot be said of the riots of 2011. Any sympathy there may have been from decent people for the disenfranchised young black men of South London disappeared when it was revealed that the man shot by police and supported by rioters was a gangster and drug dealer. In 1966 PC Norwell Roberts was treated appallingly by white colleagues, despite the attention focussed on the Metropolitan Police Force's first black recruit. Somehow he survived and retired thirty years later with the rank of Detective Sergeant. His retirement went almost unremarked, further evidence of the extent to which we have moved on. It is our political elite that have not. Along with the BNP, the real racists are the political elite who keep their client groups in thrall under the cloak of multiculturalism and diversity. Black boys will not prosper, and Irish traveller children will not learn to read and write, until unacceptable cultural practices that hold them back and practically amount to child abuse are challenged by those that affect to govern.

However, it should be noted that the oldest form of racism is actually anti-Semitism. The sporadic persecution of Jews in Europe and the Middle East is centuries older than the Euro-African slave trade. Anti-Semitism is, in part, historically religious discrimination, rooted in the fact that although the founder of Christianity was a Jew, the Jewish elders denied his divinity and connived with their Roman masters to crucify Christ and stifle Christianity at birth by the crucifixion of leading apostles and disciples. The Jewish diaspora which followed the unsuccessful rebellion against the Romans has made the concept of a Jewish race more elusive as distinctive and tightly knit Jewish communities sprang up all over Europe and the Middle East surviving and sometimes prospering as best they could. Hitler solved that problem by raging against Jews wherever they were domiciled. Their very exclusivity made them a ready target of prejudice and blame for everything from defeat in battle to famine and plague. Jews were outsiders and as such were seen both as unreliable subjects and unfit to be citizens. In Hitler's Germany, the Jews were demonised as the unpatriotic minority more interested in making money, who had stabbed Germany in the back during World War I and thus were the ones to blame for defeat. As Marx and Trotsky were of Jewish origin, Hitler could rage about Jewish inspired Communist conspiracies against Germany with equal venom. Nevertheless, faith is the common factor rather than colour or cultural practices, and many are just like nominal Christians in that they are outwardly secular and do not wear distinguishing apparel. You simply cannot tell a Jew from the colour of his skin or the mutilation of his penis. Circumcision is not a practice exclusive to Jews, indeed it also a part of the Muslim faith. It is also common in Africa and a source of interethnic prejudice. In the United States where Jews and Muslims are just minorities in the great American melting pot, 80% of American males are circumcised. However, to be German and circumcised was potentially dangerous as it raised suspicion about an individual's origins. Faced with the unreliability of using circumcision to detect Jews who hid or denied their faith, the Nazis substituted the long hooked nose.

Another feature of the animus against members of the Jewish faith is their perceived success in business. In medieval Europe the money lending community from which banking evolved was largely Jewish. Kings were frequently in need of money and raising cash for foreign adventures brought them into conflict with the nobility and rich merchants. Moneylenders were an alternative source of income and also a much safer default option than an over mighty subject with troops at his disposal. In the 20th century Hitler was able to mobilise the resentment that Germans felt about their impoverishment after the war and the great inflation against an apparently economically successful Jewish minority. In the USA, where Jews have certainly not been persecuted, there are still deep seated resentments based on their perceived business acumen, this in a country where self- improvement is part of the national DNA. This resentment is manifested not just by the WASPS (White Anglo Saxon Protestants) but also by black activists such as Jesse Jackson, who infamously referred to New York as "hymie town". The USA elected its first Catholic president in 1960, and crossed an even bigger divide when electing its first African American president in 2008. America has yet to elect its first Jewish president. Even in the music business after the explosion of rock and roll in the mid '50s which saw racial divides breached, Jewish Americans who dominated the roster of songwriters in New York's Brill Building felt constrained to downplay their origins. Thus Carol Klein who with her writing partner husband Gerry Goffin, were the most prolific songwriters of the era, adopted the surname King as her professional persona. Klein was just too Jewish. Robert Zimmerman renamed himself Bob Dylan. That taboo would only be broken in 1965 when (Paul) Simon and (Art) Garfunkel recorded and performed using their own distinctive surnames. Neil Diamond, who broke through a couple of years later, also used his own distinctive name.

In the Britain of my childhood, there was also residual anti-Semitic prejudice. Jew jokes were currency amongst small boys and were in very poor taste, often centred in concentration camps with the teller of the joke doing an impression of an SS officer. As I attended Roman Catholic schools, I have no recollection of meeting any Jews as a child although there was a small community in Blackburn which appears to have been established with the rise of the cotton trade. According to Aubrey Newman (1975), the Jewish community in Blackburn was quite well integrated as it was small and did not threaten jobs in the way that Irish immigrants were perceived to do. Nationally, some 300,000 Jews migrated to Britain in the late 19th and early 20th centuries to escape pogroms in Russia and Poland. In places where they competed for work, integration was much more difficult. Jews were portrayed as mean and grasping, and also dirty as in both unclean and lascivious. Being cheated was referred to as "being jewed". The word Jew was used as an insult against anyone considered "tight" with their money. It was a standing joke that Santa could tell a Jew's house at Christmas by the presence of a turnstile in the chimney. Nevertheless, Jews were much higher up the scale of social acceptability than the Irish but without ascending to the Rotary Club or the ranks of Freemasonry. A similar discreet bar operated in the gentleman's clubs of London. Anti-Semitic prejudice was common across all classes. As in America, Jews succeeded best in occupations and professions which were open rather than establishment dominated. They were new money not old. As in the USA, Jews were prominent in show business, but as regards British rock and roll they tended to be managers, promoters and impresarios rather than performers or writers. Britain had its first and only Jewish Prime Minister in Benjamin Disraeli as far back as 1867, but he had long been converted to Christianity, so in the most crucial respect he does not count. However, by the 1980s, an unprecedented number of Jews held senior posts in the Conservative government led by Margaret Thatcher. Sir Keith Joseph, Nigel Lawson, David (Lord) Young, Malcolm Rifkind and Leon Brittan all held Cabinet office, at one point simultaneously during her premiership and Michael Howard, who was John Major's combative Home Secretary 1993-97, in 2003 became the first ever practicing Jewish leader of a major British political party. In challenging residual anti-Jewish prejudice, Mrs Thatcher had breached yet another bastion of the old establishment.

However, in the new establishment the picture was rather different. The elite of My Generation cannot of course be seen to have anything in common with Nazis old and new. Instead their anti-Semitism, the officially licensed form of racism amongst the ruling elite, is intellectualised as anti-Zionism, which demonises Israel as an imperialist and racist state. As I have said earlier in Chapter 4, I first came across this phenomenon at NUS conferences in the mid '70s, where proposals to allow a guest speaker representing Palestinian students would be cheered, and a proposal to hear a speaker from the Union of Jewish students roundly jeered. Zionists were nothing other than Jews who sought the creation of their own nation state, in the same way as Palestinians, Zimbabweans, and Black South Africans pursued self-determination, but with the crucial difference that these latter had the support of My Generation at university. Zionist Jews were dispersed and were of common faith, rather than of common ethnicity, but in all other respects they were the same as other peoples who sought emancipation from colonial masters and the right to determine their own affairs. They have shared a common aspiration with the people of Ireland, the people of India and the people of Palestine. They have shared the same aspiration with the people of Zimbabwe, Nigeria and Yugoslavia. The examples are not exhaustive, but they all illustrate the power of the urge to be free, not just from the outgoing imperial power, but from the competing claims of others in the area or region who also seek to be free. In the Indian subcontinent the differences were religious, in Zimbabwe and Nigeria they were of ethnicity, and in Yugoslavia both ethnicity and religious faith were part of a lethal cocktail. In Ireland, it was not about ethnicity but about faith and allegiance. The plantation of Ireland was so successful that by the time of the conflict that eventually resulted in partition, around about a quarter of the total population of the 32 counties preferred allegiance to Great Britain. The point is that such conflicts cannot be reduced to banal slogans and insults if they are to be understood. However, My Generation chose to level its greatest insult at Israelis and their supporters, labelling them as racists by definition i.e. Zionism equals racism. Anti-Semitism is the racism of the respectable and the anti-Semitism of our political elite was given life by the success of Israel on the battlefield. Israel has fought four wars against various combinations of its Arab neighbours since it was founded in 1948. The first of these was fought in 1948 and was literally a battle of survival for the fledgling state. Subsequent wars were fought in 1956, 1967 and 1973 known respectively to history as Suez, the Six Day War and the Yom Kippur War. All resulted in victory, and in the case of the 1948 and 1967 campaigns, expansions of territory, which is where the controversy lies. Nevertheless, these were wars of survival not conquest and as such render redundant the accusations by student Marxists of the '70s that these were imperialist campaigns that demanded a response from liberation movements similar to those in Zimbabwe and South Africa. It is a wilful misreading of history.

An independent Jewish state in the land known as Palestine had not existed since the times of the Old Testament. Anno Domini Palestine has been part of the Roman Empire and when that declined the Ottoman Empire, apart from a brief period in the 12th century when the crusaders were in the ascendant, which extended at its height to both Eastern Europe and the Middle East. Turkish power declined severely in Europe in the 19th century and the death knell sounded for what remained of the Ottoman Empire when Turkey chose the wrong side in World War I. However, the victorious powers frustrated their former Arab allies by not granting independence, but instead elected to grant what were called mandates to imperial powers under the auspices of the newly formed League of Nations. Nationalism was the great political driving force in the 19th century, which had seen the emergence of a united

Germany, a united Italy and a number of new nation states in the Balkan region which had broken free from Turkish rule. The aspiration for self-determination was growing in the Arab lands and crucially also amongst Jews. In 1917 Arthur Balfour, the British Foreign Secretary, in what is known as the Balfour Declaration, promised the Zionist movement that there would be a homeland for Jews in Palestine. This was explicitly not the same thing as promising a nation state, but it alarmed Arabs who saw it as contradicting promises made to them about the status of Palestine and inevitably it encouraged further Jewish emigration which in the fullness of time led to inter-communal strife. The mandate for Palestine fell to Great Britain.

It is important to spell out the geographical extent of Palestine. It included the country we know as Jordan. In 1922 the League of Nations, predecessor of the modern United Nations, accepted a British recommendation that the establishment of a Jewish homeland would not be applicable to the territory of Transjordan, now known simply as Jordan. Transjordan was that part of Palestine that is on the East Bank of the Jordan River, and actually comprised 77% of Palestinian territory. The British installed Abdullah, an Arab from Hejaz, now known as Saudi Arabia, as Emir of Transjordan, thus founding the Hashemite dynasty that still rules Jordan today. The political elite have a collective amnesia about this large scale satisfying of Arab claims. The rise of Hitler encouraged further emigration and after World War II the debt to the Jews for their unimaginable suffering during the holocaust was to be repaid with an independent state. In 1946 Transjordan became independent, but the United Nations decided on a further partition of the remainder of Palestine between Jews and Arabs. Zionists accepted it but the Arabs did not, and this led to a short war in which Israel miraculously defeated its Arab neighbours. The territory allocated for Arab Palestine on the West Bank was seized by Jordan. Only after the six day war in 1967 was Israel able to add the West Bank to its territory at the expense of Jordan and put the geography of the Jewish homeland in Palestine back to what was envisaged by the League of Nations in 1922.

Thus, the notion that somehow the Zionist state denies the existence of an independent Arab Palestine is therefore demonstrably false. Independent Arab Palestine exists on the East Bank of the River Jordan in the state known as Jordan. Arabs living in the territory ruled by Israel are not of different ethnicity to those ruled by the Hashemite monarchy in Jordan. It was never envisaged by the League of Nations that Jordanian Palestine would extend across the West Bank of the River Jordan. Its successor, the United Nations, attempted the judgement of Solomon by dividing the West Bank between two new small states, Jewish Israel and Arab Palestine. This much less favourable solution was accepted by the Zionist leadership, but not by the Arabs. The failure to establish West Bank Palestine as a separate state is entirely down to the Arabs. Firstly it was seized by Jordan in 1948, and subsequently lost by Jordan in 1967 as a consequence of the ill-judged attempt by Egypt, Jordan and Syria to wipe Israel from the map. By the end of the '70s, and after a further war, both Egypt and Jordan signed peace treaties with Israel. Significantly, the Jordanian government chose to expel the Palestinian Liberation Organisation from its territory because of the threat it posed to the stability of the country. From these wars the enduring myth of a Palestinian refugee nation is derived. So deeply ingrained in the psyche of our ruling elite is the concept of Zionist imperialism that BBC news reporters persist in broadcasting their reports from what they call Palestinian refugee camps when the viewer can clearly see not a tented cholera ridden village, but domestic and business premises that are quite clearly of permanent construction. As for admitting Palestine to the UN, it is already there under the name of Jordan.

It is the nature of war that territory is lost and gained. Far sighted victors consider the long term consequences of expanding their territory if the object is to secure lasting peace. Given the religious significance of Jerusalem, Israel may have found it useful to consider the internationalisation of the city under UN supervision. Secondly, Israel may have been better served by not carrying out a provocative policy of transplanting large numbers of Israeli citizens into the disputed West Bank. However, Arab recognition of Israel's right to exist could have transformed the situation, as has actually happened closer to home in Northern Ireland. Effectively, what has occurred in the British Isles in that the de facto concession by the IRA that Ulster remains British for the foreseeable future has been exchanged for a guaranteed role in government and recognition of the Irish dimension by the UK. The Republic of Ireland government went further by abandoning its historic claim to the six counties. In addition to their ignorance of history, anti-Semitism is sustained also by a failure to understand international law. The argument is that Israel is in breach of its obligations under international law by refusing to leave the "occupied territories" in accordance with UN resolutions. It is a much oversimplified argument and a very partial interpretation of the concept of international law. For more than 40 years the USA and the USSR played out the Cold War across the world. The Middle East was no different. The USA naturally supported Israel, anything other being inconceivable because of the significance of the Jewish vote, and the USSR supported the Arabs. In any case the UN is not a law making body. The concept of International law insofar as it exists at all, bears little resemblance to the process of law making in nation states. No two countries are the same, but to a greater or lesser extent the law relies on popular consent and this applies also as we have seen in the "Arab Spring" to repressive dictatorships. By contrast, international law is comprised of treaties which have force until abrogated by one or both sides. On the basis that Egypt and Jordan have both signed peace treaties with Israel, it can be reasonably argued that they have accepted the verdict of the battlefield. On this basis, Israel is in lawful possession of the West Bank and this remains the case until such a time as the treaties are renegotiated or repudiated.

CHAPTER 10

THE EEC

The most profound and far reaching political change for this country in my lifetime is not the retreat from the Empire, or Mrs Thatcher's break with the post war consensus. It is, in fact, the entry of this country into the Common Market (as it was then called) in 1973, which has so changed over time our destiny as a nation to the extent that control of our destiny is rapidly being lost. My Generation did not set up the EU (to use its current name), it did not sign the treaty of accession, nor did it pass the single European Act. My Generation is not responsible for the Common Agricultural Policy (CAP), the destruction of our fishing industry, or for metrication. However, as a generation, we were able to vote in the 1975 referendum, of which more anon. I suspect that as a generation then between 18 and 30, this is not quite the club we had in mind.

The economic cost of membership of the European Union is terrifying. Between 1973, the year of accession, and 2007, our total trade deficit with our EU partners was £255 billion, an average of £7.5 billion per year over the period. That deficit is accelerating at an alarming rate. Over the five year period 2005-09 the trade deficit was £135 billion. In that period the deficit with the EU i.e the excess of imports over exports, accounted for 88% of our our trade deficit with the entire world. In 2011 the trade deficit with the EU was £50 billion. In the month of April 2014 the deficit for that month alone was £5.14 billion. These are terrifying figures and according to the Bruges Group the cost of this deficit in jobs exported to the continent is around two million in an economy of thirty million jobs. It's almost the reverse of Nick Clegg's ludicrous claim that leaving the EU would cost three million jobs. The fact is that the tightly regulated sclerotic single market is ruinous for British industry and commerce. Only 10% of our trade is with the EU, 80% is generated by trading amongst ourselves and the remaining 10% represents trade with the rest of the world. Yet for that 10% of trade with the EU we are 100% subject to regulation from Brussels. Our deficit with the EU is also accelerating at the same time as the EU share of world trade is falling. Its share of world trade is calculated to fall to 15% in 2020 compared to 26% in 1980. Yet My Generation in power clings to the toxic legacy of Edward Heath and keeps its wagon hitched to an organisation that is rapidly becoming a dinosaur. UKIP calculates that the cost to our economy is around £50 billion per annum. Quite properly it adds the cost of EU overregulation of British business, £20 billion, the cost to UK agriculture as a consequence of the Common Agricultural Policy (CAP), £14 billion, the cost to our fishing industry (what is left of it) £1 billion, and £2 billion in miscellaneous costs. When our contribution of £12.1 billion for the 2012 budget is added, that gives a grand total of £49.1 billion. In fairness, we should subtract the £6.7 billion we receive back from the EU and the £3.6 billion rebate we still receive, which would reduce the cost below £40 billion. However, once the annual trade deficit is added back in, the UKIP figures are actually very conservative. What is clear is that the EU needs us far more than we need them as a market. It would have no choice but to strike deals with UK.

By the end of 2013 the UK's budget deficit had fallen to £96 billion (the excess of government spending over revenue). Leaving the EU would see us swiftly into surplus. The markets of the future are India, China and Brazil. Economically, the EU is an idea whose time has long passed.

The history of our major political parties' involvement with the EEC is a tawdry story of dissembling, deceit and denying the British people their democratic rights as citizens of a sovereign nation. The Liberal Democrats get credit for consistency with regard to their stance on British membership and can escape charges of bad faith on the basis of not having held national elected office until joining the coalition in 2010. They cannot be acquitted of being wrong. The policy of post war British governments has been very closely linked across the Atlantic with the USA.This was particularly true of the Attlee and Churchill governments, which had to contend with the Cold War as it played out in Europe and South East Asia, although Churchill had flirted romantically with the kind of political union associated with Jean Monnet, the founding father of the EEC. Britain also had its declining Empire and its economic relationship with the white or white ruled Commonwealth. So, the six founding members of what was originally called the European Coal and Steel Community were left to get on with it. In any event, the economic meshing of France and Germany and what that would mean for their political relationship, well suited the traditional British concern of maintaining the balance of power. In 1958 President de Gaulle, a staunch patriot and nationalist, returned to power in France, putting dreams of European integration on ice.

Harold McMillan was the first British Prime Minister to apply for membership back in 1962. His decision was pragmatic and based on economic considerations. World War II had badly damaged British industrial infrastructure and competitiveness, and the two major defeated powers, Germany and Japan had recovered at a phenomenal speed. Although the Conservative government was by no means united on the issue, the pragmatists saw membership as an economic panacea that would keep the country at the top table. As we now know, the reality has proved very different. Unfortunately for the history of this country, McMillan appointed Edward Heath as the chief negotiator. Heath may have been a pragmatist across the rest of the political landscape, but as regards Europe, he was an idealist for whom British membership was an all-consuming passion. De Gaulle was not keen on another big player at the European table and felt (rightly) that the UK was simply too close to the USA. The French President had withdrawn his country from NATO, thus asserting his country's independence of American hegemony. De Gaulle vetoed British entry in 1963.

The official policy of the Labour party was opposed to entry. The party leader, Hugh Gaitskell, was adamantly opposed. For him, joining the Common Market would spell the end of a thousand years of history. It is one of the ironies of British politics that after Gaitskell's death in 1963, his closest acolytes, Roy Jenkins in particular, matched Edward Heath for enthusiasm for the European project. Gaitskell was succeeded as Labour leader by Harold Wilson, who led Labour to victory on an anti-Common Market platform in 1964. By 1967, with Labour mired in Britain's economic problems, Wilson changed his mind and decided to apply for membership. Like McMillan, he was thwarted by De Gaulle's veto. However, the political landscape changed swiftly. De Gaulle resigned in 1969 and was replaced by the more amenable Georges

Pompidou. More significantly, Edward Heath, Conservative leader since 1965, secured a surprise victory at the polls in the summer of 1970. Instead of heading for political oblivion, his moment had come. Heath successfully concluded negotiations and the UK formally acceded to the Treaty of Rome on 1 January 1973. Ireland and Denmark joined on the same day and the six became nine.

Edward Heath, unlike Harold Wilson before him, did at least have a manifesto commitment to negotiate for entry. However, in that manifesto he promised that Great Britain would not enter the EEC, "Without the full hearted consent of the British people." Shamefully, this promise was broken. Heath would not countenance a referendum and could not risk a General Election. This was no surprise as his government would have struggled to win an election at almost any point during its tumultuous term of office. Harold Wilson continued as Labour leader in opposition. Wilson was savaged then, and still is to this day, for his perceived opportunist reversal of Labour's position, on the basis that terms on which Heath was prepared to enter the Common Market were unacceptable. Whatever the criticism of Wilson, there is little doubt that Heath was determined to enter the club at any price and secure his place in history. Admittedly his position was not strong. The Common Market had long got used to the UK not being a member. Nevertheless, only an ardent blinkered Europhile can defend the terms. The British fishing industry was sold down the river and we have paid the price ever since. Heath was correct in his cynical calculations that Commonwealth countries, and in particular New Zealand, would find other markets for their food products. However, reform of the Common Agricultural Policy, which propped up French peasant farmers and at the time consumed 80% of the Common Market budget, was not a priority for Heath. Even now CAP consumes 40% of the EU budget. The result was that we lost access to cheap food just as price inflation was taking a stranglehold on the British economy. This was economic madness and neglect of duty to the electorate. By 1984, when Mrs Thatcher negotiated the British rebate, the UK was on course to be the largest net contributor despite being the third poorest economy of the then ten members, Greece having joined in 1981.

Wilson had his own problems in the Labour party. The pro-Common Market supporters were in favour of entry on principle and were not forgiven for voting in the same lobby as the Conservatives. Heath had a smaller number of rebels, but they were sufficient to deny Heath a parliamentary majority on entry only if Labour pro-Common Market supporters did not break ranks. It is a matter of public record that Roy Jenkins led 112 Labour members into the government lobby. It would cost Jenkins not only the deputy leadership of the party, but also the leadership when Wilson retired in 1976. This major fissure was the genesis of the split in 1981 that saw the birth of the Social Democratic party. Wilson deftly solved the short term problem by committing Labour to renegotiation and a referendum on the new terms. Labour was returned to power in February 1974 and Wilson duly delivered on the promise. In reality, the boat had left and the revised terms subtracted very little from the price Britain had paid. Collective responsibility was scrapped for the duration and Roy Jenkins, Harold Wilson, Edward Heath and his replacement as Tory leader, Margaret Thatcher, campaigned on the same side, if not always the same platform, to remain in the market. The electorate, heartily sick of the issue, and blissfully ignorant of the Federalist sub texts of the Treaty of Rome, voted 2 to 1 in favour to put the matter of British membership to bed. The Common Market had defined and contributed to the destruction of Edward Heath's career, and it also ensured that Roy Jenkins would never become prime minister. The Common Market would be the midwife of the SDP, and play a major role in the electoral disasters suffered in turn by the Labour and Conservative parties. Out of office, Labour reverted to opposition to the Common Market and pledged to withdraw in its 1983 election manifesto.

Margaret Thatcher replaced Labour's James Callaghan as prime minister in May 1979. Her stance was emphatically that the work of the European Economic Community (EEC) was essentially subordinate to the national interest. She secured a rebate on our inflated contributions that lasted until a large chunk of it was negotiated away by Tony Blair. Given her stance, it is one of history's strange ironies that Mrs Thatcher agreed to the Single European Act in 1986, which would enhance the power of the European Commission at the expense of the nation states. As the decade drew to a close, Mrs Thatcher became increasingly and noisily irritated as EEC bureaucrats became more vocal about their federalist ambitions. Although the poll tax and the perception by many Tories that it would condemn them to certain defeat at the next election is often cited as the reason for the demise of Mrs Thatcher, her increasingly strong stance against the pretensions of Brussels alarmed the Europhile wing of the Tory party, which held many senior positions. Sir Geoffrey Howe's resignation speech in the House of Commons (he had been humiliated over Europe), holed the prime minister below the waterline and was the catalyst for Michael Heseltine's challenge. As it turned out, he who wielded the dagger did not wear the crown and John Major became prime minister.

Mr Major had a sufficiently long personal honeymoon to allow the Conservatives to retain power at the 1992 election, but after that civil war erupted over Europe within the party, and that, along with the loss of their reputation for economic competence consequent on "Black Wednesday" (September 1992), precipitated the electoral holocaust of 1997. In 1993 the EEC formally became the EU, European Union, a rebranding that was a clear indication of the direction of travel. It was John Major who secured British opt outs from harmonising monetary policy and from the social chapter which dealt with workers' rights when signing the Treaty of Maastricht, which was intended to give life to the single European Act. Euro-sceptics were not impressed and neither were many of the electorate on discovering that the most public achievement from negotiations was that their employers could continue to insist on excessive hours being spent at work. The failure to see the big picture was a recurring theme of the Major premiership. As it turned out, the Referendum Party, which campaigned in 1997 for a referendum on continued EU membership, would not be the Tory version of the SDP. Nevertheless, their intervention did cost the Tories a number of marginal seats and ensured that the Conservative defeat would be the worst since 1906, when the party was also split.

By the 1990s, Labour had largely accepted that being anti-EEC was an electoral albatross. Re-branded New Labour no longer saw the EEC, now the EU, as an impediment to socialism. The bureaucratic collectivism of EU institutions well suited the purposes of politically correct New Labour. It is European institutions that keep the political class in power whatever the result of national elections. Under Tony Blair, Labour would embrace Europe, and enter the European Monetary Union as soon as his Chancellor, Gordon Brown, said that the five tests had been met. Fortunately, Gordon Brown constantly blocked entry into the Euro-zone. Gordon Brown had absorbed the lesson of what had happened not just to the Tories, but to the country as a result of the UK's ill fated two year tryst with the ERM (European Exchange Rate Mechanism), which tied the pound to the historically strong German Mark. The value of the pound was unsustainable at this level and fell prey to currency speculators on what is known as Black Wednesday in September 1992. Britain was forced out of the ERM and this proved to be the catalyst for economic recovery. Between September 1992 and the General election in 1997, unemployment fell dramatically from 10.1% to 5.3% of the workforce. Without Gordon Brown's veto, our economy would have descended to the basket case level of Greece in the aftermath of the banking crisis. Furthermore, Labour had moved on from defining its Socialism by its commitment to nationalisation and control of the commanding heights of the economy. Having conceded the economic argument to the Tories, New Labour concentrated on winning the social argument for its version of equality. New Labour began to understand that the ratchet effect of the EEC is not reversible without withdrawal. Bureaucracy, regulation, and the judicial activism of the European Court of Justice, the European Court of Human Rights, and the Supreme Court (as it was re-named)in the UK, would permanently hold back the forces of Conservatism. Membership of the EU, and the consequent acceptance of the superiority of supra-national institutions, would make it impossible for a future Mrs Thatcher to turn back the clock and rip up the cosy Westminster consensus of the political class. Thus, the further surrendering of sovereignty that took place under Blair and Brown had a domestic anti-democratic purpose; to render null and void any decision by the electorate to throw Labour out of office. One only has to look at the early performance of the Coalition and the sheer inability, inasmuch as it desires to, which is another matter, of the government to deliver on such huge issues as immigration and terrorism, as well as rather more minor vexations like votes for prisoners. Oddly enough, it is this still unresolved issue which has the potential to give real momentum to the slow burning revolt against federal Europe and supra-national institutions which have no democratic legitimacy.

Thus the major charge, even greater than the continuing economic damage of remaining in the EU, against My Generation in power in its European policy is that it has put at risk the viability of democracy in this country. It is perfectly acceptable for a government to seek to make changes that it believes can, and should endure beyond its own electoral lifespan. It's called strategic thinking. The Asquith, Attlee and Thatcher governments had that vision in the 20th century and were honest in pursuing their mandates from the voters. All those administrations have left legacies that endured, and have continued to endure to this very day. However it is not legitimate to pursue a policy that subordinates our nation permanently to the EU behemoth without ever bothering to ask the electorate. The drift of power from Parliament to Brussels and Strasbourg accelerated under Tony Blair and Gordon Brown. The handing back of most of the rebate, the acceptance of further QMV (qualified majority voting) on previously ring fenced issues, and the failure to consult the electorate on the Lisbon treaty that was the proposed European Constitution in all but name were the major strategic issues where New Labour rolled over. It happily gold plated EU policy, in particular freedom of movement. The most obvious example is the failure to make use of the 10 year "opt out" that was available from immigration from the eight former Warsaw pact countries that joined the EU in 2004. The cost in jobs of mass immigration was discussed in Chapter 9. In January 2014 unrestricted immigration from Bulgaria and Romania commenced as the privileges of membership clicked in for two of the EU's poorest members. We have also discovered to our cost that the European Commission has abrogated to itself the power to determine the single market regulations including whether there is not even a tenuous connection to free trade. This is why we are being forced to close down perfectly serviceable coal fired power stations under EU regulations to combat the global warming that ceased in 1997. The interference continues at micro as well as macro levels. One typically absurd example was the order to remove from circulation our traditional light bulbs and replace them with inferior low carbon models. Our government not only acquiesced in this classic piece of Euro meddling, it implemented the policy earlier than required. As for the bulbs, they don't provide sufficient light, they're expensive, and, by the way, half of the nation's light sockets won't take them. Additionally, they give off much less heat which of course only increases fossil fuel consumption and there is also an issue about safe disposal given the mercury content. We are therefore faced with increased burning of carbon and increased pollution as a consequence. The elite of Europe simply ignore the contradictions. This is only one example of how EU bureaucracy has encroached upon the minutiae of our lives. A far worse example is the destruction of the Royal Mail as a result of European competition law which allowed the private sector to cherry pick the most lucrative Royal Mail business, and leave it with the service no-one wants to offer, the universal daily post at the same price whether that is to Orpington or Orkney. The result as we know is the punitive costs of stamps, the phasing out of Sunday collections, and the demise of the second post. Additionally rural and small town post offices have been lost because of EU rules on the internal subsidy of loss making business units. A once enviable postal system has been wrecked by a clueless, interfering, unaccountable bureaucracy and the Royal Mail is now in private hands and will almost certainly pass in due course to foreign ownership.

On its return to power in 1997, New Labour happily adopted the public managerial face of the outgoing administration. It was fascinated by targets, outputs and objectives. Everything had to be measured. The government became a walking essay from MBA textbooks. By applying business methods to the Police, Prison Service, Health Service, Education and other areas of the public sector, it would demonstrate the superiority of New Labour. The reality is that it simply collected mountains of information that could be turned into relentless propaganda. When the machinery failed to respond it would micromanage. It substituted management for leadership, short termism and statistics for solid achievement. In all fields of government, it grew a suffocating bureaucracy. All must sing the company song and must never comment on the Emperor's nakedness. The fashion for applying the worst kind of managerial techniques from the private sector coincided neatly with New Labour's equality agenda. It was the perfect vehicle to drive it.

Europe operates in a similar bureaucratic way but the crucial difference is that power lies with a permanent European Commission, not with the Council of Ministers, and certainly not with the European Parliament which cannot initiate, amend or repeal legislation. It is a parliament only in the sense that it is a talking shop and its only value is that its proceedings are televised so at least people like Nigel Farage, the UKIP leader, can get some publicity, on the occasions the BBC deigns to allow it, for exposing the hollowness and the sham democracy of a body that was created to rubber stamp the decisions of the Commission. The Commission also maintains its power over its officials after retirement. It is not permitted to recant publicly. Pensions are conditional on not criticising the EU and its institutions. The Commission is both a civil service and a quasi government. It has no democratic accountability. You cannot vote for EU Commissioners and neither can the European parliament. They are nominees of the political classes in the member states. Indeed, it regards democracy as an inconvenience which obstructs the great project. In this way, it is very like New Labour.

Thus year in, year out, it gradually adds to its power. Every directive, which by the Treaty of Rome you are bound to obey, concentrates its power. That power is buttressed by the European Court of Justice (not to be confused with the European Court of Human rights), which rules on any disputes about the scope of the Treaty of Rome. Its default option is to intrude further into our lives. One of most recent examples is the absurd decision to prevent insurance companies from using gender as a pricing tool. It makes no difference that young men have more road traffic accidents than women. It makes no difference that men die sooner than women. The outcome of this judgement which took effect in 2012, is that young women will pay an unnecessarily high price for motor insurance, and older men will see the cost of annuities rise, despite the fact that men live, on average, four years less than women. Where is the Equality in this? The only winners will be the insurance companies who have been gifted a cast iron excuse for further scams. Contempt for democracy and contempt for the nation state that is legitimised by democracy is written into the DNA of European Institutions. We are sliding inexorably into a bureaucratic dictatorship.

New Labour habitually trumpets its superiority regarding its commitment to international development and the alleviation of poverty. How come it has nothing to say about the discarding of perfectly edible fish into the ocean which are not part of the quota that can be landed? Does it not know that fish are unable to work out whether or not they are allowed to be caught? When did you last hear a New Labour politician condemn the Common Agricultural Policy that sees mountains of food rot and productive land set aside? How can these obscenities be justified in a world where millions go hungry on a daily basis? New Labour has been silent on this issue, and they should know that silence gives consent. My Generation in power has had the opportunity to right a grave wrong. Instead it is guilty of a gross moral dereliction and added the unwillingness to provide some protection to the world's hungry to its unwillingness to protect its own people.

New Labour was also quick to trumpet its commitment to animal rights, particularly by ensuring that time was found to abolish hunting with hounds. Whether it really did so is another matter. What is inescapably the case is that the government did nothing other than protest feebly when French farmers attacked trucks carrying live sheep and burned them to death. This atrocity had nothing to do with sheep scrapie and everything to do with French farmers, tacitly supported by their government, intent on defying the EU and preventing legitimate livestock trade under the Treaty of Rome. Did our Government obtain compensation? Did our government deduct the compensation from our EU contribution? The reader knows that the answer is in the negative. Our government did nothing and let down its people. However what this dreadful episode does demonstrate is that the bureaucracy in Brussels is powerless when defied.

There is a school of thought that the European Court of Justice could prevent a member country from withdrawing from the Treaty Of Rome, on the basis that the decision of a supra-national body has the power, by virtue of power being ceded to it by member countries, to overrule a national parliament that wished to regain control of its destiny. This is legalistic garbage and totally at odds with democratic legitimacy and the right of sovereign nations to renegotiate or abrogate a treaty, but it gives an insight into the contempt in which democracy is held by those signed up to the federal ideal. Effectively, we would be the Confederates. However, unlike the American Civil War, the EU has no army (yet) and no power in the final analysis to prevent nation states from withholding or taking back powers from the EU. The next generation, personified by Prime Minister David Cameron, born in 1966, can cast off the shackles imposed by Edward Heath, and shamefully made tighter by My Generation in office. We shall discover soon enough if it has the balls to do so. At the moment Mr Cameron has committed his party to a re-negotiation of some of the terms of our membership, to be put to a referendum in 2017 which will determine whether or not the UK remains in the EEC. The truth is that Mr Cameron, along with the Labour and Liberal Democrat leaders is committed to continued EU membership. He has yet to set out his negotiating position and has recoiled from making any explicit threat to leave the EU should they refuse to negotiate or not negotiate in good faith.

Ironically what I suspect was Mr Cameron's plans for a re-run of 1974-75 when Harold Wilson successfully engaged in cosmetic and superficial negotiations in a bid to staunch the bleeding from the running sore of euro-scepticism in his own party, were dealt a massive blow by Liberal Democrat leader Nick Clegg's agreement to debate EU membership with the UKIP leader Nigel Farage live on television in late March and early April 2014. The outcome of the first debate was not wholly clear cut but even pro-EU commentators have accepted without hesitation the public view that Mr Clegg was roundly trounced by an opponent that the political class have sought to treat variously as a buffoon, a drunkard and a xenophobe. Mr Clegg stuck to his ludicrous claims that three million jobs were at risk and tried to make out that trade with the EU would cease the day after we left. To assert this as Mr Clegg did at the very time that EU immigration has had a major upward spike due to controls on Romania and Bulgaria being lifted was a significant political misjudgement. None of this deters the unaccountable EU Commission from seeking to prevent the British government from setting stiff qualifying periods in which immigrants support themselves entirely from earnings before becoming eligible for welfare benefits. No audit of the impact of mass immigration can be credible without taking this EU interference into account, alongside the more familiar arguments of wages being bid down, rents being bid up, and the pressures on local community infrastructures that have so damaged working class communities, which should not necessarily be characterised as white (error here from Mr Farage as these communities include those migrants and their families from the West Indies and the Indian sub-continent who were needed to fill unskilled jobs in the 1950s and 1960s). Apart from the mistaken assumption that the host community is homogeneous Nigel Farage deployed the cost/benefit argument superbly and brought new arguments into public consciousness emerging perhaps for the first time as a substantial political figure in his own right. This has already emboldened Tory euro-sceptics, put Mr Clegg's leadership of his party at risk, and further damaged the reputation of the political class as a consequence of both David Cameron and Labour leader Ed Miliband refusing to debate with him. Mr Farage was able to carry forward UKIP's momentum into the Euro elections of May 2014 when for the first time since 1910 a party other than the Labour and Conservative parties won a nationwide election. It remains to be seen if that momentum can be maintained when the general election is contested in May 2015.

Of course whether a referendum takes place at all will depend on the outcome of the next general election as both Labour and the Liberal Democrats have no intention of challenging the status quo on Europe. As far as the Tories are concerned, many members must wish they had chosen David Davis instead of David Cameron in 2005 to lead their party. Campaigning to leave the EU is no longer an electoral albatross, mainly because of the immigration issue, and it is unfortunate that Mr

Cameron does not grasp that. Sadly at the right time both the nation and the Conservative party have the wrong leader. It is perfectly possible that the parliamentary arithmetic will make a referendum impossible in the next parliament, to the delight of the political class. However, they should not be under any illusion that they are doing anything other than delaying the inevitable. Europe is simply now too toxic to be removed from the agenda by spin and political chicanery as public anger with venal politicians grows. In September 2014 Scotland will have a genuine referendum about its independence from the UK which will rightly fuel demands for a referendum about UK membership of the EU. This can only further raise the profile of UKIP. The party, its leader, and some of its senior figures may not be to everyone's taste but it is undeniable that there is finally emerging a credible threat to the long hegemony of our political class and with it the tantalising prospect of the political realignment that will give us back our democratic sovereignty.

CHAPTER 11

FOREIGN POLICY, TERRORISM AND THE DEFENCE OF THE REALM

On 12 May 1997 the late Robin Cook, New Labour's newly appointed Foreign Secretary, set out in broad terms the thrust of foreign policy under the new government. He set four goals for the fledgling government eager to make its mark after 18 years in the wilderness that would distinguish it sharply from its Tory predecessors. The first goal was security within NATO and the pursuit of multilateral disarmament, which took New Labour back to the traditional policy of the Wilson and Callaghan governments. There would be no return to the unilateralism and anti-Americanism that characterised Labour in opposition during the early '80s. After being treated with contempt by Republican Presidents Reagan and Bush Senior, the Labour Party had an American President it was comfortable with in Bill Clinton, and one who was comfortable with them. New Labour benefitted from the Major government's ill advised partiality in the 1992 Presidential election in which they let it become known that Downing Street preferred a Bush victory. The second goal was prosperity, not surprising at a time of economic confidence. Cook's third aim was quality of life, to be achieved by tough multilateral agreements regarding environmental targets. 1997 was the year of the Kyoto agreement. New Labour was unashamedly green and swallowed almost whole the theory that global warming was the result of industrial pollution for which the developed nations must take most of the blame. The fourth aim was gaining the respect of other nations in the world for keeping the peace and promoting harmony. Cook insisted that foreign policy must have an ethical dimension. As such, the UK must promote human rights and support demands for democratic change in the face of authoritarian regimes. An ethical foreign policy would have the high moral purpose that would be the defining distinction between New Labour and its predecessors. Cook intended to present an annual audit of progress in promoting human rights abroad. Foreign policy would not be exempt from public managerialism.

Robin Cook also laid out the strategic aims in his mission statement. We would be a leading player in Europe, strengthen the Commonwealth, promote a more effective United Nations Organisation and be a leading partner in the world community. He announced that the UK would not sell arms for the purposes of external aggression and internal repression. Cook would later argue that doing the "right thing" and promoting national self-interest were one and the same. This can be seen as illustrative of the New Labour desire to synthesise what had generally been seen as competing principles and therefore is part of the intellectual muddle that characterised the so called "third way". As an intellectual position it has obvious weaknesses. The first problem is that the right thing to do is defined by the ruling elite according to principles they believe not merely to be universal, but self-evident and derived naturally from our shared membership of the human race. The messianic urges that drive what has become known as Liberal Interventionism flow from these propositions. Thus where universal values do not pertain, there is an immediate and straightforward justification for intervening elsewhere in the world to make them pertain. As has been argued in Chapter 8 of this book, there is no such thing as natural rights, and therefore no such thing as international law deriving from these natural rights. As has been argued in Chapter 8, rights are a product of people fighting, dying, negotiating and ultimately legislating. In the same way as has been argued in Chapter 8, international law is not the product of mystically endowed inalienable rights, but rather it is the sum total of treaties between sovereign states. New Labour should not be criticised for having high ideals, but it is fair to criticise when those high ideals lack a coherent philosophical underpinning. In the final analysis New Labour in power, like any other administration, has to be judged by its deeds and omissions rather than by its words.

New Labour will forever be judged for its ill-fated forays into Iraq and Afghanistan. In the process the UK humiliatingly became the USA's lackey, lap dog and cipher all at the same time. Under New Labour, the UK colluded with torture carried out by the US authorities in that it knew about the extraordinary rendition of suspected terrorists, sent members of the Secret Service to interview them, and provided refuelling facilities for US military aircraft on route to Guantanamo Bay. This was neither ethical nor in the national interest. It is actually a national disgrace. As a consequence our citizens became a target for terrorists, just as we were starting to enjoy the peace dividend in Northern Ireland. The chance to strut on the world stage is a key perk of being Prime Minister and, to a slightly lesser extent, of being Foreign Secretary and Chancellor of the Exchequer. Being welcomed at Camp David, holding a joint press conference at the White House, and inspecting American troops are nature's way of reminding British Prime Ministers that they have arrived at the top table, feted by the leader of the world's most powerful nation. On the world stage, they affect to transcend party politics. The opportunity to be remembered as a great visionary, as one of the great movers and shakers when history is written, has a tantalising siren lure that is hard to resist, particularly as the alternative is to be a mere footnote. A place in the pantheon of great Prime Ministers beckons. The spirit of Churchill is invoked and suddenly Great Britain is a great power again. It is a heady cocktail for the star struck and for the possessors of giant egos. It was our misfortune as a nation to have been led at a time of great danger by a man who was both star struck and a consummate egotist. His handling of the death of Princess Diana gave a very early indication of how Tony Blair would perform on the world stage.

The attack on the Twin Towers in New York on 11 September 2001 was nothing less than a horrific atrocity. Had the terrorists also succeeded in taking out the White House, the propaganda value to militant Islamists of the most audacious act of war since Pearl Harbour would have been incalculable. However, unlike Pearl Harbour, there was not an easily identifiable enemy nation. Indeed, militant Islam was probably most closely identified with Saudi Arabia, a key ally of the USA and the UK. The late Osama Bin Laden, mastermind of 9/11, was a Saudi national. America's desire for vengeance was entirely understandable. I would not criticise our government for giving moral support to the USA in its hour of need subsequent to the worst atrocity visited on the innocent civilians of a first world nation since Hiroshima and Nagasaki.

The centre of terrorist activity was Afghanistan. It was here in this remote mountainous country that would be holy warriors received training to conduct jihad against infidels and non-believers. The Taliban regime, which at the time was in power in Afghanistan, practised a brand of Islam that made even Saudi Arabia appear liberal. Girls were forbidden to go to school, made to wear the burka, and not permitted, on pain of death, to talk to any male other than a relative. Culturally, Afghanistan was pre-medieval. It was the perfect place for disaffected and deluded misogynists to lose themselves in the cause of Islam as nowhere were Western values more strongly rejected than in Afghanistan. President Bush and Prime Minister Blair were not daunted by the reputation of Afghanistan as being unconquerable. It had denied the British in the 19th century and humiliated the USSR, which had been forced to withdraw in 1989 after spending ten fruitless years trying to subjugate this proud people. The involvement of the USSR came about when a client Marxist government came to power in Afghanistan. Its land reforms and its proclamation of equality of the sexes were not understood and were resisted in a rare display of cross tribal unity. In December 1979 the USSR decided to invade Afghanistan and was resisted by Mujahideen fighters. The kind of guerrilla warfare that daily claims the lives of our young soldiers was perfected in this decade. The collapse of Communism in Eastern Europe in 1989 saw Russia accede to international pressure and withdraw. Afghanistan was the last set piece battle of the Cold War. The USA had supported the Mujahideen and also taken on Pakistan as a client state. Thus, after 9/11, the USA was faced with the supreme irony when it confronted the very Islamist extremists that it had propelled into power.

Ten years of war in Afghanistan have yielded precious few results. Bin Laden was actually hiding in Pakistan and had been for a number of years before American troops succeeded in killing him. Theoretically, Afghanistan has a democratic government but its writ no more runs outside of a few heavily fortified and Anglo-American defended areas than that of the Marxist regime supported by the USSR a generation earlier. A leaked report prepared for the US government, a summary of which was published in the Daily Mail on 2 February 2012, highlighted the sheer futility of the Afghan campaign. At this juncture 397 British troops had lost their lives, mainly to snipers and road side bombs. The report painted a picture of the influence of the Taliban increasing at the expense of the government which is seen as corrupt by Afghan civilians. Weapons and vehicles given to Afghan forces have been passed on to the Taliban. Evidence was cited that the Taliban were engaging in hearts and minds exercises with civilians rather than crude terrorism. The Afghan government and the Taliban are both aware that the USA and the UK are committed to withdrawal in 2014, so the Taliban have no incentive to negotiate peace. None of this should surprise anyone with knowledge of the fate of the Soviet invasion a generation ago. What is devastating, however, is what is revealed about the collusion of neighbouring Pakistan, nominally a NATO ally. The report cites Pakistan's secret service, the Inter Services Intelligence Agency as actively colluding with the Taliban and actually directing attacks. The report states, "Pakistan knows everything... they control everything... the Taliban are not Islam, the Taliban are Islamabad (capital of Pakistan)... ISI officers tout the need for continued Jihad and the expulsion of foreign invaders from Pakistan... The government of Pakistan remains intimately involved with the Taliban." It should be recalled that the assassination of Bin Laden on Pakistani soil was carried out without the knowledge of the Pakistan government. It is obvious why and the reaction within Pakistan to the raid is also illustrative of what is really felt by Pakistan's power brokers in the military and intelligence services. The Pakistani government, of course, denies collusion. Civilian governments in Pakistan have had a chequered history. Nominally democratic governments have sadly been institutionally corrupt. The military has got used to stepping in and remains enormously influential behind the scenes, able to ignore the elected government with impunity. When reservists and paramilitaries are included, Pakistan boasts in excess of 1.4 million personnel under arms out of a population of around 177 million people.

Although losses of life are insignificant compared to the great conflicts of the last century, the Afghan war has been nothing but a huge folly and a total failure, increasingly fought in the face of public opinion that is no longer supportive. Families have historically been able to handle the loss of their sons (and now their daughters) when they have been able to see that a war had a higher moral purpose such as national survival, the reclaiming of sovereign territory, or the overthrow of a brutal dictator bent on world domination. It is difficult to find anything in the Afghanistan policy that can be described as ethical. Cook believed that doing the right thing and our national interest were one and the same. Perhaps someone could tell me how the UK has benefitted from the ten year campaign, because I can't think of any benefits. Afghanistan is never going to be a fully functioning liberal democracy any more than it was going to embrace Communism. The cost of the Afghan and Iraqi campaigns combined over ten years has exceeded over £20 billion, according to official figures which do not include the cost of soldiers' salaries and the ongoing health care costs of both wounded and mentally traumatised individuals. The cost of fighting terrorist threats in the UK is also not included. It is not difficult to think of ways in which that money could have been better spent.

In terms of shredding moral credibility, New Labour in power did the job with terrifying effectiveness by invading Iraq. I will not waste my time on arcane arguments about whether or not a second UN resolution was needed in order to make the invasion of Iraq lawful. What is at issue here is what was moral and ethical. As a former Prison Governor, Michael Howard is one of my least favourite politicians. As a voter, I have long been irritated by the slavish devotion of British Conservative politicians to American foreign policy, and disturbed by the presence of "neo-con" ideologues in the Tory party, but Mr Howard was the victim of the abuse of Privy Council confidentiality when Mr Blair gave him, as Opposition Leader, an intelligence briefing on the existence of WMD (Weapons of Mass Destruction) which turned out to be completely false. On realising he had been deceived, he called for the Prime Minister's resignation, but the truth is the opposition were hobbled by their support for the Iraq war and therefore could not hold the government properly to account. To this day no one has been punished. Thus democracy was failed by a Labour government lying to the opposition leader, lying to parliament and lying to the people, and failed by an opposition that could not emancipate itself from its uncritical pro-Americanism. What was truly stunning was the speed at which Tony Blair got into bed, metaphorically, with the US President, George W Bush. The invasion of Iraq was nothing less than unfinished family business for which 9/11 was simply the pretext. In 1990, when George H Bush was President, the UN authorised war against Iraq for its brutal invasion of Kuwait. When the Iraqi army was driven out of Kuwait and its legitimate rulers restored, the war ended and Saddam Hussein remained in power in Iraq. American neo-cons, had, however, argued for a full scale invasion of Iraq with the intent of bringing about regime change. In the White House of Mr Bush junior, the neo-cons were in the ascendant and wiser counsels were marginalised.

The facts about the regime of Saddam Hussein are simple. He was a brutal and repressive dictator, but in many respects no different to some of those supported in the past by the USA as part of its proxy Cold War battle strategy against the Soviet Union. The Pinochet regime in Chile is an obvious example. A second key fact is that unlike in Afghanistan, Al-Qaeda was not a force and nor was it taking refuge in Iraq. Indeed, Saddam Hussein was actively opposed to Al-Qaeda and would not have hesitated to suppress it had that been necessary. Thus, there were no Bin Laden acolytes worthy of Anglo-American attention in Iraq. Thirdly, Saddam was a Sunni Muslim presiding over a predominantly Shia Muslim country. During the Gulf War (1990-91) Shia Muslims had revolted in Iraq. Saddam brutally suppressed the rising once the Gulf War was over. It did not take a geopolitical expert to work out that the downfall of Saddam, in a country with no tradition of tolerance and democratic pluralism, would result in sectarian violence breaking out, which occurred in short order after his overthrow. An estimated 100,000 plus Iraqis have died in the civil war that has raged since the fall of Saddam. Although violence is now below 2006-7 levels, there are still hundreds of sectarian killings per month. In Baghdad communities live in insecure enclaves. Probably the main beneficiaries of Saddam's fall are Iraqi Kurds who now how have a large degree of autonomy. However, ethnic Kurds are significant minorities in Syria, Iran and Turkey, of which only the last can be considered a stable state. Thus there is obvious potential for more instability. There were no grounds for war against Iraq that made any sense in terms of meaningful foreign policy objectives. It was simply unfinished business. As with the decision making process that preceded the war, it was entirely devoid of ethical content, and what followed has been a humanitarian disaster. It was neither right nor in our national interest. Robin Cook, however, redeemed his reputation overnight by resigning from the government.

President Bush, unwisely, depicted the action against militant Islamists as a crusade. In doing so he angered a resurgent world Muslim community that is growing in confidence and asserting its identity. The politics of identity can be seen on our own streets. The expulsion of the Marxist regime in Afghanistan was not the first successful rejection of western values. In 1979, led by Ayatollah Khomeini, Iranian Islamists overthrew the Shah of Iran, for long an American client ruler in the key Middle Eastern Cold War battleground. To this day there is no American embassy in Teheran and British diplomats were forced to leave in 2011. The USA remains the world's most powerful nation, although China is likely to dispute that hegemony within the next two decades, but is nevertheless an insular nation whose people are remarkably ignorant of the world. This is reflected in its leadership. Some like Richard Nixon learned quickly, some like John Kennedy learned more slowly and painfully, and some like George W Bush refused to learn at all. The USA is remarkably impervious to world opinion. In allying ourselves with the foreign policy aims of the USA, we ally ourselves with a country happy to act as the world's policeman and impose its will by lethal force. We ally ourselves with a country whose name stinks in most of the world, even in countries like Pakistan that it bankrolls. New Labour in power fell into the American trap of not appreciating how the world looks to some of the other nations that share it. The combination of the most unworldly and ignorant US President in living memory, and his grinning sidekick, the most egotistical and self-righteous British Prime Minister in living memory (other than possibly Edward Heath), has been literally lethal. For all his faults Heath did not possess that soaring, almost demonic messianic streak that could make Tony Blair appear almost possessed. I can remember watching in horror as Mr Blair told the party faithful that Iran and North Korea were on his list for regime change. Quite how nations such as North Korea and Iran are to be defeated on the battlefield is an enduring mystery, given that our combat troops were withdrawn from Iraq in 2009 with the government simply unable to sustain their presence. Just to demonstrate the scale of the task, including reservists and paramilitaries, North Korea has over nine million soldiers under arms and Iran in excess of three million. At the time Britain could muster around 400,000 as a combined total for the armed forces, over half of whom were reservists. Get real Mr Blair.

My Generation in power betrayed the idealism of our youth. It was My Generation as students who demonstrated against the Vietnam War, yet a generation later My Generation in power allied itself with the country that we regarded as the biggest threat of all to world peace. This was the country that kept dictators in power, colluded in the assassination of elected leaders who questioned the American stranglehold on their countries, and bombed and napalmed innocent civilians in faraway lands that were unlucky enough to be caught in the Cold War cockpit. Of course, those views were attacked from the right of politics by those who saw that idealism as naivety on the one hand and crypto Communism on the other, although even right wing thinkers have conceded that the USA bled us dry and stole our markets as the price for their belated support in World War II. Smear was a substitute for argument then, and My Generation in power has adopted the same offensive approach to those who are not with the project. I am reminded of Animal Farm when the slogan "four legs good, two legs bad" became "four legs good, two legs better" as pigs who had deposed the farmer adopted the characteristics of their former master. I had hoped that, after the collapse of Communism in the former Warsaw Pact countries there would be an end to Cold War rhetoric and that constitutional left wing parties such as Labour could distance themselves from the USA without there being electoral consequences. New Labour did not even try.

As I indicated earlier, there is a price to pay for being perceived as the 51st state of America. We have become a target for militant Islamists. It may be that we would have become a target anyway, even without the slavish devotion to the USA, if only because we have an active fifth column in the UK that is growing exponentially like a cancer. How this fifth column grew and prospered under the protection of the post modern cultural relativism espoused by the political elite which has eaten away at our national identity, is brilliantly described by Melanie Phillips in her book "Londonistan: How Britain is creating a Terror State Within" (Gibson Square Books 2006), which should be required reading. Radical Muslims would still regard the UK as a decadent society, whether our government had behaved sufficiently badly to appear to be getting its deserts or not. The problem for our society is not decadence, but the threat to our national identity and collective self worth posed by the political elite. Radical Islam sees our country as having a soft underbelly that betrays weakness. It exploits our human rights laws, our open borders, and abuses freedom of speech to incite violence against unbelievers. Of late, there has been someone frightening examples of the brazen defiance being demonstrated by extremists. Some examples will suffice. In the East London boroughs of Tower Hamlets, Waltham Forest and Newham, posters appeared proclaiming "You are entering a Sharia controlled zone. Islamic rules apply". There were images indicating that smoking, alcohol and music were banned. In Tower Hamlets, posters declaring a "gay free zone" appeared before being removed. In Derby, the authorities actually did bestir themselves to prosecute Islamist extremists who distributed posters calling for the execution of gays and those convicted were imprisoned in January 2012.

At least on this occasion, it did not require a national newspaper campaign before the police and CPS acted, unlike in the aftermath of the demonstration against the Danish cartoonists who had published images of the prophet (forbidden in Islam). The demonstration took place in London on 3 February 2006 and a number of posters went far beyond what is acceptable as free speech and into the territory of incitement to violence. I quote some examples: "Be prepared for the real holocaust", "Your 9/11 is on its way", "Behead those who insult Islam" and "Freedom go to hell". Our political elite labels and persecutes anyone who suggests that such people should return to Pakistan or migrate to an Islamic state as racist, which is absolutely outrageous and without any understanding that this simply is another manifestation of our weakness in the face of the threat. People such as Abu Hamza (known to Daily Mail readers as Captain Hook and since extradited to the USA after a prolonged legal battle) had and have no intention of leaving voluntarily as they are revolutionaries whose work is to be done in the UK. The toleration of Madrassas and Sharia Law in Muslim enclaves is simply further evidence that the British have no will to resist and can be pressured into more and more concessions. Dr Rowan Williams, the Archbishop of Canterbury, demonstrated this perfectly when he argued that Sharia Law would need to be accommodated and no amount of backtracking in the face of public outrage can conceal the real views of a foremost member of the nation's elite. If 9/11 caught the imagination of potential Muslim radicals, then the Anglo American response in Afghanistan and Iraq caught their balls. Pandora's Box went from being open ajar to having the lid ripped off. It is ordinary civilians that will suffer and it is middle of the road Muslims that will suffer first as radicals tighten their grip on the mosques. As a consequence, we can look forward to more terrorist outrages, such as the murder of off duty British soldier Lee Rigby on a London street in broad daylight, which will act as a recruiting sergeant for groups such as the English Defence League, whose shaven headed alumni will usurp the role of protector of the community wherever people feel that the government has opted out. The multiculturalist dream of a mutually tolerant rainbow society will instead be one in which communities eye each other suspiciously with mutual hostility. The apocalyptic future is that we regress to being a larger version of Northern Ireland during the Troubles.

Finally, this chapter would not be complete without reference to our brave armed forces which have borne the brunt of the ill-starred campaigns in Iraq and Afghanistan. At the beginning of March 2014 453 UK service personnel had lost their lives in Afghanistan and 179 in Iraq. Many more have been disabled by their wounds and others, physically unhurt, are, and will be, suffering serious mental health problems. The blunt truth is that it has all been for nothing. More tragically still, many of these deaths were avoidable. Our service personnel have been sent out on patrol in vehicles that offered no protection against road side explosive devices. Former Army Sergeant Chantelle Taylor, in her book "Bad Company: A Woman Face to Face with the Taliban" (DRA Publishing 2011), offers articulate and telling insights from the front line. She describes being frustrated by the lack of resources and manpower in an area (Helmand) where the insurgents held all the tactical advantages. She recalls how the then Defence Secretary, John Reid, in 2006 stated that he hoped not a single round would be fired on the tour. Sgt. Taylor details how the Taliban took advantage of the lack of helicopters which forced the Army to use the roads where the lightly armoured vehicles were sitting ducks for roadside explosives. We know also that maps of minefields in Afghanistan were not up to date and that there was not enough body armour to go round in Iraq. Despite the government's denials, we know that Iraqi Shia insurgents were being funded and trained by Iran. The response of the USA was to send major reinforcements, the so-called surge. The UK, however, was trapped by the classic German error of two world wars, fighting on two fronts, an impossible task given the size of our forces and the resources available to them. Soldiers have always put their lives on the line. That is the nature of their profession. They were not the first, and will not be the last, to die as a result of the vanity of politicians with no experience whatsoever of putting their own lives at risk.

The truth is that My Generation at university hated the military. The army were the oppressors in Ireland. Working class boys who joined the army were class traitors particularly those who became NCO's. The educated elite of My Generation never grew out of its immature perception of the role and nature of the armed forces. As an institution it was sexist, racist and homophobic. Its modern role was to oppress Irishmen, just as its forbears had oppressed ethnic populations in the colonies. The inquiry into Bloody Sunday in Derry in January 1972 convened some 25 years later can be seen in this context. It took twelve years for the Saville Commission to report finding that the shootings of 13 men were "unjustified and unjustifiable". It is hard not to believe that at least some of the 13 victims were murdered, especially as all the victims were unarmed. That it was a shambles and that some soldiers lost their discipline is beyond doubt. Yet, in the end, there is no more point in apologising for Bloody Sunday, which David Cameron did in 2010, than there is in apologising for Amritsar. Events have to be seen in their political context. Ulster was a boil that was bound to burst at some point, it did so in 1968. This time there could be no closing of the lid and putting Ulster away for another 50 years. It also needs to be said that the Heath government was not neutral at this stage. In January 1972 10 Ulster Unionist MPs still sat in the House of Commons, and took the Tory whip. Indeed without them Heath's majority was precarious and it is to his credit that he changed course in the face of Ulster Unionist intransigence. The point is that soldiers in war situations take their cue from politicians. Not until repudiation of Unionist hegemony was official policy could the behaviour of soldiers be expected to change.

The loathing of the armed forces owes much to its resistance to the blandishments of the political elite. Service personnel are patriotic and fiercely loyal to each other in public. There is no culture of denunciation, no culture of cringing apologies for our history and no place for emotional incontinence. In the inverted world of the elite, its virtues are vices. There is no recognition that like other organisations the armed forces have purged themselves of prejudice based on gender, colour and sexuality. The army can also claim to be a disabled friendly employer. The Labour and Liberal Parties have not in recent times been welcoming places for former military officers seeking a political career, with the singular exception of Paddy Ashdown. The last officer to serve as Labour Defence Secretary was Major Denis Healey (1964-70), still regarded as the most able holder of the post since the Second World War, in which he served with distinction. Fred Mulley (1976-79), a Second World War sergeant who spent five years as a POW in Germany, was Labour's last Defence Secretary with combat experience. By contrast, Conservative Defence Secretaries were always former officers until 1992. Lord Carrington (1970-74) was the last Second World War Officer to serve in the role.

The cases of Privates Lee Clegg, James Fisher and Mark Wright exposed the deep fissure between the political classes on the one hand, and the military supported by Middle England on the other. It should be remembered that the convictions of Privates Clegg, Fisher and Wright in Northern Ireland were handed down by a civilian judge sitting without a jury. Sergeant Clegg as he now is, to the best of my knowledge is still serving 24 years after the incident subsequent to which he was convicted of murder and another lesser offence when a teenage joy rider was killed in Northern Ireland in 1990. After a vigorous campaign led in the media by the Daily Mail, and featuring very senior army officers who showed no fear of being publicly involved, Private Clegg was paroled in 1995. Finally, five years later he was acquitted of all charges. On being paroled, Private Clegg was immediately reinstated into the Parachute Regiment causing predictable riots in Belfast, but also an outcry amongst the lentil eating classes. After finally being cleared, he attempted to join West Yorkshire Police but his application was vetoed. To this day he has not received any compensation for the three years he spent in prison. The army has been more supportive and thankfully immune to the blandishments of political correctness. Sergeant Clegg received the coveted Long service and Good Conduct Medal awarded after 15 years exemplary service.

Less well known are the cases of James Fisher and Mark Wright convicted of the murder of Peter McBride in 1992. Both soldiers were paroled in 1998 and reinstated in their regiment. By then New Labour was in power and the Northern Ireland Secretary, Mo Mowlam, criticised the decision of the Army Board to reinstate the men. It should be noted that her successor, Peter Mandelson, took the pragmatic view that it was a matter for the Army Board and not for the government. Nevertheless an official who I had never before heard of, a Mr McDonald, The Independent Assessor of Military Complaints Procedures, was saying in his Annual Report as late as 2004 that the two soldiers should have been discharged and that the case was undermining the credibility of army employment procedures. Mr McDonald was given the job in 1997. I know nothing about him, but the post sounds like a typical politically correct post created in the same vein as the useless Children's Commissioners. The difference between this case and the case of Lee Clegg is that Fisher and Wright have not had their convictions overturned and are therefore on life licence. Like the Lee Clegg case, it arouses enormous emotion. There is no meeting of minds between those who regard the men as murderers and those who regard the continuing existence of the convictions as a miscarriage of justice.

In power My Generation actively sought to tame the Army and reverse the humiliations the political elite had suffered at the hands of the Generals in the Clegg and Fisher and Wright cases. In 2006 it went for a big fish, the Commanding Officer of the Queen's Lancashire Regiment,

Jorge Mendonca, charging him for failing to supervise subordinates after the death of an Iraqi civilian, Baha Musa, who was in the custody of soldiers from that regiment. As well as Colonel Mendonca, one Officer, one Warrant Officer, two NCO's and a private soldier were cleared. One soldier, a Corporal, admitted a charge of inhumane treatment and was duly sentenced to a term of imprisonment. It is unlikely that one man only was involved, but there was not a scrap of evidence against the Commanding Officer. This was a political prosecution lobbied for ferociously by the Attorney General, aimed at bringing senior officers into line and making them fear politicians. I expect as much as the next man that soldiers will behave in a disciplined manner and not like a wolf pack. It is in no-one's interests if soldiers cannot behave because if they cannot, it relegates our armed forces to third world status. However, political commissars are not the answer. The Attorney General, Lord Goldsmith, hotly denied political interference, but it was he who overruled the Commanding Officer of the 2nd Tank Regiment and insisted on the prosecution of Trooper Kevin Williams for allegedly shooting a civilian at a checkpoint in Iraq. This soldier was tried at the Old Bailey, as a Court Martial was no longer an option given that the Commanding Officer had already determined there was no case to answer. Thus, our soldiers are actually subject to a unique form of double jeopardy whereby the Attorney General can override military justice that doesn't suit politically correct imperatives. As it turned out, the CPS withdrew its evidence at the start of the trial and the jury was not called upon. Nevertheless at an earlier stage in proceedings the Judge had refused a defence submission that there was no case to answer.

The Army is not the only military institution to suffer from undermining by those who see our enemies as victims. The war on piracy in the Indian Ocean has been hobbled by lawyers arguing that returning Somali pirates to their own country for trial is a breach of their human rights, as they face possible torture and execution. Bring them back to England and they will ask for asylum and at the end of their sentence use Human Rights legislation to bring their families over. As they can't be made to walk the plank or hung from the yardarm, the traditional punishments of days gone by, the only other option is to let them go. What a farce. Yet again the criminal is treated as a victim. Undermining is also done at home. On leaving the army, soldiers find that asylum seekers and reckless breeders qualify for social housing in front of them. They are abused in civilian hospitals and have to fight bureaucrats seeking to cut their disability payments. They have even been advised not to wear their uniforms off duty for fear of "giving offence".

The more usual weapon of choice against the armed forces is economic. My Generation has always believed that the defence budget is bloated. The prime target was the nuclear arsenal, but here lay electoral oblivion, so politically that became impossible. Once in power politicians swiftly learn to love the bomb. It is the admission card to a still pretty exclusive club. Thus, it is death by a thousand cuts, that fall everywhere except on bureaucrats of whom there are actually more than there are army personnel. Morale is undermined by stealth. We have now reached the stage where any more international commitments would be completely unmanageable. Fighting a Falklands campaign similar to 1982 is now a military impossibility. We do not have enough ships and will have no aircraft carriers until 2020. Falkland Islanders are reliant entirely for their defence on the deterrent value of a couple of high tech surface vessels and one nuclear submarine, always assuming that there will be one at sea. Our only good fortune is that Argentina is a corrupt state whose sabre rattling leader has only ancient combat aircraft which HMS Dauntless could blow out of the sky before they got close. Nevertheless, if the Argentines ever resolved that problem and were able to capture the airfield on the Falklands, it would be game over. The government would fall amidst public outrage, but the political elite would have won their greatest victory, orchestrated in a moment of supreme irony by Tory defence cutters. It would be the ultimate revenge on Margaret Thatcher. Only the fall of the monarchy, which is intimately connected with the military, would give them greater joy.

CHAPTER 12

EDUCATION AND HIGHER EDUCATION

It is tempting to at least partially acquit My Generation of much of the blame for the wreckage of our system of education, on the basis that it cannot be blamed for what it inherited. The wholesale destruction of grammar schools, the phasing out of corporal punishment and the subsequent decline in discipline, and the spread of child centred classroom methods which are a key feature of the decline of reading skills, as well as the dumbing down of standards were facts of life even when some baby boomers were still at school. The central charge, therefore, against My Generation, is embracing and furthering these developments at best uncritically and at worst deliberately. It is as if the expansion of higher educational opportunities, after the Robbins report of 1963, was wasted on My Generation which has signally failed to apply intellectual rigour to what was to become the prevailing orthodoxy. I am reminded of a comment made by Ed Miliband when he was Secretary of State for Climate Change and the Environment. "The Science is settled," he said, regarding global warming. Mr Miliband is not of my generation. However he seems to be repeating the classic error of believing, on the evidence of his own words, that knowledge is a destination rather than a journey.

The tripartite system established by the 1944 Act of Grammar, Technical and Secondary Modern education did not exclude the possibility of comprehensive schooling. Essentially, the Act was about establishing secondary education for all according to "age, ability and aptitude" rather than prescribing the number of roofs under which it took place. My memory of my own studies is that there were comprehensive schools in Wales during the late 1940s. The 1944 Act, implemented by the 1945-50 Labour government, had its strengths and weaknesses. Probably the biggest single weakness in retrospect was the effective abandonment of technical education, for which our country has paid and continues to pay a high price. Despite the sterling work done by some secondary moderns, not until they were permitted to enter youngsters for examinations, did they cease to be anything other than rebadged elementary schools. Added to that was the fact that many years often elapsed before purpose built secondary modern schools were available for all children. My memory of my own primary school is that it continued to cater for 5-15 year olds until 1960. Again, it would not be unfair to describe it as a pre-war elementary school in all but name. GCEs replaced the school certificate in the early 1950s, but not until 1965 was the CSE (Certificate in Secondary Education) available for secondary modern pupils.

Entry to grammar schools depended on success in the 11-plus examinations. This was something of a postcode lottery as the provision of grammar school places depended on local provision, which could be anything between 15 and 33%. Where technical schools did not exist, which was most of the country, there was a grim finality about the 11-plus, which segregated young people for life. The lucky ones would take the GCE at 16, and have the option to go as far as their talent would take them. The unlucky ones, at least until secondary moderns were permitted to enter pupils for examinations, would leave school at 15 for a life of manual labour. Thus, those who buckled under the pressure of examination day and those who were late developers were denied access to an academic education. There was a 12-plus second chance, but in reality it had few takers. The original verdict tended to be accepted. In theory, there was a further opportunity to enter grammar school at 16 in the sixth form. However, surmounting this barrier only became possible when secondary moderns were permitted to enter pupils for public examinations. Achieving 5 'O' levels was a demanding enough target for existing grammar school pupils who were used to being driven hard in a competitive environment. My own school only relaxed the requirement for 5 GCE 'O' levels or equivalent as the minimum qualification for sixth form entry in 1969, the year I entered the sixth form.

The tripartite, or more usually bipartite system, lasted only a generation as educationalists and politicians sought to dismantle it, and replace it with a fully comprehensive provision in the state sector. In 1965, the newly elected Labour government invited LEAs to volunteer to go comprehensive, and made it financially worth their while to do so. Between 1970 and 1974, when the Conservatives were in office, Mrs Thatcher, then Secretary of State for Education and Science, was reputed to have signed off more conversions to comprehensive schooling than any other occupant of her post. The job was virtually completed by the 1974-79 Labour administration. In 1975, the government required all local education authorities in England and Wales to submit plans for comprehensive schooling to cover all pupils in secondary education. The only alternative for Direct Grant schools was to go independent and effectively join the public schools in what would be an expanded private fee paying sector. Religious foundations, which had been much more reliant on LEAs purchasing places, were left with no alternative but to join the state system. Indeed many had read the writing on the wall in the late 1960s. As for the Manchester Grammar Schools of this world, the door was firmly closed on working class pupils as they resumed their pre-1944 exclusivity. The drive for a fully comprehensive state system actually increased the size of the independent sector. The only reason any state grammar schools survived at all, the main concentration being in Kent, is because some local authorities were able to delay submission beyond the next election. The incoming Conservative government, elected in May 1979, did not disturb the settlement. What it did do was set up the Assisted Places scheme, by which state school pupils could attend participating independent schools. As it did not offer free places, it was a pretty thin substitute for the Direct Grant. Mr Blair's government swiftly abolished the scheme.

So why did the settlement of the 1944 Act not endure? It was probably a soft target. The claims of parity of esteem between the three types of school were chimerical. How could they be any other when two thirds of pupils left school at least three terms earlier than their grammar school counterparts, did not sit examinations, and indeed often experienced their version of secondary education in the same premises under the same Head Teacher as their younger siblings in the same primary school? However, the attack on the 1944 Act was not just based on the inadequacies of the secondary moderns or the vicissitudes of premature selection. For C.A.R. Crosland, Labour MP, political thinker and future Secretary of State for Education, the system was not capable of incremental reform. Indeed, Crosland vowed not to rest until "every fucking grammar school had been closed down." Crosland produced a paper in 1956 entitled "The Future of Socialism". Its central tenet, hugely controversial in left wing circles in that era, was that the battles over the extent to which capitalist organised industries should be nationalised were no longer relevant, as a managerial class was succeeding the owning class, and that Socialists should now concentrate on equality. The symbolic repudiation of the old clause 4, after Tony Blair succeeded John Smith as Labour leader in 1994, marked the posthumous triumph of Crosland's ideas and set the agenda for the Labour government of 1997-2010. One of the central tenets of this book is that in reality New Labour has only succeeded in creating either new inequalities or entrenching old ones even deeper.

Another highly influential publication of that era is Michael Young's "Rise of the Meritocracy". Young's lengthy satirical essay foresaw a world in which merit, as expressed in the early years of life through educational success rather than birth, defined the new ruling elite. The problem for Young was that the new ruling elite became as entrenched in much the same way as the old landowning one, restricted social mobility and had strict rules (political correctness?) governing membership and acceptance into the club. The principal agent of the meritocracy foreseen by Young was the grammar school.

I am happy to admit that I was a supporter of comprehensive secondary schooling. I saw it as an extension of our democracy; fluid, dynamic and responsive to the needs of all. The parity of esteem problem would be just a memory. The divide between academic and vocational education would steadily weaken and damaging social segregation would end. Selection would be a rational rather than an arbitrary process. My first full time teaching post in my short teaching career was in a comprehensive school in King's Lynn, Norfolk. It had been created by an amalgamation of a girls' grammar school and a mixed secondary modern, and my probationary year coincided with the first year of operation and the first non-selective intake. I offer no criticism, indeed quite the reverse, of my former colleagues or the head teacher in this book. As a school, it strove to cater for all abilities and provided rigorous academic education for those who could benefit from it for the four years I was on the staff. It kept Harold Wilson's promise to retain grammar school education under the comprehensive umbrella. However, for our modern day egalitarians, this was not acceptable. Selection of any kind, competition, and the pursuit of excellence for its own sake were social evils to be extirpated.

Battle commenced in schools, local authorities, and university departments training teachers up and down the land. Gradually the baby was forced down the plughole with the bathwater. The demise of Latin and Greek outside the independent sector is almost total. General Science is pushing out the separate study of Physics, Chemistry and Biology. Worse than that, experimental science and dissection have fallen foul of bogus health and safety and animal welfare considerations respectively. Climate change is taught as though it were fact and multiple choice questions containing idiotic alternatives that add to the litany of schoolboy howlers have replaced the need to learn, understand and retain. History and Geography suffer frequently from amalgamation which damages the integrity of both disciplines. Being taught separately does not make the picture any more appealing. It is now possible to obtain a good i.e. grade C or better pass in GCSE History, but in fact remain remarkably ignorant of our country's past. Instead of understanding the causes of World War I, the student will be able to sketch a trench and write a short essay from the perspective of a German participating in the Christmas Day inter-trench football match. Geography syllabuses are re-written with a pronounced anti-imperialist slant. No prizes for guessing that the UK is one of the pantomime villains. If I appear to exaggerate, it is only slightly. No subject is immune. Only recently I was made aware of another example of something even the most imaginative author would struggle to make up. A class of 13 year olds changed for PE, but instead of an hour's vigorous exercise they had to sit on the gym floor and listen to a lecture on obesity. Does that school not know that lack of exercise is the key contributor along with poor diet to that ever worsening problem? Does that school not have Domestic Science or Food Technology lessons, or whatever is the politically correct term these days, to impart such vital information? Do they not know how few calories you burn sat on your backside?

That takes me neatly to the demise of competitive sport. Cricket has almost disappeared from comprehensive schools. Rugby Union is in similar disfavour with health and safety a familiar excuse. Soccer does not suffer to the same extent, if only because the metropolitan elite have adopted it in the cause of associating themselves with celebrity. However, that has not stopped some Primary schools from trying. The papers have published a number of examples of politically correct teachers picking boys who can't tell one from foot from another in local cup finals in the cause of "inclusivity". Naturally their team loses.

Naturally skilled and competitive boys and their parents are distraught. And as for the poor kid who gets into the team without being worth a place; well, he gets the blame when the team loses and his self-esteem falls lower than a snake's scrotum. He would have been better off cheering from the sidelines and enjoying the vicarious pleasure of cheering his more talented fellows to victory; which is what we all do when we cheer on our favourite football team. You know; the one we dreamed of playing for before we learned we would never be good enough. Were we damaged by it? No we were not. But for this breed of teacher competition is evil. If all cannot have prizes, then no-one can. It gets worse. Some Primary school head teachers have even banned children (mainly boys) from playing football in the playground, again on spurious health and safety grounds. And we wonder why we have fat children on the one hand, and on the other children doped with Ritalin, and we wonder why we breed aggressive moronic boys with no safe outlet for natural male aggression.

I can tell you from my own experience just how badly boys and young men need hard physical exercise and competitive sport. I can also tell you from the same experience that the need is in inverse proportion to educational attainment. Back in the 1980s, as a very junior prison officer, I was trained as a Sports and Games Officer so that there was sufficient back up for the very small number of PE instructors. I would be given charge of anything between 12 and 24 young offenders on a Saturday or Sunday afternoon, as would other colleagues. The job was to ensure that in the space of a couple of hours these young tearaways engaged in competitive physical exercise that burned up all the excess testosterone, and then some. If evening association passed without any fights or other incidents involving aggression, then we had done our job well.

Why can't our schools understand the needs of boys? Part of the answer appears to be the increasing feminisation of our education system, although it is important to remember that feminisation is as much the fault of male educationalists as it is of women. Male teachers are fast becoming an endangered species in primary schools. Indeed there are some radical feminists who believe that children in this age group should have a female chaperone if the class teacher is male! When combined with family breakdown, it can be seen that boys are often completely deprived of positive male role models in their immediate lives. Comprehensive schooling didn't just kill off the grammar school, it killed off single sex secondary schooling. It has also effectively killed off competitive examinations as benchmarks trusted by parents, employers and institutions of Higher Education alike. Adolescent boys are easily distracted by girls. Those who consider themselves as alpha males cannot help but show off. It is peacock syndrome at work in the classroom. Fairly obviously this behaviour is distracting and wastes more than its fair share of teacher time. Boys also mature mentally and emotionally more slowly than girls. They are also more likely to be risk takers. Examinations where you have to deliver on the day actually help level a playing field now strongly biased against boys. Well, they do if boys have not already been completely turned off by a system which neglects their psychological and intellectual needs. Boys have suffered badly from the loss of Woodwork and Metalwork, and their absorption into amorphous Craft, Design and Technology courses, which is another example of feminisation which denies boys of average ability a chance to excel and increase self-esteem.

Gender differences are as much an argument for single sex teaching as differential ability is for banding or setting, or what other polite euphemism is used for streaming. But of course this isn't allowed either. Education must be dumbed down to a pace and content that is equally accessible to all, so that many more can appear to succeed. Thus, the ever increasing pass rates at GCSE ordinary and advanced levels are not a product of ever increasing untapped brain power being unlocked by better teaching, rather they are a product of easier examinations and reduced pass marks. The grade C, we are told is the equivalent of a pass in the former GCE 'O' level. The reality is that it is the equivalent of the old CSE grade 3, the mark of the student of average ability in the former Secondary Modern intake. The use of modular courses allows unlimited opportunities for downloading from the internet, for the repeating of assignments until they reach the required standard, and for teachers to turn a blind eye to such practices as it is only results that count; and it is by results they will be judged. The way they are achieved is irrelevant. It is like rigging the FA Premier League so that it is almost always won by Stoke City, rather than Manchester United or Arsenal. Thus, excellence, the academic equivalent of the beautiful game, is a key casualty. Our examination system no longer commands the confidence of employers and the public at large.

School reports would be no more helpful. The last one I saw, which was quite recently, told the parents a great deal about their daughter's social skills and emotional development, but nothing at all about her academic prowess one way or the other, and certainly no indication where she ranked with respect to her peers. The same parents were told by me, rather than by the school, that their younger daughter was probably of well above average intelligence. Don't gifted children have special educational needs? Don't the parents deserve to know the true potential of their offspring? Not in the land of conformist mediocrity they do not. And we wonder why the independent sector not only maintains but extends its stranglehold on places in top universities and the professions. And we wonder why bright working class children are less likely to be the first in their family to make it to a prestigious university than was the case with My Generation.

Social mobility is not the primary purpose of a university. It is merely a happy by-product. The primary purpose of a university is the pursuit of excellence and constant pushing of the frontiers of knowledge. They are places where existing orthodoxy should be challenged on a daily basis. The science is never settled. Knowledge is always a journey and never a destination. These are lofty ideals that soar above social engineering and drab educational utilitarianism. By living up to these ideals, elite status is earned. I contend bluntly that we do not need nor can we justify 50% of the population in higher education.

The organisation of post school education, apart from its most elite universities, is almost unrecognisable from my time in higher education. University provision was expanded as a consequence of the Robbins report in 1963. A generation of what were termed "redbrick" institutions were established and swiftly acquired credibility. My student days commenced in 1974 and around one-sixth of school leavers entered higher education. The sector itself was divided into three component parts; the Universities who awarded their own degrees, the Polytechnics which were also part of the post 1963 expansion whose degrees were validated by The Council for National Academic Awards (CNAA), and the Teacher Training Colleges, whose courses were validated either by a neighbouring university, or by the CNAA. The award of degrees to teacher training college students was only a few years old at this time and only around one-fifth of their alumni typically stayed on for an extra year to take a degree. The professional degree, the B Ed, was developed contemporaneously with the drive to comprehensive schooling. Typically in the bipartite system, virtually all grammar school teachers (PE was the usual exception) would be university graduates, not all of whom would have taken the Post Graduate Teaching Certificate and therefore were technically unqualified. The majority of secondary modern teachers, apart from the Head, would hold the non-degree standard Certificate in Education, having qualified via a three year teacher (until 1960 two year) training course at a College of Education, to give teacher training establishments their proper appellation. Primary school teachers, again, largely qualified by the same route as their as their secondary modern peers.

This system was perceived as unfit for purpose in a comprehensive secondary education world. Equally, to revisit a theme, it was perceived necessary to have an all graduate profession in order to raise its status, its attractiveness to recruits and its credibility. Looking back, it seems anomalous that it took until the mid-seventies for the decision to be taken to create an all graduate profession. The PGCE route for university graduates would be maintained, but those entering the Colleges of Education would study for the B Ed. As both the Polytechnics and Colleges of Education were Local Authority controlled, provision was swiftly rationalised, and the free standing Colleges disappeared into Departments of Education. In practical terms the B Ed route lacked the status of the BA/BSc and PGCE route, and a Masters would be de rigueur for the ambitious. Teachers holding only the non- degree standard Certificate in Education still remain in the profession, as a number of local authorities refused to grant secondments to allow their employees to upgrade. This cadre includes many fine teachers, now in the final stages of their careers.

As any school student will tell you, qualifications are no guarantee that the holder is a good or even competent teacher. We have all been to school and can recall from distances of many years the truly inspirational, the truly terrifying, and the truly terrible. The merely competent merge into relative anonymity, unless they are remembered for some eccentricity or personal peccadillo. However, I cannot allow the sepia tint of nostalgia to be the final word on classroom organisation and discipline. I have described school discipline as it was for us in Chapter 2. Much has changed and most of it for the worse. There is no doubt that very fine teachers are being driven from the profession, or at the very least having their effectiveness severely reduced by the attack on school discipline that has been conducted relentlessly by the country's liberal elite. This would have been inconceivable 40 years ago.

Corporal punishment effectively disappeared from the state system after an ECHR ruling in 1985 that children could only be physically chastised with the agreement of the parents. At the time, this was not a legally enforceable decision but the government, as signatories to the convention, felt a moral obligation. Clearly, a two tier system of discipline was untenable. In any event, corporal punishment had been rapidly disappearing from the educational landscape. It was actually abolished in the Republic of Ireland, home to the Christian Brothers, in 1983, four years earlier than the UK. An organisation called STOPP, the Society of Teachers Opposed to Physical Punishment, was particularly influential in parts of England. A newly appointed headteacher could simply outlaw the cane or strap in his or her own school. Local education authorities were not slow to appoint these evangelists. There were exceptions, and they were not exclusively Tory. The Labour leader in Swansea in the early '80s was not prepared to have their teachers operating with "one arm tied behind their backs". It is not easy to argue for the return of corporal punishment without attracting opprobrium at worst and sniggers at best, on the basis that you may be a fetishist or a pervert. Former MP Harvey Proctor was unhelpfully notorious in this respect, being forced to stand down from parliament in 1987 after his spanking of underage rent boys (the age of gay consent was then 21) came to light. However, it is a solvable problem, using the tawse rather than the cane. The tawse, used mainly in Scotland, was a strap administered to the hands rather than the backside. Thus sexual connotations are avoided and it then has the added advantage of it being a unisex punishment. I am advised by those of my acquaintance educated in Scotland, that the tawse was every bit as painful and effective as the cane. Without discipline, there is no hope of improving standards. It should be available to every secondary school teacher for a strictly prescribed list of individual infractions; violence, bullying, gross verbal abuse and disruption of lessons, thus avoiding it been brought into disrepute by being used for trivial matters or for mass punishment. As for ECHR, it can go to hell.

My generation has an immature attitude to school discipline. All of us can remember instances of injustice and unfairness from our school days. However, it hardly ranks with the 16 years in prison suffered by the Birmingham Six for terrorist crimes they didn't commit. A sense of proportion is needed. Carrying adolescent resentment of legitimate authority into adult life is not a hallmark of maturity. What my generation has done, subsequent to the abolition of corporal punishment, has been to destroy the authority of teachers in school at every turn. Let me recite some of the litany. New Labour is not responsible for the passing of the dreadful Children's Act, but it is responsible for much of the damage that has ensued. Children can make the most ridiculous allegations against their teachers with a good chance of being believed. When that occurs, dismissal, disgrace and destitution follow. Even when the allegations are not upheld, there will have been a lengthy period of suspension with all the professional and personal damage that inflicts. If the allegation were of a criminal nature, innocence is no protection against the ruin of the reputation. As it stands, details of an allegation can actually be printed even before a person is charged. All it needs is a leak to the local press. DNA will be taken and not destroyed. More insidiously, the allegation will remain on file and under the vetting and barring regulations, this information may be disclosed. So a career change won't be an option. An acquittal in court, or not even being charged, does not necessarily safeguard your employment. The standard of proof at disciplinary hearings is the balance of probability, which offers teachers little safeguard against children and their parents determined to lie to the bitter end. This is a system that is riddled with random injustice. It destroys lives and careers and does not make one child safer. We have all been children and all those of us who are parents know deep down that children lie to keep out of trouble. And if we are honest, we will all remember as children that we would have given up a week's pocket money to see a teacher sacked or a neighbour taken away by the police. As children we simply did not understand the consequences of lying and exaggerating for the victims. By institutionalising the view that children are simply another minority group deserving of vulnerable victim status, we have institutionalised the child's view of the world.

New Labour came to power promising to restore standards and school discipline. However, yet again it is by deeds that New Labour must be judged, not its words. The relentless dumbing down to which I have previously referred accelerated. Spin was the order of the day. Figures were produced to demonstrate that more youngsters than ever were achieving the benchmark 5 grade Cs. Not only were the passes easier to achieve, New Labour happily boasted about these achievements when they did not include some or all of Maths, English and Science. Given that the government and its Tory predecessor laid down the minimum standards that should be achieved in core subjects at 7, 10 and 14, and set targets for those achievements, it was clearly disingenuous to publish figures which did not reflect the same expected outcomes in the GCSE. Foreign languages are deemed too difficult for many pupils and one state school in five does not enter a single student for advanced level Physics. It is small wonder that Independent Schools are increasingly entering students for the International Baccalaureate. It is hard to believe that the Labour Party once believed that a high quality state system would make private schooling educationally, if not socially, redundant.

Given the damage done to the learning environment, it was probably essential to make examinations easier and offload study via the bedroom computer plugged into the internet. New Labour, as a matter of public policy, made it harder to expel the violent and disruptive from schools, in much the same way as the violent and the disruptive are free to prey on the nation's social housing estates. Severe financial disincentives, which could more accurately be described as swingeing fines, penalised schools who sought to expel those who assaulted, those who extorted, those who dealt drugs, and those whose behavioural problems made teaching impossible. Thus, if head teachers expelled those who would not accept even these minimum disciplinary standards, they had substantially less money to spend on those who wanted to learn, and those who would be persuaded to learn by virtue of seeing adults take a strong line against malefactors. The real victims, as ever, are working class children whose parents lack the affluence or influence to find a more congenial scholastic environment. This is the system that David Blunkett commended to the electorate.

Head teachers seeking to impose discipline by using the only meaningful sanction left open to them also have other enemies. The police do not want an army of feral youths on the streets. They infinitely prefer them in the classroom. It gives a whole new meaning to crime prevention. Next, there is the appeals panel which can overrule, and frequently does overrule, permanent exclusions. Only industrial action by teachers is effective in preventing returns to the school as a consequence, which is an anarchic state of affairs. Naturally, the problem is offloaded elsewhere, frequently to a school considered to have less than its fair share of juvenile misanthropes, or if the mainstream is lucky, to a pupil referral unit, the numbers of which have burgeoned over the last 20 years. After this, there is the race lobby who happily pedal the myth that the disproportionate number of exclusions of Afro-Caribbean boys is a by-product of racism. It shows the lack of understanding of discipline in these households, which is uncompromising and makes schools appear ludicrously weak to Caribbean boys. The race lobby also conveniently ignores the lack of suitable male role models and the baleful influence of the gang culture. The Commission for Equality and Human Rights, the country's most pernicious quango, has recommended a higher tolerance threshold of poor behaviour by Traveller children before the ultimate sanction is imposed. How this can be demonstrating equality beggars belief. Traveller children have nothing to gain and everything to lose from concessions to unacceptable behaviour, and it is in fact extremely patronising to Traveller families. The main losers in all this; you've guessed it – working class children. If this was not enough, then there is always the human rights lobby, always ready to rally behind irresponsible parents whose cherubic little dears are being denied the right to self-expression and the right to run their playground protection racket. And wherever there is a loud bleat about human rights there is a grubby firm of solicitors with an eye on further enrichment via the public purse. And incidentally, why did Michael Gove not get rid of the terminally useless Children's Commissioners?

Returning to the theme of higher education, there was one very significant development under Tony Blair's predecessor, John Major. The binary divide was abolished and the polytechnics, many of which a generation earlier had been Colleges of Further Education, became universities. By the stroke of a pen, the comprehensive system was established in higher education. I doubt even Tony Blair's cabinet believed that all should go to university. After all, increasing the school leaving age to 21 would have been a pretty extreme measure to deal with unemployment, which on Labour taking office in 1997, was at its lowest level for 18 years. Nevertheless, when coupled with easier school examinations, the road was open for the all ability university to become part of our educational fabric. In one sense it was a logical development. All ability compulsory school education, all ability sixth form education moving into territory once reserved for the further education sector, followed by the comprehensive university. Mr Blair's target for university education was 50%. It has already reached 43%. In the mid '70s the numbers in higher education were around 16%, and I have to say that even then I thought some of my fellow students were intellectually lacking.

In waging the equality war in higher education, New Labour has used three distinctive but interlinked tools. Firstly, as has been said, it has severely watered down the meritocratic principle, by making the qualifying hurdles of GCSE and advanced level much easier to jump. As with schools, it has waged class war. In the schools sector, local authorities by no means all of them Labour, have used methods such as random balloting for school places to defeat parents who have used their muscle in the housing market to get into the catchment area of perceived good schools, and just as important, avoid perceived bad ones. Parents have fought back by finding God and his churches, as faith schools have higher standards according to the league tables.

In the university sector, New Labour (and its Coalition successors) has used the power of the public purse to weaken university independence and drive through the anti-elitist agenda. They have had more than their fair share of collaborators from within. In much the same way as exam success has increased exponentially in our schools, so it is with the number of students achieving first class and upper second class honours degrees. As such the Upper Second rather than the Lower Second, (A "Desmond" in rhyming slang), has been elevated to the expected norm of achievement. However, this rather transparent method of increasing the number of sheep at the expense of goats is not to the taste of the anti-meritocratic egalitarians. For them, an increasingly vocal lobby, the abolition of degree classification and its replacement by anodyne student profiles is the goal. By devaluing the currency, university Vice-Chancellors are paving the way to the destruction of the ultimate educational kite mark.

New Labour may have been politically committed to a major hike in student numbers. However, what it was not prepared to do was to pay for it, or more pertinently, not raise general taxation to pay for it. Instead, the new generation of students who were supposedly the main beneficiaries of comprehensive higher education would be called upon to pay an ever increasing chunk of the cost. The reasoning behind the charging of tuition fees to home students was devastatingly simple. Since graduates earned higher salaries, university education conferred lifelong relative privilege, and therefore could fairly be taxed. Make no mistake, tuition fees are as much a tax as VAT. The anti-elitist zealots took no account of the contribution graduates make to society, the wealth they generate for the nation, and the higher taxes that they will inevitably pay. The crude message from New Labour was just the opposite; that graduates take out more from society than they put in. Sadly, there are signs that could become a self-fulfilling prophecy if all many of the new alumni have to look forward to, is the dole queue and the minimum wage. If that comes to pass, then the graduates of the first and succeeding decades of the 21st century will have been the victims of a giant Ponzi scheme. A spokesman from Oxford University recently called for elite institutions to be allowed to charge fees of 16k per annum, almost double the current maximum. Thus, this uncalled for and unnecessary expansion of higher education makes debtors and paupers of its recipients; social mobility in reverse.

As has been emphasised repeatedly in this book, New Labour built on the work of the outgoing government, which in higher education had replaced student grants with loans during John Major's premiership. Mandatory grants for first degree courses and the two routes to teacher qualification were made available on a means tested basis in 1962, as part of the expansion of higher education. It was these grants that enabled working class students to enjoy the benefits of higher education. I was one of those who received a full grant. New Labour made great play of the small scale restoration of grants for students from the least privileged families. However, their fiscal policy with regard to higher education throws up a couple of interesting contradictions. Firstly, for the whole of New Labour's period in office (1997-2010) compulsory education still ended at 16. Logically, New Labour should have levied fees for what my generation knew as sixth form education. After all it conferred advantage. Instead, New Labour did the opposite and introduced the EMA (Educational Maintenance Allowance) to encourage working class children to stay on at school. The cynic in me says it's cheaper than the dole. The second contradiction comes with the provision of grants, such as they were, for working class children entering higher education. After all if the life chances after graduation are equal, what is the basis for a subsidy? Working class children are no less eligible for student loans, bank loans and part time jobs. I make the point tongue in cheek to demonstrate the contradictions. It also needs to be remembered that system is skewed against two income families. A typical working class couple, where the husband earns the median wage of 19k per year and his wife around 8k from part time work, does not benefit from state help for higher education. This is another example of the malevolence of the anti-married family policies pursued by New Labour. Conversely, or should it be perversely, the cap for state help does not apply to those in receipt of benefits. It is now the case that there are families whose benefit payments are at such a level, they find themselves with an income equalled or exceeded only by a quarter of the workforce. I have examined this situation in more detail elsewhere in this book.

The coalition government seems intent on pursuing New Labour's fees policy to its illogical conclusion. Those elite universities who charge the horrific new maximum of 9k per year will be forced to take a proportion of disadvantaged students with lower qualifications from poor performing schools, virtually all of whom will be working class, at the only marginally less horrific rate of 6k per year. When living costs are factored in, how the reduction of one's debts on graduation from around 40k to 30k is an incentive, defeats me. Twenty years ago, and remember we have had low overall inflation in that period, 30k was still a mortgage for ordinary families. Now, graduates have that kind of debt before they can even think about the housing ladder. What does My Generation think it is doing to its children and grandchildren? If this is equality in action, I want none of it.

The other grim reality is that for the very rich, this policy will only have a miniscule effect on already deep pockets. Those parents that can afford Eton and Harrow will find university fees a relatively modest imposition. Oxford will still be much cheaper than Eton. Their sons and daughters were never eligible for maintenance grants in any case. No doubt the cash will come from trust funds or be found by tax advisors who specialise in helping the rich avoid paying their due. Their dominance of Oxbridge and other elite institutions will remain unchallenged and indeed enhanced. The world that New Labour made fit for bankers and other plutocrats will continue to spin happily on its axis. By making the cost of the best education truly horrifying, social mobility will continue to decline, aspiration will continue to be stifled, and New Labour will go down in history as the working class party that betrayed the working class. As for the middle classes who voted Labour in 1997 and 2001, they are also discovering that like the manual working classes, they no longer have a political party they can call home.

I believe firmly that higher education should be free at the point of use like the NHS. Fees should be charged only to foreigners, who we would not expect to be paying taxes in this country for the rest of their lives. It is simply not acceptable that university Vice-Chancellors should have a vested interest in expanding these institutions into vast utilitarian qualifications factories, turning themselves into Chief Executives and ramping up their salaries as part of the bargain. Universities need to rediscover their role at the frontiers of knowledge and, therefore, should be elite institutions. The numbers studying for degree courses should be slashed in half and those institutions which become unviable as a result should either close or be rebadged as Institutes of Further Education specialising in non-degree qualifications. The cutting of costs will allow the re-introduction of maintenance grants on a means tested basis. I favour maintenance grants for a number of reasons; it fosters a debt free culture, it prevents an over-reliance on part time work for income at the expense of study, and it allows the matching of the brightest students to courses at top universities away from their home area. Expansion of university provision would be increased in line only with intellectual demand. It would be dependent on improved standards in schools. This is what occurred in the 1950s. The expansion of grammar school provision catered for previously unmet intellectual needs and fuelled a legitimate demand for university expansion that was answered by Robbins. In education the way back is often the way forward.

CHAPTER 13

THE ABANDONMENT OF THE WORKING CLASS

Of all the things that anger me about the performance of My Generation in power it is the almost complete abandonment of the working class by the 1997-2010 Labour Government. Given that the Labour Party began life as an organisation seeking to further the interests of ordinary working people via representation in the House of Commons, it amounts to a systematic betrayal of the ideals and aspirations of the founding fathers of the party and of the work done by the Labour Government led by Clem Attlee after World War II. The lowest turnouts at election time are very much concentrated in constituencies with the greatest number of inhabitants in the lowest social classifications. I hesitate to describe these constituencies as working class given that they tend to have the highest unemployment levels. Increasingly, throughout the life of that government, those whose default option was Labour were simply abstaining or turning to the BNP as they viewed with despair the metropolitan elitism of the party that left them without a natural repository for their vote. Although Labour was re-elected with another landslide in 2001, turnout dropped nationally from 70% to 60%. In a number of urban constituencies less than half of eligible voters turned out. The working and former working classes sent a message to Labour which was simply ignored. Voter apathy cannot be linked to the outcome being telegraphed in advance by the opinion polls. There have been certain results before, notably in 1983 and 1987, which did not prevent voters from going to the polls in broadly comparable numbers to the previous election. The fall off in turnout in 2001 was unprecedented since the abandonment of a property based suffrage in 1918. In the election campaign of 2010, the Prime Minister, Gordon Brown, finally let the mask slip when he was heard referring to a Rochdale pensioner of impeccable working class origins, Gillian Duffy, as a "bigoted woman", because she had the temerity to break a Labour taboo, and challenge Mr Brown on immigration. Now we know for certain the contempt in which Labour holds its core vote. Labour voters have not deserted the party, the party has deserted them.

The Labour party has provided six British Prime ministers. Of the six, only the reputation of Clement Attlee who led the party from 1935 to 1955 stands more or less intact. Even Conservative commentators put Attlee in their pantheon of great Prime Ministers of the twentieth century alongside Winston Churchill and Margaret Thatcher. Ramsay MacDonald is either forgotten or disowned. Harold Wilson and James Callaghan are associated, fairly or unfairly, with Britain's economic decline, from which according to Conservative commentators, the nation was rescued by Margaret Thatcher. My Generation has provided two prime ministers, Tony Blair and Gordon Brown. To plagiarise the late Michael Foot's 1940 book title, they are the "Guilty Men". As the two most powerful individuals, the two of My Generation who rose the highest, they have to take the lion's share of the blame.

I was born in 1952. Gordon Brown was born the previous year and Tony Blair the year after. Although Labour had lost office In November 1951, its ethos and achievements mapped out a broad consensus that 13 years of Tory rule could not and dare not undo. 1945 had made it clear to the Conservatives that the deference vote could not be taken for granted. The Conservatives were the dominant force between the wars. In 1945 they were punished for unemployment, for means testing and for appeasement, but more than anything they were punished for mediocrity, lack of imagination and the failure to deliver anything meaningful to show for being in office almost continuously, either on their own or in coalitions they dominated, apart from two short periods of Labour minority government, from 1918 to the fall of Neville Chamberlain in May 1940. Sadly, New Labour takes little account of the lessons of history. It should not take comfort from avoiding the electoral Armageddon it deserved in 2010.

The 1945-51 Labour government was, indeed, led by a man who had attended public school and who had held the rank of major in the British army. Nevertheless, Attlee is regarded as Labour's most left wing prime minister by some distance, insofar as that term has any meaning in modern political parlance. The government also included very significant figures from working class backgrounds such as Herbert Morrison, Ernest Bevin and Aneurin Bevan. These are only the best known and the most senior of that era. All of these had left school by the age of 13, and enjoyed only an elementary education. They were living proof that working men could not only succeed in politics, but also in government. Bevin and Morrison both made their reputations as ministers during the wartime coalition. Numerically, Labour were the junior partners, but in practice they were the senior partners on the home front, and were determined that there would be no repeat of the failures to win the peace that characterised post First World War governments. Nye Bevan was not considered remotely suitable for office in the coalition, but any doubts about his ability to rise to the challenge were dispelled with the delivery of the National Health Service. It remains Labour's towering achievement and it will forever be associated with Aneurin Bevan. The Trade Union movement and Local Government provided the theatres in which able working class people could grow and develop.

The men and women of Attlee's government were staunch patriots. The prime minister was a bona fide war hero who had served with distinction in the Dardanelles in the First World War, not that he would have seen it that way. Labour's patriotism followed the style of its leader; understated. Jingoism was not a Labour value. In any case, Britain had survived rather than conquered. Labour's victory spared the Tories the agony of attempting to maintain an Empire and the former League of Nations mandates from an empty public purse. The patriotism of the Labour party was not about imperialism or its associated empty vanities. Practical decisions were taken about independence for India and withdrawal from Palestine. These were simply unsustainable commitments, given the mandate for reconstruction at home and the worsening of relations between Britain and the USA on the one hand and the USSR on the other. The British working classes had carried a very heavy burden in the war, filling the non-commissioned and quaintly named other ranks. They spoke or wrote about "doing their bit". Unlike in 1914 there was no enthusiasm for war, only a resigned acceptance that there was a job to be done and that they had to do it as the alternative could not be contemplated. Thus patriotism was about freedom, whereas for the Germans it was about conquest. Without this low key but determined patriotism the war could not have been won. It was a shared value that cut across the class divide.

The British working classes also believed in personal responsibility. Men accepted without reservation their duty to work and provide for their families. They were staunch believers in the dignity of Labour and held in contempt those who neglected their duty. The British working classes felt a sense of acute emasculation when mass unemployment stole their dignity. In many respects this loss of dignity was worse than the scourge of poverty. This is where the Labour party came in. The commitment to full employment and the use of the power granted by electoral victory formed the Government side of the bargain with working people, and where that bargain could not be kept temporarily because of the periodic failings of capitalism there would be the safety net of the welfare state. Key industries would be nationalised and run patriotically for the benefit of the people, rather than for absentee owners and shareholders who lived well off the sweat of the masses. Never again would hard working people be blamed for their plight, but at the same time work would never be optional. Labour accepted the Beveridge Report in full and in peacetime sought to slay the five giants identified by Beveridge: squalor, ignorance, idleness, disease and want. Attlee's government tackled this massive agenda with skill, unstinting commitment, and unbridled enthusiasm.

Working class communities were not physically attractive. They were despoiled by smoke, slums, and slag heaps. Nevertheless, beneath this dispiriting veneer, they were communities in every sense of the word. Crime was low and people looked out for each other. Working people, and crucially their representatives, understood that crime impacted most harshly on those at the bottom of the heap. For this reason the working classes were not liberal about the punishment of crime and were believers in the curative power of the birch. Historically, the nation's ruling classes had advocated fierce physical punishments as a means of constraining the perceived power of the proletarian mob. In 1945 they would have discovered that the working classes believed in them just as passionately. Working class people drew a distinction between those who were respectable and those who were not. In fact respectability was all important. Breaking the law, not maintaining yourself and your family, and getting pregnant out of wedlock were not compatible with respectability. Evading National Service was wholly unacceptable. People knew each other because they walked or travelled to work with colleagues on public transport. They used the same shops, supported their home town football team, and met socially in the same pubs and working men's clubs. It is not disputed that these communities were often narrow minded, inward looking, and on occasion prejudiced. However, it should be remembered that their social betters were not necessarily any better disposed to Catholics, Coloureds (then a polite expression) and homosexuals.

It should never be forgotten that working class communities were aspirational, not necessarily for themselves, but for their children. The dream for many working class families was that their children would be white collar workers, free from the danger and darkness of the mine or the deafening noise of the factory. These were not limited aspirations in 1945. Pre-World War II many working families could not contemplate grammar school education for their children. Even if a free place was won, the cost of uniform items could be prohibitive. Also, the commitment to staying on until 16 deprived a family of a working child's income otherwise available at 14. In the hungry thirties it was often much easier for 14 year olds to find work because of the huge disparity between their pay and that of adults. This is not to say that there was a huge clamour to enter grammar schools. Working class parents were realistic, often brutally, about their children's abilities and understood the concept of academic merit. It also has to be admitted that some working class families did not value education, particularly for their daughters and worried about educating their children beyond their class. For this reason grammar school places were sometimes declined and amongst those who did go there was a low rate of staying on at school beyond the age of 16. There was no sense of victimhood. In any event, white collar work was not necessarily dependent on a grammar school education. Where it was apparent that children would follow their parents into the pits and factories, what they wanted was the security of employment, that up until the election of a majority Labour government was a pipe dream.

The demise of traditional working class life and community structure had, of course, been in progress long before the 1997 election. Working class communities had been changing incrementally prior to the return of mass unemployment in the 1980s. It is undisputed that the motor car, which gradually came to be in reach of working people, brought a freedom never previously enjoyed. However, it also brought a privacy to travel which by its very nature allowed families to segregate themselves from their neighbours. Increasing atomisation was a consequence of increasing affluence. This was seen across the piece as attendances at sports fixtures declined as other options became available for the increased leisure time that was a feature of the new prosperity, traditional "bucket and spade" holidays became sepia tinted memories, and the family television gradually eroded the popularity of the cinema. For young people there was hitherto undreamed of financial freedom, particularly after the end of National Service and the explosion of a youth culture. Sales of clothes and records rocketed. It was also noticeable that young people no longer automatically supported their home town football team. Manchester United and Liverpool were rather more glamorous and fashionable than Blackburn and Burnley, a development I cannot view positively. However, one major contributor to the decline of community cannot be viewed with any degree of objectivity. That is the replacement of slums with high rise flats. Nothing did more damage than these architectural monstrosities which made whole areas look more like East Germany. Only the Trabants in the car parks were missing.

Unemployment had for the most part been rising steadily throughout the 1970s. The textile industry was already a near terminal case, heavy industries were in decline, and traditional dock working was being challenged by containerisation. Trade Union militancy in that era can be very much explained by the threat of foreign competition and new ways of working to 30 years of prosperity and apparent job security. Mrs Thatcher's government, elected in 1979, accelerated the decline rather than managed it. A train ride through the West Midlands in the mid 1980s was like a journey through a giant scrap yard. After the failure of the miners' strike in 1984-5, the industry declined with such rapidity that by 1997 the now privatised industry employed less than 10,000 men. In 1914, a million people were employed by the coal industry. The wharves of London, Liverpool, Glasgow and other seaport cities were deserted. Where they were regenerated, the housing built there was unaffordable to all but the nouveau riche. Canary Wharf is a living monument to the destruction of working class London. For the Conservatives, prosperity would be built on information technology and financial deregulation, where the traditional skills of working people had no place. The working class (defined as those in occupational groups C2, D and E which are principally manual), as a consequence of major social and economic change, has declined to around half of the population at the time of writing. Sadly that figure includes many for whom a secure full time job is a distant memory, an impossible dream or a project abandoned for a life of state subsidised reproduction for women and substance abuse and criminality for men. These are the non-working working classes, sometimes referred to as the underclass, or more disparagingly as "chavs". The result of all this was that once proud and solid law abiding communities became fit only for drug dealers and bored feral youths. In 1970 the working class constituted around two thirds of the population, itself a decline from an immediate post war peak of around three quarters. It is no coincidence that Trade Union membership declined from a high point of 13 million at the start of the 1980s, to barely half that in 2010 and it is largely concentrated in the public sector where two thirds of a six million strong workforce pay their dues. In the private sector membership is around one eighth, and the bulk of that is concentrated in the former nationalised industries such as the railways. Trade Unionism can be a controversial subject, but the decline in membership is very much part of the picture of the decline of working class communitarianism.

It would be foolish to pretend that Tony Blair's government could or should have attempted to recreate a mythical idyll circa 1960. It was no more an option than it was for the royal family to put the clock back to the world before Lady Diana hit them like a meteor. Nevertheless, the huge majority gained in the 1997 election, coupled with the self-destructive tendencies of Europe's hitherto most successful electoral force, the British Conservative party, virtually guaranteed New Labour a decade in office. The victory in 1997 like Mrs Thatcher's of 1983 went against prevailing political wisdom. In 1983 the Falklands factor and the Labour split that led to the creation of the SDP allowed Mrs Thatcher victory despite a jobless toll of 3 million. In 1997 a buoyant economy did not save the Tories. The charge against New Labour is that it systematically betrayed those whose interests it was created principally to promote; those on the lowest rungs of our society.

Like most people, I welcomed the introduction of minimum wage legislation. I believe it was too low and that there should have been a higher rate for London. Nevertheless, it was a start and the government did raise it annually above inflation. The state is not there to cover the gap between what the worst employers feel they can get away with paying and that which it is reasonable for them to pay in any given labour market. Sadly, what has happened is that the payment of the minimum wage by employers, along with other statutory entitlements, has become some sort of kite mark, rather than a badge of shame. How did we get here? It's simple. New Labour's policy of promoting large scale immigration drove down wages ever closer to the legal minimum. Between 1997 and 2010, 85% of new jobs created were taken by immigrants. This occurred in a country where the Job Seekers Allowance claimant count rose from under 1 million to over 2 million in that period. This statistic shows only the top soil of unemployment. Once incapacity benefit and those no longer drawing Job Seekers Allowance are taken into account, the true unemployment tally was in excess of 5 million, a figure admitted to in a moment of stark candour by the incoming Coalition Work and Pensions Secretary, Iain Duncan Smith. There were half a million adults who had never held official paid employment in that period. Youth unemployment amongst the educationally unqualified is at third world levels. Even amongst new graduates unemployment was running at 20% in certain parts of the country. The Labour party should hang its head in shame for presiding over 1930s levels of unemployment.

Labour's own inheritance in 1997 was a relatively buoyant economy. Although the economy lacked balance and was already too dependent on Finance and IT, unemployment was at its lowest point over the life span of the outgoing Tory government and it would only be in Labour's third term that it would start to rise again significantly. In short, there was an opportunity for New Labour to carry out its promise "to think the unthinkable" on the welfare state and put the work back into that hard core of the working classes who had lost the habit. History records what has happened. Frank Field, the minister responsible for welfare reform, was effectively neutralised by being made subordinate to Harriet Harman, the high priestess of new bourgeoisie political correctness. Instead of acting to ensure that the new jobs were taken by the unemployed and hence tackling poverty of aspiration head on, New Labour opted instead to allow hundreds of thousands of migrants to come to the UK and fill those vacancies. The aim of creating an irreversibly multicultural country and thus dishing "the right", we now know was official but secret policy, pushed through by Labour's ruling elite at the expense of those it was created to represent with no semblance of a democratic mandate. No-one is pretending that cleaning, fruit picking and waiting on tables are attractive jobs. These are jobs now filled almost exclusively by migrants who aren't too proud to work, aren't too proud to share rooms, and aren't too proud to serve others. They do not feel in any way diminished. We cannot have a functioning society in which people are too proud to carry out menial jobs and expect their lifestyle to be funded from taxes. The immigration policy has created a labour market that the unemployed can opt out of with the only too willing connivance of employers who quite naturally prefer a workforce that is well motivated, docile and unorganised.

By no means is this the whole picture. The wages and employment opportunities are being driven down for skilled tradesman, most notably, according to the popular press, by workers from Poland. A supposedly socialist party spent its term of office conniving with rogue employers to take advantage of situations where Trade Unions were not strong enough to enforce the payment of nationally agreed pay rates. Finally, not only did New Labour import workers from abroad, it exported jobs to other countries, particularly India. The Mumbai call centre for our banking is now an established feature of British business. Incredibly, Patricia Hewitt, one of New Labour's most prominent ministers, sought to defend outsourcing as part of the UK's contribution to developing countries. Not only did New Labour have no mandate to export jobs, this was also incredibly naïve. Did Ms Hewitt not realise that what banks and financial institutions were doing to British jobs today, would be done to Indian jobs tomorrow when a cheaper and more compliant source of labour became available? If New Labour had chosen to say that its ability to prevent the export of jobs to stable developing countries in a global market is beyond the wit of nation states, it is a proposition we may choose to accept, albeit with ill grace. But for a Labour government to try to pretend that global capitalism and the needs of developing countries are working in a harmony that we should applaud is nothing short of ludicrous. No British citizen would wish to see the people of India starve, but the fact is that the Indian economy is growing at a ferocious pace. By the standards of countries such as those on the Horn of Africa, India is rich and prosperous. The people of India would be angry if we were to describe them as third world. They need neither our patronage or to be patronised. In defending the outsourcing of call centres to India's rising bourgeoisie, New Labour did no more than pay hypocritical and self-serving lip service to international development. Patricia Hewitt's argument was bankrupt both morally and intellectually, and a dereliction of her duty as a democratically elected politician.

Large influxes of immigration, of necessity, place strains on resources and on social cohesion. Not unreasonably people will try to bring their families at some point if they are intending to settle permanently. The basic rule of thumb is that the poorer the community from which they hail, the more likely the intention to settle. An equally valid generalisation is that the poorer the migrant community, the larger the family. A third valid generalisation is that the poorer the migrant community, the less it will bring in the way of scarce skills. During the major wave of immigration that characterised the period prior to the first Immigration Act of 1962, unemployment was at unimaginably low levels, and there was a high demand for unskilled labour. The building of new homes was one of the main priorities of the Conservatives in the 1950s, as it had been for Labour after the war. Crudely, the indigenous workforce could move into the vast council estates, and the new arrivals go into the privately rented sector. Thus, the triple whammy of immigration that now bears down on the British working class was not present in the 1950s. In our era the skilled migrant still fills a hole in the labour market. The unskilled migrant competes not only for work, but for housing, education and dental care. A percentage of the British working class (by no means exclusively white), may have opted out of the competition for work, but the absence of affordable housing and NHS dentists is felt acutely and actively resented. London, as the nation's capital, is the principal magnet, and British families are finding their schools are packed with non-English speakers, who for fairly obvious reasons make a major call on scarce resources at the expense of indigenous families. It is plain that for an economy with unacceptably high unemployment, it is suicidal to be engaging in policies that will exacerbate the problem in a way that is irreversible. It is just crazy to hand control of a large part of immigration to the EEC, or as in the case of bogus asylum seekers, to a judiciary using Human Rights laws as part of its challenge to parliamentary sovereignty.

It should be noted that the original immigrants and their descendants are often equally distrustful of excessive immigration. The original immigrants bore the brunt of racism. Pakistani immigrants have, to some extent, taken shelter behind their faith and closed cultural mores. This luxury was not available to Christian anglicised immigrants from the Caribbean. This community of black Britons remains very much at the bottom of the social pile and as such the continued migration of the low skilled is a huge threat. Islamist radicalism is a complex beast, but at least part of it is rooted in the disenfranchisement of working class Pakistani and Bangladeshi youth. Secure employment and a measure of social mobility are powerful antidotes to a disaffection which simply breeds criminality of one type or another. Britain's working classes can no longer aspire. (This was dealt with in more detail in the chapter on Education.) On top of this, it does not help to import criminals. Sadly, not all migrants come to work and provide for their families. Some come to take advantage of our generous benefit system, and for the opportunities to commit crime, which is self-evidently bound to be more lucrative in a developed country. Immigrants like the indigenous population commit a full range of offences, but people trafficking, controlling prostitutes, and organised pick-pocketing using children, are crimes particularly associated with the dregs of migrant communities. All this is notwithstanding the attractions of the drug trade.

As has been said, it is the poorest communities who suffer the most from crime. They are much more likely to be mugged or burgled for their meagre possessions. The vast majority of poor people are law abiding, whether employed or not. Indeed being employed can actually make you a target in this world of inverse morality. Thanks to New Labour, they are much more likely to be living in communities whose principal business opportunities are fencing stolen property, prostitution and drug dealing, and where the streets have been abandoned by the police to the effective control of feral gangs of uneducated and unemployable young thugs.

Ernest Bevin and Herbert Morrison would be turning in their graves.

CHAPTER 14

THE POLICE STATE: THANK GOD FOR OUR PROSTITUTED PRESS

Growing up, it never occurred to me that we lived in a Police State, Northern Ireland apart, which in many respects was a different world. The deaths of Kevin Gateley and Blair Peach at demonstrations shocked me to the core, but were not evidence that a crucial threshold had been crossed. I can recall being uncomfortable with aspects of the case against the Guildford Four, in particular the sheer impossibility of one of the defendants identified as being in London, 45 minutes before she was supposed to have detonated explosives in Guildford. Put it this way, it cannot be done on a Friday evening. I was appalled at the police assaults on the Birmingham Six and totally disgusted by the fact that prison officers were prosecuted for assaults on the Irishmen as a device to screen the police from blame. This was in the days when decisions to prosecute were taken by the police. The Crown Prosecution Service was still a decade in the future. It should be noted that the prison officers were acquitted, although it can hardly be denied that some physical abuse by staff took place at Birmingham Prison. It is not possible to second guess the thinking of the jury in this case, but it is hard to believe that they were not influenced by the breathtaking cynicism of this prosecution.

The 1970s was an era of miscarriages of justice with the three Irish terrorism cases, Guildford Four and Maguire Seven, Birmingham Six and the Judith Ward cases, the best known. It is absolutely shocking that the British political and legal establishments were determined to uphold these convictions long after they had unravelled. The Skuse test, which provided the key evidence against the Birmingham Six, ostensibly demonstrating that four of the accused had handled explosives, had been shown to be utterly flawed years before the convictions were quashed, when it was discovered that the handling of playing cards and cigarette packets would give a positive reading. The accused had been smoking and playing cards on the train to Heysham, where they were due to embark on a ferry for Northern Ireland. As a result, the defendants in the Birmingham Six and Guildford Four cases served around 17 years of their life sentences. Judith Ward would serve more than 20. At the Guildford Four and Maguire Seven's final appeal, the prosecution did not even have the decency to withdraw their evidence. I am obliged to a then serving Wakefield prisoner, Kevin Callan, himself a victim of a miscarriage of justice before being cleared, for drawing my attention in 1994 to the Judith Ward case, which like the media I had forgotten. Kevin Callan also drew my attention to the case of Stefan Kiszko, who was released on appeal in February 1992, after serving 17 years of a life sentence for the murder of Lesley Moleseed, a crime he did not commit. The ordeal had destroyed his mental health. He lived only until December 1993 as a free man before succumbing to a heart attack at the age of 41. The appalling feature of this case is that the senior officer in-charge of the case, and the forensic scientist, both knew that Mr Kitszko could not produce sperm, which made it impossible for the semen stains on Lesley's dress to belong to him. Sadly, a magistrate prevented retired senior police officers from being prosecuted by throwing the case out at the committal stage. For reasons beyond my comprehension, the CPS did not seek to have the case reinstated. The other notorious case of the 1970s was that of the four defendants in the case of the murder of 13 year old paper boy, Carl Bridgewater. Three were convicted of murder and one of manslaughter. The three surviving defendants were not acquitted until 1997, 19 years after the offence. It transpired that the police had fabricated evidence in a bid to take a group of career criminals off the streets forever.

A less well known case of a man with a history of petty crime involved Liverpool man John Kamara, convicted of the murder of a betting shop manager in 1981. He was cleared by the Court of Appeal in 2001 where the public learned that over 200 documents had been withheld from the original defence team in the case. Both of these cases found their way back to the Court of Appeal via the Criminal Cases Review Commission set up in 1995 following the Criminal Appeal Act (1993), itself the result of the Royal Commission on Criminal Justice set up subsequent to the release of the surviving members of the Guildford Four. The CCRC was a long overdue reform. However, it is worth noting that the Court of Appeal itself was set up as recently as 1913. Only after the execution of Derek Bentley in 1952 did it establish its independence properly. Bentley was posthumously cleared of murder more than 50 years after the CCRC sent the case back to the Court of Appeal. Astonishing as it sounds, given that this case is within living memory, Lord Goddard presided at both the original trial and appeal.

The two preceding paragraphs, of necessity, contain only some of the best known examples where the legal system failed defendants and the police did not behave well. There was no independent police complaints authority in those not so far off days. Notwithstanding those events which caused me considerable discomfort, there is little evidence of the tests for a police state being met. A police state can best be described as "one in which the government exercises rigid and repressive controls over social, economic and political life." In such a state there is little distinction between the law and the exercise of political power by the executive. There are restrictions on mobility and the freedom of expression. Policing, sometimes carried out in secret, operates outside of constitutional boundaries. It is vitally important to remember also that the police are not the only paid agents of the police state. From the above, it can be seen clearly that Northern Ireland operated as a police state. Indeed, from its foundation in 1921 until Paul Rose broke the taboo in the mid-sixties, there was a convention that Northern Ireland affairs were not discussed in Westminster. The advent of the troubles in 1968 exposed the seedy underbelly of gerrymandering, corruption over public housing, and sundry discriminatory practices. The police, supported by the paramilitary B Specials, served the community in a brutal and wholly partisan fashion. The purpose of the police was to ensure the survival of the Orange dictatorship, a task they undertook with obvious delight. There was virtually no distinction between the law and the exercise of political power by the Ulster Unionists. It would take a generation before Northern Ireland ceased to bear the hallmarks of a failed state. Despite Bloody Sunday (January 1972) and the internment farce (August 1971), I am prepared to acquit the Westminster government of actively supporting a police state. Indeed, Heath's government was desperate to find a solution that would make the six counties governable and command assent from the population. William

Whitelaw met the IRA and the following year a power sharing executive was set up. A generation later, this solution would finally be accepted as the hard men came to the table. Bloody Sunday was a disaster, but the British Government did not order troops to shoot nationalist demonstrators. The internment farce, which saw not a single arrest of loyalist extremists, has to be laid politically at door of the indolent, drink sodden Home Secretary, Reginald Maudling, whose political antennae had long since been lowered to the point of invisibility.

On this side of the water, life was rather different. From the late sixties through until the end of the miners' strike in 1985, there was social ferment that only ended when demoralisation set in. Strikes and demonstrations of varied intensity were a feature of that period. Nevertheless, the deaths of Peach and Gateley were isolated incidents, which were as indicative of the inability of the police to manage demonstrations as it was of the attitudes of some low ranking officers to a class of people, students in particular, whom they saw as both privileged and unpatriotic. The police were totally unable to prevent the Arthur Scargill led pickets from closing Saltley Coking depot in 1972. Trade Unionists were not routinely arrested, beaten up or otherwise harassed. Neither were the various Marxist splinter groups which could always be found on any demonstration or picket line sloganising, chanting and taunting the forces of law and order. Troops were not seen on the streets, nor did they act as strike breakers unless one counts the manning of fire appliances during a fire fighters strike. By the mid-seventies censorship was a private war waged by Mary Whitehouse, rather than a state sponsored activity against what she saw as the forces of depravity. However, where the state was active was in terms of surveillance. It could not resist opening and maintaining files on activists, including future Archbishop of Canterbury Rowan Williams, even if did nothing with the dossiers. Twenty five years on, when long haired students had become New Labour ministers, they amused themselves by using Freedom of Information to examine their own MI5 files.

The most obvious exception to the contention that the UK (apart from Northern Ireland), did not come close to meeting the tests for a police state, is the miners' strike of 1984-5. For Mrs Thatcher's government it was an opportunity to expunge the folk memory of 1972 and 1974 and avenge itself for the demise of the Heath government. It was a test of virility to equal that of the Falklands given that their opponent,

Arthur Scargill, was a revolutionary socialist rather than a pragmatic trade unionist. Police forces were ruthless in arresting pickets and magistrates granted bail only on condition of staying off picket lines. Mr Scargill himself was arrested. The mobility of flying pickets was hindered and restricted. Those collecting for miners' families were arrested and taken off the streets, and the cash confiscated. The shouting of the word "scab" became a criminal offence long before the shouting of the word "Paki". The state moved to sequester NUM funds. Although Arthur Scargill was a determined and principled foe who espoused a revolutionary creed, it was as hard then as it is now to see this man as a threat to the survival of the nation as we know it. He was no Lenin. Police officers earned fortunes in overtime. It is hard to avoid the conclusion that the distinction between the execution of the law and the exercise of political power by the government became dangerously blurred. However, police chiefs were savvy enough to refuse entreaties by the Prime Minister to get personally involved in meetings regarding police tactics against mass picketing. Mrs Thatcher and her ministers forgot that the state and the government are not one and the same. Their opponents would note the precedent.

In history, it is important to remember that dates which are used to demarcate major social, political or economic change do not of themselves give a full picture, and are perhaps better seen as the point at which pent up forces or trends already in train are released. Using 20th century British political history to illustrate the point, the dates 1945, 1979 and 1997 are seen as significant turning points, but it isn't sufficient to say the world changed because of the general elections of those years. The Labour victory of 1945 may have stunned the press and the Conservative Party, but the collectivism espoused by the Labour Party was not only an idea whose time had come, but an idea already tried and tested to win the Second World War. Planning, the gearing of industry to the needs of the nation, and the subjugation of class interest to the war effort, were a template for the future. Similarly in 1979, the country was much more receptive to what is loosely labelled neo-liberal economics than it had been at the beginning of the decade. Heath's U turns may have been derided by the Tory press and some backbenchers, but they commanded assent in the country, even if the government's competence did not. It should be remembered that the monetarist ideas of Milton Friedman were already being trialled by the Labour Chancellor, Denis Healey, who was in post continuously from February 1974 to May

1979. Mr (now Lord) Healey had already restricted the money supply and introduced cash limits for government departments. Although the bulk of the Labour party was in denial for at least a decade after their defeat, there is little doubt that the key figures in the Callaghan government were either openly or grudgingly accepting that Keynesian economics had no answer to stagflation and that new gurus had to be tried. The election of Mrs Thatcher opened the dam.

Similarly, the drift towards what is more recognisably a police state, but more laced with political correctness than at any time since Cromwell was Lord Protector, didn't just land on our doormats like unwelcome junk mail in May 1997. Both trends, although of necessity working separately given that the Tories were in power, were apparent before My Generation grabbed the parliamentary levers of power. Conservative Home Secretaries traditionally have a hard time from the Tory press. One can only speculate what the reaction would have been had David Maxwell-Fyfe done the right thing and reprieved Derek Bentley in 1952. In more recent times, Willie Whitelaw was re-christened Willie "Wetlaw" for his allegedly insufficiently robust approach to law and order, despite the introduction of the "short, sharp shock" for young offenders during his tenure (1979-83). Leon Brittan attracted ferocious criticism for paroling serving prisoners to deal with an overcrowding crisis. Michael Howard, Home Secretary from 1993 to 1997, however, was the real deal for the Tory press, a genuine hard liner on crime, punishment and penal conditions. He was seen as the perfect antidote to post Manchester prison riot (1990) liberalisation and open purse strings. Michael Howard would set a benchmark for his Labour successors Jack Straw, David Blunkett and John Reid, all three of whom seemed determined to appear as tough, if not tougher, than the Conservative hard man.

The 1994 Criminal Justice and Public Order Act aroused ferocious opposition from civil liberties campaigners. Ominously the then Shadow Home Secretary, a certain Tony Blair, persuaded his party leader, John Smith, that Labour should not oppose the bill on its third reading, presumably so that the party could not be accused of being soft on crime. With the benefit of hindsight, it is perfectly possible to impute a more sinister motive. Among the more contentious clauses of the Act were those which increased police powers to restrict freedom of movement and association; (football fans were particularly worried and they were duly targeted), the right of prosecution appeal against the granting of bail by magistrates thus forcing an individual into prison pending a hearing in a higher court; the abolition of judge's warnings about the dangers of uncorroborated evidence; the stunning abolition of an accused person's right to have no adverse interpretation placed on his/her silence; criminalisation of non-violent protest and other previously civil matters; and most terrifyingly of all the Act paved the way for a national DNA database which is the ultimate aim of our Liberal authoritarian masters. Tony Blair was absolutely open in his belief that all of us should be on a DNA database. Mr Howard's legislation did not create a police state, but it ensured that the criminal justice system now bore some of its features, particularly the restrictions on movement and the huge widening of police powers to take intimate and non-intimate body samples. Under the Police and Criminal Evidence Act (1984), the power to take samples was restricted to those charged with arrestable offences, normally (but with a supplementary list) those for which the penalty prescribed was five or more years' imprisonment. Under the 1994 legislation, this was extended to recordable offences, i.e. any offence of which the police are bound to keep a record for the purpose of crime statistics. Effectively this excludes only the most minor offences such as speeding, littering or dog fouling for which a sentence of imprisonment is not available. At this stage samples could only be taken from those charged, and those who were acquitted had their samples destroyed. Campaigners warned that this was the foundation stone of the forensic police state.

The removal of the requirement to warn juries about the absence of corroboration opened the way for feminist New Labour to permit rape cases to come to trial without corroborative evidence. Whilst it is readily conceded that this allowed women who had been too scared to report an alleged rape, or had felt so violated that they destroyed clothing or showered away forensic evidence, it reduced such trials to gladiatorial showdowns between barristers, with the appearances in the witness box of complainant and accused part of the blood spectacle put before the jury. Warren Blackwell, whose case is referred to elsewhere in this tome, became the most high profile casualty. We have moved on from appeals against the granting of bail to appeals against lenient sentencing. How long will it be before some bright spark wants to allow the prosecution to have a routine right of appeal against the verdict of properly empanelled juries? With the abolition of the double jeopardy rule, we are now well on the way. The recent successful prosecution of two men acquitted of the racist murder of Stephen Lawrence in 1993 on the orders of the trial judge, is clear proof of that. The nationwide revulsion at the fact that it took almost two decades for someone to be convicted of this appalling offence made a very effective smokescreen for what was, in reality, a very sinister development. The police state begins when the seesaw begins to tilt under the weight of illiberal measures against the ordinary citizen. That significant tilting began under Michael Howard's stewardship and would accelerate under New Labour. My Generation, seemingly so anti-authority in the 1960s that are so despised by Lord Tebbit, matured into the new authoritarians.

Terrorist atrocities are no respecter of the form of government in an affected state. Democracies and dictatorships are equally vulnerable to a form of warfare with a long pedigree conducted on a "hit, run and hide" basis. By its very nature, terrorism invites governments to seek additional and extraordinary powers against those who prosecute their particular cause at the point of a gun or from the fuse of a bomb. Citizens expect their government to protect them and are not surprised that there may be some restrictions on liberty. Since the events of 11 September 2001, airport passengers have willingly accepted tiresome security measures in exchange for a feeling of security from being blown up in an aircraft at 35,000 feet, such is the fascination of Bin Laden and his followers with aviation. The problem is the ratchet effect on police powers over the citizen. Currently a suspect can be detained for 28 days under anti-terrorist legislation. New Labour actually wanted 90 days, the effective equivalent of a six month prison sentence, served without trial or charge. This is a very strong negation of habeas corpus.

The ratchet has also turned further notches away from our traditionally unarmed police. In reality armed police have been visible on our streets for some time now, and there are those who would trace this back to the abolition of the death penalty, and hence the abolition of the ultimate deterrent. As an argument, it is probably too simplistic. After all we do not arm our police with knives as a response to knife crime. More than two decades of the IRA campaign are a more plausible explanation. Jean-Charles Menezes, shot dead by armed police on an underground train at Stockwell tube station in the hysterical aftermath of "7/7", was not the first victim of armed police nor will he be the last. Victims have typically been temporarily deranged individuals in armed sieges who have either already killed their fellow citizens, and/or pose an ongoing threat to the police and the community by refusing to hand over what police reasonably believe to be a firearm. In these situations (at least until the riots of August 2011) only the relatives mourn the deceased and the rest of the community is quietly relieved that order has been restored and the bad guy has got his deserts. However, in the case of Jean-Charles Menezes an innocent man was cold bloodedly executed. The mark of a police state is not that a mistake was made, but that no-one was held accountable. Citizens do not expect anti-terrorism legislation to be aimed at them indiscriminately. At a lower level, the removal of an octogenarian member of the party from the Labour conference for the crime of heckling was an outrage. Powers of search have also been abused, notably by the creation of zones in which searches can be conducted on the basis of reasonable suspicion i.e. just being there, and the searching of people who don't remotely fit a terrorist profile, in a bid to avoid claims of discrimination. In a police state, the informal contract and mutual trust that should exist between the police and other legitimate authorities and the law abiding citizen breaks down, creating a situation which unchecked leads to a failed state. Citizens who have experienced freedom will only contract into a dictatorship for a period of time before they want their freedoms back. The Roman Republic understood this; the Empire did not. In due course it declined and expired. My Generation, however, as I have said elsewhere, does not value history.

New Labour moved with terrifying speed over the creation of a DNA database. No-one batted an eyelid when serving prisoners convicted of serious offences were compelled to give their DNA. By their very nature they were those who had begun their term of imprisonment before the Leicester University team lead by Professor (now Sir) Alec Jeffreys discovered DNA profiling in 1985, and saw it trap Colin Pitchfork, the "Black Pad" murderer in 1987. However, in 2001, the Government determined that the DNA samples of those charged but not convicted would go on the database. An innocent citizen can request the destruction of a sample, but unless you are an MP, forget it. Somewhat surprisingly, the legislation survived a challenge under Article 8 of the European Convention on Human Rights. Emboldened New Labour took the most illiberal step of all in 2003 and empowered the police to take and retain samples from those simply arrested, even if not subsequently charged. By 2009 there were over 5.5 million samples on the database, including children. This compares with the USA which has 9.4 million people on its database, from a population four times greater than the UK. Proportionately, therefore, we have a database more than twice as large as the USA, a country that imprisons two million people. As race relations campaigners were quick to point out, 75% of black males between the ages of 18 and 35 are now on the database. Learned Judge Sir Stephen Sedley had a neat solution to what appeared to be a highly discriminatory practice. He suggested that the whole population be put on the database. Mr Blair publicly agreed with him. One can only speculate whether New Labour would have attempted to take that step, but the Human Rights Act then came back to bite them when the ECHR sitting in Strasbourg ruled that the 2003 legislation failed the tests of necessity and proportionality. Thus, we had the unedifying spectacle of a foreign court protecting our freedoms, which of itself is virtually unique, and a Labour government refusing to obey Strasbourg, despite the fact that it ceded final authority over our laws to that body by virtue of the 1998 Human Rights Act.

The Coalition did eventually respond to the court but the 2012 Protection of Freedoms Act was a half hearted affair. Persons arrested but not charged can have their DNA retained for three years with the approval of the biometrics commissioner and for a further two years with the permission of a District Judge. Those charged but acquitted automatically have their samples retained for three years with provision for a further two years if approved by a District Judge. However, the Act did also work retrospectively meaning that many samples taken since 2003 were destroyed.

Generally speaking, I absolve the ordinary bobby and their supervising sergeants from my criticism of the police. I normally ascribe the faults of low ranking officers to the minority of idiots who lack common sense, or use the uniform to conceal their own psychological inadequacies. Higher ranking officers are normally better educated and have imbibed politically correct notions on their way up the ladder. Like the prison service, the road to the top is open only to those who can chant the mantras of inclusivity, diversity and the victim status of minority groups and feral children. Like the prison service, there is little meeting of minds between the ordinary copper and the most senior ranks whose idea of management is producing mission statements and the achievement of meaningless targets. At an event I attended towards the end of my prison service career, I recall one senior civil servant declaiming that only that which is measured is valued. I can only say that well adjusted men do not measure their penises; they leave that sort of thing to Sue Townsend's wonderful creation, Adrian Mole, aged 13¾, but they sure as hell value them. However, when it comes to DNA retention, senior and junior ranks are as one. They truly believe it is the ultimate crime fighting tool, the magic bullet that will enable them to solve myriad previously unsolved offences at the click of a mouse. They truly believe that the public will be better protected from rapists and murderers long undetected who can no longer sleep easily in their beds. They will also tell you that only those with something to hide will object, thus smearing anyone with a legitimate civil liberties objection. There is simply no understanding that it is not the legitimate business of the state to hold DNA records of all its citizens. There is no democratic mandate for that position. There is no understanding of the concept of policing by consent, unless of course it is a victim group that must be appeased. Equally, there is no understanding that compulsory sampling on arrest and subsequent retention opens up a whole new field not just of potential police corruption but of wholesale abuse by the state as the database grows. You cannot, even in a democracy, assume that government is essentially benign. Much less can you assume that will always be the case in the future. The police need to remember they are citizens in uniform. The issue of consent, and the relationship between the police and public, is critical to a functioning community. There is anecdotal evidence that police forces have DNA targets. A superintendent exposed this recently but, predictably, it was denied by ACPO. However if you have arrest targets and we know many forces have for their front line officers then, ipso facto, there are DNA targets. One thing you can be certain of is that this superintendent's career is finished and that everything he says and does, every penny he claims in expenses, every complaint made against him will be scrutinised in depth. This is part of how the police state works, and it operates across the Civil Service.

To make life easier for the police, New Labour via the Serious Organised Crime and Police Act (2007) obligingly abolished the distinction between arrestable offences and recordable offences. In fairness the list of arrestable offences that was part of a supplementary list of offences that did not command a five year plus sentence but were nevertheless considered serious, had become unmanageable. Thus, only the most minor offences which are not recorded for the purpose of crime statistics, such as littering or dog fouling, protect you from having your collar felt and your DNA taken as opposed to receiving a summons to attend court. Needless to say, police spokesmen have sought powers to include these offences and even take DNA on the street, which is much more sinister, if not more risible, than marching yobs to a cash point to cough up a fixed penalty fine.

The Act laid down the conditions for arrest. The standard test is reasonable suspicion, i.e. the officer must genuinely suspect that an offence has been committed by the individual, must have reasonably justifiable grounds, and it must be his/her judgement as an individual. This is important because it means that the German General's defence of only obeying orders is insufficient. The second test is necessity. A number of criteria are adduced in the Act: the need to ascertain a name and address; prevent the person causing injury, damage or offending public decency; prevent obstruction; protect a child or vulnerable person; facilitate a prompt investigation; and prevent the individual from doing a disappearing act. On the face of it, this is reasonable. The problem is that in the rush to get someone's DNA on the register, the test of reasonable suspicion is downgraded to the mere existence of an allegation. The most familiar scenarios are those involving anti-social behaviour by children. Adult tells off child for bad behaviour, child claims that the citizen has hit him, threatened him or worse still exposed his self, and the police response is to arrest despite the fact that there are no reasonable grounds to believe a manipulative child above a responsible citizen. This happens time and time again and also happens between children. Our police on the ground are taught that children are vulnerable and what they say must be taken at face value. They are taught that they have to be neutral and therefore on that basis arrest is a reasonable response, but they do not understand that apparent neutrality is just another ideology, but crucially one that seeks to rebalance the relationship of the private individual with the state and its agents in a way that is adverse to the respectable citizen. In this way, the police become the Gestapo without electrodes. The new breed of politically correct senior officers believe that the nation's respectable working and middle classes are full of criminals who dare to believe that their property should be respected. There are serious academics who question whether property should be included in their list of universal human rights.

Of course, the abuse of powers of arrest does not apply to all citizens. A few years ago Mohammed Al Fayed, high profile owner of Harrods and Fulham Football Club, was the victim of an unsubstantiated allegation of sexual assault on a 15 year old girl. Was Mr Al Fayed arrested? Was Mr Al Fayed's DNA taken? Actually, he was invited to give a voluntary interview which he duly did and the ludicrous allegations went no further. One wonders why the same consideration cannot be given to other respectable citizens. One has to speculate that the proper presumption by the Metropolitan Police in Mr Al Fayed's case that there was no evidence to support the allegation was not the real reason for not using powers of arrest. One can only speculate the extent to which they were fearful of a powerful individual who would sue the arse off them, and also one can only speculate the extent to which Commissioner Blair's officers were influenced by Mr Al Fayed's Muslim faith. Contrast the treatment of Mr Al Fayed with that of 20 year old Abby Podmore, reported in the Daily Mail on 9 July 2011, who sadly discovered her 3 year old son dead in his bed. He had already been sent home from casualty where doctors had failed to diagnose pneumonia. Before any toxicology tests could be made, West Midlands Police had turned her home into a crime scene, arrested and detained her on suspicion of murder, and of course taken her DNA. A post mortem revealed death from natural causes, or as natural as it can be when a hospital and its staff have failed to do their jobs. There were no grounds whatsoever for this arrest and only a post mortem could have supplied them. This was a truly appalling way to treat a grieving mother. It is small wonder that police forces up and down the land are paying out taxpayers' money in compensation for wrongful arrest. However, given the reluctance of the judiciary to order the destruction of DNA samples, ACPO probably believes it is well worth budgeting for. Let us hope that Ms Podmore receives an award that blows their budget out of the water, as I can see no other way to stop these outrages until the law is changed.

Even if you succeed in getting your DNA destroyed, it may be too late. Thanks to the information that can be included in Criminal Records checks, your employer or potential future employer will have what he believes are good grounds to dismiss or not to employ you. After all, if the employer is made aware that the allegation involves children, then it is an invitation to take no chances. This is truly a Kafkaesque nightmare for the innocent citizen. It gets worse. Safeguarding legislation, when fully enacted, will allow an employer to dismiss you on the basis of information you cannot see, cannot challenge, and cannot pursue at an employment tribunal, as the law says your dismissal is automatically deemed to be fair. This is the dreadfully legacy of the murders of Holly Wells and Jessica Chapman by their school caretaker, Ian Huntley, in Soham, Cambridgeshire. This dreadful tragedy had the press in full cry about CPS and police incompetence and led directly to the forced retirement of two Chief Constables, and political powers to dismiss Chief Constables being seized by the Home Secretary, David Blunkett. The right wing press, normally libertarian as opposed to Liberal, forgot that you should beware of what you wish for, as the hue and cry played a major role in subsequent legislation about the use of information regarding individuals who have had contact with the police, but not been charged. In doing so we have reached a point where low ranking police officers can wreck lives simply by the way in which they write up an allegation. It is truly terrifying power.

In a previous paragraph, I referred to the ambivalence that some human rights proponents have towards private property, on the basis that it is exclusive and restricts the rights of fellow citizens. The failure to respect private property is a hallmark of the totalitarian police state which does not accept the distinction between the public and the private sphere. The insidious spread of this doctrine from our political elite through to the police and other key public sector agencies largely explains the exponential growth of powers to enter private homes without a warrant and why criminals who put householders in fear of their lives and then pay the ultimate price, are treated as victims rather than as the scumbags they really are. To challenge this doctrine, it is necessary to put the concept of property into its historical and psychological context. It is important to remember that private property isn't simply about the ownership of a lump of real estate for which you spend 25 years paying an extortionate price, unless you are a canny or lucky player of the housing market. I should add that, for those who rent the home in which they live, it is just as much their private domain, and it is this notion of a private domain that is crucial to understanding the significance of private property and its inviolability in all but the most exceptional circumstances. The front door (back door in Yorkshire) is your barrier against the world. Behind that door is where individuals and families live their private lives, relax after a hard day's work, and where they expect to feel safe from intrusion both from criminals and from the state. Private property is not simply bricks and mortar, the family car and household goods.

Property also includes acquired rights such as the right to vote, the right to a pension and welfare benefits, and rights at work, and of course, your job itself. As I recall, Arthur Scargill believed very firmly that jobs in the pits were the property of mining communities. For people like me there is also intellectual property. These are rights held in common with others, but form part of private property in terms of the relationship with other members of the community and the state. Private property is also psychological rather than purely acquisitive. This need to have time and space to separate ourselves from our fellow human beings, for at least part of the day, has been part of the human psyche since we lived in caves. It also works within the home. Ask a child from a large family what they would like most for Christmas. The answer would be "a room of my own". This does not mean they do not love their siblings or that they are anti-social. They are simply displaying a prime human need for personal space. All that people want is their own retreat so that they can re-charge their batteries. I note with interest that foster parents are required to give the child his/her own room by Social Services, the agency perceived by some to be the quickest to violate the family home.

It is unarguably true that property is inequitably distributed both at home and abroad. It may have been acquired by an inheritance or by theft and expropriation as is the norm in dictatorships, or by a product of wealth acquired as you make your way in the world. The last of these is not necessarily straightforward as talent and social value are not rewarded in proportion in a market economy. Thus, if you are a banker or senior executive of a FTSE 100 company you can expect to be lavishly rewarded whatever the toxicity of your company's ethics. If you are a Premier League Footballer or a rock star, the same applies, except that unlike the banker you can't buck the market and there is actually a price for failure. There is also a new public sector plutocracy, not as lavishly well rewarded, but still drawing salaries many multiples in excess of that earned by the former Town Clerks. The adoption of private sector management methods in the public sector has brought with it the adoption of the salaries, bonuses and perks that form a culture of entitlement. New Labour in power happily embraced the private and public plutocracies, and the celebrity culture of the music business and the Premiership football club. De Tocqueville coined the phrase "all property is theft", and one can see the emotional force of the argument when so much of the world's wealth goes to so few people with little relationship to hard work, merit, and social contribution.

The connection made by academics, between capitalism and the development of the sanctity of private property, is actually rooted in the decline of feudalism. Under the feudal system, all land was owned by the monarch. The magnates held their land in return for services rendered, usually military, and in turn granted land to the knightly class below in return for military service. At the foot of the pyramid were serfs who were not free and owed labour services to their lord. It was a system in which every man had a lord, including the King who answered only to God, although Popes did beg to differ. Gradually as the un-free bought or were granted freedom, they purchased property which they held on sufferance to no-one. Although the Peasants Revolt of 1381 failed in the short term, the defeat of Wat Tyler and his followers only delayed the inevitable victory of the social forces that replaced serfdom with yeoman farmers, the most socially mobile of whom ascended to the ranks of the gentry. Two hundred and fifty years later, the battle between Charles I and the property owners who dominated the House of Commons would lead to civil war and confirm the rebalancing of relationships between the monarch and his most influential subjects.

Thus, private property existed long before capitalism, although it certainly created the conditions in which it could flourish. However, the ruling classes of My Generation seem wholly unable to make the distinction between the private property of the ordinary citizen which preserves individual freedom, supports plurality, and impacts minimally on the freedoms of others and the corporate property of big business, public and private, which systematically negates individual and collective rights, devalues labour, and destroys communities. A few examples will suffice. The Campaign for Real Ale was set up in 1970 to combat the oligarchy of six big breweries that controlled the market and reduced choice for the consumer. CAMRA has been a magnificently successful pressure group, but the big breweries and pub chains continue to lobby for an alcohol duty system that would leave small breweries unable to compete and thus be forced out of business. Companies like Pfizer and Kraft can, as evidenced in Sandwich and Somerset, destroy whole communities by moving business abroad. Our banks, building societies and insurance companies export jobs to call centres in Mumbai. My Generation in power has allowed British firms to be taken over by global giants who take advantage of this naive approach to capitalism that would never occur in France and certainly not in the world's foremost capitalist country, the USA. Big companies take advantage of privatisation legislation to force down wages and negate the influence of trade unions, while the taxpayer picks up the bill in child tax credits and other forms of outdoor relief that subsidise low pay. Early 19th century politicians reincarnated would have recognised this as the rebirth of the Speenhamland system. EEC competition rules also conspire to thwart working people. The opening up of postal services to competition is a perfect example as businesses such as TNT have cherry picked the profitable bits and undercut the Post Office by hiring workers on lower pay. TNT bosses actually believe that postal workers on 18k per annum are overpaid. This is how corporate property works and the EEC is the biggest hoarder of corporate property in the world at the expense of working people, consumers and voters whose possession of the franchise is rendered meaningless by this remorseless bureaucratic engine. This is the world of corporate property and its attendant asserted rights that have been embraced by My Generation in power. In classic Orwellian terms, this could be styled, "Private property bad, Corporate Private Property better." Our political masters wax lyrical about social inclusion, but the reality is that in conceding the economic arguments to Neo Liberals, they have created a society in which the rich have got richer and more citizens are excluded from private and social property than at any time since the 1930s.

The police state does not bear on these lucky few. Instead it bears down on people like Norfolk farmer, Tony Martin, who in seeking to protect his humble farm and tumbledown property in the summer of 1999, shot two burglars, one of whom, a sixteen year old boy, bled to death on Mr Martin's property. Having lived in West Norfolk, it is open to speculation whether a jury in Kings Lynn would have been prepared to convict. West Norfolk people have little time for gypsies, and it is not inconceivable that they would have taken the view that Brendan Fearon and Fred Barras, the boy who died, got their just deserts. Needless to say, the authorities manufactured a reason to transfer the case to Norwich, where a jury was likely to be less sympathetic, and so it proved, as he was found guilty of murder and given the mandatory life sentence. In 2001, the Court of Appeal reduced the conviction to manslaughter and substituted a 5 year prison sentence. Mr Martin's ordeal was not over yet as the Probation Service and the Legal Aid system both kicked a man when he was down. Mr Martin was refused release on licence, parole, on the basis that he may be a risk to burglars (!!!). Sir David Hatch, a high ranking member of the Probation Service, described Mr Martin as a danger to society. The nation's liberal authoritarian elite went further when Fearon was granted 5k worth of legal aid to sue Tony Martin for loss of earnings due to his wounds. That this disgraceful taxpayer funded legal action was not ultimately pursued can be credited to "The Sun" newspaper which photographed Fearon cycling and appearing perfectly capable of work. After that bit of adverse publicity in Britain's bestselling daily paper, Fearon dropped his legal action. Three cheers for our "prostituted press". That an individual can actually sue for injuries sustained in breaking the law using public funds is a total outrage, one that My Generation in power did nothing to resolve and everything to perpetuate.

Tony Martin was eventually released with maximum remission for good behaviour and the "Daily Mirror" reputedly paid him £125k for his story in 2003, and no thieving toe-rag was able to get their hands on a penny of the cash. It is fair to say that Tony Martin is not a sympathetic character, particularly as he is reputed to have flirted with the BNP. In that sense he is the ultimate flawed hero. Eccentric and reclusive does not come close. I would not remotely expect him to express remorse for the death of Fred Barras, but would expect a least of tinge of regret for the loss of life of someone so young, particularly as there was no intent kill Fred Barras, which was accepted by the Court of Appeal. It has to be accepted that the shotgun was illegally held, although most households contain potentially lethal weapons such as carving knives and pokers which are held perfectly lawfully. The case caused a furore, which is still ongoing 12 years hence, about the rights of householders to defend themselves and their property.

There have been two further high profile cases in recent years which have kept the pot boiling; firstly that of Munir and Tokeer Hussain in 2008 who received custodial sentences for the injuries they inflicted on a burglar, whose two accomplices were never traced. The problem for the Hussain brothers was that their victim was beaten after he had been apprehended outside the home, which made the argument that they had used reasonable force more difficult to sustain. Both men had the sentences reduced on appeal and a third defendant was acquitted at a later trial, after the jury failed to agree. It is impossible to know what happened in the jury room in the later trial, but it is fair to speculate that there are jurors who will put the principal of defending one's home before any evidence placed before the court. It is interesting to note that the prosecution in the case of the Hussain brothers, disingenuously in my view, told the jury that the brothers would not have faced prosecution if the burglar had been beaten in the house by terrified family members, drawing a distinction between behaviour they were prepared to tell a jury was lawful, and that which they said was unlawful in order to secure a conviction.

The resolution of the case regarding the Flanagan family of Manchester suggests that the CPS has finally got the message, firmly reiterated by the Justice Secretary, that the public want a more generous interpretation of the notion of reasonable force in self defence. Fifty nine year old grandfather Peter Flanagan, his adult son and his girlfriend were arrested after one of a gang of three burglars who invaded their modest Manchester home was stabbed to death in the melee. Nevertheless, the traumatised Mr Flanagan still spent three days in police custody, and the family members several weeks on police bail, before common sense finally prevailed after the attack in June 2011, for which the surviving offenders subsequently received long prison sentences. There have been several similar cases since, yet there seems to be no recognition by the chattering classes of the horrendous ordeals suffered by law abiding householders who have to live with the memory that they were forced to kill in order to survive and that the forces of the state sought initially to treat them as criminals rather than victims.

The Flanagan case had our supposed intellectual betters racing to man the barricades against those who want only to be secure in their own home. Interviewed on "Daybreak" on ITV, Shami Chakrabarti, head of the organisation "Liberty", perhaps better known by its earlier name, "the National Council for Civil Liberties", used inflammatory language, accusing those who wished to extend or at least clarify the rights of householders, of wishing to grant powers to execute burglars to those whose homes are violated. This is typical of the way our governing elite debate issues, using hyperbole and smear when faced with an articulated desire by ordinary law abiding people to have their rights respected and put first. Like most people, I am of the view that if we were to have the death penalty at all, and I would prefer we did not, it should be imposed judicially. This is a world apart from the instant decisions that have to be made by terrified householders who believe, not unreasonably, that they are about to be murdered in their beds. I would not wish burglary on Shami Chakrabarti, but as ever with our ruling class, she does not understand how the other half live and that crime impacts disproportionately on people much further down the social scale than her good self; subsistence farmers like Tony Martin, immigrants like Munir and Tokeer Hussain, working class families like the Flanagans in their modest terraced home. Ms Chakrabarti then went on to make herself utterly ridiculous by saying that other members of the households would be at risk of death when returning home from a night out at the hands of gung ho heads of household. As the interviewer, I can't recall whether it was Kate Garroway or Fiona Phillips, rightly said, there is no record of such a case. My own memory of coming home late was that I let myself in with a key, and if I had forgotten to take a key, then I braved my father's wrath and knocked on the door. I imagine this is entirely typical. If Ms Chakrabarti could be ripped to shreds in this way by gentle breakfast time interviewers, then she needs to avoid Jeremy Paxman. Liberty is another example of a once proud and independent organisation subverted by the politically correct version of victimhood with all its attendant perversity.

The point that Shami Chakrabarti failed to make, or perhaps doesn't get, is these incidents arouse the ire of the public because they perceive that they are being failed by the police. It is as much a characteristic of a police state that the police fail to protect, and even conspire against the public and the sanctity of their property, as it is when they act in an openly repressive way on behalf of the regime. This point was brought home with a vengeance with the events of August 2011, when the police were unable to control riotous mobs in London, Birmingham, Manchester, Liverpool and other cities. Four nights of mayhem, much of it planned using social networks, exposed in full colour the damage done to our society by My Generation in power. As the comfortable middle class districts of Notting Hill, Camden and Ealing were invaded by their underclass neighbours on the evening of 8 August 2011, Notting Hill discovered Johannesburg and the affluent were confronted by the effluent. The chickens of failure to think the unthinkable about welfare, the failure to have a strategic vision about the poverty of ambition amongst our underclass, and the failure to stop the haemorrhage of job opportunities to migrants, have come home to roost. The police were originally founded to keep the peace and protect the public. The impotence of the police, the inability to protect shops and homes, the initial paralysing fear of using legitimate force to grip the situation, brought home the total lack of respect for any form of authority, that family breakdown, the destruction of the education system, and the fostering of the myth that the criminal classes are victims rather than villains has wrought on our society. The maintenance of the Queen's peace is their primary duty; not dining with former "News of the World" executives, not flying rainbow flags at police stations, not wasting their time on meaningless mission statements. The reality is that failure in the primary duty which goes all the way back to the founding father, Robert Peel, has been apparent for some time.

For all the prattling about non-discriminatory policing, partnerships and social inclusion, Leicestershire police flunked the acid test of modern policing when it let down Fiona Pilkington and her disabled daughter Francesca who, when they could take no more bullying from local youths which had gone on for years, committed suicide in a burning vehicle. The local Superintendent took the view that anti-social behaviour was a matter for the council. It will be of no consolation that Napoleon's dictum almost certainly applies in this case; "Never ascribe to malice that which is adequately explained by incompetence." Since when did the police contract out law enforcement other than parking to local authorities? Virtually all anti-social behaviour is unlawful if one looks carefully enough. In this case the Public Order Act (1986) which forbids causing harassment, alarm or distress, would have sufficed nicely. So also would the Protection from Harassment Act (1997). There were ample police powers, but there was a lack of will and the slavish adherence to the misguided ideology of protecting young people from the rigours of the law. For the Pilkington family, their lives would have been no less miserable if they had lived on a remote farm in Zimbabwe, a true police state in which the supposed forces of law and order conspire with a twisted ideology in a corrupt state.

The picture I paint of the UK may lack the presence of the ranting syphilitic dictator and his hired thugs, but this is not a reason to sleep soundly in our beds especially when one considers just how many people have the right to enter your home. They may not wave clubs or apply electrodes to your genitals, but your freedom and security is no less violated. Lord Selsdon, speaking in the House of Lords in January 2010, calculated that there are 1200 powers under different Acts of Parliament to enter your home. The "Daily Mail" has reported that New Labour in office created 430 new powers for council inspectors. The "Sun" discovered, using Freedom of Information, that 14,793 council officials have been given powers of entry by council bosses. Extrapolating these figures to include the councils that failed to respond to the survey, the paper calculated that 20,000 council officials can enter your home without a warrant. The fact that they usually need to give notice is irrelevant. As ever, there is an array of penalties for failing to co-operate with council jobsworths. Among the reasons available to officials for wishing to enter your home are; to check for illegal hypnotism, to check if your pot plants have pests, to check for injurious cross pollination of seeds (this from a government that permitted GM crops), to search for weapons of mass destruction and to see if you own rabbits. Needless to say, there are powers derived from Brussels diktats. Your local council can enter your home to check that your fridge/freezer is compliant with EU energy regulations (2004). It does not matter that these powers are rarely if ever made use of - it is the fact that they are available. The Childcare Act of 2006 permits officials to enter your home to check on the welfare of children. Needless to say these powers were not used to save Baby P.

To reiterate, the police state is not administered solely through the police. Social Services, the Judiciary, the aforementioned Local Authorities and the Civil Service are powerful agents of the state. The public sector is a crucial battleground for those seeking to establish the politically correct police state. Diversity directorates and departments in public sector organisations are key players in tightening its grip.

Mercifully, most citizens will have little to do with Social Services, at least not until they are very old and very frail. However, it only takes a fall at home for your child and a trip to Casualty for precautionary treatment, and you run the risk of the doctor notifying Social Services. They have a terrifying array of sanctions, ranging from placing your child on the At Risk Register, through requiring a parent to leave the family home, to the ultimate sanction of removing the child or children from the home and placing them for adoption. I think very few people would dispute that there has to be a mechanism whereby parents who starve, brutalise and sexually abuse their children lose all parent rights and also their liberty. The problem is that they discharge their duties with a mixture of incompetence and malice. The most disadvantaged children, as we have seen from many high profile cases going back to Maria Colwell in the 1970s, are the most vulnerable. The murder of Victoria Climbie in 2001 was supposed to be the case that ended all cases. It was not. In the last couple of years, the nation has been shocked by the murder of Baby Peter, a case that couldn't stay off the front pages as the dismissed Head of Haringey Social Services, Sharon Shoesmith, fought her case successfully for unfair dismissal and breach of contract. Why do these cases keep happening? The demise of the traditional family, documented elsewhere, is the key cause. Social Workers are expected to be neutral, non-judgemental about lifestyle choices, and at all costs avoid the taint of racism. Quite how being neutral justifies the tolerance of drug addiction, takeaway diets, and a succession of interchangeable low-life step dads in young lives defies belief. In their eagerness to avoid racism, social workers are actually guilty of it. By not taking action against families in which children are battered black and blue to beat the devil out of them, by not taking action against families known to be contemplating forced marriage for under age daughters, by not taking action against families who import a culture of genital mutilation, they are letting down those they are employed to protect for no other reason than their ethnicity and culture. It is in clear breach of Race Relations legislation and no-one is prosecuted. There are sometimes more basic reasons why social workers do not challenge scumbag parents; the presence of the family pit-bull and the overpowering smell.

Malice becomes a factor when dealing with respectable citizens. It is a key tenet of the politically correct that violence and abuse in the family home is as much the province of the respectable as they are of the criminal and disreputable, or disadvantaged as it is called in the official language of our elite. At the first sign of anything resembling abuse in a respectable family, Social Services descend like carrion on a corpse. The respectable believe in co-operating with the authorities and suffer the true disadvantage of not being eligible for legal aid. Worse than this, the proceedings of family courts are secret. There is no way of knowing how many families have been destroyed by family courts acting on allegations which are not subject to challenge in open court. Ostensibly it is to protect the children. The reality is that it protects the system. Those caught in the Kafkaesque nightmare are prevented, under pain of imprisonment for contempt of court, from seeking assistance from a newspaper, or even from their Member of Parliament. Although it is almost certainly contempt of parliament to prevent a constituent from discussing the matter with their MP, families are naturally intimidated from taking the risk, and of course the system will be all the more determined to enforce the removal of children. The courts have thus far refused to reverse adoptions clearly carried through in error and there is no sanction for doctors and social workers who commit these massive miscarriages of justice.

The sad truth is that unless a child dies, evidence will not be tested in front of a jury, and the light of publicity will not shine on supposed experts. Shaken baby syndrome, if indeed it exists at all, is the nightmare that will see the hitherto respectable in court. There has been a series of high profile cases in which many of the initial trials ended in miscarriages of justice, so great was the disadvantage under which the defence laboured. Sir Roy Meadow's doctrine, that the mother is the best place to look for an explanation of a repeat cot death in a family, has been massively influential. In doing so the finger of suspicion was pointed firmly at mothers in all cases of Sudden Infant Death Syndrome. The police have bought so deeply into this particular politically correct mantra that they are now challenging the expertise of defence experts to try and prevent them from giving evidence at all! It seems that they have learned nothing from the tragedy of Sally Clark, wrongfully imprisoned after the cot deaths of three of her children. Mrs Clark was eventually cleared on appeal, but her life was ruined and what was left of it terminated by alcoholism. Hers is simply the best known case, probably because her husband was an articulate professional with more ability to push the right buttons than the averagely educated.

Returning to Local Authorities, these buttress the police state in more visible ways than just their Social Services departments. Two examples will suffice; refuse collection and parking. It is utterly monstrous that local councils can place tracking devices in your rubbish bins. It is utterly unacceptable that they have the power to levy draconian penalties more than ten times in excess of what drunken hooligans could expect in a court, for failure to recycle in a way acceptable to the authority, and without recourse to a magistrate. Local authorities have become the prime abusers of the Regulation of Investigative Powers Act, another grossly illiberal measure (474 of the 653 state bodies with RIPA powers are local authorities), using surveillance for what they call environmental crimes such as dog fouling, breach of recycling rules, and controversially checking that parents really do live in the prospective school catchment area. Speaking as one who is not a dog lover, it is readily conceded that dog fouling is deeply unpleasant and that some dog owners are selfish and anti-social. However, the enforcement of the law would be much better served by a police constable pouncing on dog owners who are happy to leave Fido's mess for others to clear up. Dog walkers are creatures of habit. Thus, they are easy to catch and a message enforced by visible policing would soon penetrate the rest of the canine owning community.

Like dog owners, car drivers can be anti-social in their parking habits. A recent dispute between the police and local council in Aberystwyth regarding the employment of traffic wardens, brought about a situation where neither was responsible for enforcement of parking restrictions and regulations (as opposed to unlawful parking which is still a police matter). Residents, particularly those with small businesses, were soon crying out for the return of traffic wardens. The problem arises where parking enforcement is privatised. Wardens who have targets to meet will behave badly as their job depends on it. The local authority is laughing as they collect a wedge off the private company for doing no work. It is a classic example of power without responsibility, as Stanley Baldwin put it when criticising the Beaverbrook newspaper group in the 1930s, the prerogative of the harlot throughout the ages. It gets worse when wheel-clamping is contracted out, as these companies are often run by or employ criminals. And worse still, the DVLA can give your details to these outfits. As has been said, handing over data and getting criminals to do the dirty work of the state is a prime characteristic of a totalitarian regime. My Generation in power loathes the motor car, although former Mayor of London, Ken Livingstone, is one of the few who does not indulge in hypocrisy over the matter as he does not drive.

The Civil Service is one of the nation's largest employers. The public sector as a whole employs around 5.5 million people, about 15% of the nation's total potential workforce. The public sector polices its employees diligently and tightly. The public sector was the test bed for political correctness and it is here that it is most deeply embedded. It is impossible to obtain a senior managerial role in the public sector, and increasingly many junior ones, if the employee does not publicly subscribe to the doctrine. As I have said, the vast majority of us subscribe to dignity at work and believe that those who bully and harass should be brought to book. The vast majority of us are opposed to discrimination on irrational and irrelevant grounds. The vast majority of us are opposed to abuses of authority by police and prison officers. What we do not subscribe to is a revolutionary ideology that is steadily subverting the institutions we once trusted, that gives criminals victim status and special privileges as part of the war on private property, and promotes mass immigration without a mandate and smears with a racist tag those who challenge the policy. Like all totalitarian ideologies it encourages and rewards informing under the guise of challenging canteen, locker room and gate-lodge cultures in the Police, Fire and Prison Services. It is important to remember that the Civil Service, Emergency Services, the Health Service, Local Authorities and the other constituent parts of the public sector can, and do, inflict the most draconian penalties for breaches of disciplinary codes that control behaviour both in and out of the work place.

On occasion, even very senior staff can be caught in the net. The Chief Constable of North Yorkshire, Grahame Maxwell, received a final written warning after being found guilty of gross misconduct. His alleged crime was nothing more than ensuring that an application from a relative would actually be received as the electronic system for handling applications broke down under the strain. Note that the Chief Constable played no role whatsoever in the short listing or final selection process of candidates. What he did was the equivalent of bringing a written application to the place of work and handing it to the personnel department instead of trusting the post. Who reported this supposedly heinous act? Sue Cross, Assistant Chief Constable. Mr Maxwell's Deputy was also disciplined in the same case. One can only speculate on the atmosphere and the state of working relationships at the top table in North Yorkshire Police. I would not for one minute wish to suggest that Sue Cross behaved in this way to enhance her career at the expense of her two immediate superiors, but her actions show a complete lack of proportion. There is a difference between reporting wrongdoing and engaging in a culture of denunciation.

A similar case occurred in the Prison Service in 2010. The Acting Governor of HMP Elmley was dismissed for a disciplinary infraction reported by someone not present at the incident, and not the subject of a complaint by the alleged victim. I am not seeking to defend the drunken behaviour of the individual involved, particularly as it cast genuine doubt on his suitability for high office in the prison service, but the manner in which it was ventilated and the fact an individual stood to benefit from the removal of a career rival, is deeply disturbing. Again, I am not for one minute suggesting that the dagger was wielded for that reason, but this high profile case within the service, like the North

Yorkshire case, will have been noted by malcontents for the ease by which an individual's downfall can be procured. Even where malice is not present, there is a breed of public sector manager for whom zealous enforcement and placing the worst interpretation on behaviour is a means of impressing your bosses, a trait which has a nasty habit of ensuring that commonsense and proportionality do not prevail.

Managers are under pressure to inform. Indeed, failure to do so is a grave offence. It is important to remember that the financial penalty a dismissed public sector professional suffers can be hugely disproportionate to the infraction committed. Unless the unfairness of the dismissal falls under the ambience of the politically correct categories for which damages are unlimited, the cap on an award will not come close to covering loss of earnings and pension for an employee who could have expected to continue for another 15 years. Two further examples will serve to illustrate how public sector discipline operates.

During Jack Straw's tenure at the Home Office he was called upon to hear the appeal of PC Steve Hutt, dismissed when reported for using the expression "black bastard" about a recalcitrant ethnic minority prisoner. Under an arcane procedure, a dismissed officer has a final right of appeal to the Home Secretary. PC Hutt was reported by his Sergeant for a remark made under the extreme pressure of restraining and arresting a man who had no intention of co-operating with the police. The prisoner himself made no complaint. What he said was wrong and undeniably it was a racist remark. The expression "black bastard" is rightly considered to be deeply unpleasant with no mistake as to the power of its meaning, yet the suspicion lingers that had PC Hutt used the expression "fucking bastard" or "vicious bastard" it would have passed virtually without comment. PC Hutt's dismissal attracted considerable debate in the media and it took 14 months before Jack Straw reinstated the officer and substituted a stiff fine. In the interim, Tariq Ghafoor, a Deputy Assistant Commissioner at the Metropolitan Police, attempted to influence proceedings by pronouncing his view that PC Hutt should remain in the dole queue. As a serving officer of very high rank, he had no business commenting on the case and abused his position. He was not disciplined. The same officer would attempt to sue his employers some years later for racial discrimination, when the higher rank to which he felt entitled did not materialise. Even Sir Ian Blair, the Met Commissioner and a man with a reputation as the UK's most politically correct policeman, was exasperated. The case ultimately went nowhere and Mr Ghafoor took his pension. PC Hutt was unprofessional for a split second. No account was taken of his exemplary service and there was no suggestion that he was a closet racist. The response was simply hysterical. Instead of the case being judged on its merits, which Mr Straw ultimately did, PC Hutt was called upon to be the blood sacrifice that would expiate the guilt of senior officers over the failure to bring the killers of Stephen Lawrence (1993) to justice and demonstrate the Metropolitan Police's commitment to racial equality. The Aztecs would have been impressed.

The prison service operates in broadly the same way, with prison service bosses happy to engage in high profile human sacrifices of little people to demonstrate their enthusiasm for the cause. Like the senior ranks of the police, prison service bosses view the rank and file as potential enemies of the people (i.e. the politically correct state), rather than as colleagues. In the prison service, this has been exacerbated by the notoriously poor industrial relations climate, particularly with the Prison Officers Association but also sometimes with the Prison Governors Association. Possibly the worst example of the police state mentality occurred back in 2003 when Officer Colin Rose of HMP Blundeston was dismissed for an alleged racist remark. This case made me ashamed to be a Prison Governor, as by implication, as a cadre, we were associated with the decision to hound Colin Rose out of the service. The incident itself was trivial. Officer Rose slammed his keys down the key chute and made a comment about Osama Bin Laden. Unlike the case of Steve Hutt, there was no racist remark. Within sight, but not hearing, were female Muslim visitors waiting to visit a prisoner. Other than gate staff, the only person who heard the remark was the Deputy Governor. Instead of issuing a swift verbal reprimand for a minor piece of unprofessional behaviour, the Deputy Governor chose to report the matter to his immediate superior, the Governor, a man named Jerry Knight who later decamped to the private sector. Mr Rose was dismissed and his appeal failed. At the subsequent employment tribunal, the prison service was absolutely lambasted by the tribunal judge. Jerry Knight was labelled "vindictive" and the appeal authority condemned as "lazy and incompetent". The Deputy Governor had persisted with the party line at the tribunal and with no sense of irony told the panel he was "offended" by Mr Rose's remarks. The settlement was not disclosed and Mr Rose was reinstated.

The fact that a member of staff can be dismissed simply because a senior manager is offended is truly terrifying, yet this is the situation throughout the public sector. Any chance remark can be interpreted in a grotesque way that brings Stalinist retribution with the dole queue the equivalent of Siberia. I can recall one case I dealt with at HMP Dover back in 2001 where an Anglo-Asian officer claimed he was the victim of a racist remark when his supervisor told him that if he didn't like the job, there were vacancies outside for bus conductors. The fact that in certain parts of the country Asian immigrants took jobs on the buses was being used cynically to target a supervisor who had done nothing other than take him to task for his poor attitude. Suffice to say, that with the support of my Governor, it was squashed flat, as indeed it should have been at Blundeston. What Blundeston's Deputy Governor believed he was doing by claiming to be offended by a non-specific remark about a mass murderer is beyond comprehension. We reached a stage where the perversity of political correctness plumbed undreamed of depths, protecting an Islamist terrorist from imaginary offence. What happened to a sense of proportionality? The career of the said Deputy Governor has blossomed since. I would not for one moment impute baser motives to the individual concerned, if only because he was once a junior colleague who I believed to have integrity, if not higher intelligence and judgement, but his work in the cause cannot have failed to impress top management.

After the tribunal, the Director General of the Prison Service, Martin Narey, condemned the tribunal decision in a statement and went on to defend the indefensible on David Frost's Sunday morning programme. Mr Narey truly believed that this case was about fighting racism. He had already angered staff by falling over himself to associate the prison service with the newly discovered label of institutional racism. It is scarcely believable that a senior civil servant was permitted to go on television and attack the verdict of an Employment Tribunal, particularly one that condemned the behaviour of Prison Service managers unequivocally. Moreover, it is utterly monstrous for the head of a law enforcement agency to be seen publicly to dispute the verdict of a duly constituted court of law. This is the sort of behaviour one would expect in Zimbabwe. Those of us in the service were used to Martin Narey's totalitarian ways. At one point he sought the power to overrule local disciplinary hearings which of course would have allowed him to intervene and dismiss people he believed had been treated with undue leniency at local level. For an otherwise intelligent man needing to be told that this is a blatant breach of employment law is extremely disturbing. Fortunately Martin Narey departed for Dr Barnados but his management style survives as a legacy. The fate of Colin Rose can be contrasted with the way in which the departure of a senior member of the Prisons' Board was handled. This individual under the influence of drink, a frequent occurrence, can charitably be described as a sex pest, yet instead of the public humiliation of a disciplinary hearing and potential dismissal, was quietly paid off. Somehow this case slipped below the radar of the media.

A more high profile case occurred when five governor grades, including the two in-charge governors of HMP Wandsworth and HMP Pentonville, and the Deputy Governor of Wandsworth, faced disciplinary charges with respect to a complaint that there had been prisoner exchanges to facilitate a more favourable report for the often under fire Wandsworth prison. Two staff received final written warnings and charges of complicity against the two in-charge governors were not substantiated. The Deputy Governor of Wandsworth received "Advice and Guidance," a non-disciplinary award and was duly promoted to an in-charge governor role two grades higher a mere three months later. This was an unusual case in that the two most junior governor grades, the Head of Residence at Wandsworth, who came up with the idea for the prisoner swap, and the residential governor at Pentonville, with whom the swap was arranged, were not the fall guys in the media firestorm that was unleashed by the Inspectorate when they found out about the matter some months after the actual inspection of Wandsworth. I do not believe that they were saved by full and frank admissions, genuine contrition or superb advocacy on behalf of their union representatives. This was politics pure and simple. A disciplinary hearing is a private organisational matter and the media is told only what the organisation concerned believe it needs to know, whereas an employment tribunal is held in a court with no ability to suppress allegations, evidence and management decisions that an organisation would prefer not to be publicly ventilated. The Prison Service had learned from the Rose case. Nevertheless, the Prison Service was fortunate in that there were no leaks to a strangely incurious press. Secrecy is a classic hallmark of the police state as is the protection of upward career trajectories for the chosen few.

Finally, it must be proclaimed loud and clear that the best defence against the police state is a free press. Once the press is muzzled, there is no effective challenge to the absurdities and calculated vindictiveness of the police state. It is easy to criticise the press. The obsession with the sex lives of so called celebrities, the misleading headlines and the crudest political partisanship are unappealing characteristics, but freedom is of little value if external forces such as governments determine when that freedom strays into the territory of licence. It disappoints me that certain newspapers are simply dishonest about public sector pensions. The treatment of Neil Kinnock by the Murdoch press was appalling. There is nothing appealing about press barons such as Rupert Murdoch, himself in many ways a reincarnation of the late Lord Beaverbrook. However, without brilliant journalists such as Richard Littlejohn, we would be substantially less free. Week after week the powerful are lampooned, ridiculed and their pomposity pricked. For all the garbage that appears in newspapers never forget that they have exposed scandals such as cash for honours, the MPs' expenses racket and the flawed strategy for tackling foot and mouth. The Conservative press have shown no mercy to greedy bankers, rather than just concentrating on their usual pantomime villains. Whether or not our press is the "most prostituted in the world," we owe it a great debt. The warts are a price worth paying.

I firmly believe that without our "prostituted press" a measure even more illiberal than the DNA database would have reached the statute book, the introduction of ID cards. Only the press stood against a government with a huge parliamentary majority that could have railroaded the measure through the House of Lords using the Parliament Act. New Labour tried to tell us they would be voluntary. Of course if ID cards are voluntary, then they have no point. We would have crept incrementally towards compulsion as everyday matters such as renewing passports, claiming benefits and purchasing a house became subject to the production of a valid ID card. Your friendly government would have needed to charge around £100 per card as costs spiralled. My Generation in office would have created its own version of the pass laws in South Africa under apartheid, a regime it affected to despise, but without appreciating the irony. As I have said, a characteristic of the police state is that it fails to protect its citizens. In 2003, the Blair government signed the one sided extradition treaty with the USA and the following year opted into the Euro arrest warrant. Both these procedures allow British nationals to be extradited to the USA and to EU countries respectively without a prima facie case of an offence being made. Were it not for the ceaseless agitation of the press, these legal devices would by now have become part of the constitutional furniture. Needless to say ECHR has proved no help against extradition to the USA. Even Abu Hamza (immortalised as Captain Hook by Richard Littlejohn) was finally extradited.

I stand by these comments, despite the emergence of the full horrors of the phone hacking scandal since the first draft of this chapter was written. The affair itself had begun in a low key way with the convictions in January 2007 of Clive Goodman, royal affairs editor of the News of the World, and Glen Mulcaire, a private investigator working under contact with the News of the World, for the hacking of royal telephones but also those of other public figures such as Simon Hughes MP, and Gordon Taylor, Chief Executive of the Professional Footballers Association. In a decision that would ultimately cost him his career, in July 2009 Assistant Commissioner John Yates of the Metropolitan Police refused to reopen the case when The Guardian made allegations that there were a much larger number of victims of phone hacking by the News of the World. The dam burst in 2011 when The Guardian revealed that it had information from a police source that the mobile phone of murdered schoolgirl Amanda (Milly) Dowler had been hacked by the News of the World during the search for her when her family still nursed the hope that she would be found alive. There was public outrage. The country was further appalled when it was revealed that the phones of the 7/7 bombing victims had also been hacked. The nation was united in its disgust and Rupert Murdoch was forced to close the News of the World. Suddenly newspaper editors and journalists were being roused from their beds by posses of police officers carrying out dawn raids and carting away computers. Eventually in June 2014 all the defendants in the News of the World trial who contested the charges were acquitted with the notable exception of Andy Coulson, former editor and more pertinently former spin doctor to the Prime Minister, David Cameron. Four others pleaded guilty and four of the five guilty defendants received immediate custodial sentences. There are further cases involving the press in the pipeline. A very expensive sledgehammer was used to crack this particular nut but it is perfectly clear that the existing criminal law is more than adequate to deal with allegations of press wrongdoing. (Which leaves open the question, when is it the bankers' turn to have their collars felt?)

The Prime Minister, Mr Cameron, in a decision he may live to regret, announced the Leveson inquiry into the press long before the court cases began. In doing so he ensured that this was a political trial. His action released the genie from the bottle and predictably sparked off a campaign by celebrities aggrieved at their dubious private lives being carved up for public consumption in the tabloid press. More pertinently the subsequent ongoing inquiries into the phone hacking affair have also revealed the true colours of politicians seeking to get their own back for press exposure of the expenses and cash for access scandals. It is terrifying that at the highest level of politics, press regulation is favoured by an unholy trinity of the Prime Minister, the bulk of the Labour shadow cabinet and the leadership of the grossly misnamed Liberal Democrat party, which seems dedicated to making our country an even more illiberal province of greater Europe. The political elite have connived across the party divide to use the evidence of a culture of criminality in one newspaper group to impose statutory regulation of the press via a Royal Charter. It is important to remember that Leveson did not recommend statutory regulation. Quite properly the press are refusing to register under its ambit. Once they register they have by default accepted political regulation. The idea that the charter preserves press freedom as it can only be amended by a two thirds majority in parliament is garbage, as MPs can simply vote by a simple majority to remove the requirement. The celebrities campaign group, "Hacked off", no doubt believe they have won. However it is of limited significance that sexually incontinent actors, singers and footballers support press regulation. As Mandy Rice-Davies might say, "They would, wouldn't they." It is the political class we need to fear.

If regulation does come to pass then the police state achieves its victory and the political class are triumphant. The capture of the BBC would be consolidated by the neutering of the press. Wrongdoing by the rich and powerful, particularly if they are members of the political elite, will henceforward be concealed. The brief window of opportunity finally prized open by the press for an inquiry into an alleged historic paedophile ring that may well have gone right to the heart of Westminster and included well known political figures, some of whom may still be alive, will once again be slammed shut. Instead of the political classes being held to account, we will have to settle for a travelling circus of celebrity prosecutions coming to a crown court near you. Needless to say at a lower level we will continue to be fed a diet of tittle tattle about minor celebrities. I find it as distasteful as anyone that singer Charlotte Church's phone was hacked when she was 16 in order to obtain a scoop about the loss of her virginity. We don't need to know and we have no right to know. The point I am making, and it is one that "Hacked off" don't seem to get, is that in a brave new world of regulation the privacy of individuals and the sanctity of their property from press surveillance will continue not only to be breached, but will be trumpeted by politicians as the continued freedom of the press when at the same time real scandals will be concealed from view. We will be told there is no privacy law, but never again would we find out about government complicity in torture by its main ally, the USA, dodgy dossiers about weapons of mass destruction, or the unnecessary deaths of our brave troops because the Ministry of Defence cannot competently organise its procurement procedures. Indeed the Coalition has gone further and legislated for secret criminal and civil court hearings on grounds of national security, however it chooses to define the term. We can forget the exposure of misconduct and corruption by senior police officers, although no doubt some junior officers will be publicly sacrificed at intervals for breaches of the politically correct code. The norm, however, will be secrecy. It will be classic mushroom management of the public, keep them in the dark and feed them shit.

The behaviour of the Metropolitan Police in this messy and tawdry affair, from which few escape with any credit, sheds light on another murky aspect of police culture. What we have suspected for some time that junior officers receive payment for tipping off the press about the arrest of celebrities so that newspapers can scoop their rivals, was exposed. Thus, singers such as Paul Weller and Mick Hucknall found that false sexual allegations were reported in the press. Neither man was charged. A simple legal ban on reporting the name of alleged offenders until charges are brought would solve the problem. The press needs to understand that this is in their interest. Celebrities such as the late Jimmy Savile and those arrested in the subsequent moral panic, even when behaving criminally, are a distraction and are merely crumbs from the table. It is the equivalent of Roman bread and circuses. Contrast this with the failure of the Met to get to grips with the phone hacking scandal until the exposure of the treatment of the Dowler family. Contrast it further with the continued failure to deal with illicit hacking, blagging and surveillance carried out by private detectives on behalf of "blue chip" firms in law and commerce, something in which the Leveson inquiry seemed uninterested. For all its faults, the press must be self-regulating or we make the final descent into the full panoply of the police state.

Finally what both Leveson and our political class have left unaddressed is the issue of press ownership. The real problem with the Murdoch press was that its ownership of The Times, the News of the World and the Sun simultaneously concentrated too much power in one pair of hands in the newspaper market. Tory and Labour politicians alike had no incentive to deal with this issue when the papers favoured their party. They failed to see just how unhealthy this situation was. A rule that no-one individual or group can own more than one national newspaper is long overdue. This is the only form of press regulation by the government that we genuinely need.

CHAPTER 15

THE PRISON SYSTEM, PUNISHMENT AND THE VICTIM CULTURE

Having worked in the prison service for the best part of 27 years, this chapter has something of an inside view. Until 1990, the general public took remarkably little notice of the nation's prisons, and the politicians not much more. There had been notorious prison escapes in the 1960s, most notably trainer robber Ronnie Biggs and the spy Gordon Lonsdale. The high profile escapes led to the Mountbatten report (1967) and the Radzinowicz report the following year. The government opted to disperse Category "A" prisoners rather than house them in one "Supermax" prison favoured by Mountbatten, but none of this prevented the complacency that led to the escape of armed robber John McVicar from Durham gaol in 1968. There were prison riots in the 1970s, most notably at Hull, but they did not lead to improved prison conditions. Industrial relations worsened and there was significant damage to a number of prisons, and the complete loss of Northeye in East Sussex in 1986, during an overtime ban by prison officers. Yet none of these events led to anything like the media hysteria that can swiftly envelope the prison service and the Home Secretary (since 2005 the Justice Secretary) whenever there is a high profile escape, suicide or other major incident. The catalyst for change was the Manchester riot of April 1990, which lasted for 25 days and was the subject of non-stop media coverage. Although there is no excuse for wanton destruction on this scale, it is true that our prisons were neglected by politicians. Local prisons with a remand function were simply squalid. Not until 1994 was Manchester re-opened, refurbished and won by the public sector in a competitive bid. The light of publicity was shone on the prison system like never before, and that light has never dimmed since. The Wolfe report into the disturbances was largely accepted by the Home Secretary, Ken Clarke, and for a brief Prague spring there was money available for improvements in conditions, and the recognition that squalid accommodation and non-existent regimes only served to harden the criminal and did not offer long term protection to the community. The nadir of the "nothing works" era was finally reached with the Strangeways (as HMP Manchester is familiarly known) riot. After the riot prison numbers fell as the courts made use of the non-custodial disposals available to them whenever practical. It is hard to believe that in 1993, when Ken Clarke handed over the reins to Michael Howard, the prison population was around 43,000 inmates, around half of its current level.

It is worth remembering that holding those sentenced to a period of custody did not become the principal function of prisons until the 19th century. Rather, their main function was to hold prisoners on remand pending trial at the Assizes (replaced by permanently sitting Crown Courts in 1972) and thereafter hold those condemned to death or transportation until those sentences could be carried out. They would also hold those sentenced by lower courts to be publicly whipped at the cart's tail. Whippings were part of the undercard on execution days at Tyburn. In addition, prisons also housed debtors until they discharged their obligations. Further up the social chain, barons who displeased the king and captured foreign nobles would languish comfortably in the Tower of London. Public executioners did not just hang or behead those condemned to die, they also carried out floggings and burned banned books. However, the cessation of transportation and the abandonment of the "bloody code" just prior to the end of the Georgian dynasty saw the growth of imprisonment as a punishment for crime. Prisons were harsh places in the 19th century and conditions eased only gradually. They were places of punishment, hard labour and atonement. The deterrent value was unquestioned, like so many Victorian values. Outside of the Borstal system for young offenders, rehabilitation did not come seriously into vogue until the 1960s, and its apparent failure to check the relentless increase in crime led to the predominance of a doom laden "nothing works" view.

Mr Howard was not remotely a disciple of "nothing works". Indeed he took very much the opposite view - that "prison works". His view was that prison conditions should be "decent but austere". Mr Howard refused to permit in-cell television as part of the Incentives and Earned Privileges scheme piloted in 1995, and newly drafted prison standards were implemented only on an advisory basis. Although Mr Howard's successor, Jack Straw, swiftly approved in-cell television as an earned privilege and made standards auditable, the "prison works" policy remained effectively in place under a series of hard line incumbents. Mr Straw was succeeded by David Blunkett, who in turn was followed by Charles Clarke, and when he was forced to resign was followed by the exceptionally combative John Reid. The popular press led by The Sun, the Daily Express and the Daily Mail have kept up such relentless pressure on the Home Office and then the Justice Ministry, when responsibilities were transferred, that it is almost impossible to envisage a figure such as Roy Jenkins having political responsibility for the criminal justice system ever again. Mr Howard's position opened the floodgates for the courts to use imprisonment without regard to capacity. The prison service budget was reduced under Mr Howard, and the main method of handling the rise in numbers was "doubling up", unsurprisingly as the building programme always lags behind the rise in population. Inevitably this raised tensions as prisoners competed for space, facilities and places on programmes. The general public would remain indifferent if prisoners were stacked on pallets.

Under New Labour the acceleration would continue, until some sort of plateau was reached towards the end of their thirteen years in power. Financial pressures forced Labour and the Coalition which followed to abandon plans for a prison population exceeding 100,000. Labour eventually achieved population stability at some political and popular cost. Very firm sentencing guidelines now constrain judges and magistrates and this remains the case under the coalition as the Ministry of Justice lives within its reduced budget. The irony is that in immigration and human rights cases the judiciary appear to be out of any semblance of political control; unless of course you are a cynic like me who believes that the protests of former Labour ministers regarding judicial interpretation of the Human Rights Act lack sincerity.

There are, of course, those who will argue that the rise in the prison population was necessary, and that the plateau reflects the success of the "prison works" mantra, in that offenders are finally getting the message. For those of this persuasion, you continue to spend on custodial places regardless of cost until there is a demonstrable downward trend in re-offending, and then hold spending at the level necessary to maintain the trend, which explains why the world's largest democracy, the United States of America, has over a million offenders in custody. This is the formula that billionaires use to bankroll football clubs such as Chelsea and Manchester City. It has a compelling simplicity, but it neglects accountability, competing financial pressures, and if the private sector is involved, a vested interest in the use of imprisonment. The coalition already has a problem that it inherited from both New Labour and the Michael Howard era, in that most of the private prisons have 25 year contracts, which are basically mortgages taken out by the state whose operators cannot be forced to accept reduced reward for the lucrative work they do on behalf of government until the contracts expire and the establishments finally become debt free government property. The public sector as a whole has a lamentable record when it comes to negotiating contracts. Companies treat the public sector like gangs of rogue travellers offering roof repair services treat the senile, as mugs waiting to be fleeced. IT contracts are far and away the most glaring example when taken across the public sector as a whole. It costs £3,500 per desktop PC, around seven times what one would pay for a decent model from a reputable high street chain.

On a much smaller scale of incompetence, during my time as Deputy Governor of Ford Prison, I discovered that our Library contract made no provision for the Library Service to cover sick leave taken by the Librarian they employed. The whole purpose of Library contracts was to put an end to the practice of using long serving prison officers for the much prized soft number of prison library officer. Needless to say, the provider was not prepared to re-negotiate. That is a small example which involves two public sector organisations, but across the public sector the prison service has to bear the private sector's burden of cost cutting as well as its own, because of these watertight long term contracts that seemed such a good wheeze at the time, despite the fact that these were basically expensive and rigid mortgages that no sensible householder would entertain from their own lender. This might be tolerable if the private sector was less costly to the taxpayer, but it is not. This is the logical consequence of New Labour reneging on its promise to take back private prisons into the public sector. There is now no realistic prospect of this immoral policy of privatising prisons being reversed in my life time.

Michael Howard and his Labour successors will feel they have every right to claim credit for the steady drop in crime that has taken place over a period of about 15 years that now seems to have settled on a plateau. Although causational factors affecting crime are complex and much debated, it is undeniably the case that longer sentences have a positive impact on re-offending. Eoin MacLennan-Murray, now President of the Prison Governors Association, quoted these figures from 2004 in a debate on the proposed abolition of short sentences at the 2009 Annual Conference. For adult offenders serving four years or more, the reconviction rate had fallen by 13.1%. For those serving between 2 and 4 years, reconviction rates had fallen by 10.1%. For those serving 1-2 years reconviction rates had fallen by 6.3%. There was no change for those serving 6 months to a year, but below 6 months the rate of re-offending actually increased. Community disposals were more effective than custodial disposals for those serving up to 12 months in reducing re-offending. At the time, the PGA's position was distorted in the press including a headline that suggested Prison Governors were seeking to abolish custody. The reality is that the motion which was approved by Conference was a timely reopening of the debate on the purpose of imprisonment. The upward trend of sentencing for more serious offences reflected a desire both to see offenders punished, but also to allow the prison service to offer rigorous programmes designed to address offending behaviour. The statistics suggest that this policy was making a positive impact, and the failure to achieve more was down to variables that could not be addressed by a combination of retributive sentencing and cognitive behaviour programmes in isolation from factors affecting the offender's behaviour once returned to the community. Without the offending behaviour programmes, it is likely that the trumpeted deterrent effect of exemplary sentencing would be much reduced. This factor is clearly at play with very short sentences. Proponents of short sentences usually draw attention to the supposed deterrent effect, protection of the community, and it being the last necessary resort when other disposals have failed. Although prisoners serving very short sentences account for only about one-eighth of the prison population at any one time, they account for around half of the annual throughput. Thus, sentences of this nature are very expensive to the public purse, estimated as costing the economy around £10 billion per year, and the government therefore stands accused of throwing good money after bad. The argument for short sentences being a deterrent is easily exposed as false. If serial petty offenders were deterred by the prospect of custody, then clearly re-offending rates would fall rather than rise.

The protection of the public argument is also flawed. It is true that if an offender is in prison, then the community gets a rest from that individual's criminal behaviour. However, it needs to be remembered that a six month sentence can be as little as six weeks with almost automatic half remission and the availability of Home Detention Curfew. If that offender continues to offend, as we know he does, what we have is revolving door syndrome. The community in which he lives may gain a short respite, but in our most blighted communities there will be others between sentences causing mayhem. It should also be noted that there is no little scope for criminal activity within prison, usually smuggling, dealing and indulging in unlawful substances, given the ready availability of easy to smuggle mobile phones. The offending pattern is simply reinforced. Proponents of the public protection argument also forget that the completion of a rigorous community programme, say 240 hours community payback, will, unlike a six month prison sentence, take a full six months to complete. If the offender does not re-offend in this period, it has actually been more successful than a short prison sentence. Much of the time, this is what happens. What the courts don't always appear to grasp is that if this individual re-offends, as sadly serial petty offenders do, he is no less suitable for a community disposal. It has to be accepted that where offenders refuse to co-operate with community disposals such as fines and community paybacks, then they should face short terms of imprisonment for the civil offence of contempt of court. Those that offend whilst carrying out community orders deserve imprisonment, and for rather longer than six months.

In July 2010 the Scottish Daily Mail carried a large feature on a number of offenders sentenced to six months or less complete with mug-shots and details of some genuinely unpleasant offences. The point the paper sought to make was that these offenders would not have gone to prison at all if proponents of "soft" community orders were to prevail. In fact the Scottish Daily Mail missed the point. Each of those offenders should have received significantly longer sentences but did not do so, either because judges and magistrates were too lenient, or more likely tied down by sentencing guidelines. This is one of the ironies of New Labour in office. It became increasingly unwilling to invest in longer sentences that have proven value, yet continued to waste money on short term custodial disposals for those who merited longer, as well as those who could have been adequately punished within the community. New Labour could actually have done better and missed an opportunity to do so. Part of the problem is an unhealthy relationship with a newspaper industry many of whose denizens have a simplistic view of the effectiveness of imprisonment. There is no doubt that Labour suffered badly at the hands of the press from around the mid-seventies until Tony Blair became leader in 1994. The fear factor was real after the 1992 election. However, it is another thing altogether to allow powerful press barons (not just Mr Murdoch) to make penal policy when you have the kind of majority in the House of Commons that requires no sacrifice of principle. Of course you have to principles to start with...

My Generation in power should not have its record on crime and punishment judged solely on overall crime figures, as there are very significant areas of failure. I have noted in the chapter on the family how social workers and police chiefs seem to be almost paralysed by fear of being accused of racism when dealing with the abuse of children in mixed race or BME families. The reality is that if a poorer service received by these families is based on race it therefore meets the definition of racism. Understanding this requires no great intellectual ability, but this is the price we pay for educating people beyond their intelligence. If religion is involved, the situation is compounded. We live in a country which tolerates Madrassas in which children are beaten and indoctrinated in the same way as the Republic of Ireland tolerated the Magdalen Sisters and their appalling laundries. The difference is that in Ireland the last Magdalen laundry closed in 1986. There are now pockets of Great Britain where Sharia law operates unofficially. In Sharia courts the evidence of a woman is valued at half that of a man. The point being made here is that despite the 1989 Children's Act, an early triumph for My Generation, numerous initiatives to safeguard and elevate the rights of children, and the creation of Children's Commissioners, the innate racism of a "hands off" policy with dysfunctional BME families and religious extremism, has led to My Generation creating a ghetto in which crime within the family can flourish un-policed. These are the consequences of a victim culture that instead of ameliorating disadvantage actually embeds it. Further evidence of the failure of family policy is readily found in the gangs of young black men, virtually all from families where no father is present, who give human life no value and have no compunction in using knives and guns to avenge the smallest of slights, so important within this subculture is the notion of "respect". Instead of exposing this perversion, the New Labour establishment embraces it. The creation of an organisation within the prison service, set up with the entirely laudable aim of providing an officially approved self-support organisation for BME staff, was named (you've guessed it), with no sense of irony, "Respect".

As has been said, My Generation's family policy is detailed elsewhere in this book and is inextricably linked to its failings on crime. Another key failing is the infantilisation of children in terms of personal responsibility for their behaviour. The age of criminal responsibility remains 10 despite pressure from penal reformers to increase it. Had they succeeded, the two 10 year old boys who killed James Bulger would not have faced a court. As it was, Liberal orthodoxy that these boys were as much victims as James Bulger won the day. Despite the demand of Denise Fergus, James's mother, that the killers Robert Thomson and John Venables continue to serve out their life sentences in the prison system on reaching 18, Venables and Thomson were released into the community having served all of their sentences in children's homes. This is exactly what would have occurred had Thomson and Venables been too young to face a court, and it is this denial of justice that will haunt James's parents to their dying day.

At the start of my career in the prison service in 1984, youth detention centres with quasi-military discipline were still part of the armoury available to the courts in dealing with youth crime. They were divided into Junior (14-16) and Senior (17-20) establishments. William Whitelaw, Home Secretary 1979-83, was a great believer in the efficacy of a "short, sharp shock".Under his tenure, the 3 month, 6 month and rarely used 9 month sentence was replaced by a minimum of 21 days and a maximum of 4 months, with up to one-third remission available. More serious offenders were sent to Youth Custody Centres which replaced the old Borstals in 1983. It should be noted that Detention Centres were first provided for in the 1948 Criminal Justice Act, passed by a Labour Government. Both these and the Borstals had a strong military ethic with parades, inspections and bull the order of the day. The vast majority of staff were ex-services and found running an unbending regime, in which the few available privileges had to be earned, straightforward and congenial to deliver. The regime was intended to both punish and deter. Indeed, I believe that some offenders could have been released the following morning as the fear factor was never greater than on the first night. The DCs as they were known, were a target of the Guardian reading classes. The BBC exposed brutality in one particular establishment, New Hall near Wakefield, long since re-rolled as a women's prison. At the time, there were no officially approved control and restraint methods for restraining violent and recalcitrant prisoners. The absence of these techniques until the mid '80s led inevitably to the use of more rough and ready methods which not unexpectedly aroused the ire of penal reformers. However, the demise of the DCs was in the end down to the courts. At Christmas 1984, my own establishment, HMDC Werrington, where I was then a probationer, had only 34 of its 110 beds filled. Numbers did increase in the New Year but re-rolling was inevitable. The courts preferred the longer sentence of youth custody and what they perceived as a more constructive training regime. Werrington re-rolled as a Youth Custody Centre in August 1985, but no money was spent on improving an impoverished regime; so much for meaningful training. The other issue was the re-offending rate which added the argument of futility to that of being uneconomic to run. However, as has been said, the courts have to be cited for their role in consigning the Detention Centres to the status of penal footnote. They could not resist imposing further DC sentences on offenders, and moreover imposed DC sentences on young offenders who had already served time in Borstal/Youth Custody or even worse than this, had been held on remand. For this type of sentence to succeed, it had to be available once only, and then only to custodial virgins. Needless to say, statistics of this nature were never collected. The abolition of the Detention Centres in 1988, and their replacement by Young Offender Institutions, was an early victory for My Generation in the cold climate of Thatcherism. Although the new sentence was named "Detention in a Young Offender Institution", it would soon bear as much resemblance to the old style DC or Borstal sentences as Open Prisons do to a Soviet Gulag.

Over time, the penal reformers would consolidate their victory, inasmuch as they could tolerate young people in custody at all. Young people are yet another victimised minority group in the eyes of the elite. The 1989 Children's Act was the catalyst for what followed. The juvenile delinquent made way for the vulnerable child. In 1999 the sentence of "Detention in a Young Offender Institution" was replaced by the "Detention and Training Order". The minimum age for a custodial sentence of this nature was raised to 15 and the age of juvenile status was raised to 17, the latter being an understandable rectification of an anomaly. Much more significant, however, was the abolition of the governor's powers to award loss of remission, or to use the technical language of the time, award added days. I became aware of this proposed change in the autumn of 1998 when working at the Prison Service Training College and was, very briefly, a member of a working party on the proposed Detention and Training Orders (DTOs) for young offenders. My protests saw me promptly removed from a working party. At a stroke, the most meaningful disciplinary sanction available in a penal establishment was removed and professionals sidelined in a classic coup by our ruling elite, who always affect to know what is best for us, whether we like it or not. This was the precursor of the loss of governor's powers to take remission from adult prisoners for poor behaviour in 2002, after a prisoner successfully convinced ECHR that this should be outlawed. Thus, we now had a foreign jurisdiction interfering in the administration and discipline of our prisons with the consent of our now fully ensconced new ruling class. Loss of remission, or added days to use the modern term, can now only be awarded by a District Judge.

More would follow in the revamped Young Offender Institutions. The traditional smart prison officer's uniform was replaced by polo shirts and glorified track suit bottoms. Trendy governors abandoned their suits. Some enterprising governors have rebranded their establishments as Secure Colleges, a development which has my wholehearted support since education is sadly lacking amongst this client group. Young Offenders were addressed by their forenames rather than surnames. Privileges were increased and the presumption was that they were given rather than having to be earned, a complete reversal of real life (or maybe not given the prevalence of the benefits culture). At disciplinary hearings, young offenders were given the services of an independent adult to speak up for them and challenge the governor. At every turn legitimate authority was dumbed down.

The Inspectorate under Anne Owers (now Dame Anne Owers) reinforced the undermining of authority. In particular, HMIP declared war on the use of force, bewailing its use and slandering caring prison staff as ill-educated brutes. In 2007, Phil Wheatley, then Director General of the prison service, was forced to publicly rebut part of an HMIP report subsequent to an inspection of HMYOI Werrington. During their visit an incident took place in which force was used. The inspectors were unhappy and an independent investigation led by Gerry Hendry, Governor of

HMP Shrewsbury, convened. Despite the fact that Mr Hendry's report found that the use of force was necessary, proportionate and otherwise carried out within procedures laid down for its use, the Inspectorate refused to accept the verdict and published their attack on Werrington staff. It was this slur on the integrity of prison staff and the investigation team that forced Mr Wheatley to issue an unprecedented public rebuttal. (HMIP reports are public documents and can be accessed by any citizen on the internet.) Anyone who knows the first thing about handling this age group in custody in a custodial setting will tell you that the adolescents concerned are mainly of low intelligence for whom violence is frequently the first resort. Not losing face in a fight is critical. Hence they are frequently staged in front of staff, knowing that the staff will intervene swiftly before any real injuries are sustained. It is also part of the culture that intervening staff should face some resistance in order to retain peer group credibility. These are the conditions under which YOI staff work, where gross personal violence can erupt without warning. HMIP also have a history of being critical of reduced association and the use of segregation. This is despite the fact that measures such as reducing the numbers on association and segregating the most vicious and anti-social children (because as I have said this is what penal policy liberals call them) are vital tools in making the environment safe for the majority of incarcerated youngsters. Safety is one of four key headings that HMIP use when evaluating an establishment. Thus, what is happening in YOIs mirrors what occurs in our schools where every obstacle is put in the way of Heads who strive to enforce discipline and where well behaved youngsters and the genuinely vulnerable are not safe from predatory, congenitally anti-social thugs in their midst whose demeanour is not improved by the provision of five portions a day of fruit and vegetables. In terms of reducing re-offending, "softly, softly" has yet to demonstrate its worth. Given that the politically correct are no more willing to challenge the underclass culture of dependency, single motherhood and ignorance, this is only to be expected.

My Generation's appeasement of young offenders in custody merely mirrors what is occurring out in the community, and not only in disreputable neighbourhoods. One of New Labour's much trumpeted weapons against petty youth crime was the Anti-Social Behaviour Order, forever known by its acronym, the ASBO. This was the magic bullet that would make communities safer. The strategy was flawed because it decriminalised anti-social behaviour until such a time as the order was breached and gave responsibility to local authorities. At a stroke it invited the police to opt out. The most notorious case occurred in Leicestershire where Fiona Pilkington reached a point where she could take no more after eight years (!) of abuse of the family on account of her daughter Francesca's disabilities. Fiona and Francesca were found dead in their burned out car. The street in which they lived in Barwell was not notably rough. Journalists scouting the street where the Pilkingtons lived noticed that most of its inhabitants went to work, and that this included white collar workers. This was not a sink street, but it is what happens when the police surrender control. When a crass Leicestershire Police Superintendent stated that anti-social behaviour was a matter for the council, the gaff was blown. Local authorities are ill-equipped to deal with anti-social behaviour as most of it occurs out of office hours. They are also constrained by legislation that forces them to re-house scumbag families they evict if there are children in the family. It does not seem to occur to them that eviction coupled with taking the children into care would get the message around sink communities at great speed.

The underlying priority behind the ASBO is not safer communities, but keeping children out of court. The number of juveniles receiving custodial sentences has fallen sufficiently for some of the capacity to be converted for adult use. This is not because juvenile crime has fallen; it is because the courts have got the politically correct message that children should be kept out of custody wherever possible. Inevitably ASBOs were swiftly breached in order to test them out. Young people walked from court un-penalised. The law was exposed as a paper tiger. The juvenile courts had already been dumbed down by removing the formality, and therefore the fear factor. The fact that the law is not feared was amply demonstrated by the riots of August 2011. Under the new mantra, if children had to go to court at all, they had to be child friendly. My Generation on its way to power absorbed a different lesson from James Bulger's murder than respectable citizens. They saw Thomson and Venables as victims because they had to face the full panoply of the law. For our Liberal authoritarian soon to be rulers, the grief of Denise Fergus, mother of James, would open the way to a wrecking spree in the juvenile justice system. Needless to say, disrespectful young thugs saw no reason to behave respectfully in court and even less reason to leave alone those they had tormented who were now labelled as "grasses" and were ripe for further intimidation. Look at the agenda of any meeting of the public with their local beat constables. Anti-social behaviour by young people is almost invariably top of the agenda. Yet further up the police food chain senior officers have either swallowed or been forced to swallow the mantra that children must not be demonised. Every child matters means that every child must be appeased, and appeasement only invites the bully to continue his foul behaviour. Thanks to My Generation in power, there are places where communities live in fear of children and young people knowing that to challenge their behaviour invites being arrested themselves, or end up dead like Gary Newlove, kicked to death by thugs outside his Warrington home. We feel powerless. The riots of August 2011 have exacerbated that fear further. This is why the fear of crime has grown when overall recorded crime has fallen. It remains to be seen whether the riots will prove to be the catalyst that forces our ruling elite to remember who they represent.

However, returning to the prison system, it does need to be made clear that prison conditions are immeasurably better than 25 years ago. Sadly, it took the Manchester riot to get rid of "slopping out", a disgusting thrice daily ritual whereby prisoners walked along the landing when their cells were opened, pots in hand, to empty the contents down a sluice. Prison officers were taught always to unlock cells starting from the recess so that prisoners carrying pots were never walking behind them. "Potting", as it was called, was also a handy prisoner on prisoner form of revenge. In remand centres and on remand wings prisoners could spend all day other than an hour's exercise and the short time taken to collect meals, in their cells. These cells frequently housed three prisoners in accommodation designed for one. Oddly enough, the Victorians initially provided integral sanitation. However, the Victorians believed in single cell accommodation to allow malefactors ample time to contemplate the error of their ways. Only remand prisoners were permitted to wear their own clothes. For the rest of the population, prison issue socks, underwear and shirts were changed just once a week. Visits for remand prisoners were restricted to 15 minutes, although these were permitted daily. Convicted prisoners were entitled to one 30 minute visit per month, although in practice the length of the visit was greater in training and young offender establishments. Prisoners had no official access to telephones, (although the Chaplain could sometimes be persuaded) and there was no in-cell television, only radios. One prison issue letter was given freely, any more had to be purchased, although additional free letters were available for legal business or contacting a probation officer. Constructive regimes were almost wholly absent in local prisons (those with a remand function), though better in training establishments. Education classes in local prisons were frequently cancelled if more officers were required to staff the courts. It is not necessary to be a liberal reformer to understand that prison conditions were squalid and regimes impoverished to know that this was unacceptable.

After the Wolfe report, the most obvious manifestations of reform were extended visiting opportunities, including evenings, and much more time out of cell. In more recent times, this has been clawed back on account of financial stringencies, with purposeful activity being prioritised over free association. Prisoners have access to card phones, which was being experimented with pre-Manchester riot, and since 1997, rather more controversially, in-cell television, in theory a privilege, in practice virtually a right. Prisons themselves are much cleaner environments. No longer is it necessary for a party of prisoners to be employed to collect and dispose of shit parcels hurled from cell windows. There are now usually facilities for prisoners to do their laundry. Prison healthcare, bureaucracy aside, has improved by a quantum leap. Twenty five years ago prison healthcare was run by a doctor, usually known as the Senior Medical Officer, supported by largely untrained prison hospital officers. The regard in which they were held can easily be guessed at by the fact that they were nicknamed "scab lifters". Gradually they were encouraged to gain nursing qualifications, but that development was relatively short lived as nurses were firstly recruited from local hospitals and employed as civil servants, and then when prison healthcare was handed over to the Primary Care Trusts nurses either moved to or were appointed on NHS conditions of service. I doubt that many people of any political persuasion would object to these reforms, apart perhaps from in-cell television.

I loathe the existence of the private prisons sector and therefore rarely praise it, but they do have the advantage of the kind of freedom governors in the state sector have not enjoyed in nearly a generation. The innovative Director of Lowdham Grange (a Category B establishment housing virtually all of its population in single cells) Guy Balfe, went further than in-cell television and also installed in cell card-phone facilities. It is easy to hold up one's hands in horror, but this allowed Mr

Balfe to have an uninterrupted and longer working day for prisoners and allow free association only at weekends, thus saving on staffing costs and cutting down opportunities for bullying. For prisoners, the ability to contact their families was restricted only by how much credit they had left, with plenty of opportunity to earn it, rather than having to wait patiently in a queue on the wing avoiding bullies and hoping and praying that an incident wouldn't see everyone "banged up". A predictable and reliable regime does much for staff and prisoner safety.

However, My Generation in power could not resist taking reform beyond the pragmatic and the decent. As prisoners are human beings, the passage of the 1998 Human Rights Act could not fail to have implications. Prisoners joined the gravy train as another client group, another victimised minority to enrich lawyers and enrage the public. Had prisoners simply been given codified limited rights under the control of parliament, it would have been much less contentious. Instead, the Act put our laws at the mercy of an international institution that has no democratic legitimacy; the European Court of Human Rights. Domestically, because there was no codification of prisoners' rights, the judiciary was able to make it up as it went along in much the same way as it did with immigration. Eventually, even ECHR went too far for a section of our political class when handing down a verdict that ruled that prisoners should have the right to vote. The political class does not seem to be aware that the franchise was excluded from the original treaty and the judgement is therefore ultra vires. The judgement has produced an impasse in parliament in that there is no majority to support the measure. It has the potential to be a turning point, but it needs to be remembered that the coalition can accept the judgement without recourse to parliament, in which case only a successful motion of "no confidence" can possibly prevent the judgement being enacted. I would love nothing more than to be proved wrong, but I cannot see any of the main parties either singly or in combination putting the spoils of office at risk for the sake of votes for prisoners (or at least some of them) when the crunch comes.

Of course, this case may never have wended its way to Strasbourg if unlimited legal aid under the Human Rights Act had not been extended to prisoners to fight this and other causes that lack any merit, and evince no sense of shame. Prior to the implementation of the Act, prisoner legal aid ran out when the appeal in their case was dismissed. Any other legal action had to be self-funded or they had to find a solicitor willing to take on the case on a pro bono basis with the hope of obtaining costs later. The extension of legal aid removed the risk from solicitors and gave a green light to litigious felons. The Legal Aid Board views them as just another disadvantaged minority that deserves favour, taking no account of the heinous nature of their offences. Thus a notorious prisoner could sue over the hardness of his bed. A paedophile in Lewes Prison obtained an award of £47k (!) for breaches of the Disability Discrimination Act. On his next sentence, he commenced another legal action under the Act. To fight this, it was necessary to keep an exhaustive log of all occasions the prisoner was offered a shower, taken to the library, and pushed promptly to visits to demonstrate that reasonable adjustments were being made. Costs to the taxpayer from these proceedings far outweigh the awards given. The Disability Discrimination Act is notoriously easy to abuse. The prisoner legal aid bill now exceeds £23 million per year compared to only £1 million in 2001. It remains to be seen if coalition plans for reform are actually implemented in the face of fierce opposition from the legal profession.

Despite the media explosion of interest in the prison system, my experience of speaking engagements brought home how little the public know about prisons. The same applies to opinion formers such as respected journalists. Prisoners are referred to in the press as lags or convicts. It is normal for staff to be referred to as warders, despite the term having been changed to prison officers as long ago as the 1920's. Warders are in fact a Museum grade, usually found at the Tower of London. Open prisons are familiar targets for tabloid stings, whereby the public are invited to believe that felons live a life of luxury of substance abuse, SKY TV, and smuggled in strumpets. Indeed, the term "Open Prison" is something of an oxymoron since there is nothing to stop the inhabitants walking out any time. A fortunate few are never apprehended. The absconding rate at around 5% of throughput is not high and indeed has been falling for a number of years.

Although it was an exaggeration, open prisons once had the image of being the prisons provided for gentlemen felons such as Lord Brockett and Jonathan Aitken, crooked businessmen such as Ernest Saunders and errant but well loved ex professional footballers such as George Best. Indeed HMP Ford, where I was Deputy Governor from 2001-05, boasted of its ability to cure senile dementia, which was advanced by Saunders'

QC, George Carmen, as a reason not to put him on trial for insider trading. Open prisons did house these characters and many other white collar offenders. Bent policemen and prison officers, corrupt solicitors and lesser white collar criminals such as dishonest building society or betting office clerks, all found their way swiftly to open conditions in just the same way as a handful of corrupt MPs have done recently. The papers do not seem to understand there is no queue. There is no point keeping demonstrably low risk white collar offenders in closed conditions for a day longer than necessary. It is a simple waste of scarce resources, a familiar charge against My Generation in power. Eligibility for Category D status is defined simply as "can be trusted in open conditions". It surprises me that even the right of centre press seems to see this as some form of class distinction. Others on the opposite side of the political spectrum see discrimination at work, replicating middle class privilege that exists within the community. This is why allocation procedures are now covered by the Equality Act and the prison service is required to test its procedures to ensure no discrimination against minorities occurs for these much prized places in these idyllic rural and coastal havens. The primary purpose of open establishments is resettlement, which is why they also house life sentence and other long term prisoners moving down the system towards final release. Open prisons therefore house some once notorious characters and play a vital role in bridging the gap from long term incarceration to reintegration into the community. If we do not have the death penalty, and only a small number of people serving whole life sentences, then society is committed to integrating the bulk of murderers, rapists and other serious malefactors back into the community. Although I accept that there is a legitimate public interest it does not help when prisoners are "outed" in high profile headlines in much the same way as MPs caught in flagrante with rent boys. Open prisons do the job of resettling these offenders very well.

However, the successful work of open establishments with long termers and white collar criminals masks a major change in the function and population of open prisons. In April 2001, when I took up post at Ford, only 300 of its 500 beds were filled. It was a similar picture at other open establishments. However, the population spike encouraged by Michael Howard and continued by his New Labour successors was biting and the empty beds were attracting the attention of prison service bosses. In 2002, HMP Downview re-rolled from a male Category C prison to a women's establishment. Increased female incarceration is one of the unintended consequences of greater gender equality, much to the chagrin of radical feminists. A significant number of Downview prisoners, who obtained Category D status on completion of the RAPT program (designed to counter substance abuse), were transferred to Ford, an establishment that had no support mechanisms for prisoners trying to live a drug free life in a community which did not necessarily share that aspiration, and which was not funded for that support. Naturally a number of prisoners relapsed at a cost to them and inevitably at a cost to the estates to which they returned on release. In short order, the need to fill beds led to their being a target of 95% occupancy in open conditions, and this was 95% of a higher number of places created almost invariably by doubling up single accommodation. Closed establishments were given targets for the number of prisoners categorised initially or re-categorised as Category D in order to fill the spaces. In the target culture, targets not hit affect careers adversely. In much the same way as insurance salesmen and bank staff have their values warped by targets, the prison service moved inexorably towards a system where risk assessments were devalued and open establishments were actively discouraged from challenging these risk assessments and re-categorising prisoners back up the system. The result of this was a massive influx of offenders serving short sentences who had major issues with drugs and/or alcohol, whose prison terms were too short for any meaningful work to take place and who were simply dumped in open conditions on the basis that they were not particularly likely to abscond. Given that these offenders could swiftly replicate the facilities of their own sink estates, drink and drugs for all those who could pay (or whose relatives were forced to pay), absconding was dis-incentivised for experienced savvy petty offenders who now found themselves in pleasant penal environments that were once beyond their dreams. The only surprise is that it took until the early hours of New Year's Day 2011 at HMP Ford for this policy to be exposed as drunken inmates torched significant parts of the prison. Open prisons are another British institution debauched by New Labour; My Generation in power. For better and for worse, we live in a society where deference has almost been abolished, where shame is a concept from a bygone age, and one where people are assertive of their rights independently of their obligations. These characteristics are at their most marked in the nation's underclass.

There is almost no greater guarantee of policy failure than cross party consensus. Where the radical right and the Liberal left are in apparent harmony be very afraid and very suspicious. Two examples will suffice; care in the community and prison privatisation. To the radical right, care in the community obviated the need to staff and maintain expensive staff intensive institutions. It was massively cheaper and provided a fund for tax cuts that would enhance consumer choice. For those on the opposite side of the spectrum, mental hospitals were outdated relics of an age where families could commit family members with learning difficulties and unmarried pregnant daughters, where the mentally ill were classified as feeble minded, idiots and imbeciles, and beyond that as full blown lunatics. If they were not mentally ill when they got there, they would be soon enough. It would be foolish to deny that there were not abuses, but it is pointless to pretend that there was not a hard core of people whose learning disabilities were so great that they could not cope in the community. In a recent dreadful case in Warwickshire a young woman with severe learning difficulties, Gemma Hayter, was murdered by sadistic neighbours on the sink estate where she had been dumped. This case should have engendered the same level of anger as the case of Baby Peter, but it has not. The policy and its interpreters at local level will survive. Local authorities will continue to waste money on equality and diversity advisers who aggressively pursue wolf whistlers and appease Islamist extremists, but who do not deliver any sort of service to a minority in dire need of positive action. The public tends to be more concerned about schizophrenics in the community, who have no supervision as regards their medication, and have committed some high profile murders. Quite rightly, the view is taken that these are people for whom secure residential care is a must. Finally, it must be noted that the explosion of the drug culture has adversely affected the numbers of the mentally ill. My Generation remains in denial about the hugely damaging effects of skunk cannabis. The spike in mental illness has been felt severely in the hard pressed prison system, which in the absence of sufficient residential mental health provision has become the default option for the courts. It should be obvious to any half-wit that prisons are not the sort of environment in which the seriously mentally disturbed should routinely be housed. Prisons are for the bad, not for the mad and the sad.

The biggest single change doing my career as a custodian of those committed to prison was the exponential explosion in drug abuse. The smuggling of drugs into prisons was not that frequent an occurrence in

1984. Ten years later the prison service was forced to introduce random mandatory testing. During my time on the staff at Woodhill Prison (1995-98), "snatch squads" patrolled the visits room ready to respond to messages from the CCTV room about the imminence of drug passes. Now only open prisons in the adult estate do not use CCTV for social visits. In urban locations, packages of drugs are simply hurled over prison walls to be collected by work parties. Large sums of money have had to be spent on netting to combat this form of smuggling. When all these methods fail, then solicitors, contractors' employees, and sadly prison officers who of course have daily contact with prisoners are targeted. The general public, the press and even some MPs with prisons in their constituency struggle to understand why prisons are not drug free. Partly it is about expense. Non-contact visiting facilities would cost serious money to construct and it would probably be money wasted as it is likely to be found unlawful under the Human Rights Act. All establishments, not simply the high security estate, would have to spend money on X-Ray equipment and on staff to carry out searches as each shift entered the prison. External patrols with dogs would be needed to guard the external perimeter. Significantly more drug dogs would need to be used and they are expensive to train and maintain. It is no good sections of the press excoriating the prison service for its poor security, if they do not support the taxes needed to pay for it. The same applies to MPs. It also has to be reiterated that prisons only reflect what is happening in the felonious part of the community. Testing of new receptions at one local prison where I served revealed routinely approaching 60% of newly received prisoners had traces of narcotic substances in their system. The true figure for substance abuse amongst the offending classes is certain to be higher. The causal link between drug abuse and acquisitive and violent crime could not be better evidenced. Prisoners are not going to allow a small thing like prison rules to get in the way of obtaining a fix. Yet the public are only given the figures for the easily manipulated system of random testing, where the failure rate is around 10%. The target culture encourages sharp practice such as putting a string of your best known drug abusers on frequent testing, thus removing them from the pool of prisoners eligible for random selection.

The public also needs to be aware that perfectly lawful drug abuse goes on in our prison establishments. A judgement a few years ago rendered the imposition of "cold turkey", unlawful. This gave stimulus to the now official policy of methadone maintenance for heroin addicts. This is the policy of the NHS in the community, and having taken control of prison healthcare, they were able, as the professionals, to make it the policy in a custodial setting. Morally, I am uneasy about maintenance as it is supporting addiction by another name. Nevertheless, I would make the pragmatic point that our drug ridden prisons are a shade easier to manage as a consequence, and in the community maintenance has contributed to a fall in acquisitive crime, although the proliferation of burglar alarms and much improved vehicle security also has a significant role. It is also the case that tobacco remains a legal drug in prisons, unlike most of the USA. Indeed in 2006, Phil Wheatley, then Director General of the National Offender Management service, lobbied ministers successfully for prison cells to be excluded from the smoking ban. Only in the juvenile sector is tobacco prohibited. The Prison Officers Association supports the withdrawal of the tobacco privilege. Drug policy is therefore mired in confusion and inconsistency. My Generation as students were exposed to the drug culture when it was the property of intellectuals, rock stars and other socially well connected bohemians. The working classes stuck to beer and tobacco. This ambivalence to the drug culture has rendered My Generation in power not merely incapable of responding to its continued favour amongst the comparatively well heeled, but more pertinently incapable of responding to the destructive power of the drug culture on the nation's underclass. Keith Richards, in his recent autobiography, clearly could not come to terms with the fact that the Prime Minister (Tony Blair) regarded him as a hero. Mr Richards could, of course, afford his habit. Wrong messages were sent out when cannabis was downgraded to class C, and a de facto zone of tolerance was created for street corner dealing and public consumption of cannabis on the streets of Brixton. New Labour's war on drugs fought with weasel words rather than weapons has predictably come to nothing. Cannabis has since been regraded as a Class B narcotic, but the damage has already been done.

Privatisation was originally bitterly opposed by My Generation in opposition, and condemned in the strongest possible terms on moral grounds when it was introduced into the penal system. Labour actually promised to reverse it in the prison system; a promise it did not make with regard to any other former state enterprise. Instead it did the opposite and indeed went further inviting private sector bids for existing public sector prisons, not just new builds. Jack Straw was excoriated at

POA and PGA conferences for the offence of changing his mind. Various reasons have been offered by New Labour politicians for changing their minds. Cost, efficiency and union intransigence are regularly cited. Yet the fire service, which has an equally challenging trade union to deal with, has never been seriously considered for privatisation. Neither has the ambulance service. The Tories were undoubtedly impressed by prison privatisation in the USA, and it was a useful stick with which to beat the Prison Officers Association. Yet New Labour took its antipathy to the public sector prison service to a new level. An explanation, I think, lies shallowly buried in the baggage of My Generation. The Prison Officers Association is perceived as part of an ongoing racism that it is desperate to eradicate from society. No other trade union is labelled in this way. Some of it goes back to the 1970s, when a small number of prison officers at a London gaol were seen to wear National Front badges. More recently Feltham prison officers were the subject of allegations at the public inquiry into the murder of Zaid Mubarak by a racist cell-mate in 2001, that they deliberately put known racist white young offenders with black young offenders and then stood back to watch the fun. It is important to remember that these allegations were neither substantiated nor were they made by individuals with any credibility. Nevertheless, mud sticks. We also know that Paul Boateng, a British born former lawyer of Ghanaian extraction, Prisons' Minister at the turn of the millennium, was determined to privatise Brixton prison, although in the end there were no bidders. There is no doubt that the target of this ill-fated venture was the Prison Officers Association.

For those of My Generation who cannot forget their Marxist past, prison officers like the police and non-commissioned officers in the Armed Forces, are class collaborators who help capital subjugate labour. Of the above mentioned groups, significantly only prison officers were permitted to join a free trade union. Prisons, therefore, are institutions that oppress working people, ethnic minorities who are numerically over-represented in custody, and increasingly, women. It is another example of how My Generation has had difficulty growing up from junior common room rhetoric. For the record, the POA is unequivocal in its opposition to racism. Its members elected and then re-elected a black national chairman, Colin Moses, who stood down in 2010. It is also not the only trade union that in the past, in the age of flairs, loon pants and shoulder length hair, has had members it would not wish to highlight in an official history. Back in 1968 it should be remembered that

London dockers marched in support of Enoch Powell after his notorious "rivers of blood" speech in April 1968. New Labour had the chance to strangle the private corrections sector before it became established. On the basis of prejudices imbibed in the university seminar, we have been further lumbered with expensive PFI contracts for an underperforming, almost secret system that operates without the transparency and public scrutiny characteristic of the public sector.

The popular press gives the prison system little respite. Governors and senior civil servants are accused of appeasement, of running holiday camps, and of bumbling incompetence caricatured by the governor of the fictional Slade Prison, from the oft repeated classic 70s comedy, "Porridge". It should be remembered that appeasement was trialled first in the private sector. It was in the first private prisons where inmates were addressed as "Mr", where in-cell television was pioneered, and prisoners were out of cell until 22.00 if they wished. It was in the private sector that the revolutionary agenda of treating prisoners as equals and victims, rather than as transgressors, was trialled. The policy was smuggled under the radar by the socially desirable objective of decent and humane conditions which had been exposed as lacking by the Manchester riot. It was these establishments that trialled lower staffing levels and salaries 7-10k less than public sector staff. The result was that prisoners were not safe and corruption levels amongst staff were unacceptably high. One private establishment, HM Young Offender Institution Pucklechurch, suffered the indignity of a public sector governor being brought in to sort it out. Staff turnover remains horrendous throughout the private sector and its un-unionised workforce is under constant and often intolerable pressure to cover the shifts of those staff which have voted with their feet and found another job. More recently the Coalition has abandoned privatisation in favour of an aggressive programme of benchmarking, using the unsuccessful bid by the public sector for HMP Birmingham as the template for forcing staffing levels down to those common in the private sector. New recruits are employed on salary scales that are much closer to those that prevail in the private sector. Pragmatism has replaced dogma as the means of dumbing down only because it delivers budget cuts almost immediately compared to expensive and protracted competitive bidding processes.

I don't believe that you can have an effective prison system on the cheap. Politicians with ambitions for office need to understand this essential point and be honest with the electorate. If they wish to go further and reintroduce stricter and more punitive regimes alongside a rehabilitative ethic, then they have to be prepared to pay for it. They need to understand that a clampdown will provoke a reaction and they need to be prepared to face it down. Keeping drugs out of prisons requires investment in physical security, staff and dogs. Keeping mobile phones out of prisons, an enormous menace as it allows users to continue organising criminality from behind the prison walls, requires technical investment. Preventing prisoners in open establishments from going to the local off licence requires investment in technology and staffing. Preventing high profile prisoners from killing themselves requires 24/7 cover, and Norman Baker, MP for Lewes, who criticised HMP Lewes for not preventing a remand prisoner from cheating justice, knows this very well. Just 100 prisoners in the system, less than one per establishment, being observed constantly a la Ian Huntley would add around £15 million per year to the budget for the prison service on staffing costs alone. Like their Tory predecessors, New Labour was happy to follow a populist demand for greater use of custody, but it was not prepared to fund it. Prison policy has been a series of tactical shifts that have obscured or negated a coherent strategy. It was New Labour that introduced the End of Custody Licence which released short term prisoners 18 days early (and paid them for the privilege), and it was New Labour that introduced Home Detention Curfew (HDC), up to a maximum of 135 days. Thus, a prisoner serving an 18 month sentence, obtaining the full tariff of 50% remission for good behaviour, plus HDC, is actually released after four and a half months. A prisoner sentenced to 6 months can serve as little as 6 weeks. The prison service can do nothing meaningful with this type of individual. Needless to say, all bar a small number of prisons housing those not eligible for this perk, employ staff in a variety of grades to devote a greater or lesser part of their working week to risk assessment, administration, and the inevitable case conferences.

When I joined the prison service in 1984 conditions for staff left much to be desired. The basic wage was poor and high earnings were obtained from high overtime. Prison pfficers were not a healthy crew by and large. A diet of long hours, junk food and beer in the prison officers' club was not conducive to a long life. In many ways it replicated military life without a rifle, the vast majority of uniformed staff having served in the forces anything from 3 to 22 years. Staff lived in communities clustered around the prison, socialising only with each other, with the prison officers' club taking the place of the mess on the military base. To this day staff canteens are called messes. Lunchtime drinking only fell out of fashion gradually and only when governors closed clubs at lunchtime was the practice marginalised. In recognition of the fact that prison officer grades lived on average 5 years less than other workers, the POA had negotiated the right to retire at the age of 55. This changed after what was called "Fresh Start" in 1987, when the retirement age for new recruits was set at 60. In 2005, new recruits were contracted until 65 years of age. Thus, just among uniformed staff alone, there are three separate groups with different conditions of service.

As described in Chapter 7, the 1984 service was stratified in a similar way to the armed forces in that there were two methods of entry; as a prison officer or as an assistant governor. An internal competition was run annually for prison officers seeking entry to the governor grade, but the norm was no more than a handfull of staff passing what was referred to colloquially as the "Country House Test". The majority of prison officers were former members of the armed forces, either as regulars or in the case of older staff (mid-40s and up) as National Servicemen. This gave the uniformed ranks a very distinct ethos. The summit of promotion was to Chief Officer 1, seen as the equivalent of a military RSM. Promotion was very slow for both officers and governor grades. I was very conscious of being in a minority, not having a military background and having the benefit of higher education. Governor grades were virtually all university educated, whereas prison officer grades were mainly secondary modern educated, left school at 15 and were resolutely working class. The preponderance of military men gave this working class community a very Conservative (with a large and small "c") outlook. Despite the fact that most staff had served in the forces where trade unions were not permitted, and despite their admiration for Mrs Thatcher, prison officers were staunch trade unionists. In 1987, the Chief Officer rank was scrapped and the grade structure unified, thus allowing people to climb from prison officer to in-charge governor and beyond into the Senior Civil Service with no barrier other than merit, for the first time. This gave the prison service a career structure more akin to the police than the armed forces.

The political class do not like merit as a principle, nor do they like the ability to think and conceptualise beyond the narrow confines of their post Marxist ideology. They are especially wary of those who have risen from the lowest ranks, on the basis that they may still carry some of those values. They might have that very traditional value: commonsense. Too much experience is actually considered dangerous, as this means there is a group of people who command sufficient authority to point out what will not work and what has failed before. Such people are dangerous and need to be neutralised. It is sometimes stigmatised as the canteen culture. My Generation in power has deployed its full range of weaponry on an outwardly meritocratic structure in a bid to ensure that its elite values dominate the prison service. Internal applicants now find it exceptionally difficult to get on fast track schemes, whereas for a number of years after the introduction of the Accelerated Promotion Scheme in 1988, they were positively encouraged. The whole mindset is that appropriately educated graduates fast tracked to senior ranks and therefore loyal to the values of the political class rather than to the values of prison officers, are the future.

The prison service also recruits from outside industry direct (rather than fast tracked) to senior ranks. These people are supposed to bring with them a proven track record of management that they can apply to the prison service. Inevitably, the results are variable. The most high profile direct recruit was into the top job. This was Derek Lewis, former Head of UK Gold, a minority TV Channel who was appointed by Kenneth Clarke. Although Mr Lewis worked hard to master his brief, the rank and file regarded the appointment as a gimmick and Mr Clarke's successor, Michael Howard, unceremoniously showed what he thought of the appointment, when he fired him peremptorily after high profile Category A escapes from HMP Whitemoor and HMP Parkhurst, although Mr Lewis quite properly won legal actions against the Home Office for breach of contract and wrongful dismissal. One of the unintended consequences of the scheme is that seriously good recruits at this level (and there are a few) are then attracted to the private prison sector where the pay is better and they are not stifled. At the other extreme, there are those inevitably who cannot cope in a custodial environment and find their way into well paid desk jobs in the regional bureaucracies. The organisation is so sold on this policy that it actually has far more people on the scheme than there are posts, so many of these recruits are set to become disillusioned as they carry out lower grade work, but of course get the higher grade pay to keep them onside. Without the opportunity to return to their original profession because of the employment situation, they are well paid captives. The prison service is busily culling the ranks of experienced deputy governors promoted from the ranks to make room for those whose values are not tainted by a significant spell in uniform. When challenged by the Prison Governors Association, Phil Wheatley, then Head of the Prison Service, justified this expensive, wasteful and unproductive form of recruitment on the basis that it helped the service achieve its targets for ethnic minority recruitment. In the politically correct world diversity trumps efficiency.

The policy of external recruitment to senior ranks is one that reformers also seek to impose on the police. Soldiers respect their officers because they share the danger and because they know that officer training at Sandhurst is even more demanding than their own. In the prison service, graduate entrants do a meaningful stint as a prison officer and then as a first line manager on a wing. They have the opportunity to gain respect. Direct entrants are very much on their own. They have no peer group and no roots. Yet this ludicrous policy is espoused both by the Tories and New Labour and, as I have said, a policy of this nature when it commands cross party support, means you should be very afraid. Can you seriously see someone who was managing a Tesco store a year ago commanding a police operation around a high profile football match? Subsequent to the Winsor report on policing, this could become a reality. It's a bit like expecting a probation officer to perform a liver transplant, and it would normally have been derided as an ill thought out gimmick from yet another management consultant. However, following press criticism of the police response to the August 2011 riots, and the exposure of too comfortable relationships between senior Met officers and News International, a revolutionary policy of direct entry into senior police ranks is now more likely given the current political vulnerability of the police. In time, politicians may come to regret hounding out Sir Paul Stephenson and John Yates, Commissioner and Assistant Commissioner of the Metropolitan Police respectively. The Met Commissariat and their provincial counterparts, the 43 regional Chief Constables, are high profile powerful public figures with a high degree of operational independence, but this power is constrained by ministerial (in London Mayoral) favour (the Home Secretary has the power to get rid of them), and now by locally elected Commissioners which have replaced police committees. Thus, there is some accountability even though sometimes it may only be to another branch of the ruling elite.

However in the prison service, which operates under the civil service umbrella, the feudal barony that runs the organisation above establishment level operates without any checks and balances and without public scrutiny. The Director General of the service is much less well known than police counterparts. Governors in charge of prisons do have a public profile and a press campaign can result in exile to the prison service equivalent of a Siberian power station, a desk job in Head Quarters. However, at senior civil service level, the occupants of the senior managerial ranks above prison governors and below the Director General, have no public profile and no public accountability at all.

Until 1992, the prison service was divided into five regions; the norm being that the head of each region was a career civil servant rather than a former prison governor. The Director General was also a career civil servant. This structure, whereby the service was administered by generalist mandarins rather than the professionals, was replaced by an area structure in 1992. The job of area manager became available as an avenue of promotion for serving in-charge governors and gave them access to the senior civil service. This development was welcomed by professional practitioners and completed the process begun five years earlier when military style segregated entry routes to the service were abolished. Geographical boundaries were re-shuffled at intervals, but in practice around a dozen areas replaced five regions. At first, area offices were all based in London and lightly staffed with the support team consisting of little more than a staff officer, a secretary and a clerk. Once they moved out of London, again a move that on the face of it was totally logical, the area managers built vast bureaucratic feudal empires funded by top slicing prison budgets. Small armies of advisors, diversity managers, investigators, performance teams and clerks laboured away collecting statistics, designing Excel graphics, and generally irritating the hell out of management teams in prisons who were forced to neglect the day job in order to service the voracious bureaucratic monster. Without a Freedom of Information request I cannot be sure of the cost of the area (now regional again) structure, but I would estimate conservatively that staffing costs alone were £15 to £20 million per annum. Many buildings were rented so these costs would need to be added. The cost of paper, IT, and other consumables would also need to be added. Area managers were also granted the power to move in-charge governors and their immediate subordinates around the system. This power of patronage has been abused ruthlessly in the near two decades since it was devolved. It is the corrupt means by which political correctness is imposed. In 2005, the prison service, by now renamed the National Offender Management Service, introduced a parallel bureaucracy headed by Regional Offender Managers (ROMS). Within a few short years the now doubly expensive structures were amalgamated under a new tier of management, 10 Regional Directors of Offender Management (DOMs). Area managers who were not promoted to this level were renamed Regional Custody Managers, stripped of their budgets but crucially not of their powers of patronage. If you want to know how the taxpayers' money is wasted, just apply these shenanigans across the entire public sector, calculator in hand. The Coalition did at least get rid of the DOM's. However the former area managers got all their powers back and were given a grander sounding title, Deputy Directors of Custody.

I use the prison service as an example because that is the part of the public sector known to me. It is pretty certain that the higher echelons of the police, the fire service and other significant public sector employers outside of the civil service operate in a way that would be equally recognisable to dissidents like me in those organisations. So anyone who, like me, thought that the main jobs of our police forces (sorry services!) are to prevent crime and catch criminals, and anyone who thought that the main jobs of the prison service are to secure incarceration and rehabilitation of the criminals caught by the police, has got it wrong. Their first job is to deliver on the revolutionary ideology of the nation's political elite and what constitutes crime and what constitutes punishment have to be seen through that prism.

CHAPTER 16

ENERGY AND THE ENVIRONMENT

In 1920 coal industry employment peaked at 1.2 million workers. After the 1974 coal strike it still had a 200,000 strong labour force. The incoming Labour government that year intended to invest further in coal mining and enhance the rôle of the industry, rather than manage its decline as alternative energy sources, including nuclear, came on stream, which effectively had been the policy for two decades. Harold MacMillan, Conservative Prime Minister 1957-63, had appointed Lord (Alf) Robens, a former Labour minister, to manage the decline in a consensual way. Coal had powered the industrial revolution, two world wars and post war reconstruction, but the slagheaps scarred the environment and industrial smogs afflicted the lungs of the very old, the very young and the infirm. On the day I was born, December 4th 1952, polluting smog descended on London and blanketed the capital for five days. I can just about remember smog in Blackburn when I was very young and clearly remember the smoke belching from mill chimneys. All that changed with the progressive implementation of the Clean Air Act that created smokeless zones. In 1968 came a symbolic tipping point in the UK's love affair with coal when the last British Rail steam hauled passenger train completed its journey. After 1968 steam would become the province of nostalgic private sector enthusiasts who reclaimed disused railway lines and built a new and lucrative tourist industry. The end of steam had been heralded in the 1955 modernisation plan which it was envisaged would take 15 years to implement. In the case of dispensing with steam hauled traction, the deadline was achieved with 16 months to spare. Two years earlier the Aberfan disaster occurred, when a coal waste tip engulfed a primary school like an avalanche and claimed 144 lives of young children and their teachers. This was another hammer blow for the industry. Harold Wilson, the Prime Minister, had waxed lyrical prior to the 1964 election about the need to modernise and the need to forge a technological revolution. Anthony Wedgwood Benn, as he was then known, was Minister of Technology at the time of the Aberfan disaster. The same Mr Benn, ironically, was Secretary of State for Energy when his department produced the Plan for Coal.

So what provoked the renewed importance of coal? The answer lay in the volatile Middle East. The Yom Kippur War of 1973 was the fourth in a series of wars fought by Israel since its founding in 1948. The Israelis were on this occasion themselves the victims of a pre-emptive attack, but despite the war being harder fought the Israelis were victorious again within a few weeks, and Egypt and Syria were again left to lick their wounds. The USA and its Western European allies were unequivocally pro-Israel. However, the usually disunited Arab countries were able to fight back against the West using the one economic weapon available to them: oil. Under the guise of OPEC (The Organisation of Petroleum Exporting Countries) the price of a barrel of oil quadrupled overnight. Non Arab countries were just as keen to extract higher returns from rich countries like the USA and the UK who were not self- sufficient in oil. At a stroke the fact that the UK was no longer self-sufficient in energy was exposed. In many respects the timing could hardly have been worse. For Edward Heath's embattled government, already buffeted by soaring inflation, massively increased oil costs were swiftly reflected at the petrol pumps in a society where private motoring was now the dominant mode of travel. In 1972 the miners staged their first national strike since 1926, as they saw their wages not only eroded by inflation, but eroded in comparison to other workers who had once earned rather less. There was considerable public sympathy for the miners, not least because the public recognised the ever present danger of their work. The notion that they were not adequately rewarded struck a chord. The Yom Kippur War and its aftermath radically altered the market position of the miners and their trade union, the NUM, lost no time in taking advantage. Unfortunately, for Edward Heath as it turned out, this put them into direct conflict with the government's incomes policy. There could only be one winner of this second strike and it was not the Conservative government. Heath called a general election and his party used the slogan "Who governs?" The answer was "not you". Heath's campaign was undermined from his own backbenches. Enoch Powell, sacked from the shadow cabinet by Heath in 1968, was a thorn in the

Prime Minister's side on a number of issues principally immigration, Common Market membership and economic policy. Powell argued, from a free market perspective, that the miners' demands should be met on the basis that (for now) they were in a strong market position, and resistance to market forces was useless. He also detonated an even bigger bombshell, resigning his seat and urging voters to vote Labour on the simple basis that they had promised a referendum on Common Market (as it was then known) membership.

In truth the outcome of the February 1974 election was less than clear cut. Constitutionally Heath had no need to go to the country until July 1975, but in practice his comfort zone had been eroded by lost by-elections and the defection from the Tory camp of the Ulster Unionists, which had reduced his effective majority to single figures. The coal strike and the defiance of government presented an opportunity to shore up an administration in danger of not being in control of its own parliamentary fate. The Conservatives actually won the most votes, but in terms of seats trailed Labour by 296 to 301. After an attempt to woo the Liberal leader, Jeremy Thorpe, failed, Heath bowed to the inevitable and resigned. Labour governed, as a minority, until October 1974 when a general election gave it a majority of three. By 1976 by-election defeats had reduced Labour back to minority government status. The Plan for Coal can be seen through the prism of a renewed role in energy provision, but it was also Labour paying its debts to a resurgent NUM. Labour was enthusiastic about the North Sea. Already providing the natural gas that was rapidly superseding the provision of town gas, the North Sea was the new Klondyke for Britain, potentially emancipating the country from Arab potentates. Tony Benn set up BNOC (British National Oil Corporation) to protect the interests of the state in what could be described as the forerunner of public-private partnerships, which would intellectually occupy the minds of New Labour two decades later.

Critics from the free market right of the political spectrum have never accepted the validity of the Wilson-Callaghan governments' energy policy, and in particular the plan for coal. Their position, which is based on dogma and the triumph of neo-liberal economics under Mrs Thatcher and Mr Major, and accepted by their New Labour successors, forms a major part of the toxic brew that is now the UK energy situation. The privatisation of energy has seen control of our resources pass out of the hands of government responsible to the electorate into the hands of multi-national companies, for whom Britain is simply another market. As a country we no longer own most of our energy and are at the mercy of inadequately regulated, predatory companies who are perfectly happy to restrict supplies to the British taxpayer and, instead, export the resources of our territorial waters on a preferential basis to foreign countries. Therefore, we effectively import most of our gas as well as our oil. The only issue is whether we import it from foreign controlled firms or foreign countries. The situation is worsened by the lack of storage facilities in the UK. Thus if the gas companies have sold our resources abroad, gas has then to be imported via pipelines controlled by other countries, and in particular Russia. Under President Putin, Russia has already flexed its post Soviet era muscles by cutting off supplies to the Ukraine. The privatisation of energy is possibly the most toxic legacy of the 1979-97 Conservative government.

As for the coal industry, it went the way of all traditional industrial flesh. The final decisive battle between the Tories and the miners was fought in 1984-5, and this time the Tories came out on top. The outcome was such that by 1994, when the coal industry was privatised, there were only 15 working pits, concentrated almost exclusively in South Yorkshire and Nottinghamshire, left. Under New Labour, the number of deep mining pits would contract further to single figures. Just 7,000 men remained employed in deep mining by 2007, compared to 160,000 at the commencement of the strike. By 2011, this had fallen to around 3,000 in 6 pits with another 3,000 or so workers employed in open cast and drift mining. In 2013 the largest private company, UK Coal, entered administration. At the time of writing, April 2014, it is becoming apparent that by the autumn of 2015 there will only be one deep mine left operating in the UK.

The dramatic decline in coal mining can be attributed to economic factors, but the Thatcher-Major governments chose to accelerate the decline. Germany, for example, employed 166,000 miners in the deep coal industry in 1985. By 2007 that figure had declined to 35,000. In that year, Germany decided to close its deep mining (black coal) industry entirely by 2018, but its open cast industry has actually been increasing production. In 2012 Germany actually mined 5.1% more brown (dirty) coal. France closed its last mine in 2004, but it should be remembered that France embraced nuclear power like no other EU country, 80% of its energy is generated in nuclear power stations. In the UK this peaked at 26% in 1997, but had dropped back to 19% by 2004. However, even France became concerned at ever increasing energy prices and only two years later a licence was granted to an open cast (surface) mining company, thus undercutting the price of imported coal from South Africa. It is expected that resumed open casting will meet 1% of France's energy needs. In Britain the demise of the steel industry, which was well under way at the time of the strike, slashed demand. The British mining industry was competing against French and German deep mining industries which received subsidies of three times and four times respectively greater than the British coal industry. Open caste industries in Poland, South Africa and Australia could all produce and ship coal for export cheaper than deep mining in Britain. As a consequence, we import two thirds of our coal consumption. For market economists the demise of the domestic coal industry was a no brainer.

Another nail in the coffin came in the early 1990s with the "dash for gas". By 1990 coal's share of electricity production had declined from around 90% immediately post war to around 67%. By 2011 this had fallen to around 44%. In one sense it is remarkable that such a tiny industry in employment terms still provides the fuel to generate more than 2/5ths of our electricity. However, that most malevolent of forces, the EU, in its infinite lack of wisdom put in the final nail by ruling that coal fired power stations must be closed down on environmental grounds unless equipped with carbon capture facility (CCF). Unless this is reversed the UK will lose half of its coal fired generating capacity by 2015, and all of it by 2023. It seems as though the EU is determined to put out Britain's lights and freeze its homes in winter and our government seems happy to roll over. As ever, EU rules only apply to the UK. Germany opened two coal fired power stations in 2012 and is scheduled to open six more in 2013. None of these are equipped with carbon capture facility.

By contrast to the tiny workforce in the coal industry, UK oil and gas industries combined employed 265,000 people in 2007. On the other side of the generating coin, electricity produced from gas had been a minimal 0.05% in 1990, but a mere 14 years later this had risen to just over 39%. The "dash for gas" was largely occasioned by a change in EU regulations to permit the wider use of gas for electricity production. Both the Conservatives and New Labour appeared to take no heed of the fact that North Sea gas is a finite asset, and what remains will be more expensive to obtain. In 2005 the UK was almost self-sufficient in its gas needs. By 2010 this had dropped to 60%. The UK has a gas storage capacity of only 15 days' supply. By contrast, Germany can store 99 days' worth of gas, and France has capacity for 122 days. As a consequence of the Lisbon treaty, so disgracefully signed by Gordon Brown in 2009, a further threat looms, predictably from the EU which seeks to get its hands on our energy supplies as a reaction to the Russian gas pipe blockade. If this threat is not resisted, our energy resources will go the same way as our fishing grounds, so appallingly handed over by Edward Heath. It should be noted that 64% of the world's energy resources from fossil fuels derive from coal, enough to last 164 years. Oil and gas represent 18% each, although these figures could be radically altered by the development of hydraulic fracturing, known colloquially as "fracking". However, remarkable economic growth in two of the world's largest countries, India and China, has quite naturally led to increased energy consumption by these countries and increased competition to burn oil and gas. In Britain, coal reserves run at around 90% of the 1950 figure although the official calculation is 12%. The gap between the two figures is explained by the consequences of the abandonment of deep mining. It does not take long for flooding and subsidence to render former collieries beyond use without major upfront investment to get at the seams of coal safely. Even at the lower figure, recoverable assets are calculated to last around 20 years. That investment would also need to find a way of re-creating a skilled workforce, given that many former miners from the great contraction that has taken place since 1985 are retired or dead and that the average age of those remaining in the industry is 50.

The conduct of British energy policy over the last 30 years borders on criminal. The deliberate abandonment of coal assets to flooding, subsidence and general neglect has taken place despite reserves of gas declining at a much faster rate than that of coal, and despite the fact that losing our self-sufficiency in terms of fuel has put us at the mercy of a potentially hostile Russia and a predatory EU. The extent to which we depend on rapidly dwindling gas reserves is terrifying. At the same time, both Tory and New Labour governments have refused to invest in the obvious alternative to coal and gas, nuclear power. The situation with oil is not comparable to that with gas, as the former contributes only a little over 1% to electricity generation. However, the petroleum resources which we cannot do without to facilitate private and public transport are in the hands mainly of despotic and potentially unfriendly regimes, a concern exacerbated by the slavish following of American foreign policy.

The truth is that we have had the ability to protect our electricity supply and the politicians have flunked it. Before the end of the decade it is easy to imagine routine power rationing during harsh winters as a consequence of the combined doctrines of the free marketers of the right, and the environmentalists and nuclear rejectionists of the left. To reiterate what has been said before in this book, when the right and left wings of politics pursue similar policies, albeit for very different reasons, then voters should be very afraid. New Labour was only too happy to mainstream the veganomics of the beards and sandals brigade, who traditionally have inhabited the Liberal Democrat and Green Parties. Having abandoned proletarianism, New Labour was only too happy to consign the mining industry and its remaining workforce to the status of an industrial footnote. It was interesting to discover, when researching this chapter, that New Labour in office proposed to invest £100 million in what was left of British mining. In terms of a whole economy, it is a trifling sum and can rightly be slated as gesture politics. Yet even this virtually irrelevant gesture was criticised on the basis that mining was outdated, inhuman and inherently in conflict with protection and enhancement of the environment. Elsewhere on the political spectrum, to post Marxists who have rejected class conflict as the route to socialism, the environment is another revolutionary battleground along with race, gender and sexuality. For them, the non-revolutionary groups and influential individuals who have adopted the "green" agenda are Lenin's "useful idiots". Underpinning and popularising the Green agenda is the seizure of climate science by those who have convinced themselves that man-made global warming is both an established fact and a source of mortal danger within the remaining lifespan of the baby boomer generation.

The "warmists", like their revolutionary brothers and sisters, the feminists and the race and gay rights lobbies, operate as a theocracy. Their central tenet is that man-made global warming is taking place and can only be reversed by the most stringent measures to curb the emission of greenhouse gases or carbons, as they are now most commonly known. No opposition to this point of view is tolerated. Scientists who challenge this orthodoxy are marginalised and denied both tenure and promotion. We are told that the science is settled and of course this is accepted by our political elite. As one would expect, given that that political elite long since captured the BBC, it spews out warmist propaganda at every opportunity and virtually ignores alternative views, and when these are given airtime their proponents are portrayed as cranks, flat-earthers, and moral defectives. It was in 2006 that Lord May, formerly of the Royal Society, told BBC bigwigs that the science was settled. Henceforth, editorial policy has proceeded on that assumption, despite the incontrovertible fact that there has been no warming since 1997. Only on a minority channel, Channel Four, has any serious challenge been permitted. Nothing is more anti-science than a claim that the science is settled. The "warmists" have conjured the ultimate oxymoron into pseudo- intellectual existence. Ever since an email trail revealed a data rigging scandal at the University of East Anglia (UEA), we have known that research findings that do not fit into the new environmental bible, are either binned or massaged. In the same year, the BBC held a review into whether or not they were biased on the issue, and it concluded that they were not biased enough! The BBC has breached its charter and trashed the historic mission to inform bequeathed by Lord Reith. In our schools they terrify our children by telling them unless we act now the Arctic ice cap will melt and the much loved polar bear, the great white icon of the frozen north, will be extinct. In former US Vice-President Al Gore's award winning (!) documentary (!), "An inconvenient truth", there is the unforgettable scene of a solitary polar bear stranded on a piece of broken iceberg. In fact, polar bears are excellent swimmers and have been observed swimming continuously for 62 miles (100km). There is also no evidence of a decline in the polar bear population. It is true that Arctic summer sea ice has been declining for around 30 years with record low levels in 2012, although there was a dramatic reverse in 2013. It is this continuation of the trend beyond 1997 that has kept the "warmist" cause alive. By contrast in the Antarctic as observed by the National Snow and Ice Data Agency of the USA, sea ice reached record levels and the expansion is considered to be a long term trend.

It is sometimes forgotten that back in the 1970s scientists were actually worried about the consequences of global cooling, in particular whether or not the earth could be heading for a new ice age, albeit some 4000 years hence. There is geological and historical evidence of warmer and cooler periods. Ask yourself why Erik the Red gave the name Vinland to the territory we now know as Greenland. Ask yourself how it got the name Greenland. We know also that a little ice age actually occurred extending roughly from the mid 16th to the mid 19th centuries. NASA dates the little ice age as circa 1550 to 1850, whilst other experts have it lasting until the end of the 19th century. The balance of evidence is that it was a worldwide phenomenon. It is known to have followed a period of warming. As one would expect, events were better documented in the northern hemisphere. The well documented frost fairs held on the River Thames are ample evidence that winters were routinely much more severe than in the lifetime of the baby boomers. The last of these frost fairs was held in 1814. Interestingly, only two winters during the little ice age, 1683-84 and 1739-40, rank as colder in England than that of 1962-63 since records began in 1659, which demonstrates the singular nature of that winter. Elsewhere, in 1680 New York Harbour froze completely, and in the same winter sea ice extended several miles out to sea around Iceland completely cutting off the island. Famines were endemic in Europe as both spring and summer were often cold and wet and, as a consequence, there was an absence of a reliable growing season. There is ample geological evidence of the little ice age being mirrored in the Southern Hemisphere.

Various theories have been advanced as causes and these are often submerged by the intellectual tyranny of man-made global warming enthusiasts. Solar activity, because the sun also warms and cools, is probably the most persuasive and volcanic activity can certainly be blamed for the "no summer" of 1816. One of the more interesting theories is the shutting down of the ocean conveyor, known as thermohaline circulation. This is believed to be a consequence of excess fresh water entering the North Atlantic during the medieval warming period that preceded the little ice age. This theory is particularly interesting, as the entry of melted fresh water ice during the recent warming period could potentially have the same effect according to this theory by disrupting the gulf stream that keeps our climate temperate. Three moderately harsh winters in the last four years (to 2013) are not themselves evidence of climate change towards cooling, but a sequence of them would require scientific explanation. However, the Canadian style winter of 1962-63 was not caused by any temporary defect in the gulf stream. It was caused by a "blocking high" that lasted an extended period and prevented prevailing westerly winds from exerting their normal moderating influence. In short, it was a weather feature, albeit an extreme one. Our most recent winter 2013-14 which was exceptionally wet, is an extreme example of the opposite phenomenon, caused by the position of the jet-stream which led to a constant stream of wet and windy Atlantic weather systems reaching our shores.

There is no dispute that there was significant warming in the period 1977-97, since when it has ceased. Needless to say, the climate change theocracy regard it only as a pause in an inevitable process, regardless of the absence of evidence. The bigger dispute is over the cause. As has been said, the climate change industry is determined to blame man -made carbon pollution. The theocracy also ignore the fact that global warming has been detected by astronomers on Mars, Jupiter and Pluto as well as one of Neptune's moons, Triton. Given that none of these planets boast heavy industry or methane producing cattle it is no surprise that other scientists have looked for the most obvious candidate; the sun. Russian astronomers were satisfied that global warming on Mars was evidence that the sun was also responsible for global warming on earth. We know that satellites that measure the temperature of sunlight have recorded increases in the sun's temperature. In 2004 the Daily Telegraph cited research by German and Swiss scientists who claimed that it is increasing radiation from the sun that is resulting in our current climate change. Given the criticality of the sun for the survival of the planet as our one natural source of heat and light, these conclusions should come as no surprise. Yet the UN Intergovernmental Panel on Climate Change (IPCC) ignores the evidence as does our own national broadcaster. It is important to understand that the IPCC is a political organisation, not one of neutral truth seeking scientists. Al Gore's film actually distorted the findings of scientists who had concluded that a rise in CO2 actually <u>follows</u> a rise in temperature rather than the other way about as claimed by the "warmist" establishment. It should be noted also that carbon emissions rose dramatically after World War II as the major world economies surged back into peace time production. Yet for nearly four decades after 1940 the global temperature actually fell.

Dr Timothy Ball from Canada felt moved to make this very depressing comment on the climate change debate (insofar as debate is permitted). He said "sadly my experience is that universities are the most dogmatic and oppressive places in our society. This becomes progressively worse as they receive more and more funding from governments that demand a particular viewpoint." This can be described as nothing other than totalitarian. In a completely different field, Dr Andrew Wakefield was struck off for challenging the prevailing and well-funded orthodoxy that the triple MMR vaccine was safe. The fate of Dr Wakefield underlines my point perfectly. Dr Wakefield now works in the USA, but it would be a mistake to believe that American academia is necessarily the land of the free. When universities are reduced to the level of a market place, then scientific respectability and more to the point the academics who provide it, can be bought, sold and lent to governments and powerful lobby groups who will stop at nothing to trash the reputations of those who oppose their creed. This is the very antithesis of the academic freedom that expands knowledge and protects democracy. Dr Ball was himself the victim of a crude smear, being accused of being in the pay of the oil companies. Perhaps the most disgusting smear of all is the one that appeared in the Boston Globe written by a certain Ellen Goodman: "Let's just say that global warming deniers are on a par with holocaust deniers." As denial of the holocaust is a criminal offence in some fully functioning western democracies like Germany and Austria, and is capable of being construed as incitement in others, Ms Goodman is effectively comparing those who doubt that global warming is man-made with genocidal racists, and by implication calling for their freedom of expression to be curtailed. It is a world that Galileo and Copernicus would recognise from their battles with the late medieval papacy. In my own former profession, sex offenders who refused to admit their offences were referred to as "deniers". So in the most appalling totalitarian misuse of language those who challenge the man-made nature of global warming are boxed alongside Jew baiting war criminals and paedophiles.

On the basis of science that is at best hotly disputed and at worst thoroughly bogus, My Generation in power declared war on the householder, the motorist and the holiday maker. Householders have to put up with the local council bin police and EU directives forcing them to buy expensive low energy light bulbs. This is another well intentioned measure that neglects the law of unintended consequences, as the low energy light bulbs give off 90% less heat thus forcing householders to turn up their central heating and burn more fossil fuels! Those trying to sell their home were forced to purchase Home Information Packs (HIPS) at around £300 a throw. Although the energy rating of your current or prospective home is not entirely useless information, there is no evidence that it has any meaningful effect on the behaviour of buyers and sellers in the housing market. Mercifully, the Coalition government swiftly abolished this requirement. The British motorist pays the highest fuel duties in the world. When VAT is included, 80p of the 130p price per litre is taken by the government in tax. Indeed, the higher the price per barrel of oil in the international market place, the greater the tax take. As for the holiday maker hammered by Air Passenger Duty (APD), well according to Oliver Letwin, prominent Conservative member of the cross party ruling elite, we cannot have more families from Sheffield jetting off on foreign holidays. In the early years of Victoria's reign, the Duke of Wellington expressed his concern that the development of the railways would encourage the "lower orders" to travel about. I can only assume that the otherwise erudite and open minded Mr Letwin has been well and truly got at and hopefully regrets sounding so dreadfully patronising. Whether Sheffield was mischievously singled out as it is the location of Nick Clegg's constituency, is a matter of idle speculation. Air Passenger Duty, like all the other taxes, charges and fines relating to emissions, simply goes to the Exchequer. For example, petrol duty in 2009-10 raised £27 billion from motorists. Only a third of this was spent on the nation's roads. In December 2011 the Coalition government defending itself against criticism of high petrol prices, stated that in scrapping New Labour's fuel accelerator it had relieved motorists of the burden of a further £4.5 billion in fuel duties. Put simply, My Generation in power had been planning to raise petrol duty by 16% in the space of 18 months, way above the rate of inflation. This was nothing short of a declaration of war against the private motorist and against businesses which are wholly dependent on road transport. This is a typical abuse of the tax system and part of the overriding hypocrisy of environmental taxes.

As cattle are responsible for more methane emissions than industry, prominent vegetarians such as Hilary Benn have been quick to advocate the abandonment of meat. The Centre of Alternative Technology, in its manifesto for a carbon free Britain by 2030, calls for amongst other things a 90% reduction in the number of cattle and sheep. No doubt our vegan friends, given their total opposition to all things dairy, would regard 90% as lacking in ambition. As ever, the swivel eyed fanatics have missed a crucial point. Without an alternative source of milk from dairy animals, babies unable to access breast milk for whatever reason will be condemned to death. My message is beware of what you wish for. Given that CO2 rises as a result of temperature increases rather than the other way round as claimed by the "warmists", then all the carbon neutral measures in the world have been and will continue to be futile. It will have all the impact of pissing in the wind and the blowback will be the negative effect on our industrial competitiveness and ferociously hiked domestic energy bills that make fuel poverty the norm for British families. If we are hitting a sequence of hard winters, then green policies could hardly be worse timed.

In the 2011 autumn statement, The Chancellor of the Exchequer, Mr Osborne, was clear that putting British industry out of business was not going to save the planet. He has also acknowledged the costs piled on businesses and households by environmental laws. Indeed, the UK is no longer in the top ten of world polluters, our emissions contribution being less than 2% of the world's total. In 2005, China led the way with 17% with the USA just 1% behind. The Climate Change Act of 2008 passed in the House of Commons by 463 votes to 3, further proof that the political elite transcend party labels. Using the government's own figures, it will cost £404 billion to implement, or £760 per household per annum over four decades. New Labour committed the country to a reduction in carbon emissions of 20% by 2020 and 80% by 2050 from the 1990 figures. The Kyoto Convention signed in 1997 used 1990 as a benchmark year as it was helpful to major industrial countries in being seen to get their emissions down, particularly the newly reunited Germany tackling the pollution left by the former Communist government of East Germany, a filthy inheritance readily acknowledged by this author.

The change in EU regulations that year set off the aforementioned "dash for gas" in the UK, which emits significantly less greenhouse gas than coal. However, the figures committed to by the UK are achievable only by shutting down the economy. Needless to say, China and the USA have no intention whatsoever of flagellating themselves and their economies by pursuing such grandiose and indulgent schemes. New Labour's Climate Change Committee in 2008 recommended a switch to less carbon intensive food production, i.e. away from beef and lamb. Lord Turner, the Committee Chair, also called for 40% of all cars on roads to be powered by electricity within a decade. Given that a mere 1100 were on the road at the time, cloud cuckoo land does not begin to describe it. The same committee was happy to follow the dictates of the EU and prevented the construction of a new generation of coal fired power stations unless they were fitted with the aforementioned carbon capture, an experimental and as yet unproven technology being funded by a £3 billion levy on energy bills funded by, you guessed it, the hard pressed taxpayer. The likely effect of this technology (even if it works) would be to double electricity prices, and without a massive expansion of the industry, would have little impact on imported energy. As it is, we face an increase in electricity prices of 41% in real terms between 2012 and 2020 as a consequence of subsidies to expensive green energy generation. This is in addition to the 44% increase in energy costs in real terms over the last decade. It should be noted that we now (2011) import 70% of our energy with all the signals this gives out about our national weakness to our suppliers, in particular countries like Russia which has discovered the power that comes with controlling thousands of miles of gas pipes.

The contribution of the EU was typically bureaucratic. Industries were taxed per ton of fossil fuels used. The mechanism was enforced purchase of carbon credits and firms could actually trade surpluses. Each year the availability of carbon credit would be reduced, therefore firms would have to compete for them, theoretically forcing them to be more energy efficient year on year. The competition was not limited to the private sector. Government offices and even hospitals were included so one can only speculate how many more bureaucrats hit the public sector payroll. The government actually spent money purchasing carbon credits for NATO bases abroad, thus raiding the defence budget when British troops were short of kit in Afghanistan. Inevitably, in the private sector, two things happened. Firstly, costs were passed to consumers, raising prices by as much as £300 per annum. Secondly, companies that could do so relocated abroad. For example, huge tranches of the aluminium industry left these shores. One big firm relocated from Anglesey to the United Arab Emirates. So, we had the spectre of a Labour government deliberately destroying manufacturing industry and with it the jobs of skilled workers. The disgraced former Coalition Energy Secretary, Chris Huhne, very recognisably of My Generation, went further by making Britain purchase carbon credits at above the market rate, thus handing a free gift to our EU and other competitors. As one would expect with this nonsense, our chemical industries are at major risk. They can happily relocate to South Africa, India and China while British workers lose out yet again from green ideological profligacy. Astonishingly, under a global credit scheme, we actually subsidise these firms in that they receive credits which they can sell back to our remaining domestic industries at a profit. Madness doesn't begin to cover it.

However, for pointless ideological subsidies, then the wind turbine is in a class of its own. Of all the renewable sources offered up as the future, wind power is the biggest waste of money of all. The Adam Smith Institute recently demolished the case for both wind and solar power as the replacements for gas, coal and nuclear energy in a piece entitled, "Renewable Energy: Vision or Mirage?" Current targets for wind turbines require the installation of 5 turbines per day until 2020, the bulk of them offshore. This is simply unrealistic, but even if this was a credible building target it would not change the fact that wind and solar power make only a marginal contribution to reduced carbon emissions. This is for the simple reason that back up generating capacity, which inevitably comes from fossil fuels, is needed to compensate for the inherent intermittency of these sources. As we all know the sun does not always shine, particularly in our northern latitudes, and the wind does not always blow and so the turbines and solar panels stand as idle monuments to mankind's helplessness in the face of the elements. Even when it does blow, we lack both the capacity to store the energy and the ability to get it to the grid in optimum conditions which, of course, takes us back to generation using fossil fuels. Additionally, as we also know, wind turbines cannot operate in very high winds and indeed in Scotland, during a violent storm in December 2011, one caught fire, a scene spectacularly captured on film. The fact is that wind farms have a capacity of only 25%. They also only have an operational life of 20 years, far less than that of coal mines and significantly less than that of zero carbon nuclear power stations. Which other industry would tolerate 25% capacity? Would you buy a machine for your business that only delivered a quarter of the goods it was designed to produce? Would you buy a photocopier that would only reproduce a quarter of the page? No business would contemplate such folly. Additionally, would you then expect a taxpayer funded subsidy to produce such useless equipment, always assuming there were businesses daft enough to buy it. Well, this is where we are with wind power.

Solar power has similar built in fault lines. As has been said, it is inefficient in high latitudes and it is high cost. So far, subsidies have been spent on small scale domestic installations, which are intrinsically less cost effective. There is the same storage problem as with wind. Additionally, large solar farms would require far greater land areas than coal fired and nuclear power stations. For obvious reasons, solar farms cannot be situated in the sea or the Scottish Highlands.

Although it is impossible to conceive of a revived coal industry there are serious alternatives to the green follies. One of these, hydraulic fracturing, better known as "fracking", has already attracted the ire of environmentalists and exposed the weakness and the unwillingness of senior police officers to deal with intimidation, criminal damage and eco-terrorism by green protestors. Without being too technical, fracking is a method that allows the extraction of oil and shale gas (and also uranium) from rock. The first experiment was conducted as long ago as 1947 and commercial use began two years later. By 2010 some 60% of new gas and oil wells were using the method. Fracking was used in the UK sector of the North Sea from the late 1970s onward. Its first use on land in the UK was as long ago as 1963 and a small scale industry has existed below the radar ever since. The fact is that fracking for shale gas has transformed the United States energy market and prices to the consumer have been slashed. The shale gas industry is expected to create a further 250,000 plus jobs in the USA within the next two years alone. North Dakota, in particular, is experiencing a major boom. The oil finds also promise to free the USA from the power exercised ruthlessly by hostile oil producing countries in the Middle East. In the UK there are vast deposits of shale gas awaiting exploitation in West Lancashire and other parts of the country. The environmentalist lobby has reacted furiously to the threat to the green dream. As well as the unlawful activities carried out by protestors in Sussex, there has been a sustained propaganda campaign. The green lobby has been peddling untruths that fracking is dangerous in that it causes both water pollution and earthquakes. Seismologists will readily confirm that the West Lancashire area around Blackpool is an earthquake zone, with small tremors felt up to 100 miles away a regular occurrence. The American experience also exposes the pollution argument as a lie and a fallacy. We also need to beware of the EU where the green lobby holds considerable sway, giving it the capacity to seriously obstruct an industry that has the potential to restore our energy fortunes in the same way as it has done in the USA.

Oddly enough, our usually more practical Gallic neighbours have banned fracking. However, they always embraced the other and better known alternative to fossil fuels, nuclear power. The French generate 80% of their energy from nuclear power, four times the energy share of nuclear in GB. Despite growing evidence of an energy gap and its consequences in terms of dependence on imports, New Labour in power set its face firmly against nuclear energy as the green lobby conjured up apocalyptic images of Hiroshima and Chernobyl, and more recently Fukushima in Japan. The Fukushima episode in Japan appears to have spooked Germany into giving up nuclear energy altogether. However, the UK (like Germany) is not an earthquake zone, so there is no risk of a similar occurrence. Equally, British safety standards are so high that the risk of a catastrophic nuclear accident on the scale of Chernobyl is extremely low. The bombing of Hiroshima is wholly irrelevant. Nuclear power stations are about fusion, not fission. The most significant risk is actually terrorism, which can be countered by good security and a high state of vigilance. It is readily conceded that the potential consequences of a nuclear accident are much greater and longer lasting than those from an accident in a coal mine, potentially another Buncefield and perhaps even Bhopal. The likelihood, however, is far lower. Nuclear power generation is a safer and far greener activity than power generation from fossil fuels. Again, it is conceded that toxicity from nuclear waste is a significant issue, not least because of the length of time that materials remain radioactive. Nevertheless, the amounts of radioactive material are not large when compared to the old coal tips or modern landfill rubbish sites, and the methods of sealing and disposing of radioactive waste have proved to be safe. Its overall record, in terms of environmental damage, is far superior to the oil industry with its unfortunate history of repeated marine pollution. Nuclear generates electricity a little more expensively than coal and gas, but is vastly cheaper than wastefully subsidised renewable sources such as wind and solar power. It is not disputed that nuclear power stations are ugly, but so also are oil derricks and pit head winding gear. Electricity pylons are an acquired taste, but wind turbines disfigure the landscape in a completely different way. They are utterly intrusive on an otherwise peaceful rural landscape. Protruding from the sea, they look even more unappealing. The number of monstrosities that will be needed to move from the current figure of 6.6% of electricity generated by renewables to just the 20% target will entail the wholesale disfigurement of whole swathes of our environment. Additionally, there is the low level noise pollution that penetrates the senses and irritates chronically like tinnitus. Truly, wind turbines are the new environmental pollutants.

My Generation in power stood and watched as nuclear power stations approached the end of their life span. Most current power stations will have to be decommissioned by 2023, along with their coal fired cousins. New Labour simply let them wither on the vine. Chris Huhne, one of the high priests of green energy, became Energy Secretary in the Coalition government. We can offer perhaps one and a half cheers for his partial conversion to nuclear power, although he retains his misplaced faith in the sun and the wind. In June 2011, Mr Huhne announced the building of eight new nuclear power stations on existing sites. However, the sobering truth is that because New Labour sold off our technological expertise, the new power stations will be built by the French and the Chinese, the first of these on an existing site in Somerset. As a consequence, the Franco-Chinese consortium whichis led by the French power company EDF, has been able to extract from the government a guaranteed price of twice the current wholesale cost of electricity rendering very hollow the boast of Ed Davey, the Energy Secretary, that these will be the first power stations not to be built using British taxpayers' money. The first new facility will not open for business until 2019 and the program will not be complete until 2025. By 2020, as a consequence of decommissioning, we are set to have a further 20% shortfall in our energy needs. My Generation's legacy will leave our country hugely vulnerable to power cuts from around 2015 onwards and dependent on the good will of countries whose friendship cannot be guaranteed to bridge the gap. It is no exaggeration to say that My Generation has created the perfect storm. All we can do is wait helplessly for it to make landfall.

CHAPTER 17

THE MORAL VACUUM: SEXUALITY, FEMINISM AND THE FAMILY

Briefly defined, morality is a code that lays out the principles and standards of conduct expected of the community that it covers (and communities that it does not). Although religion is not a necessary condition of morality, historically organised religion has laid down a moral code be it the Bible, the Koran, or the Witch Doctor who interprets what does or does not please the gods. Morality, therefore, defines right and wrong in absolute rather than relative terms. Moreover, a moral code rewards the virtuous (not necessarily in this world), punishes transgressors and protects the innocent. When it fails to do those things, the community becomes less safe, less stable, and less cohesive. The traditional moral code in these islands, as in other European countries, stems from the Judeo-Christian inheritance handed down through the generations. However, it should be pointed out that claims made by a particular moral code of being the true path will not always stand scrutiny. Authority over right and wrong is truly awesome power. It is also the case that moralists have taken it upon themselves to prescribe regulations in great detail and add a cultural stamp to the moral code. The enforcement of the burqa in some Islamic communities is a classic example of what is essentially a repressive cultural practice cloaked in religion. Moralists can be great control freaks obsessed with the behaviour of fellow human beings. It is fair to say that morality has not always co-existed with freedom, as opposed to co-existing in Christian terms with an autonomous conscience. There is nothing fundamentally wrong with challenging the validity of moral codes; indeed not to subject them to rigorous examination invites ossification, retrogression and tyranny. The moralist cannot be the self- appointed arbiter of what is good and bad. However, this does not mean that moral codes will not withstand scrutiny. Indeed, I would expect many definitions of what is right and wrong to stand scrutiny on the basis of historical success, empirical evidence, and the social cohesion of or even the survival of the human race. As one would expect, moral codes are often, but by no means always as they are frequently unwritten, translated into law, although again it should not be assumed that it automatically validates the code in question.

As far as Western Europe was concerned, there was one Christian church only until the Reformation destroyed the hegemony of the Catholic Church. However, despite no longer having a monopoly on Christian worship, the Catholic Church maintains, albeit in a more muted form, its universalist claims up to this very day. The Church is clear that its path is the right one, and the only one that guarantees admission to heaven after death. It is difficult to ascribe organisational and doctrinal disagreements as a battle over a moral framework. The Christian message does not rely on adherence or otherwise to the doctrine of transubstantiation. It is also difficult to ascribe a moral purpose to religious or denominational wars that result in the mass slaughter of innocent people. Closer to home, the Church of England was founded simply to legitimise the adultery of England's powerful ruler, Henry V111. However, fratricidal Christianity gradually gave way to religious tolerance in stages from the 17th century onwards, and Christianity has been forced to accommodate democracy. Islam also is a split faith with its Sunni and Shia adherents often living in a very uneasy peace. Islam has not accommodated democracy, and its most fervent adherents hate it with a passion because it challenges directly their power and cultural sway rather than their moral code. Turkey is an apparent exception, but it may be more of a case of democracy accommodating Islam.

Nevertheless, despite perfectly reasonable reservations about the negative features of organised religion, Judeo-Christianity successfully prescribed a moral code which actually thrived under the pressures of industrialisation and only began to break down significantly from the 1950s onward. In the second half of the 19th century, crime fell significantly. The gradual abandonment of the "bloody code" began in the 1820s and was complete by 1868, when public executions were abolished. In 1861, capital offences were reduced to those of murder, and the very rarely prosecuted offences of piracy, treason, and arson in a naval dockyard. This settlement endured until the 1957 Homicide Act split murders into capital and non-capital categories. Acquisitive crimes and drunkenness also fell. It is noteworthy that penal liberalisation and a fall in crime went hand in hand, but even more noteworthy is that crime fell despite the uncompromising capitalism of the era. The Poor Law was as good as it got in terms of a welfare system. There were indeed cesspits of squalor and utter misery in every city, but this decline in criminality is a walking rebuttal of contemporary Marxism. Even the conduct of the upper classes improved. Although as a body they were still broadly contemptuous of bourgeois sexual ethics, they were more discreet. The public debauchery of the 18th century young male aristocrats could not withstand the gaze of stern Victorian morality, although Queen Victoria and Prince Albert certainly despaired of the Prince of Wales who still practiced a public hedonism that was becoming something of an anachronism. The universities revived as seats of learning and the public schools, much influenced by Dr Arnold, acquired a moral purpose.

On this basis there was broad acceptance of a moral code that proscribed murder and theft, excoriated public drunkenness and loutish behaviour, and preached the sanctity of marriage. The moral virtues of honesty, industry, conscientiousness, personal responsibility, punctuality and sobriety were much prized and were the intangible indicators of good character. The virtuous worked hard, malefactors were punished, and the state impinged little on the lives of ordinary people. In terms of the most heinous of crimes, most murderers were caught and around 60% executed. The execution rate was only that low because of the reluctance of the state to hang women who committed infanticide, the vast majority being reprieved. Until 1922, when a separate offence of infanticide was created, the pronunciation of the death sentence was mandatory. People therefore felt protected, a sine qua non of an effective moral code. It is here that the effectiveness of a moral code is demonstrated empirically to support the underpinning principle. The other empirical plank of a moral code is the extent to which its absence would undermine society. Clearly if murder, sexual abuse of children and theft, to give some obvious examples, went unpunished or were condoned, then society could not function effectively as there would be no basis of trust between its members. Thus, it can be seen that the Roman Empire undermined itself as its Senators and putative

Emperors could not be trusted to keep their daggers sheathed. Modern dictatorships are essentially malfunctioning societies, governed by capricious and immoral rulers. Zimbabwe is an excellent example of a failed society because there is no security for your life or your property, both of which are forfeit on the dictator's whim.

Moralists typically seek to regulate sexual behaviour in favour of fidelity and continence. Indeed, they are at their happiest regulating sexual behaviour. The view is very much that this protects the family and best socialises the next generation. However, although gay sex cannot seriously be argued to have threatened the family, it has been traditionally regarded as deviant and sinful by Christian (and Muslim) society. Prior to the English Reformation, sodomy was dealt with by ecclesiastical courts. Henry VIII determined that from 1533 it would be tried in the King's courts and that the penalty would be death. Sodomy would remain punishable by death until 1861, the last execution being carried out (in public) in 1835. In 1806 the number of hangings for sodomy, actually exceeded by one those for murder. It should be remembered that the law did not discriminate between homosexual and heterosexual buggery, for which the penalty after 1861 could still be life imprisonment. Indeed section 61 of the Offences against the Person Act of 1861 was entitled "Sodomy and Bestiality" and made reference to "the abominable crime of buggery, committed with either mankind or beast." This continued the precedents set by the courts in defining the 1533 Buggery Act as anal penetration or bestiality. Thus sodomy was perceived as every bit as depraved as intercourse (by either a man or a woman) with animals. This was the context of debate. Indeed, buggery only disappeared from the legal landscape in 2003 when the distinction between vaginal and anal penetration was abolished.

The outlawing of all forms of gay sex for men did not come until 1885, when the law was extended to cover the full range of sexual practices, as a consequence of what is called the Labouchere amendment. Offences below sodomy were punishable by two years' imprisonment, the fate that befell Oscar Wilde. Lesbianism remained lawful as reputedly, Queen Victoria could not be persuaded that women engaged in such behaviour. There was another unsuccessful attempt to criminalise gay female sex in 1921. There the law remained until 1967. In 1957 the Wolfenden Commission had recommended legalisation, but the House of Lords remained obdurate. The Lords was the most conservative estate of the nation. They believed that legalisation threatened the character and moral efficacy of the nation. Religion provided the crucial prop of Leviticus in the Old Testament.

> "You shall not lie with a man as with a woman. You shall not have sexual intercourse with any beast or make yourself unclean with it..." Leviticus 18: 22-24

> "If a man has intercourse with a man as with a woman, they both commit an abomination. They shall be put to death, their blood shall be on their own heads." Leviticus 20: 13-14

By 1957, the Anglican hierarchy were veering towards a more pragmatic approach. Indeed, Anglican Bishops were often more concerned about pre-marital and extra-marital sex amongst heterosexuals as moral issues. The Archbishop of Canterbury, Geoffrey Fisher, proposed the repeal of the Labouchere amendment, but still wished for sodomy to remain unlawful. Looking at Leviticus, it not only explains the link in English law between homosexuality and bestiality, but also the apparently contradictory attitude of Archbishop Fisher.

The 1967 Act was piloted through the House of Commons by the late Leo Abse, a prominent Labour backbencher. As private members bills require government benevolence to become law, the support of Home Secretary, Roy Jenkins, was crucial as it was for the legalisation of abortion. Abse would later pilot the seminal reform of the Divorce laws through the House in 1969. Although Jenkins was no longer Home Secretary by the end of 1967, and indeed had not yet been appointed Home Secretary when the death penalty was suspended, for contemporary moralists and those with long memories, Jenkins was the villain of the piece; the man who started the rot that destroyed the nation's moral fibre. It is difficult to see how liberalising legislation against a small and then unthreatening minority of between 2 and 5% of the population could be held to be the road to Sodom and Gomorrah. There was nothing that essentially disturbed the peace of the bulk of British citizens going about their daily family lives. That would come later. Divorce law reform was much more significant and far reaching in its effect.

However, the legalisation of homosexuality was not instantly liberating. As has been said, if one reads the language of debate, for many of those in favour of tolerance, homosexuality was still an abomination and still a disease rather like leprosy. Toleration was granted only on the basis that this particular breach of the moral code did not merit the attention of the courts as it was not necessary for minimisation of harm. Equality was not the intention of the act. Moreover, the new law restricted tolerance to consenting adults in private, and then only two. Gay men could still be prosecuted for group sex, and the age of gay consent was 21, which at the time equated to the age at which citizens obtained the franchise. Sexual activity in public remained unlawful for both sexes, not unreasonably as we are not describing a spectator sport. Thus gay men continued to be prosecuted, particularly for "cottaging" in public toilets and rather less frequently for group activity. Indeed prosecutions for gay sex offences actually increased in the immediate aftermath of the 1967 Act. Ancient laws forbidding licentious dancing were used to close down gay clubs and prosecute offenders. As well as the remaining rigour of the law, there was also public policy. Those whose sexuality was discovered or suspected were usually discharged discreetly from the army, albeit without a suitable testament to their conduct, rather than court martialled. Shrewd employers are well aware that any conduct rating below "very good" for someone leaving the armed forces is suspect. After the various spy scandals of the '50s and '60s, suspected homosexuals had no future in anything remotely connected to the secret services. I recall that, in 1975, a teacher was dismissed when he declared his homosexuality. This became a cause celebre within the National Union of Students. However, in the teacher training institutions, assuming that my own was typical, student teachers were uncomfortable with gay men in the classroom, thus adding paedophilia to bestiality as an additional vice attributed to homosexuals.

The press appeared to get particular pleasure out of homosexuals who either broke the law or were deemed unlikely to have any chance of a successful libel action. Ironically, prior to legalisation, famous men who happened to be homosexual could successfully withstand press allegations. In 1959 American entertainer Liberace successfully sued the Daily Mirror. Even after legalisation the press remained remarkably reticent for a number of years. Labour MP Tom Driberg was a notorious cottager yet the press deferentially made no mention of his behaviour until after his death in 1976. Jeremy Thorpe's homosexuality was also no secret to journalists and only Private Eye, in 1974, breached the tacit embargo. The voting public did not have a clue. This would all swiftly change. The sensational trial of Jeremy Thorpe, Liberal Party leader 1967-77, for conspiracy to murder his alleged former gay lover, Norman Scott, effectively allowed open season when Mr Thorpe's barrister conceded his client's previous homosexual inclinations. The "red top" coverage was never less than lurid. The trial took place during the 1979 General Election campaign and Mr Thorpe refused to stand down as a candidate. Despite his acquittal, his majority of over 6,000 in North Devon, which he had represented since 1959, was overturned and replaced by a Tory majority of over 8,000. It is impossible to say with any accuracy what the effect of his admitted homosexuality, or at least bisexuality, had on the result. Jeremy Thorpe's credibility was already damaged by a financial scandal and in any event the Liberals did badly nationwide, probably not forgiven by voters for the "Lib-Lab" pact which propped up the Callaghan government. Nevertheless, on the basis of an admission in the trial, 1979 was the first General Election in which there was an openly gay male candidate. It is unarguably true that the swing against Jeremy Thorpe was well above average.

The next time homosexuality intruded upon elections was in the bitterly contested by-election at Bermondsey in 1983. This time the Liberal Party was the beneficiary. Labour selected Australian born gay activist Peter Tatchell as their candidate. To say that the atmosphere was febrile would be an understatement in post-Falklands Britain. For the right wing press, Peter Tatchell's selection was a gift, allowing them to portray the candidate as a sexually degenerate Trotskyist who symbolised everything that was wrong with the Labour Party that could safely be labelled unpatriotic, unmanly and unelectable. The treatment dished out on a personal level to Peter Tatchell was nothing short of a disgrace. However, it cannot be denied that the moribund Bermondsey Labour Party had been easily infiltrated by ultra left elements, which had changed its stance from condemning the Labour party and ignoring it from the point of view of revolutionary social change, to one of "entryism". In the years that followed, Neil Kinnock declared war on the visible, noisy Trots of the Militant Tendency, but quietly, beneath the surface, the infiltration of the party and other key citadels of power outside parliament, was taking place. After 1997, they would surface like a fleet of previously undetected submarines. As for the Liberal party, it fought the by-election in the no holds barred manner that became its trademark in such contests, and also behaved with breathtaking hypocrisy, as it eventually emerged many years later that the victor at that election, Simon Hughes, was bi-sexual on his own admission .Mr Hughes remains in parliament to this day. One can only speculate, but it seems likely that the long term concealment of his sexuality from the public, if not from his party, ensured that he would never be its leader.

Homosexuality also intruded briefly on the 1987 election, although in this case the candidate stood down. Harvey Proctor had been MP firstly for Basildon and then for Billericay since 1979. He was a hard line right winger in most respects, but ironically enough was an early supporter of a Freedom of Information Act. Proctor had been hit in 1986 by a Sunday newspaper story of his penchant for spanking under age rent boys, the age of gay consent at the time still being 21. He was duly prosecuted the following year. Proctor pleaded guilty and stood down from parliament, and disappeared thence into well merited obscurity. Peter Tatchell would find himself rehabilitated as the climate changed, but given his bravery in protesting against the persecution of gays in Zimbabwe and Russia, at considerable personal risk, he emerges as a man of principle, even if you reject the agenda, and I am confident that most of us reject an agenda that calls for the age of consent for sexual intercourse, straight or gay, to be reduced to the age of 14.

As the '80s wore on, there was no escape from homosexuality in the press as the "AIDS" storm broke. The disease, originally known as GRID (Gay Relative Immunodeficiency Syndrome) was first identified in 1981. The original title was swiftly replaced by AIDS, but it is now more usual to describe sufferers as HIV positive. Despite the name change, the original colloquial name was the Gay Plague. Its translation into public consciousness provoked no little hysteria. In my own profession, the prison service, there was a high level of ignorance of the disease. I can recall staff demanding protective clothing and for medical confidentiality to be abandoned when admitting HIV positive prisoners. As well as being a touch hysterical, it was also impractical. There was no guarantee that prisoners would be aware that they had the disease, or even minded to disclose it. My other particular memory of the time is the huge official efforts that were expended in countering any notion that AIDS was restricted in the main to active homosexuals and intravenous drug users. Despite the very low incidence of transmission amongst the heterosexual population, there was a deluge of propaganda warning straight men and women about the dangers of promiscuity and unprotected sex. The condom became the symbol of our age. Trendy young professionals, who had not been noted for their love of barrier methods, submitted themselves for AIDS tests as the ultimate pre-nuptial ritual. It must be conceded that in Africa, AIDS is as much a disease of the heterosexual population as it is of the gay male population. There are studies to suggest that there is an intrinsic factor in the vaginal walls of African women, but there is also a more prosaic explanation. Using anal penetration as an alternative method of contraception is fraught with danger.

In one sense I can understand why in the western world we were fed blatantly untruthful propaganda about this disease. It would not have been the mark of a civilised society to go back in time to an era when gay men and gay sex were demonised. It would not have been the mark of a civilised society to create what would have effectively been leper colonies and deny sick people who posed little or no threat to the general population their civil rights. It would not have been the mark of a civilised society to create a climate in which religious ranters about divine retribution got an attentive hearing. All of this is fair and reasonable, but it is important to understand that part of My Generation's agenda in power was to adopt the politically correct gay agenda laid down by the Post Marxist thinkers of the original Gay Liberation Front, founded in the USA in 1969 after the Stonewall riots in Greenwich Village, New York, whose rise and subsequent influence roughly coincides with the baby boomers' university years. It needs to be emphasised that the agenda of the GLF, as it is of Stonewall today, goes far beyond civil rights. GLF proclaimed heterosexuality to be a remnant of cultural inhibition. Social institutions had to be dismantled and rebuilt without sexually defined roles. GLF attacked the traditional nuclear family and traditional gender roles. Thus, one can see that they are the ideological first cousins of feminists. I am clear that homosexuality is not of itself inimical to the family; it is the militant gay activists and their allies who have infiltrated the professions and positions of power and influence, who pose the ongoing threat to our social stability. The intellectual children of Gramsci have come into their inheritance.

Identifying the tipping point precisely at which homosexuality gained wider acceptability is difficult. What is the case is that our society is dramatically less prejudiced against gays than it was 40 years ago. We have reached a point where 54% of those polled now find gay marriage in church acceptable, whereas back in 1967 only 12% of those surveyed found homosexuality even tolerable. It is rare that public opinion runs ahead of liberalisation of the law. A key factor has to be the retreat from Christian sexual mores which itself is part of a religious decline dating from the mid 1950s which has accelerated over the last 25 years. The evidence can be found in the decline of church attendance. For the Roman Catholic Church, the decline came later, but the dramatic trend was the same. The almost entirely Catholic Republic of Ireland went through the same phenomenon. If the Almighty is no longer heard to condemn gay sex, it is logical that the broad community will not do so. The vast majority of people no longer participate in a weekly service where the priest or vicar tells them sexual expression outside of heterosexual marriage is wrong and sinful. Active churchgoing Christianity is now very much a minority pursuit, perhaps even more so than gay sex. Those that do attend are much less likely to hear fire and brimstone sermons from traditionalist clergy as priests with liberal views on homosexuality are now a significant force in the Church of England.

Opposition to the gay agenda switched its emphasis to the threat to the family. The infamous "Clause 28", prohibiting the promotion of homosexuality in schools as part of a pretended family relationship, was actually tacked on to a Local Government bill. An argument based on Christian morality would not have had the same weight as 20 years previously, but the threat to the family from sex education in general, and gay sex education in particular, was argued successfully in both the House of Commons and the House of Lords by family campaigners such as Jill Knight MP from the traditional right of the Conservative Party. Whether their opposition to gay sex education for children was based on an intimate intellectual understanding of the deeper Gay Rights agenda, opposition to the sexualisation of children, or from a thinly disguised anti-gay prejudice, would necessitate an in depth study of the speeches in the parliamentary debate. The Conservative government of that era was not noted for its intellectuals.

That the Conservatives were not switched on to the agenda is demonstrated by the way that gay fostering and then adoptions slipped under the national political radar. Taken piece-meal, much of the Gay Rights agenda is unexceptional and, indeed, would be readily conceded by all except those with strong religious objections and the few genuine homophobes who simply hate anyone who is different. Few would object to gays being able to take their place openly in the community, to protection from discrimination on the grounds of sexuality, and to the right to live in peace with one's neighbours and work colleagues. Although civil partnerships introduced in 2004 raised a few eyebrows, they allow gays to make binding commitments with their fellow human beings and to protect property and assets in a way that was not previously open to them, as the law did not even recognise gay relationships to the limited extent that it took note of cohabiting unmarried couples. It is ironic that conservative arguments about protecting property were deployed as part of what is in reality a revolutionary agenda. With the Church of England already successfully infiltrated and the public for the most part apathetic, the way is open for gay marriage in church. This can appear outwardly confusing given the professed secularism of the gay adherents of Comrade Gramsci. Ultimately, this will destroy the Church of England as we know it, and this is the real objective. Legislation for secular gay marriage in 2013, which has followed remarkably swiftly behind the legislation for civil partnerships, is the gateway. The Catholic Church has even less room for manoeuvre as it does not have anything like the same capacity for doctrinal flexibility given the doctrine of papal infallibility. Catholic adoption societies simply closed rather than allow gay couples to adopt children in Catholic orphanages, but it can hardly close its churches. Putting aside briefly the revolutionary agenda, how much this matters depends on the extent to which a successful society needs a moral underpinning that derives from religion. Nevertheless, what can be said with confidence is that gay marriage will not be demanded of Islam.

Gay adoptions are the visible part of the revolutionary agenda. They are also the point at which the man or woman in the street, who has no issue whatsoever with an individual's sexuality, unfamiliar with Gramsci, unfamiliar with the war aims of the GLF, tends to draw the line. Except that they dare not do so publicly as organisations such as Stonewall and their supporters amongst the elite, have in the same way as anti-racists have with immigration, stifled any debate by controlling the language and aggressively policing the boundaries, smearing those who challenge their domain with insults such as homophobe or racist. Legitimate criticism of the Gay Rights agenda is rebutted in the same crude sub-intellectual way that Islamists rebut all legitimate criticism of Islam as the start of a modern crusade and label critics as "Islamophobic". When the homophobic (literally translated fear of homosexuality) label doesn't work, then the high priests of political correctness will accuse their opponents of latent homosexuality. It's all very neat and circular. Thus, debate is closed down and political correctness enters the mainstream as challenging it puts livelihoods and reputations at risk. Freedom of expression is a key casualty of this revolutionary war as a totalitarian environment is gradually created. The real threat of gay adoptions is to the nuclear family. Its proponents, like their feminist allies, have a hatred of heterosexual men and see the family as the private power base of the counter revolution. Individually, and collectively, gay people do not threaten the family, but the revolutionary gay activists do. The demonisation of heterosexual men and the traditional attributes of masculinity are the sine qua non of a new society that is feminised and homosexualised. The so called "metrosexual" and his illusory predecessor, the "new man", are the glossy advertising hoarding for this not very brave new world.

Revolutionary gay activists will claim that they have not yet achieved equality. As has been said, that is not their real aim. The word "equality" is deployed on the basis that it is considered to be the mark of a moral defective to oppose it. This results in deliberate intellectual marginalisation. There is actually evidence to support an argument that Gay Rights has achieved a position in excess of equality and now has privileges. The position of the Christian hoteliers, who lost a discrimination case against two gay men having denied them a hotel room on the basis that they were not married, is instructive. I have no quarrel with the judgement which stripped away the biblical fig-leaf used to conceal prejudice. The hoteliers were clearly discriminating irrationally in terms of the provision of goods and services. The law has not unreasonably put Leviticus in his box and decoupled buggery and bestiality. Two things, however, do concern me; firstly, an unmarried heterosexual couple would have no legal redress against being turned away by the hotelier and, secondly, the Commission for Equality and Human Rights provided financial and legal support for the complainants, and until wiser councils prevailed were prepared to back an appeal in order to seeker a higher level of damages. Thus, there is clear discrimination against straight couples on the one hand and on the other CEHR provides alternative non-means tested legal aid for its pet causes. This is not a level playing field.

The same pattern can be determined with regard to what are perceived as "hate crimes". On the face of it, focussing the attention of the police on offences that take place against minorities such as gays and BME people is laudable. Crimes known colloquially as "queer bashing" and "Paki bashing" have no place in a civilised and tolerant society and it is right that the law bears down on ignorance and prejudice. However, once again the law is applied partially rather than impartially. The Public Order Act can, and should, be used against gangs of youngsters terrorising streets or estates. However, we know that a Leicestershire Police Superintendent believes that "anti-social behaviour" which is criminality pure and simple is a matter for the council. That attitude cost Fiona Pilkington and her daughter their lives. The Public Order Act has been used against an eccentric Christian preacher in Bournemouth who used his platform to deplore homosexuality. At the level below the criminal law, teachers are encouraged to pounce on schoolyard name calling that bears the slightest taint of homophobia, despite the fact that very young children are using words they don't understand and cannot possibly be considered to have an identity in terms of sexuality. Contrast this with the inability of many schools to get to grips with bullying. Suddenly "boys will be boys" and "girls will be girls".

Very much below the parapet is another arena of privilege for gays: Her Majesty's Prisons. It is necessary to qualify my forthcoming remarks by making it clear that homosexuality and lesbianism have long been practiced in prisons. Sadly, an un-measurable proportion of this homosexuality occurs under duress and some of this goes as far as outright rape. What occurred and continues to occur is an inevitable by-product of confinement which lawfully takes people away from their husbands, wives and partners. It is also an inevitable by-product of an environment in which anything not legitimately available comes at a cost. Sexual services are a currency. Selling your arse is a means of acquiring drugs or tobacco for those with no external resources who lack a high place in the prison pecking order. On the face of it, this tawdry existence cannot be described as privileged. However, if your orientation is firmly gay, then your lot is very much improved. Prison governors no longer have the power to prevent the issue of condoms to prisoners. When the senior medical officer was an employee, and therefore subordinate to the in-charge governor, there the matter rested. However, since prison healthcare was contracted out to Primary Care Trusts, prison governors have no say in the matter. In custody, homosexuality has therefore been medicalised. Although the reason for the issuing of condoms is to prevent the spread of HIV, a prison cell or for that matter a prison shower facility, are not private places as defined by the 1967 Act. Indeed the 2003 Sexual Offences Act, while it abolished the strictly gay offence of gross indecency, continued to forbid sexual relations in public, a proscription applying to both gay and straight people. PCTs are therefore accessories to unlawful activity.

The general public may be surprised to learn that there is actually no direct means of charging a prisoner under Prison Rule 51, the prison disciplinary code. This is because the disciplinary offence "is indecent in act, language or gesture," is no longer provided for under Rule 51. The reason for this is that the specifically gay male criminal offence of gross indecency was abolished in 2003. The only offences against the code which offer the potential of disciplinary action is paragraph 23 "disobeys any rule or regulation," or more usually paragraph 20 "uses any threatening, abusive or insulting behaviour." However, for the former to succeed, the governor must publish a specific Governor's Order forbidding homosexual acts. In our politically correct times, no prison governor could expect to survive above a further 48 hours in office if he or she did so. Yet on the other side of the coin, quite properly prison governors enact local rules against sexual touching in the visits room, and therefore charges under Rule 51 can be laid. There is, of course, the option to refer the matter to the police. It goes without saying that no police officer would risk his career any more than would a prison governor.

Instead the prison service has moved in the opposite direction. In its guidance to staff on the disciplinary code it recommends the use of paragraph 20 thus defining public sexual acts as insulting behaviour, but says that disciplinary charges should not be laid if prisoners are in bed together during the night as they are entitled to a degree of privacy! I stress this is not confidential official information. I found it without difficulty on the internet. Interestingly, there is potential for the dice to be loaded even further. The previous Director General, Phil Wheatley, won an argument with ministers in that a prisoner's cell was to be treated as his/her home, which allowed prisoners to retain the privilege of smoking in their cells when smoking prohibitions were radically extended in 2006, an issue to which I shall return. This leaves clear wriggle room for Stonewall and a smart lawyer, although the de facto legalisation that I have described above is likely to be left undisturbed in the current climate. The other danger in a cell being treated as a private place is that searching would require a warrant.

There is also anecdotal evidence to suggest that poor behaviour in the work place by gay people is either condoned or attracts a lesser sanction. My former profession the prison service, which I joined in 1984, was historically a safe haven for lesbian staff when compared to other professions. The prison service was one of the few walks of life in which lesbians could be open about their sexuality, on the face of it healthy and progressive. Consequently, they were disproportionately represented amongst female staff. Until 1988, female uniformed staff did not work in male establishments and vice versa. The prison service in those days was also heavily influenced by a military ethic which saw bullying through the prism of the weak character of the unfortunate recipient, rather than as an inevitable by-product of the macho culture. These factors combined ensured that female establishments were dominated by a gay culture in which bullying could flourish. Despite cross sex postings and a huge change in the ethos of the service, lesbian bullying remains an issue in some large establishments, HMPPentonville being the most recent high profile example. The service elected to tiptoe around the matter with extreme caution, for fear of disturbing a hornet's nest of political correctness and unleashing a tide of litigation. On the other hand, being an openly gay man in the service was exceptionally difficult given a military ethic that was adamantly opposed to male homosexuality. This too has changed for the better, but has also unleashed the gay male sex pest. Again, whereas the straight sex pest is treated with zero tolerance and often assumed guilty until proven innocent, the gay sex pest is at least partially protected by political correctness. In recent years the prison service chose to pay off a very senior gay male sex pest when the individual concerned could and should have been dismissed without compensation. The case is widely known through the service and sends a very ambiguous message to staff and trade unions about the reality of its commitment to eradicating workplace bullying. These are only a few examples of the moral inversion and relativism spawned by what is a revolutionary agenda.

It must be remembered that gay rights exist only where a cultural boundary is not crossed. In January 2006 Sir Iqbal Sacranie, one time General Secretary of the Muslim Council of Gt. Britain, expressed his distaste for civil partnerships, his view that homosexuality was wrong, and also said that gays spread disease. Was he prosecuted under the Public Order Act for "words likely to cause alarm, distress or harassment thereby?" Was he deprived of his knighthood? Has he ceased to be a fully paid up member of the great and the good who reign over us? Has he ceased to be one of the most influential men in the UK? Naturally none of these things occurred. This must be a real comfort to gay men in the Islamic community, as it must to gays in the Traveller community where homosexuality is equally despised. Thus, acceptance of sexuality depends on the colour of your skin and cultural background. Correct me if I am wrong, but isn't this the racial discrimination that My Generation affected to fight. I should add that the police did investigate (but did not arrest or take DNA from) Sir Iqbal under the 1986 Public Order Act. The Act was not designed to deal with thought crimes and restrict freedom of expression so quite properly Sir Iqbal was not prosecuted, but as we know the same consideration is not necessarily extended to all citizens. Not only is freedom of speech under assault, so also is equality before the law. The black community is also less tolerant of homosexuality than the indigenous population. The courts will not deport those who claim to be gay to Jamaica and some African countries.

Contrast the treatment of Sir Iqbal Sacranie with that of Dr Hans Christian Raabe who was removed from his position on the Drugs Advisory Council in February 2011, when his association with academic work linking homosexuality and paedophilia was disclosed. Speaking personally, I don't regard paedophilia as capable of being divided into gay and straight; it is simply a perversion. On that basis I don't believe that statistics that purport to claim that homosexuals are more inclined to child molesting than heterosexuals takes us anywhere helpful in terms of expanding human knowledge. However, it must be said that the radical gay agenda to reduce the age of consent to 14 makes it a soft target for this kind of science. Nevertheless, as a supporter of academic freedom I am clear that Dr Raabe's association with this esoteric branch of science is not sufficient grounds to remove him from an area of work which is almost wholly unrelated and one in which he has demonstrable expertise; substance addiction.

Feminism has had a place in public consciousness longer than gay rights, if only because women are obviously more numerous than gays. Its threat to the family has always been more overt. Our politically correct masters hate the traditional nuclear family of mother and father married to each other, living under their own private roof with their children. Naturally they make exceptions for their own family. Almost all of the major politicians of the New Labour ascendancy from Gordon Brown,

Tony Blair and John Prescott through to the feminist wing of Harriet Harman and Patricia Hewitt are conventionally married with children and without a divorce between them. Our leaders from the next generation who worship in the same temple of political correctness are, now that Ed Miliband has joined them, also married with families. Despite the preferred bourgeois respectability of the elite of My Generation, it has waged war against the conventional family. As I have pointed out in an earlier chapter, in New Labour the male politicians are the ones who wear the pseudo-intellectual pinnies, (John Prescott definitely excepted) having adopted feminism without stopping to consider its essential contradictions and the damage this philosophy has wrought on the class it was formed to represent.

The central tenet of feminism is that society is patriarchal and is inherently oppressive to women. Therefore, women are always victims. To feminists, patriarchy restricts female autonomy to boundaries controlled by men. They are oppressed by child rearing, by male violence and sexual demands, and by male control of the economic levers. Women are unable to achieve their potential. The vehicle of oppression is the nuclear family. So how accurate a picture does the feminist paint?

It cannot be denied that women suffered from significant legal disabilities as compared to men as we embarked on the industrial era. A series of Contagious Diseases Acts passed in the 1860s to control the spread of venereal disease in naval ports and garrison towns rendered any woman liable to be seized, forcibly examined, and if found to be infected, compulsorily confined for treatment. Soldiers and sailors meanwhile could continue to roger with impunity. After a campaign led by Josephine Butler, these Acts were repealed in 1886. Male suffrage was enhanced gradually from its upper class base through a series of reform acts; 1832, 1867, 1884 and finally in 1918 the property qualification was abolished and universal male adult suffrage arrived. The same year women could vote for the first time ever, but the franchise was restricted to women over 30. This was not amended until 1928 when women finally got the vote on the same basis as men. A woman's property was forfeit to her husband on marriage. It took the two Married Women's Property Acts of 1870 and 1882 to rectify this situation and give a married woman a separate legal identity to her husband with access to the courts. Only in 1925 was the law of intestate primogeniture, which automatically awarded an intestate widow's property to her eldest son, repealed.

In 1937, women gained equal legal status with men in divorce cases in that they could now also sue on the basis of adultery, previously a male privilege. During the early part of the 20th century, women gained access to the medical profession as doctors and to study at university on the same basis as men. The convention that a woman resigned from professions such as teaching or the civil service on marriage disappeared with the onset of World War II. By the middle of the 20th century women had full political and legal equality, and had full access to the professions, except the clergy of the established church, which came later. In that sense the traditional liberal agenda of legal and political equality had been delivered. The major remaining battle was for equal pay in the workplace. This was (and is) a battle that had to be fought almost exclusively in the private sector.

However, modern feminism is not liberal. Liberals and liberal feminists did not analyse power relationships. Modern feminists perceived the liberal values of rationality, self-determination and equal competition as male, as opposed to the female values of empathy, nurturing and co-operation, a generalisation I shall return to in due course. Post modernism, which now dominates the academic world, is a reaction against the post enlightenment faith in rationality and progress, so as academic thinking with its implicit relativism, it creates the perfect climate for radical feminism which deals in emotion rather than logic, assertion rather than argument, and denunciation rather than discourse. For Marxists, the position of women must be understood in terms of capitalism and class, which over time replaced agrarian feudalism and caste. For orthodox Marxists, gender conflict will always be subordinate to class conflict. To get gender conflict on the table as a primary concern rather than one that would miraculously be sorted come the revolution, feminists have to commit heresy as regards the great teacher and lo! we have Post or Neo-Marxism to re-interpret Marx for an industrial society, (and beyond to a post-industrial society) that steadfastly refuses to overthrow capitalism, despite its recurrent crises. However, Marx and Engels re-interpreted do not help us with female oppression in non-industrialised societies, not that the modern New Labour feminist cares a damn about women forced to endure the burqa, arranged marriages or female circumcision,because this would be cultural imperialism. White educated middle class post -modern feminism is irrelevant to the lives of ethnic minority women. It should be remembered that re-interpreting Marx is not new. Lenin contributed the elite that pilot the revolution (ringing any bells), and Mao gave us revolution through the peasants, long thought to be a non-revolutionary class.

For radical feminists, the sex war is fundamental and it is a revolutionary war. It is one that in many respects they are winning. As with radical gay rights campaigners, the agenda is not widely understood. Just as reasonable people are opposed to unfair discrimination against gays, they are opposed to unfair discrimination against women, not least because most families need two incomes and an absence of equal pay provisions would hit the family exchequer. Only unreconstructed Neanderthals expect women to be banished to the kitchen. I would not know how many women would describe themselves as feminists, but I would be confident that most of those who make the claim do so in respect of an agenda of legal and economic equality, sexual freedom, and equality of opportunity at work. All women, whether feminists or not, would expect legal protection from violence and rape, which is another battleground. As has been said, for radical feminists, legal equality and equality of opportunity are important only in that they were stepping stones, or to use the language of the Viet-Cong, transitional demands. The workplace remains an important battleground, the education system has been insidiously infiltrated, but the cockpit of the battle is the nuclear family. Women can only be truly emancipated when the two parent nuclear family is destroyed. In brief, for radical feminists the nuclear family sustains male dominance and male power which is reinforced by violence and control of financial resources. It is perpetuated through these values being passed down the male line. Childbirth confines the mother to the home which further reinforces dependence on the father. The radical feminist engages in a reverse misogyny. Thus, we have the critique and we have the ideal. All that is needed is a programme and the capture of the citadels of power so that it can be implemented. My Generation captured the House of Commons in 1997, but it has also taken over to a greater or lesser extent other estates of the realm. Feminism and the other "isms" that make up the lexicon of political correctness now dominate all the major public sector services such as the emergency services, the correctional services, the health service, social services and local government. The BBC has pretty well been taken over, the Church of England is in thrall, and mastery of the universities is all but achieved. Even Conservative newspapers such as the Daily Mail find themselves, perhaps unwittingly, propagating parts of the feminist agenda. Even the military has not been immune, as radical feminists seek to re-define masculinity in their own image.

Radical feminism is an ideology without intellectual content. It is mired in contradiction, has no appreciation of biology, evolution and history, and is traduced by the aggressive heterosexuality of many of its adherents. Germaine Greer's "The Female Eunuch" was a seminal and hugely influential work. It brought feminism close to the mainstream. However, The Female Eunuch is not a work of great intellectual merit; it is in fact a brilliant polemic, possibly the finest ever written. Professor Greer was unabashed about her promiscuity. Indeed, during her time as a rather more junior lecturer at Warwick University in the early '70s she was reputedly prepared to sleep with any male member of the university, in return for being permitted to post a public record of the man's sexual prowess and performance. In fairness, it must be said that heterosexual feminists generally recoil from promiscuity, and Professor Greer has herself recanted. In any event post-pill promiscuity amongst the chattering classes and the denizens of "swinging London" must be seen through the prism of a more buttoned up and sexually conservative society which invited rebellion. Feminists do not wish to be reminded about some of their number wanting to shag on the same basis as men. The point to take from this paragraph is that heterosexual feminists cannot live without men. They have to make their accommodation. Heterosexual feminism is brilliantly satirised in David Lodge's novel, "Nice Work". The central character, Robyn Penrose, is a feminist university teacher who lives with her male partner. During her time as a student, she progressed rapidly from virginity to promiscuity and thence to monogamy but, having progressed to the Senior Common Room, insists that their sexual relationship is non-penetrative. As part of a mutual understanding project between the University of Rummidge (based loosely on Birmingham) and local industry, she shadows the Neanderthal (in her eyes) Vic Wilcox, Managing Director of a local engineering firm. Despite having contempt for all that he espouses, Penrose sleeps with Wilcox, who is a married man, on a foreign trip. They have full sexual intercourse, although she insists on going on top. Penrose could neither stay her curiosity nor defy her intrinsic sexuality, any more than could Professor Greer. In the 1993 TV adaptation the lead characters were superbly played by Hayden Gwynne and Warren Clarke.

Nevertheless, poking fun at feminists for needing to fuck like anybody else, serves only to scratch the surface of their destructive ideology. Fundamentally, they do not understand biology and evolution. I am obliged to Melanie Phillips' book "The Sex Change Society" (1999) for giving intellectual clarity to those of us who wish to carry the fight to radical feminism. The union of man and woman in marriage is fundamentally a bargain; a finely defined equilibrium of sexual, biological and emotional considerations. Marriage gives a man regular sex, love and companionship, and the ability to pass down his genes. Although pre-marital chastity is no longer observed in our society, most women do not have sex with any available man. Firstly, a promiscuous woman, however desirable she is for a one night stand, offers no guarantee of exclusivity to potential mates, which is essential if the male is to be sure that he is the father of the children he brings up. This is why women will underplay their sexual experience when Mr Right comes along. However sexually liberated a woman may consider herself to be, sex is withheld from unsuitable men, those not seen as strong enough to protect and provide, those whose genes appear weak, or those whom a woman simply prefers as a friend without emotional complications. Inevitably some women have to take what is left. Once the woman has successfully competed for a suitable mate, she will want the union formalised. Male promiscuity is constrained by an unspoken bargain with other men in his circle that each other's wives and girlfriends are off limits. As with choosing a woman with a limited bedroom track record, this offers the certainty a man seeks that he is the father of the children he supports. This is why men are critical of Ryan Giggs for having a clandestine affair with his brother's wife, rather than his adultery with a two bit reality TV trollop. Giggs breaking his marriage vows is human weakness that need not have threatened his marriage, whereas screwing his brother's wife breaks the rules of male fraternity. Let me be clear that my short analysis of the Giggs affair owes nothing to Melanie Phillips and I would not wish to imply that she would agree with it.

Melanie Phillips is clear that the bargain between the sexes is cross cultural. It has a history going back to pre-historic times. Men are breadwinners, women are nurturers. Feminists fundamentally object to male breadwinning, which they see as demeaning and evidence of skewed power in a relationship. However, feminists do not object to breadwinning when a marriage has broken up. Their hypocrisy, combined with John Major's government's desire to reduce welfare bills, led directly to the founding of the Child Support Agency. The legislation that brought in the CSA can fairly be compared to medieval Acts of Attainder, the only difference is that the family is beheaded rather than the individual. As Melanie Phillips says, "Feminists are caught between their desire to do without men and their desire to make men pay for their children. The latter opinion of course means admitting that the mother's independence is a myth." This succinctly encapsulates the feminist contradiction. It would be obvious to any visiting extra-terrestrial that women nurture the children. It begins with breast feeding for which female mammals are uniquely equipped. Pregnancy and the bond it creates are unique to the female of the species. One only has to read the tortured accounts of women who would like to spend much more time with their children, but cannot because their career has greater priority. In the small but increasing number of families where the man stays at home to bring up the children, it is often resented by women who cannot deep down handle the role reversal. They are either highly critical of their man's parenting skills, or losing respect for him for ceasing to be masculine, or both. Few men and few women can truly defy biology. Role reversal of this nature heightens the risk of affairs and marriage breakdown. The cynic in me says that this would delight radical feminists, as it would remind women that role reversal in the nuclear family is a poor substitute for its destruction.

There is no satisfactory substitute for a fully functioning nuclear family. It provides love, companionship, support, and effectively socialises children. The nuclear family has proved remarkably adaptable since the dawn of time. Feminists are up against history as well as biology. None of this is to suggest that every nuclear family is perfect or that every single parent family, or family headed by gay parents is doomed to failure. Human beings are not perfect. I would not wish to pretend for one minute that there are not traditional two parent families in which there is domestic violence, sexual abuse or physical neglect. I would not wish to pretend for one minute that there are not traditional families where love is absent, one sibling is favoured above others, and where there is constant friction between the parents. I would also accept that what I have described can, and does, occur across the class divide. A high IQ does not guarantee emotional intelligence, any more than a low IQ would be an indicator of its absence. In my own family, my own father could not relate to me properly until I presented him with his first grandchild. In my teens I loathed him, as he could not understand that a grammar school education made a boy more questioning rather than more docile. However, take away the role model even with the flaws typical of working men of his generation, you take away the work ethic, the sense of duty, and the requirement to make the most of your talents passed down from father to son. You also deny daughters the opportunity to discover what real men should be like long before they meet their first boyfriend. The whole point of marriage is to nurture and protect the next generation. Fatherless families breed girls who reject committed relationships with men. On the other side of the coin, I would not wish to pretend that there are not single parents who do a superb job, and as a society we should be grateful for their efforts against the odds. We should also remember that single parenthood is not a new phenomenon, but historically was one that was created by death rather than by divorce.

What you have to do is look at families across the piece. There is indisputable evidence that, on all known indicators, children from traditional two parent families fare the best. They are better adjusted, less likely to be bullied, and have higher self-esteem. They do better at school, earn more in adult life, and take less illegal substances. They have less contact with the criminal justice system and are more likely to produce stable families when their own turn comes. These are facts born out repeatedly by respected academic surveys and they are not gainsaid by those children unfortunate enough to have two married useless or at least inadequate parents. Homogeneity is a general concept, not one with universal application. Feminists are obsessed with male violence and see the traditional family as a place where violence is institutional, condoned and suffered in silence. If your analysis is confined to a society where single parent families are a rarity, it is an argument that can be understood given the private nature of the traditional family, even if it is un-provable. However, the state supported single parent family much beloved of radical feminists is providing plenty of anecdotal evidence to suggest that the sink estates, where these families tend to congregate, are where male violence is at its most prevalent. Violence comes not from married men but from the serial baby-fathers who drift from woman to woman siring children that neither of them can afford without the welfare state. The violence is meted out mainly to step-children and the women either join in or stand idly by. The major child abuse cases showcased in the press are strong anecdotal evidence. The men are excluded from society by their criminality, substance abuse, poor education and general fecklessness. The women with their large broods by different fathers are little better. Watch ITV on a weekday morning and you can view these families on the Jeremy Kyle show without having to take the risk of being attacked by a pit-bull terrier on the estates where they live. Sadly, this condition is now inherited. The children may be born of woman, but they are also the bastard offspring of feminism.

According to Melanie Phillips, the families (if they can be called that) described above are the product of an absence of restraint. Men denied a meaningful role in society revert to a default promiscuity which manifests itself in the type of serial fatherhood with numerous low status female partners. The brakes are off sexually as well as socially. Women who indulge these men have thrown away their most important mating trump card; restraint. As such, they are left with the dregs. How did we get there? Feminism exploited the opportunities given to it by other social and economic developments. The decline of Christianity detailed earlier in this chapter is a key factor. The Christian churches taught chastity, abstinence and restraint. No comparable secular moral code has filled the vacuum. Feminists have taken full advantage of the decline of the established church and are busy accelerating it. Socially, the concept of shame has disappeared. I think few of us would want to see mothers of illegitimate children, as they were once stigmatised, wearing sackcloth and ashes or being sent to a Magdalene Laundry. However, I think most right thinking citizens would want to see released prisoners slink out of the gates in shame on release, rather than climb into a stretch limo and celebrate with champagne. A person who is not ashamed of wrongdoing operates in a moral vacuum.

A hugely significant liberalisation of the Divorce Laws was enacted in 1969, a subject to which I shall return later in this chapter. A year earlier, the contraceptive pill was first prescribed to unmarried women which gave a freedom never previously enjoyed and undreamt of a decade earlier. It took some time to take root amongst the wider female population. In the physical sense, it removed a key plank of the restraint to which Melanie Phillips refers. The grim irony is that the availability of the pill has little impact on the underclass, which theoretically should have benefited the most. Here economic factors come into play. A brood of illegitimate children entitles the mother to free housing and generous welfare benefits at the expense of the taxpayer. Instead of families supported by a father, we have families sponsored by the state.

The tax and benefit systems are skewed against the married family. Again, the dogma of equality and non-stigmatisation of alternative families is exposed for the myth that it is. The non-traditional family is the one with the privileges, as it is perceived to have victim status. Feminism has not given us women's liberation. Instead, at the lower levels of society, it has increased female dependence through what amounts to the nationalisation of the family. The traditional married family represents the hated private sector. This is the consequence of a proscription on male breadwinning by radical feminists.

Just as My Generation was beginning to make its way into positions of influence in our society, we had the dramatic decline in manufacturing which turned once vibrant communities into workless deserts. Fathers could no longer carry out their traditional role and were thus emasculated. Traditional male virtues of leadership, initiative and competitive spirit were nullified by the economic forces. Feminists seem to forget that whereas women are reminded of their femininity on a monthly basis, men have to construct a role of social value. This is achieved by work which grants status. Men had the option to leave their home area and many did, whilst others accepted their fate and stayed put, hoping for better times. When better times did come, jobs were usually much lower paid and more suitable for women. Sadly, male virtues were sometimes put to criminality as a means of prospering in a country which no longer valued them. This is extreme male risk taking. Even when a recovery of sorts came, rents and house prices went through the roof. The need for two incomes circumscribed male providing to a far greater extent than previously.

Thus, a complex cocktail of factors coupled with New Labour's victory in the 1997 election brought radical feminism to power. It has not used its victory wisely. Within New Labour there were those concerned about the wider social impact of welfare dependency on the nation's underclass. Tony Blair promised to think the unthinkable about welfare, and fortunately for him the party had an acknowledged expert, Frank Field. Did Mr Blair appoint Mr Field to the cabinet? No chance. He made him number 2 to radical feminist Harriet Harman, who blocked any meaningful change. Mr Field retreated to the backbenches in fairly short order. So during 13 years of Labour rule we continued to grow a workless, dependent underclass that struck fear into the neighbours as gangs of feral youths and drug dealers ruled the mean streets. As we saw in a case in the Whitebirk area of Blackburn, the girl gangs were equally terrifying, if not more so.

The feminisation of the education system must also take some of the blame. It is a feminist mantra that masculinity is inherently anti-social. Their answer is that masculinity is tolerated only on terms acceptable to feminists. This is why we have feminist teachers preventing boys from playing football, cowboys and Indians, and war games. In examinations, the rewards do not go to the risk takers, but to the diligent for whom continuous assessment methods are made; girls. Feminists expect boys to do dance in mixed sex PE classes rather than competitive sport. Male teachers are disappearing from primary schools almost in the way that teaching orders of nuns have done. Boys have to define their sexual identity by breaking away from the mother. The absence of the father and the feminisation of father figures in school had the effect of pushing boys, particularly those of low intelligence, towards extreme behaviour to reinforce masculinity. It has become the only way they can validate themselves. The inadequate socialisation of working class boys, a massive and growing social problem, can be laid firmly at the door of feminism. Radical feminists are actually responsible for a growth in male aggression and general anti-social behaviour. Our male children have become their hostages.

Over a 26 year career in the prison service I have seen at first hand the change in the young offender population. That change is the massively increased propensity to violence as the first resort. Permanent volatility now defines that population. The gang warfare now endemic amongst young black men is fought with once unimaginable violence. Amid the hand wringing, radical feminists still say that families do not need fathers. I regard their approach to the Caribbean community as bordering on racism. They need to have a long hard look at the ethnic Caribbean population of this country, which is precisely where the family with two parents married to each other is the least numerous and compare their attainments (or tragic lack of them) to the ethnic Chinese population, or any sector of the population where strong families and a strong moral code is the order of the day. Yet the feminists still plough on with their irrelevant and immoral agenda. IVF is now available to single women without a regular male partner and to lesbian couples not in civil partnerships, notorious for their instability. The only reason a father's name still has to appear on a birth certificate (if known) is so that he can be pursued for maintenance, not so that he can play a meaningful role in a child's upbringing. Lastly, do feminists have the first idea what they are doing to their own sex condemning them to a life without fathers? If they do, they don't care.

The seminal change in Britain's divorce laws, enacted in 1969, cannot be attributed to radical feminists. It is simply too early in our history. Nevertheless, it has been massively exploited by them. Again, I am obliged to Melanie Phillips for her intellectual clarity. Until the 1969 Act came into force there were only three grounds for divorce; adultery, cruelty and desertion. Breaches of marital obligations were clearly identified by the law, were well understood and commanded general assent. The pre-1969 Divorce Laws were an excellent example of a successful secular moral code. Divorce petitions were listed in local newspapers by the court reporter. They named the parties, indicated who was cruel or had bolted, and in adultery petitions, identified the co-respondent. The concept of fault was firmly embedded. Like any other form of contract law, there were penalties for those who breached it. Thus, a woman deserted by her husband could expect maintenance. A woman who left her husband could expect none, unless she had been forced to leave the marriage by virtue of his adultery or cruelty. The parties got what their behaviour merited.

Contrary to popular belief, the 1969 Act did not introduce "no fault" divorce. That had to wait until an Act passed in 1996, the relevant clauses of which have never been activated. However, the Act was radical nonetheless, especially when combined with the extension of legal aid. Divorce became a female phenomenon. A divorce could now be obtained unopposed if a couple had lived apart for five (later reduced to three) years, but much more significantly, a divorce could be obtained on grounds of unreasonable behaviour, which theoretically was set at being so intolerable that the petitioner could no longer be expected to live with the respondent. Six examples had to be given. Consider this list; plays golf every Saturday, is rude to the mother-in-law, was drunk at Christmas, farts too frequently, spends too much time at work, is boring. All of these examples have been used individually or in combination by women seeking divorces on numerous occasions and been accepted by the courts. It is pointless to oppose a petition, because it will be granted no matter how spurious the grounds. The bar of unreasonable behaviour has been set so low that you could crawl over it. What has happened is that the petitioner, in two-thirds of cases the women, can abrogate the marital contract on trivial grounds and be rewarded for it. The man will be expelled from a home he continues to pay for as well as being landed with a fortune in costs, while she gets legal aid.

Divorce laws redistribute income by legalised expropriation. The changes to the legal aid system since 2010 whereby legal aid is no longer available for divorce except where there is domestic violence or sexual abuse do not in any way alter this as an accurate summary. It only levels the playing field as regards proceedings, not the ultimate outcome. Furthermore the exemption for domestic violence and sexual abuse within a marriage opens the way for another American import, the smearing of a partner with untruthful allegations in order to obtain a more favourable settlement and the exclusion of the father from any children's lives, whose interests are frequently subordinate. The courts are totally biased in favour of the mother. She can make any allegation she wishes against the man and expect it to be believed. If the man cannot support his ex-wife and family, then the state will step in via the social security system. Thus, a woman's boredom, a woman's inability to negotiate within a relationship, a woman putting herself before the needs of her children is rewarded by the taxpayer. The essential moral underpinning of the Divorce Laws has been systematically shredded.

As has been said to the radical feminist, men are intrinsically violent. It is easy for them to point to war as evidence, but how does that explain female war leaders such as Boudicca, Golda Meir or Margaret Thatcher? More pertinently, how does it explain the cruelties perpetrated by female members of Roman nobility, or in the 20th century the appalling Irma Grese, or the loathsome Myra Hindley? How do they explain violent girl gangs? How do they explain female domestic violence? They either can't or blame it on men. Intellectually, they are snookered behind the black. Obviously men have the greater potential for causing physical harm. They are stronger and since time immemorial fighting has been a male duty to defend their homeland, their way of life, and believe it or not, feminists, their womenfolk. Outside of those circumstances, most men exercise remarkable self control. Those men who most often fail to exercise self control have lacked the father figure that our radical feminist friends say is unnecessary. If male violence is on the increase, feminists must take their share of responsibility. However, just because women have a lesser propensity to physical violence, it does not mean they are not capable of abuse. Women can and do wreck the esteem of their partners by psychological abuse. Belittling, nagging and making unreasonable demands are well recognised for what they are if they occur in the workplace; bullying. The ultimate nightmare for a man is the ultra needy woman. Unfortunately, they appeal to the chivalrous instinct in a man. The reality is no-one can make them happy and nothing he ever does is good enough. God help him if there are other ways he needs or wants to fill his time. Think of Princess Diana and you will recognise the type. It is the nearest any man gets to the fate of the male praying mantis. Only when the man in this situation is brave enough or sharp enough to realise that he is not the problem, is an escape route visible. The emotional scars are as lasting as any physical marks.

The fact that rape is a uniquely male crime (I am assuming that no women have been convicted of rape using a strap-on dildo) is deployed as their strongest card in their ongoing animus against men. The prevalence of gay rape is irrelevant as it is still male violence. No-one would pretend that rape does not occur and that it has a history as long as human kind. It is the ultimate violation. It is also a crime that shocks most men, the vast majority of whom understand the word "no". Amongst the criminal fraternity in our prisons, only paedophiles rank below rapists. Although I would accept that having someone below them in the pecking order is very welcome to prisoners, long experience tells me that most of them genuinely have the same contempt for sex offenders and their offences as the non-criminal population, the only difference being they are more likely to take the law into their own hands in a bid to dish out justice. In other words, standards of decency prevail even amongst some of our worst felons. It is virtually impossible to engage feminists in a rational discussion of rape. Even allowing for the emotional nature of the subject, a man can expect to be howled down by the representatives of the screeching sisterhood. It happened recently to the former Justice Secretary, Ken Clarke, although his own ineptitude and failure to master a brief made him the author of his own misfortune. For his junior minister to use rape as an example of how a 50% discount for a guilty plea was crass, and upset most of the population, not just the professional feminists.

One of the battlegrounds is the conviction rate, which all parties wish to raise. Even the Daily Mail peddles the line that only 6% of rapes result in conviction. This is a bogus statistic. Once a case comes to Crown Court, the conviction rate is comparable to any other indictable offence. The sad truth is that very many of the alleged rapes reported to the police are either not rapes at all, or stand no chance of passing the CPS threshold of a 50% chance of conviction. Nevertheless, a recent joint report by HM Inspectorate of Constabulary and HM Inspectorate of the Crown Prosecution Service criticised the extent and disparity between forces of the recording of rape allegations under the category, "No crime". Rape is not necessarily like burglary where the evidence is clear. Like any other offence it needs to be proved according to objective criteria and beyond reasonable doubt. Radical feminists take the view that if a woman says she has been raped, then she has. This is guilt by denunciation, an essentially totalitarian concept. However, a major change in the law which has allowed cases to go ahead where there is no corroborative evidence and it is one person's word against the other, takes feminists into the territory where guilt by denunciation can become a reality. What this change in the law has achieved is to reverse the burden of proof; a man is now guilty until proven innocent. It is allowing cases to come to court that are placing an awesome responsibility on juries, and judges are more or less compelled to let these trials go ahead. For the most part, juries are seeing through the flimsiness of prosecution cases and applying common sense. Juries will not allow, for instance, women to attempt to conceal their infidelities behind a smokescreen of alleged rape. Juries are not buying the notion that a woman who admitted willingly giving a man oral sex was later raped. Juries will not allow women to claim that they could not possibly have had consensual sex with a man because he is too ugly, a fact they only seem to discover the morning after when the effect of beer goggles has worn off. Juries have needed to be fully satisfied that a woman could not possibly have consented when drink is an issue. The tightening of the law as regards consent does not seem to be increasing the conviction rate, because juries are well aware of what is at stake when a man is on trial for rape. Juries are not fooled by a woman claiming that she couldn't possibly have slept with a man because he was only a friend, albeit a very close one. The verdicts of juries have quite rightly emphasised personal responsibility rather counterfeit victim-hood. All of the above relate to actual cases without naming the names of acquitted defendants, people who deserve anonymity denied them at the time. It is, of course, perfectly possible, that some of the juries got it wrong, and a rapist escaped justice. That would be extremely regrettable, but in a fully functioning criminal justice system, more guilty defendants will be acquitted than innocent defendants convicted.

However, in the case of Warren Blackwell, a miscarriage of justice waiting to happen actually occurred. In this case, a woman promptly reported a rape and identified Mr Blackwell. Despite their being no forensic evidence, the CPS went ahead. The police were too idle to check out her background. If they had, they would have discovered that she had a history of false sexual allegations. I'm not sure that the police have ever recovered from the 1980s documentary which showed the appalling disrespect given to women alleging rape. As a consequence, proper professional detachment is being put to one side. In the case of Warren Blackwell, only after he had served his sentence did these facts emerge and his conviction was quashed. This was a truly shocking case and a perfect example of what happens when essential safeguards in the justice system are eroded. I still have some difficulty believing that this case was ever prosecuted or that the judge did not stop the trial. What occurs in a case where there is no corroborative evidence is that it is often down to who has the best barrister, but even that is no insurance against convincing theatricals in the witness box as happened in the Blackwell case. Radical feminism sends innocent people to prison. In Mr Blackwell's case, consent was not the issue. It simply never happened. Stranger rape is still pretty rare. 80% of rape cases boil down to a dispute about consent between people who know each other. What seemed a good idea the night before often seems a bad one the next morning .There is nothing unusual about men and women having regrets, particularly where infidelity is involved. However, it is not the purpose of the legal system to purge the guilt a woman may feel for having a one night stand that may make her a short term topic of gossip at work or in the pub. The purpose of the law is to send men who demonstrate their hatred of women by violating them to prison. Every woman who cries rape, when it is nothing of the sort, is letting down her gender, because all they are doing is hardening the attitude of juries, thus encouraging violent men to believe they can commit rape with impunity. Radical feminism actually lets down women who have been raped.

I cannot close this chapter without commenting on the latest outburst of Professor Greer, who on question time on 9 June 2011, seemed to suggest that British troops could commit rapes in Libya. It is readily acknowledged that rape has been a weapon of war since wars began. Fundamentally, it is about imposing the seeds of the victors into those of the vanquished. This can only be done via the women. It is about conquest, perceived superiority and triumphalism. I emphasise that I am explaining not justifying. Recent examples can be found in the Rape of Nanking, the Soviet advance into Germany in 1945, and Srebrenica in 1995, where ethnic Serbs murdered Bosnian Muslim males and raped the women. The Congo is the rape capital of the world. What Professor Greer failed to grasp is that the examples above were officially sanctioned. British troops in Libya or Afghanistan are there under UN resolutions. The UN would never sanction rape. Professor Greer seems to think that the UN or the UK may do so, yet felt that the allegations that the Libyan dictator was giving his troops Viagra rations was propaganda. It may be, but what we have here is yet another example of a western liberal berating our own culture, but at the same time refusing to believe that a man who murders his own people is not capable of arranging for them to be raped. For the record Britain and the USA have always taken a strong stand against rape. During World War II, the Americans executed servicemen convicted of rape at the military prison in Shepton Mallet in Somerset. The British are also known in the same conflict to have executed troops convicted of rape by firing squad on the battlefields of France after a swift court martial. Ever pragmatic, the British did arrange for mobile brothels for the troops. It was helpful that brothel keeping was legal in France, and remained so until 1958. No doubt Professor Greer would have a view about that.

CHAPTER 18

TELEVISION AND CELEBRITY

The simplest definition of celebrity is "fame", which on the face of it is value free and merely a statement of fact. However, the reality is that the term is value laden. A celebrity is an individual to be celebrated, which implies merit. According to the dictionary a celebrity is popular, which can imply vulgarity but can also be someone of repute. A celebrity is also a "star" or even a "megastar", which implies a celestial status beyond that of ordinary mortals. Merit and popularity are not necessary conditions for each other and frequently exist independently. The word celestial is synonymous with heavenly, which takes us into the realms of the divine and implies worship. In this way celebrities move into the vacuum left by the decline in religious belief and observance.

The concept of celebrity would have had no meaning when Queen Victoria died in 1901. I cannot pin down a point at which the word became an integral part of the lexicon, but I can pin down the point at which the process began. Film made the first celebrities. Charles Chaplin was the first celebrity, created by celluloid as silent movies took hold of popular imagination at the beginning of the last century. It was the beginning of mass popular culture as we know it. Fatty Arbuckle would be the first to be destroyed by the sort of celebrity excesses that are now commonplace and easily forgiven by the individual's fan following, the strictures of socially conservative commentators going largely unheard or unread. Chaplin himself had to survive scandal and the McCarthy purge of suspected communists in the USA but his personal longevity and the outliving of all his contemporaries (Chaplin died on Christmas Day 1977 aged 88), conferred not only forgiveness but the historical status that was rightly his due. It is easy to underestimate the significance of the cinema between the wars, a significance it would only lose when television ownership became widespread from the mid '50s onwards. The cinema was a shared public experience. It provided a perfect escape mechanism from the drudgery of working life that was the lot of the bulk of the population. American film stars provided unattainable glamour and films like "Gone with the Wind" gained iconic status. Where Chaplin had led, Clark Gable and his contemporaries followed. As many films were love stories the route to stardom was open for women. Jean Harlow, Joan Crawford and Bette Davis all broke through in the 1930s and were admired and possibly even worshipped from afar. The new stars of film were popular not populist, they were remote figures tightly controlled by the industry moguls who ensured that off the set they mouthed only acceptable platitudes and this would not change until after the war. Film industry power brokers were also very vigilant for scandal. Many famous actors and actresses were sufficiently wealthy and socially secure to opt out of the very conservative morality that typified and still does typify small town America. Thus, their real private lives were artfully concealed. The public were not aware of the huge sexual appetites of Errol Flynn and Joan Crawford, and certainly not aware of the homosexuality of Randolph Scott, James Dean or Rock Hudson. Only after their deaths was the truth widely known. The industry absorbed rapid lessons from the demise of Arbuckle. Nothing must be allowed to intrude on the magic. To the contemporary observer, as much used to the baring of souls as the baring of breasts, this must seem alien. The truth is that virtual abolition of restraint and the blurring of boundaries between public and private lives, as in so many other walks of life has profoundly affected the acting profession. It is not just life in a see through goldfish bowl, it is one where life is one great archive open for unrestricted public consumption. On the face of it the exposure of false gods is a good thing. The reality is that the lack of restraint and the exposed human weaknesses of the modern deities of the screen, the stage and the soccer field, provide deeply flawed role models for young people and contribute to our ongoing social ills.

Following hard on the heels of the big screen were the gramophone and the television. The 78 RPM record would make a huge star out of Frank Sinatra in the 1940s and Elvis Presley in the 1950s. It would no longer be necessary to see your favourite singer live or sit by your radio all day in the hope of hearing his music. If you could afford a gramophone and afford to buy records, then you could listen to Sinatra or Presley to your heart's content. In this way you could by-pass the restrictions imposed on your access to popular culture. By the end of the fifties the 78 RPM record was replaced by the 45 RPM record and these could be played on a Dansette record player which was small enough to be perched on a desk. The wind up gramophones the size of a fridge, which occupied a corner of the house, followed the equally bulky wireless, replaced by the transistor radio in the sixties, into the antique shops. As has been noted earlier, record sales grew from around 4 million per year in 1955, to some 64 million singles sold in the peak year of 1965. It would take more than four decades and the advent of cheap digital downloading for that figure to be exceeded. The Beatles exploded on to popular culture in 1963. Prior to the Beatles, the biggest celebrities were almost universally American. British popular singers or actors were almost too much like the rest of us, too down to earth, too much like the boy or girl next door, with Diana Dors as the obvious exception. The mystique of Elvis Presley was only added to by his failure to tour the UK. The Beatles captivated America in 1964. On 4 April 1964, they achieved the unprecedented feat of holding all the top five positions in the Billboard hot 100. The following week the Beatles would have 14 singles in the American chart. Even Presley only managed nine at any one time. The Beatles would enjoy three consecutive number ones, uninterrupted by any other artist. Only Presley had previously succeeded himself at Number One, but even he could not manage the hat trick. These achievements in what is the biggest music market in the world remain unsurpassed. The influences on the Beatles and on acts such as the Rolling Stones and the Kinks who followed them into the pantheon were unashamedly American. The British acts brought American music home and established British cultural hegemony as Americans embraced British stars, recording studio, and screen for the first time.

There would be a price to pay for celebrity. John Lennon would ultimately pay with his life at the hands of an assassin in 1980 and George Harrison was fortunate to survive a knife attack in his own home in Henley on Thames over a decade later. Lennon had an unhappy habit of making himself a target of conservative America. In 1966 he was forced to issue a grovelling apology for remarks that appeared to indicate to conservative America that the Beatles were more important than Jesus Christ. The damage was done, despite Lennon's retraction. The Beatles were relieved to get out of America safely and would not play another live concert date again after 29 August 1966. The furore provided a convenient get out. The Beatles were heartily sick of not being heard above the hysterical screams and took the opportunity to become a studio band, and experiment and develop the album as a genre, a process already underway with critically acclaimed albums such as Rubber Soul and Revolver. Record companies were delighted with the development. Albums cost five times the price of a single, and therefore generated far greater profits in a growing market. Commercial imperatives were in harmony with artistic expression. Lennon himself cared little for the trappings of fame and had no business sense. It was his second wife Yoko Ono who took control of Lennon's business affairs and put an end to his talent for being ripped off, as happened to so many artists of that era.

Elvis Presley's perceived threat to the health and morals of the USA was much dissipated by him accepting conscription into the US Army. Fortunately, middle America was not aware that its foremost cultural icon, Sergeant Elvis Presley, was engaged in sexual activity with the 14 year old daughter of one of his senior officers. On leaving the Army in 1960, Presley abandoned rock and roll at the behest of his manager for the image of the all-round artist who could master any song. Musically, he gravitated from the orbit of the aggressive sexuality of black inspired rock and roll into that of a middle of the road family entertainer like Sinatra or Perry Como. None of the Beatles, and only one Rolling Stone, Bill Wyman, was conscripted. Lennon and the Beatles drummer Ringo Starr could theoretically have been caught in the net. Paul McCartney and George Harrison were just too young, as indeed were all the Stones bar Wyman and virtually all their contemporaries in the major groups (they were not known as bands in 1963). In that sense their experience was closer to that of My Generation, whom they so profoundly influenced. The Beatles also refused to be apolitical. Lennon and McCartney had no compunction about expressing their opposition to American involvement in the Vietnam War. Celebrities with opinions were a new phenomenon. To conservative America they were not merely being rude to their hosts, they were seen as closet communists. After marrying Yoko Ono in 1968, Lennon made full use of his position to campaign for peace, inviting ridicule not just from the older generation but also from fans who simply wanted the Beatles to get on with the business of making great music. To these record buyers, Give Peace a Chance (1969) and Happy Christmas War is Over (1972) recorded as the Plastic Ono Band were just tunes whose lyrical content was irrelevant. Although John and Yoko did not invite the cameras into their bedroom again after the 7 day "bed in" of 1969, the press genie was out of the bottle and from 1971 to his death in 1980 Lennon lived in New York where he believed he would be left in peace. In the USA he had implacable enemies in President Nixon and the CIA. The collapse in morale of American institutions, brought about by the Watergate scandal and the impending defeat in Vietnam, saved Lennon from deportation. Lennon continued his political activities in the USA irritating the hell out of conservative America until he disappeared from public life after the birth of his son Sean in 1975.

For many Beatles fans the villain of the piece was Lennon's Japanese wife, Yoko Ono, who had first come to the notice of at least some of the British public in 1966. It is probably fair to describe Yoko Ono as a minor celebrity herself. Yoko Ono's idea of art was not religious images in the Sistine Chapel and her first encounter with a Beatle was actually with Paul McCartney in 1965. McCartney, perhaps sensibly, has never commented on whether or not he slept with his friend and fellow Beatle's future spouse. Lennon, an exceptionally jealous man, is reputed to have demanded that Yoko confess to all her previous lovers. Whether his jealousy was tempered by the reputed sexual encounter he had with McCartney's future wife, Linda Eastman, is a matter for speculation. I can recall, for some reason, being allowed to stay up (I was 13 years old at the time) to watch a programme that in 1966 I think was called Cinema, the direct ancestor of a programme later presented for many years by Barry Norman, which featured clips of Yoko's latest film, "Bottoms". As a piece of cinema it did what it said on the tin, an 80 minute long piece of celluloid showcasing numerous waggling naked buttocks. I don't recall being allowed to watch this programme again for some time. However, when she met Lennon, Yoko ceased to be simply an eccentric oriental curiosity. Her marriage to Lennon (he ditched his first wife for her) and her enormous political influence on him attracted adverse comment in the press that bordered on vitriol and barely disguised racism. A British icon paired with a woman from a country not yet forgiven for its brutal treatment of prisoners of war was too much for large sections of the press and public. Additionally, Beatles' fans blamed her for the demise of the group, refusing to see that the band they revered could no longer contain three massive egos and work in harmony. In harness, the apparent desire to shock became more marked. Lennon recorded an album track, "Woman is the nigger of the world". Unlike 1966, there would be no apology. Lennon made it acceptable for men to be radical feminists. Yoko Ono would appear on Top of the Pops as part of the Plastic Ono Band, despite having nothing to contribute musically. On one notorious occasion in 1970 as the Plastic Ono Band performed Instant Karma, Yoko could be seen using a sanitary towel as a blindfold. Initially, she was dismissed by the Beatles as "flavour of the month" and her presence in the studio was resented, but later, after the formation of Wings, Paul McCartney would follow his friend's example and bring his wife into his band, to the consternation of rock critics.

The main rivals to the Beatles would also pay a price for celebrity. They did not enjoy the advantage of the image of lovable mop tops and did not have the same apparent immunity from drugs busts as the Beatles. The Rolling Stones were the celebrity antidote to the Beatles, its members being exactly the sort of people you would not want your daughter to marry. They were portrayed as uncouth sexual degenerates, despite the fact that as a unit they were no more or less promiscuous than any other artists of the era, and certainly no different to the Beatles. Yoko Ono has said that John Lennon had the most phenomenal sex drive which had to be satisfied. Bill Wyman, who kept a precise record of the Rolling Stones members' sexual conquests, revealed that drummer Charlie Watts was totally faithful to his wife. The Stones early efforts on record suggested they had a limited shelf life. Once Mick Jagger and Keith Richards discovered the confidence to write their own songs, rather than rely on covers of their personal favourites, the perception of their ability and longevity swiftly changed. The infamous drugs bust at Redlands in 1967, home of Keith Richards, saw Jagger and Richards imprisoned for quite minor drug offences. Richards' conviction for allowing pot to be smoked in his home was overturned on appeal. Jagger was in possession of some pep pills that actually belonged to his girlfriend Marianne Faithful, and had been bought legally abroad, which he gallantly claimed to be his own. His sentence was reduced to a conditional discharge.

An individual present at the party who had a suitcase full of drugs was never prosecuted and disappeared. Prior to the party, Jagger had announced his intention to sue the News of the World for claiming he was involved with drugs. The newspaper claim can be attributed to band member Brian Jones' loose tongue. Not present at Redlands, the police would be at his door in three months. Time has lent weight to conspiracy theories, one being that the News of the World and/or senior police officers and/or MI5 set up the bust via David Schneiderman, the man allegedly planted in their social circle, the man who had a suitcase full of drugs not even searched by the police, the man allowed to disappear. Marianne Faithful believes that the police knew not to open Schneiderman's suitcase as it would expose rolls of film to the light. The notoriety of the event was added to by Marianne Faithful herself, who, having just got out of the bath, was naked under a large rug and had to demonstrate that fact to the police woman who wished to search her. Someone could not resist leaking that story. Miss Faithful explicitly denies the lurid story, which has done the rounds for years, that the police arrived to find Jagger eating a Mars Bar protruding from her vagina. There are no grounds for not believing that she is telling the truth. Marianne would become a celebrity casualty descending into the hell of heroin addiction, which took her the best part of 20 years to kick. Brian Jones, whose addictions were already out of control, was no longer capable of contributing to the band by 1969 and later the same year was found dead at the bottom of his swimming pool. Britain's establishment were in full cry and deplored the influence on Britain's youth. However, in class conscious Britain, working class youth had yet to really discover illegal narcotics. They stuck to beer and tobacco like their parents. More pertinently there was no underclass of note in the late sixties. However, the future movers and shakers of My Generation absorbed a different message. Even if they had only a passing acquaintance with the drug culture at university, they were relaxed about its existence as they went about the business of being educated beyond their intelligence. Drugs acquired a social cachet and sophistication that was not granted by mere alcohol. It was what their heroes, rock stars, avant-garde artists and other celebrity Bohemian figures did. The moral ambivalence about substance abuse is one of the worst bequests of My Generation in power.

The world of sport also generated its first celebrity, a man who came to epitomise the swinging sixties as much as any actor or rock musician. He was even filmed dancing at a recording of Top of the Pops in 1965. His name was George Best and for the remaining 40 years of his life the media could not get enough of him. Alcohol ensured that he was finished as a top flight footballer by the time he was 30, although he would continue to prostitute his talent in low grade zero world profile soccer in the United States for almost another decade. Best's ability to bed reigning Miss Worlds, and his very public love affair with the booze, maintained him as a tabloid staple. However, like his celebrity contemporaries in the Beatles and the Rolling Stones, his talent was sublime. Unlike them it would be wasted. Prior to Best, the nearest approximation to sporting celebrity had been England cricketer Denis Compton and his Australian counterpart, Keith Miller, on field adversaries for a decade after World War II. The latter was a bona fide war hero. Compton and Miller were dashing figures, playing hard on and off the field. Neither saw fidelity as a virtue and both are reputed to have bedded the young Princess Margaret. However, both were active in an era where gentlemen never told and journalists did not pry. Thus, England wicketkeeper Godfrey Evans' legendary sexual appetite was completely unknown to the public, and presumably to Mrs Evans. According to legend, Evans aimed for a century off the field as well as on, seeking to bed 100 women on the tour of Australia, which in those far off days began and ended with a month's voyage across the world on a cruise ship. Pre-war, Wally Hammond's VD, caught in the West Indies, remained a close secret. As late as 1965 when the Best era began, not a word of England soccer captain Bobby Moore's testicular cancer found its way into the press, something almost inconceivable today. Compton and Miller were not celebrities as we know them. They were famous but did not have their lives dissected in the way that has become the fashion since Princess Diana, of whom more later, burst on to the scene in 1981 . Cricket's first real celebrity, Ian (now Sir Ian) Botham , the hero of the 1981 Ashes series, would find no peace as the media sought to hack down the tallest poppy of 1980s British sport.

Until 1963 when the Beatles broke through, being working class in a class based society made celebrity impossible. The immediate post war era's two greatest footballers, Stanley Matthews and Tom Finney, both subsequently knighted, were as far away from celebrity as you could get. After training Finney would don the overalls of his alter ego, the Preston plumber. Thus, an England international footballer could be the man sorting out your burst pipes during a harsh winter in Preston. Matthews, from Stoke-On-Trent, was equally self- effacing. Virtually all professional footballers were working class boys who carried the traditional virtues of their class; modesty, respectability and personal dignity. Only after 1961, when the maximum wage was abolished and professional footballers could be paid what they were worth in a free market, did they acquire social mobility. Only after 1961 were professional footballers able to move out of the working class districts in which they lived side by side with supporters. It seems incredible that within living memory footballers caught the same bus to the match as spectators. Without the abolition of the maximum wage George Best could never have become a celebrity. Sadly, after his predilection for drink ended his football career prematurely, he would become the template for celebrity excess better known for his sexual escapades with holders of the Miss World title, marathon boozing sessions which could make him violent towards the women in his life, and a stint in prison. However, unlimited earning capacity is not a sufficient condition of celebrity. Bankers are certainly not celebrities and Tiger Woods apart, neither are professional golfers whose leading lights are every bit as wealthy as top professional soccer players. Television exposure changed George Best's world.

Until 1964, there was virtually no televised soccer. The FA Cup final was televised live on the first Saturday of May... and that was it. There had been an attempt to get live league games on screen in 1960-61, but it was quickly strangled at birth by reactionary club chairmen who believed that television coverage would adversely impact attendances that were already falling. Thus, if you wanted to see Finney or Matthews every other week it helped to live in Preston or Blackpool. Failing that you keenly anticipated the annual visit. If you supported a lower division club then you would never see Finney or Matthews live. Matthews would play in three FA Cup finals, 1948, 1951 and most famously 1953. Finney would make his only (losing) appearance a year later. Television ownership was still a minority pursuit at this stage, although the Coronation in 1953 televised live, gave it considerable stimulus. Change came in 1964 when recorded highlights came to our screens, with Match of the Day on BBC on Saturday nights, initially on the fledgling BBC2, but on BBC1 a year later. ITV also acquired rights on a regional basis for Sunday afternoon screening. All televised football needed was a new star and in George Best it got one. Another tremendous fillip for sporting celebrity was England's world cup win in 1966. Although league football would not be televised live until 20 years after Match of the Day began, the World Cup of 1966 marked the end of the era when the only live game screened was the FA Cup final. The World Cup and the European Championships would hit our screens alternately every two years and be given wall to wall coverage. TV pundits, usually football league managers, also became celebrities as a consequence. Manchester United's successful campaign for a first league title since the Munich Air Crash in 1958 coincided with the launch of Match of the Day. As has been noted earlier, young people with more money and more freedom to travel were lured by glamour away from traditional town clubs. Twenty years later a televised advert for Hovis bread would be filmed on a cobbled street in Blackburn round the back of the home end at the Rovers ground. Accrington Stanley would be satirised even more cruelly in a milk advert in the same decade. Television was on its way to graduating as the arbiter of social cachet and cultural cool, and specifically the lack of it.

The marriage of Diana Spencer to the Prince of Wales changed the whole notion of celebrity. Prior to that hugely significant event for the Royal Family and British Society, celebrities, and those who could be retrospectively defined as celebrities, were individuals of considerable merit with perhaps only Marilyn Munroe standing out as a significant exception whose acting abilities were in inverse proportion to her beauty. The few sportsmen who made it to celebrity status were men and women whose excellence was universally acknowledged. The names of those whose world was opened up by television rolled off the tongue; Bobby Moore, George Best, Ian (now Sir Ian) Botham, Stirling (now Sir Stirling) Moss, Brian Clough, Malcolm Allison, Bjorn Borg, Lester Piggott, Mary Peters and Sebastian (now Lord) Coe need no introduction. Botham and Moss earned their knighthoods for their contribution to the community after their sporting careers were over. Malcolm Allison may be less well known to modern readers and, like Best, it would be hard to describe him as other than a deeply flawed human being, and trashy stunts such as inviting glamour model Fiona Richmond to strip and join his players in the communal bath at Crystal Palace anticipated what celebrity would come to mean. Nevertheless, Allison was the most innovative soccer coach of his generation. The 1968 Olympic Pentathlon champion, Mary (now Dame Mary) Peters, will also not be well known outside of Ulster where she embodies the spirit of community reconciliation. Lester Piggott, who would go to jail for tax evasion and as a consequence was stripped of his OBE, was surely the greatest jockey of the last half century. My apologies to fans of Manchester United for leaving Bobby (now Sir Bobby) Charlton off the celebrity list, but this innately modest man is much more a throwback to the working class footballer of the pre-television era rather than that of the celebrity era spawned by the televised triumph of 1966.

As with the sportsmen, stardust landed on a new rock and roll aristocracy born with the Beatles in 1963 and television was the catalyst. Although there had been some televised pop music before the Beatles, 1963-64 was when television recognised rock and roll as part of the cultural mainstream. In 1963 the BBC screened Thank Your Lucky Stars on Saturday evenings and ITV launched Ready Steady Go on Friday Evenings. In January 1964 the BBC launched the most successful music show of all, Top of the Pops, which ran until 2006. Without an invitation to appear on one of these programmes, particularly TOTP, it was exceptionally difficult to launch a successful music career. It invested enormous power in TV producers. As with the sportsmen, celebrity was accompanied by merit. The compositions of Lennon and McCartney, Jagger and Richards, and my own personal favourite, Ray Davies, have stood the test of time, providing enduring proof that popular music culture can contain work of as much merit as that of Bach and Beethoven. Like actors and sportsmen, individuals could be deeply flawed and dysfunctional to the extent that there was genuine concern about the example being set, but the music business is capitalism in the raw. Those who satisfy only trends and fads are swiftly relegated to historical footnotes and ten minute slots on retro tours. Like the Rolls Royce, enduring appeal is achieved only where there is enduring class.

Diana Spencer changed the rules. With her we got not only our own Marilyn Monroe, but more pertinently our own Eva Peron. Like Marilyn Munroe and Eva Peron she died young in tragic circumstances, thus adding to the legend. To this day, 17 years after her death, the Daily Express periodically carries front page Diana stories, a symbol of how far a once mighty newspaper has fallen. In fairness, Lady Di, as the press called her before her marriage to the Prince of Wales, has to be placed in the context of the times. Britain was not a happy country in that year. Unemployment was on its way to levels not seen since the 1930s and our inner cities were powder kegs that exploded on to the streets. The cure for Britain's ills prescribed by Mrs Thatcher was painful and unpalatable for the communities that bore the brunt of neo-liberal economic thinking. 1981 was the perfect year for a royal marriage. Such an event was perceived as mood enhancing and unifying. Prince Charles had enjoyed more than a decade of royal bachelor pursuits in his leisure time, principle amongst which was making love to as many aristocratic young women who could be persuaded to his bed. The problem was that the British public were perceived to want a virgin for the heir to the throne's bride. On this basis a host of eligible aristocrats had disqualified themselves. This would not have mattered had the traditional solution of a foreign princess been acceptable. However, the days had long gone when British monarchs could communicate in French or German, and two wars with Germany had made our monarchy keen to disguise its Germanic origins. Thus, as Prince Charles got older, it was inevitable that his new bride would be much younger since twenty something virgins were found only in convents. Whether or not the 19 year old Diana Spencer was really a virgin is not known to provenance, but the press were content so nothing else mattered. Maiden aunts could sleep safely in their beds knowing that the Royal Family were protecting traditional values... except of course that the traditional values of the aristocracy, where infidelity and discretion went hand in hand, were rather different.

Diana Spencer broke the celebrity mould and created a new template which has been adapted throughout the class structure. As an individual, it is hard to find any tangible merit. I would concede that she was attractive, but in no sense was she a classical beauty. Besides, when you have the world's top fashion houses clamouring for your endorsement, you have no excuse for not looking good, unless of course you are the Duchess of York. Intellectually she was dim, which she admitted herself, although some of the press described her as a nursery school teacher when in fact she was an unqualified assistant filling in the hours before the next aristocratic party. Diana did not play sport, did not play a musical instrument and said or wrote nothing that implied a higher wisdom. What she did do was lend glamour to that fustiest of British institutions, the Royal Family. In the early years of her marriage she was the royal clothes horse as famous for what she put on as Samantha Fox was for what she took off, but there was no substance behind the glitter. Aristocrats collectively have always taken out more than they put in, but the British monarchy had built a serious reputation for duty and service, Princess Margaret being the exception. During the war the Queen (after the King's death in 1952 she was known as the Queen Mother) said that the Royal Family remained in London during the blitz so that they could look the East End in the face. For this reason, her well known extravagance was indulged. She was perceived to have paid her dues. The Princess Royal carries out more engagements than any other member of the Royal Family. The much criticised Prince Andrew, and more recently Prince Harry, put themselves in harm's way in the Falklands and Afghanistan respectively. The key point is that members of the Royal Family carry out civic duties and/or give military service out of a sense of obligation. They understand the feudal concept of noblesse oblige, the unwritten covenant between monarch and subject that enhanced their status and secured the crown. Diana Spencer did not understand this at all. Elevation to royal status unleashed her inner vacuity, neediness and desire to be adored on the nation. Her life was played out daily on TV as a live soap opera whose longevity was surpassed only by Coronation Street. As the first member of the Royal Family to embrace popular culture, in this case the low grade pop music of the early 1980s, she democratised the notion that you can have fame without talent which is a pernicious part of our modern culture. Although topless models had appeared in newspapers since 1969, only with the advent of 16 year old Samantha Fox in 1983 did it become a career that offered potentially life changing earnings over a few short years. All you needed were big breasts and a perky smile. In fairness, Miss Fox and her biggest rival Linda Lusardi went on to launch successful music and acting careers respectively. Most disappeared without trace, and one, Tracy Kirby, ended up in prison. Clare Short MP, an arch critic of Page 3 on the grounds it exploited women, perhaps missed a more significant point. Page 3 offered the opportunity to be someone without having to work for it, to have fame that did not have to be earned. All you needed was to be discovered, and when all else failed the NHS would pay for breast enhancements.

Diana Spencer's most poisonous bequest to our society was the victim culture which she embodied. Legend will have it that she was deserted by her mother, then by her husband and finally by the Royal Family. For her supporters, Diana is the naive, innocent, virginal victim of an evil royal mafia which sought to destroy what it could not absorb. The truth is a good deal more complex. What is clear was that Diana was hopelessly needy and a chronic attention seeker with the deeply manipulative streak which typifies the species. Thus her charity work visiting AIDS victims and campaigning against landmines, laudable though it was, has to be seen through the prism of her personality. The game was given away comprehensively in the notorious interview with Martin Bashir, where she spoke of being Queen of Hearts in lieu of being Queen of the nation, a job she would never have on account of leaving her husband.

Princess Diana was not the first modern royal divorcee. Indeed, she was beaten to the courtroom by both the Princess Royal and Prince Andrew. However, there were three crucial differences. Firstly, the birth of Prince William and then Prince Harry ensured that neither

Prince Andrew nor Princess Anne could ever expect to succeed to the throne unless a terrorist attack eliminated a number of key members of the Royal Family in one fell swoop. Secondly, Princess Anne and Prince Andrew stuck to the royal mantra of "never complain, never explain". The Princess of Wales conducted a lengthy proxy war against her husband via sympathetic newspapers only too happy to collude with her attention seeking and self-imposed victimhood in the name of selling newspapers. Thirdly, she went public in the notorious TV interview with Mr Bashir, telling the world that there were three people in her marriage. Thus, the taboo of aristocratic discretion about adultery was blown wide open. Ripping up the rule book had the consequence of expulsion from polite society leaving Diana dependent solely on popular acclaim. Her death cemented forever her role as the British Eva Peron. The truth is that the royal couple had ceased marital relations soon after Prince Harry was born in 1985. With no apparent way out of the marriage (the Queen's permission is required for a royal divorce), it was inevitable that both would find solace elsewhere. There is actually some debate as to who was the first to commit adultery, since Diana's affair with her royal protection officer seems to have begun at roughly the same time as Charles returned to the arms of Camilla Parker-Bowles whose cheerfully cuckolded husband was himself a former lover of Charles' sister, the Princess Royal. There is little to suggest that Prince Charles took any further mistresses, but his estranged wife forged an eclectic collection of lovers which included other people's husbands, notably Oliver Hoare and allegedly England Rugby Captain, Will Carling, whose marriage broke up as a consequence. Carling, sensibly, has never commented but the significance of his wife calling time on their short marriage cannot be underestimated. Yet no matter how gross and un-sisterly her behaviour towards other women, her iconic status remained undisturbed. For radical feminists, her real value was as one of Lenin's "useful idiots" whose proclaimed victimhood was helpful in their war against men and against the privilege that the monarchy represented.

The monarchy suffered badly from the Diana era. The aura and magic that surrounded the monarchy was drained away by Diana, and, along with Mrs Thatcher, she played a key role in the decline of deference. I am not by nature a monarchist. However, I am comforted by the existence of an institution whose purely symbolic power requires the nation's political elite to take cognisance. I am content that there is an office to which our politicians cannot aspire, and an institution that they struggle to subvert to their own ends. The independent life of the constitutional monarchy is a bulwark against totalitarianism. The Civil Service and Armed Forces are loyal to the Crown, not the Government. That would change if we were a republic. None of this means that I excuse poor behaviour from elsewhere within the Royal Family. Although it was leaked, there was something deeply demeaning about the heir to the throne telling his mistress that he wished he was a tampon. It is notable that even papers such as the Daily Mail are stern critics of Prince Charles for his extravagance, his lack of people skills, and at times his lack of awareness of constitutional propriety. The fact that Diana was able to do the traditional job of producing an heir and a spare before marital relations ceased gave birth to a new breed of star, the hereditary celebrity complete with royal status. The clamour from sections of the media, mainly but not exclusively from female journalists with feminist leadings for the monarchy to skip a generation and install the Duke and Duchess of Cambridge in Buckingham Palace when the Queen dies, is based as much on the perceived glamour of the young royal couple compared to the fustiness of the Prince of Wales and his second wife, the Duchess of Cornwall, as it is on the grossly distorted perception of Diana Spencer as the beautiful butterfly crushed by the royal wheel. The Duke of Cambridge's younger brother, Prince Harry, who has already seen combat, would almost have to die in Afghanistan to be accepted as an individual on his own merits.

The death of the Princess of Wales in August 1997 ushered in a week of collective madness that exposed how we had changed for the worse as a nation. It is important to emphasise that the emotionally incontinent women and weak metro sexual men who held vigils, laid wreaths outside Kensington Palace and prostrated themselves in fake vicarious grief constituted only a minority of the nation, as the rest of us looked on in sheer bewilderment when the death of a well-heeled trollop closed shops, cancelled sporting events and caused lawn mowers to be confined to sheds on a beautiful summer day. The majority were held hostage for several hours on the first Saturday in September. Somehow Diana managed to close down the nation when Buenos Aires came to London in the late summer of 1997. I was 12 years old when Sir Winston Churchill died. I remember watching the funeral on a Saturday morning in January 1965. Shops remained open and FA Cup ties went ahead in the afternoon. It was inconceivable that the nation could grind to a halt even for the death of a titan such as Churchill. Yet, in 1997, it was allowed to happen. It was as though the audience had joined the cast of Evita on stage when the song "Oh What a Circus" is performed.

Unhappily, 1997 was the year My Generation formally gained power. In fact Tony Blair was able to extend his honeymoon on the back of the death of Diana. Even papers such as the Daily Mail praised his handling of the near constitutional crisis precipitated by the fatal Paris car crash. The reality is rather different. Tony Blair unashamedly rode the tiger, milking the emotionalism, stoking the inebriation. He gave in to every demand of the nation's self-appointed opinion formers in the media, lent credibility to the poor deranged individuals (mainly but not exclusively women) who treated Kensington Palace as though it were Lourdes, and subjected the Royal Family, in particular Prince Charles and his two young sons, to the most horrifying public ordeal at the state funeral. Supposedly reputable TV presenters spouted drivel. One who shall be nameless screeched "Your Majesty, your people need you," as the pressure grew for the Royal Family to leave the seclusion of Balmoral and return to the goldfish bowl of London. Another said that William and Harry should be at home having lots of hugs and cuddles. Anyone would have thought they had just got out of kennels rather than being adolescent boys. Worse still was the totalitarian demand for tears at the funeral to "show that they care". Mr Blair could and should have dealt with this nonsense. He could have given employers carte blanche to discipline those who were absent from the office or factory. He could have encouraged the withdrawal of benefits from the ranks of the unemployed gathered outside Kensington Palace, as they were clearly unavailable for work. He could have insisted that the Royal Family were allowed to grieve in private at Balmoral and deployed extra security to keep out the paparazzi. He could have refused a state funeral and insisted it was a private affair for the Spencer family. The presence of television would then have been a matter for them. He could have made it perfectly clear that Britain remained open for business on the Saturday of the funeral and that sporting events should go ahead. He could have stopped the emotional spasm dead in its tracks and let the self- appointed opinion formers fulminate in impotent rage. He could have supported and buttressed the monarchy against the forces of emotional anarchy that concealed the closet republicanism of the lentil eating classes. It was his opportunity to demonstrate real leadership, with all the security that a majority of 179 affords, but Mr Blair blew it. He deemed it far better to have the celebrity company of Mr (now Sir)

Elton John at Westminster Abbey. In truth, that is no surprise. As the leader of a party committed to bringing Britain into the orbit of ECHR, it is only to be expected that he supported the emotional rights of the individual in preference to stiffening the backbone of the nation. At infrequent intervals there is an opportunity for an unlikely individual to become a great Prime Minister. Churchill, Attlee, Lloyd George and Margaret Thatcher took theirs, Mr Blair did not.

The way was now open for nonentities to become celebrities. It is a national tragedy when there are superb role models available for girls such as Carol Vorderman, Kelly Holmes and Rebecca Adlington. Instead we have to endure endless media tittle tattle about the tedious, the talentless, and the totally self-obsessed. For celebrities we now have Cheryl Cole, Victoria Beckham and the late Jade Goody. Magazines such as Hello promote the culture of vacuity. Celebrity now comes courtesy of outrageous behaviour on reality TV programmes such as the "X Factor", "Britain's got Talent", (surely an oxymoron), "I'm a Celebrity, Get Me out of Here", which is filmed in the Australian tropical forest and most insidiously "Big Brother", where the daily interactions and conversations of the participants are recorded in full, and uncensored. Notice me, adore me, pity me, for my needs must always be satisfied. New depths were plumbed in August 2011 when the wife of the Speaker of the House of Commons entered the Big Brother house. Thankfully, Sally Bercow did not demean her husband's office further and follow the example of Miss Goody and strip naked for the ever present camera. Possibly the most gruesome programme of all is "The Jeremy Kyle Show". For the uninitiated it is chav TV where members of the underclass get their fifteen minutes of fame in front of a live audience replete with tattoos, muffin tops and cheap leggings. The highlight is usually the DNA test that reveals the true paternity of some hapless infant whose future is likely to follow the same predictable path; petty crime and unemployment for the boys and single motherhood and welfare dependency for the girls. My Generation, in charge of the TV stations, now serves up the modern equivalent of Roman bread and circuses. The sets of "Big Brother" and "I'm a Celebrity, Get Me o ut of Here" are the amphitheatres. The viewer at home, who decides who is evicted on a weekly basis until only one survives, has the role of the Emperor, giving the thumbs up or thumbs down. Reality TV is the new opium of the people that will keep them quiescent and away from politics. It is the perfect metaphor for the contempt in which the political elite holds the electorate.

CHAPTER 19

THE ECONOMY, TAXES AND THE WELFARE STATE

The 1992 General Election reinforced the conventional wisdom that the economy was Labour's Achilles heel with the electorate. This was an election that should have been won, but was not, because crucial swing voters who had been in work continuously since Mrs Thatcher's accession in 1979 did not feel ready to trust Labour with the economy. The defeat came as a shock to the party, not least because the Tories were forgiven by the electorate for the "Lawson boom" and its associated house price hikes, for the return of inflation, and for the rate of unemployment climbing again, with even the South East having brakes applied to its prosperity. It is true that Labour has had a history of unfortunate encounters with the economy. MacDonald's minority 1929-31 administration was overwhelmed by an economic crisis over which it had no control and no answers. It could not and would not leave the Gold Standard which overvalued the pound and crippled our exports. The consequences were a catastrophic party split with a small number of ministers, led by Ramsey Macdonald, entering into a Tory dominated National Government which implemented brutal cuts in a then ungenerous benefits system. The Means Test replaced the Workhouse Test as the scourge of the deserving poor. Within weeks of taking office the National Government was forced off the Gold Standard.

After 1945 the Attlee government energetically tackled reconstruction in the face of the massive economic dislocation and debt that it inherited as a consequence of World War II. In 1949, the government was forced to devalue the pound, a blow to both national and Labour party pride. In 1967, a Labour government was again forced to devalue the pound. In truth it should have been done on taking office in October 1964, but a combination of pride and the political reality of a slim majority kept it firmly off the agenda. In 1970, as in 1951, Labour lost office partly as a consequence of the damage that devaluation did to its credibility. Labour was damned if it did, and damned if it didn't and the electorate remained unimpressed despite the genuine mitigation offered by its inheritances. In 1972 the Conservatives abandoned the fixed parity of the pound to the dollar and allowed the pound to float. In this way it found its own lower market value, de facto devaluation without the associated stigma. Returning to office in February 1974, Labour inherited an economy that was both stagnant and ravaged by inflation, and one in which organised labour was determined to maintain the value of pay. By the summer of 1976, the new Leader of the Opposition, Margaret Thatcher, was able to excoriate Labour with regard to 24% fall in the value of sterling against the dollar. Humiliatingly, the government was forced to go to the IMF for a loan and accept prescribed spending cuts in return. Labour would lose whatever grip it had gained on inflation towards the end of the life of the government when the trade unions refused to accept a 5% norm for pay. The infamous Winter of Discontent would ensue and the long 18 year hegemony of the Tories would begin in May 1979.

For Labour's Conservative critics the crises that beset the post war governments of 1945-51, 1964-70, and 1974-79 were evidence of the congenital weaknesses of socialism, the idealistic incompetence of Labour ministers, and their overreliance on what they perceived as the discredited economic thinking of John Maynard Keynes. As an analysis, it is much too simplistic. The Labour Chancellor 1974-79, Denis Healey, abandoned Keynesian teaching in 1975. Critics to the left of Labour approached from a different angle. To them, Labour was either not socialist enough or not socialist at all. To them, Labour ministers lacked ideals, vision and courage. At worst, Labour ministers were class traitors who worshipped a false god in Keynes, and therefore only managed capitalism rather than applying the principles of the great socialist thinkers, Marx, Lenin and (according to taste) Trotsky. Their analysis is no more helpful. Two rival visions of Utopia have failed: take as examples the rural poor of Mississippi where the American dream is just that, and the urban poor of Moscow for whom the workers' paradise is just an illusion. It must also be remembered that the Labour Party is not and never has been a revolutionary party, and therefore its socialism is of necessity constrained by constitutional and electoral reality. The original clause 4 of the constitution, drafted by Sidney Webb and adopted by the party in 1918, therefore left it vulnerable to criticism from both ends of the political spectrum. The original clause 4 read as follows:

> "To secure for the workers by hand or by brain the full fruits of their industry and the most equitable distribution thereof that may be possible upon the basis of common ownership of the means of production, distribution and exchange, and the best obtainable popular control of each industry or service."

From the right, it is read as a commitment to nationalise the whole economy. However, it can also be read as a commitment to other forms of public ownership such as municipal ownership, workers' co-operatives or consumer co-operatives. The Co-operative movement was already a member of the socialist family in Britain by 1918. It should also be remembered that Webb was an elitist Fabian who distrusted popular democracy. Socialism was something that was imposed from above. Much of the language is aspirational, leaving very much open what constitutes the full fruits of their industry and equitable (note not equal) distribution and does not seek to define the nature of popular control. It is a matter of record that the post war Labour government adopted nationalisation as its model of public ownership, a policy for which it had a clear mandate and appealed as a modern solution to the massive problem of post war reconstruction. It was an idea whose time had come. However, Old Labour settled only for nationalising what it saw as the commanding heights of the economy. For example, it nationalised the Bank of England, it nationalised coal which in 1947 either supplied or powered 90% of our energy needs, it nationalised health, it nationalised the docks, it nationalised the railways, it nationalised road haulage, and finally it nationalised the iron and steel industry. The Attlee government chose not to nationalise the high street banks, it did not nationalise agriculture, it permitted the continuation of private beds in NHS hospitals, it left whole swathes of private enterprise including the car industry, engineering, and brewing (apart from a nationalised brewery in Carlisle) in private hands. In short, the Attlee government was more pragmatic than ideological, although the socialisation of the docks and mines were also historic debts being paid off to a much abused workforce. As long ago as 1919 the Sankey Commission had recommended the nationalisation of the mines. De facto nationalisation of the pits had occurred during World War II. The industry was inefficient and uncompetitive and the rapacious coal owners regarded the miners with contempt. The Attlee government looked at the big picture. That which was nationalised was necessary for national regeneration and for the benefit of the wider community. The health of the working classes was a badly neglected area. The nation simply could not afford an unhealthy population. The Attlee government left private industry in private hands where it was profitable, efficient and paid decent wages, although in the car industry efficiency and industrial relations would both go into a decline. Equally, the government was well aware of the failed collectivisation of agriculture in the USSR.

Of the 1945-51 Labour government nationalisations, only iron and steel was returned to the private sector during 13 years of Tory rule. Despite the huge row over Crosland's "The Future of Socialism" and it's demonising as a betrayal of socialist ideals, the Wilson government 1964-70, tacitly accepted at least part of the revisionist argument, showing no appetite for further nationalisation, settling simply for the re-nationalisation of iron and steel. However, those on the left felt that Labour in office had been sabotaged by the forces of capital which caused frequent runs on the pound and by investment strikes. The former forced Labour to cut public spending and the latter forced up both imports and unemployment. In office in 1974-79, Labour set up the National Enterprise Board. Even though Labour never did take stakes in the twenty largest companies, for the right wing press this was virtual communism. On the revolutionary left, Labour was vilified for yet more management of capitalism. Labour also devised plans for the newly arriving North Sea oil and also for coal. I stand by my view that as a country a generation later we would be better off if these apparently socialist energy measures had not been abandoned by the Conservatives for ideological reasons.

Nevertheless, the nationalised industries were coming under fierce ideological fire as well as enduring a certain amount of public disillusion through the life of the Wilson-Callaghan governments. The Labour manifesto of 1983 called for more nationalisation, including the banks, compulsory planning agreements, and the unilateral abandonment of nuclear weapons. In the aftermath of the Falklands war, the last was electoral suicide not only because it allowed Labour to be portrayed as soft on defence and crypto communists, but also because of the employment consequences. As Labour endured two further defeats in 1987 and 1992, nationalisation and public ownership generally became ideas whose time had gone. Labour's problem was to catch up and re-think its strategy for economic management, which amounted to re-thinking its socialism if it was to survive as a potential party of government. Within the Labour party, Neil Kinnock, leader 1983-92, turned increasingly to a new generation within the party. Tony Blair and Gordon Brown, both elected in 1983 at the nadir of Labour's misfortunes, and Peter Mandelson, who became the principal strategist, emerged as the leading figures amongst the modernisers. Figures previously associated with the extreme left, such as Patricia Hewitt, moved into the modernising camp. For feminists such as Miss Hewitt, the abandonment of the economic high ground to the neo Liberals, who now dominated the Tory party, was their opportunity to promote their vision of equality in a party purged of its socialist economic baggage. These figures were promoted rapidly within the party and the unexpected death of the popular and respected John Smith, leader from 1992-94, who was viewed as an obstruction to modernisation, opened the way for Tony Blair to seize the crown and rebrand Labour as New Labour.

Only in the literal sense that all political thought is ideological could Tony Blair be given that label. Mr Blair will not go down as a great thinker, much less of an original thinker. The Labour party in New Zealand, which had already returned to office on a programme barely recognisable as that of a party of the left, provided tactical inspiration. Mr Blair's "third way" was not new either. Back in 1938, Harold MacMillan, then a Tory backbencher going nowhere in his party, published his book, "The Middle Way". Mr Blair moved swiftly to jettison the old clause 4 and succeeded where Hugh Gaitskell had failed 35 years earlier in eerily similar circumstances i.e. a series of morale sapping electoral defeats. The new clause 4 read as follows:

"The Labour Party is a democratic socialist party. It believes that by the strength of our common endeavour we achieve more than we achieve alone, so as to create for each of us the means to realise our true potential and for all of us a community in which power, wealth and opportunity are in the hands of the many, not the few, where the rights we enjoy reflect the duties we owe, and where we live together, freely, in a spirit of solidarity, tolerance and respect."

Since its promulgation, the new clause 4 has become something of a historical footnote. It no longer excites the Tory press, unsurprisingly as the commitment to common ownership has gone. Intriguingly there is no mention of equality, which may appear surprising in view of how events have turned out although there is mention of freedom and opportunity. Socialism is tempered by democratic legitimacy, as indeed it should be. In short, there is very little to frighten the horses and enough to give comfort to those of all political persuasions with any kind of social conscience. In any event the word "socialism" would disappear from the New Labour lexicon. The revised clause 4 betrayed few clues as to the plans of the new patricians of My Generation. There have been attempts to engage the party in further debate as to what its core values are. It would appear that Labour (Mr Miliband has dropped the "New") prefers to leave that sort of thing to the Liberal Democrats, rather than spell out for all to see the true agenda of the ruling elite and risk another debacle on a par with 1983.

New Labour was therefore free to accept as much of neo liberalism, now the dominant economic strain, as it wished or needed to do in order to get elected. The party promised to abide by the outgoing chancellor's spending plans during its first term of office; a move that was both politically and economically shrewd. For an opposition to seek to win an election against a background of an improving economy, counter intuitive thinking was required. New Labour only believed that the Tories had really self-destructed when it was confirmed by the voters. Within days of its historic victory, Chancellor Gordon Brown handed control of interest rates back to the Bank of England. This move, not revealed in the manifesto, won huge approval from the Tory press. For much of Labour's first term, the party enjoyed unprecedented good will from this quarter. Mr Brown was admiringly nicknamed "Prudence" and lauded for his admiration of American economic dynamism. Yet barely a decade later Labour's political opponents were able to lay the charges of wrong-headed ideology, incompetence and ineptitude at the government now led by Mr Brown, as debt soared to unprecedented levels and threatened national creditworthiness as the threat of virtual bankruptcy loomed.

It is important to be clear that there is one thing that Mr Brown as chancellor got unequivocally right. As a people we should be eternally grateful that Mr Brown resisted cabinet colleagues, including the prime minister, who wished for Britain to join the single currency. To do so would, of course, have completely negated the handing over of control of our interest rates to the Bank of England. It is no exaggeration to say that this resistance to the blandishments of the Euro by Mr Brown saved this country from the kind of economic meltdown suffered by countries such as Greece and the Republic of Ireland. Mr Brown should also be given credit when, as prime minister, he showed real world leadership in getting to grips with the world banking crisis. However, this has to be tempered by the near catastrophic failure to regulate the banking industry adequately. His career in office is in part a story of the inner intellectual tensions within the man. Gordon Brown was an admirer of the way in which the USA was a job creation machine but at the same time, unlike most Americans, he retained his belief in the power of big government. Mr Brown revelled in the nickname "Prudence", but in reality resorted to what were frequently described as stealth taxes to raise revenue for New Labour projects. He also had a gift for making the simple complicated; a gifted intellectual with a bureaucratic mindset. No doubt in due course and perhaps during his lifetime, Mr Brown will be the subject of an appropriately scholarly biography.

As has been said, Socialists, Social Democrats, Liberals and others on the constitutional left had surrendered the economic high ground to neo liberalism. The process was painful but was a legitimate response to the years spent in the electoral wilderness. Thus, New Labour willingly accepted an economic settlement based on lower direct taxes, the privatisation of publicly owned industry and some fringe privatisation of public services, and of legal constraints on trade unions. However, there is no evidence that the electorate wanted Labour to preside over an economy in which the very rich were permitted to gorge themselves, to avoid the reduced taxes demanded of them, and to export jobs from once thriving communities either abroad or to migrant labour. There was simply no mandate for policies which turned Labour values on its head. A 2011 report from the High Pay Commission shows that executive basic pay rose by 63% in the last decade, whereas pay for the average worker rose only by 27% in this time. However, the situation presided over by Labour in power is actually far worse when pay packages that include share options and bonuses are taken into account. In 2002, 48% of the pay of FTSE quoted companies executives was comprised of bonuses and share options. In 2011 that figure is 90%. In the period under study, share prices of those companies rose by only 21%. Since 1980, the remuneration packages of some chief executives, most notably in banking, have risen by over 4000%. In the same 30 year period the average salary in the UK increased from a little over 6k per annum to around 25k per annum, an increase before inflation is taken into account of around 400%. Thus, the pay of the top 0.1% has been sprinting ahead at a speed at least ten times faster than the pay of ordinary working people. Another slant on executive pay is provided by the independent High Pay Centre. It found in December 2013 that the pay of FTSE 100 CEOs had risen from 60 times to 160 times the pay of the average worker over the previous 20 years. It is important to remember that only one third of the workforce earn in excess of the average salary. At the present rate of progress, the pay of the top 0.1% will consume 14% of national income by 2030 compared to around 5% at the time of writing. This will take this particular inequality back to where it was at the outbreak of World War II. Peter Mandelson is quoted as being relaxed about people becoming rich. Looking at these figures, the word 'relaxed' borders on comatose. New Labour in office stood, watched and admired as income inequality continued to accelerate.

Only Utopian socialists argue for identical incomes and totally communal property. Moreover, it is not possible for a society to insulate itself against the rest of the world and pretend that global capitalism does not exist. It is certainly not possible for a society that can feed only half of its population from its own resources to institute a siege economy as that society needs to earn money from selling goods and services just to buy food, unless that society is prepared to endure North Korean style poverty. Sharing out the nation's assets (or the world's assets) equally, even assuming that a formula could be found to achieve that, would see equality achieved only temporarily. The selfish and dissolute would drink and gamble away their share, the un-enterprising, which is most of us, would soon run out of money and be forced to work for those who had made their share of the resources work for them. One only has to look at the disaster in Zimbabwe where a policy of expropriation of farmers on egalitarian grounds has led to hyper -inflation and famine in a country that was once the bread basket of Africa. The so called "war veterans" do not have the first clue about agriculture. Like most of us, they take it for granted on the supermarket shelves. Of the majority forced to work for others a hierarchy of talent would soon emerge. If you accept as I do that some individuals contribute more than others to society and others have greater responsibilities, and if you accept as Labour has historically done, that a thriving private sector is essential for the economic wellbeing of a nation, and if you accept as I do, and Labour did historically, that work is a virtue, then you must accept that gradations of income can be morally justified. This is a basic position that is not simply pragmatic, but has sound historical, economic and anthropological underpinning. Socialism emerged as a political and ethical force precisely because the impersonal market economy lacks a moral compass. Those who controlled the market as the factory owners did in the early part of the industrial revolution, controlled prices, wages and the lives of millions. The means of production, distribution and exchange were almost entirely in their hands. Only a land owning aristocracy that dominated parliament and a few prominent wealthy philanthropists stood in their way. The mass of people were wholly disenfranchised. For socialists, and indeed for others who would not wish to be labelled socialists, this was morally untenable. A society in which the ruling classes made just enough concessions to stave off violent revolution was not one they could support. Socialist movements divided into those that sought change by violent proletarian revolution, and those who sought a remodelled society via constitutional means with representative and participatory democracy as the chosen vehicle.

The charge against New Labour is that in respect of its economic and socio-economic policy, as with so much else of its record, moral principles were abandoned along with socialism. It would be ludicrous to argue that those on the left have the monopoly of moral principles in politics, not least because some very dark deeds have been done in the name of socialism. I would never attempt to deny that supposedly socialist countries have been dominated by self-perpetuating wealthy and corrupt elites who have assumed the kind of privileges associated with the capitalists they affect to despise. However, the kind of ethical co-operative Christian Socialism once associated with the Labour Party can be fairly said to have occupied high moral ground, bearing down on the unregulated cesspit in which reward and punishment in the economic sense bore no necessary connection with virtue, merit and hard work. The market economy can and does reward virtue, merit and hard work, and is an engine of prosperity, but it also rewards disproportionately, and not just the greedy and the unscrupulous. The investment banking industry can fairly be described as an unregulated cesspit and the country came perilously close to total economic disaster because of New Labour's moral dereliction in turning a blind eye to its excesses.

I consider myself to have sufficient political and economic literacy, to have enough understanding of the human condition, and to be sufficiently steeped in democratic principles to understand the constraints that there are in creating a society that is at the same time more equitable, more egalitarian, and yet has more opportunities for social mobility. I accept that these are hugely difficult principles to reconcile and that it will always be a journey rather than a destination. New Labour, however, simply gave up. It presided over the further erosion of our manufacturing base and it permitted our economy to become even more dependent for its wellbeing on the casino capitalism of the big banks. It failed to have even the most elementary regulation of their activities, putting small savers, which is most us, at huge risk. The spectacle of queues outside Northern Rock as ordinary voters sought to get their hands on their own money, which had been gambled away on the sub-prime market by irresponsible lenders and then packaged up as marketable securities, will live in the memory forever. New Labour did not cause the banking crisis, but as has been said it did nothing to either prevent or at least ameliorate its worst vicissitudes. It preferred to follow the example of President Clinton in the USA, who reversed decades of federal government policy designed to prevent the great crash from ever happening again, and presided idly and complacently over an almost wholly deregulated banking sector. It was a rational decision in the face of a changed electoral landscape by New Labour to abandon the talisman of public ownership of industry and it had no mandate for bank nationalisation as proposed in the 1983 manifesto, but it did have a moral duty to embrace regulation in the interests of the communities it purported to represent. Despite the banking crisis, bankers continued to pay themselves obscene salaries and bonuses, not forgetting pensions for those such as Fred Goodwin, who was forced to resign and see his company RBS bailed out so deeply that the state now owns 83% of this institution. Why were no bankers prosecuted? What has happened to the Labour party that it is happy to fund the cushioned retirement of this dreadful man out of taxpayers' money? What has happened to the Labour party that Fred Goodwin was recommended for a knighthood at all? What has happened to the Labour Party that there was no recommendation for Fred Goodwin to be deprived of this honour immediately the Royal Bank of Scotland (RBS) crisis broke? Why was the Labour Party unable to make any positive use of the fact that the government had an 83% stake in RBS in its last 18 months of office? This was an opportunity to demonstrate the value of public ownership to a public looking for the government to ride to the rescue. The movers and shakers of the baby boomers who had all the answers at university, had none when they came into government and this is because they jettisoned the moral compass, which despite its flaws had made the party a national movement rather than the chosen vehicle of what can fairly be described as a self- righteous, dictatorial political elite.

Taxation is one of the clearest ways that a political party can spell out its philosophy and priorities. It is also the area most keenly scrutinised by the electorate. The simplest division between left and right on the political spectrum is about tax. Conservatives and neo Liberals within the Tory Party deride Labour as the party of high, confiscatory taxes and as the party of high public spending, the party that knows better than the individual how their money should be best spent. They see low taxes as inherently virtuous, enhancing freedom and personal choice, and good for the economy in that business has the money to invest. Those on the left see the tax system as the vehicle for redistribution of wealth, the promotion of equality and the means for the state to stimulate economic activity when the private sector is on one of its periodic investment strikes.

Under New Labour the gap between the very richest and the very poorest in society has grown rather than been narrowed. Where the gap has narrowed is between working families on lower and middle incomes via the tax credit system. More notably, the gap between larger unemployed families and working families with average incomes has been bridged and often crossed by a benefits system which no longer rewards work, but does reward irresponsible reproduction. The very wealthy, however, who flocked to the New Labour banner have been amply rewarded through the honours system, tax concessions and inaction to tackle the most blatant tax dodging. Fred Goodwin is simply the worst example of honouring those who have expropriated the national wealth. The Coalition government's first budget of 2010 calculated tax revenue to be around £589 billion and forecast expenditure of £711 billion, a deficit of £122 billion, down from a terrifying £146 billion in Labour's last budget, money which of course had to be borrowed. Under New Labour, government expenditure grew from 39% of GDP during its first term, only marginally higher than under the Tories, to a historic peace time high of 47% in its final term. Even in the dark days of hyper-inflation, stagnation and strikes when Britain was dubbed the sick man of Europe, the worst recorded figure was 45%. Servicing this debt was forecast to consume £50 billion of revenue.

An estimated £42 billion of taxes is evaded annually, some of it legally, some of it illegally. This figure is more than the annual Defence budget and represents around 7% of revenue. It is a far cry from the scale of evasion in bankrupt Greece which is estimated at around 25%, but it is still an enormous sum, virtually all of which, outside the low level cash in hand black economy, is avoided by the super-rich. Staggeringly, New Labour even gave the super-rich a helping hand. Private equity companies, which have a shocking record of asset stripping, benefitted from a 10% tax rate. Why is it that it takes a Tory led Coalition to take action to tax Swiss bank deposits? Why is it that a Labour government could not prevent simple legal frauds such as FTSE company chiefs setting themselves up as companies for remuneration purposes and therefore paying lower taxes? New Labour did not even prevent former BBC chief, John Birt, from being hired by the national broadcaster on a similar self-employed basis. Instead they ennobled him and adopted his ludicrous bureaucratic ideas about internal markets. I have just discovered that former leadership candidate David Miliband uses exactly the same scam as John Birt, in that his income from speaking engagements is paid to a company and thus attracts corporation tax of 26% rather than income tax of 50%. New Labour also hired people directly into the Senior Civil Service on the same terms. How on earth can ordinary working people be expected to take Labour seriously as a party that preaches greater equality as its primary moral position, when those who seek to lead it behave in this way? Surely a Labour government could have evolved a simple principle that if you are a British citizen running an ostensibly British company, as an individual and as a company you pay British taxes regardless of where you (or your wife) choose to live and regardless of the tax haven in which the company is registered. The reader may not be aware that an author whose book has been printed and distributed by an American self-publishing company will have his royalties subjected to 30% tax at source. The fact that you are not an American citizen is irrelevant. The American company has made a profit from you so it is liable to US taxes, which not surprisingly it passes on. Capitalist America will not let its biggest companies dodge taxes, so why should we? Equally it should not be difficult to tax foreign owned and registered companies on the business they do in the UK. Starbucks are not about to up sticks and leave. Amazon is not going abandon the British market. And surely there are financial experts who could have helped the government unravel the complexity of trusts. I would accept that legislation that completely eliminates all forms of tax evasion and minimisation is a chimera, but it cannot be beyond the wit of a government with a powerful moral purpose to reduce this £42 billion by at least two-thirds. What happened to the commitment to greater equality? Contrast this with the rate of benefit fraud which runs at around £3 billion, an unacceptable figure but one that in percentage terms of spending on major benefits runs at around half the rate of tax dodging.

In reality, what constitutes lower taxes is a matter of degree. In terms of tax take, the Tories are only marginally a lower tax party when viewed through post war economic history. However, what is indisputably the case is that the balance of direct to indirect taxation swung dramatically in favour of the latter during the ascendancy of Margaret Thatcher. At one point during the 1974-79 Labour government the highest rate of direct tax was 98% although it did fall to 83%. The Conservatives cut the basis rate of income tax from 33% to 22% (now 20%), but conversely raised the rate of VAT from 8% under Labour (reduced from the original Tory rate of 10%) to 15%. When Norman Lamont was chancellor VAT rose to 17.5% and later, under Labour, it fell back to 15%. The Coalition has since raised VAT to a record 20%. The highest rate of income tax was cut back to 40% under Nigel Lawson (Chancellor of the Exchequer 1983-88) and only in 2009 did it go back up to 50% where it remained until April 2013, when it fell to 45%. The Conservatives also capped rates, introduced and scrapped the poll tax and then introduced Council Tax in 1991, but retained capping powers. The direction of travel has been towards taxes on spending with prescriptions, stamp duty on house purchases, petrol, tobacco and excise duties all outstripping inflation and new taxes on insurance (Conservative) and air travel (Labour) being lucrative new sources of tax expansion. Subsidies and services have been reduced or abolished and therefore train fares have constantly outstripped inflation and bin collections have been reduced to fortnightly. These are taxes in all but name. Indirect taxes, flat rate charges and the abolition of subsidies hit the poorest members of society the hardest. My Generation in power has permitted deficit financing on an unprecedented scale, introduced stealth taxes and ignored or allowed to develop new injustices that would have once roused it to furious anger. Alongside these measures it has built a dependent clientele, half of whom will not bother to vote at all but who can be relied upon not to vote for other parties at the election which matters; the General Election.

Perhaps the most disastrous stealth tax was the planned £5 billion per year tax raid on private pension funds when Gordon Brown in his first budget in 1997 abolished tax credits paid to pension funds and companies. Previously, private sector pension funds were so healthy that employers were actually taking "pensions holidays" and suspending employer contributions. Mr Brown's tax raid came at around the point at which pension funds were starting to do less well on the stock exchange. According to the Office of Budget Responsibility, the tax raid has taken even more than envisaged and between 1997 and 2014 it raised revenue of £118 billion for the exchequer, on average just under £7 billion a year. Its true value to pensioners when reinvested would be at least twice that. In short, what had been a healthy situation changed to one in which funds were in debt due to a combination of taxes and declining share values. In 1997, around a third of private sector workers were covered by final salary scheme occupational pensions. That figure is now down to around 10% and artificially inflated by workers in former public sector employment such as telecommunications and the railways. Final salary schemes were first closed to newly recruited employees. Subsequently, they were closed to existing staff, and in the worst cases went bust. The government set up only a very inadequate compensation scheme and a number died before they could receive the compensation. The sheer mean spiritedness of this parsimonious behaviour was on a par with the worst excesses of their Tory predecessors. New Labour stands accused of a major role in the wreck of a once vibrant industry. It simply stood on its hands. Gordon Brown has been described by Richard Littlejohn of the Daily Mail as "the man who stole your old age". The Coalition has not surprisingly continued to collect the money, estimated to raise over £9 billion, (around 2p in the pound in income tax terms). Next time you hear a politician ranting about how cosseted pensioners have been protected from cuts, perhaps you should remind them about the decimation of the private pensions industry by New Labour and the continuing collusion with that of the Coalition government.

New Labour also did nothing for those in receipt of the state pension, in that it refused to restore the link between pensions and pay inflation taken away by the previous government which linked them to prices. Between 1980 and 2000 average earnings increased three and a half times, but the state pension rose only two and a half times. Thus, pensioners did not share the prosperity of those fortunate enough to remain in work. Additionally, as anyone with even a limited knowledge of economics will know, pensioner inflation always exceeds the RPI. Instead, Mr Brown introduced the ludicrously complex pension credit scheme, which many pensioners simply can't or won't claim. I can remember my own grandmother's reluctance to claim means tested supplementary benefit to beef up her less than basic pension back in the 1960s. Today's pensioners are no different, in that psychologically they believe means tested benefits to be an updated poor law rather than an entitlement. Oddly enough, income tax rebates recycled as credits into the pay packet were originally Liberal party policy. Pension credits are simply a logical extension. However, the party of beards and sandals had the good sense to jettison this policy and substitute significantly higher personal allowances to take the poorest pensioners out of direct taxation altogether. There was a time until the Second World War that the labouring classes did not pay income tax, the only tax on their income being the "stamp" introduced in 1909 that provided some protection against sickness and unemployment. The exigencies of war have never been put back in their box. Only now, more than 65 years later, is serious work being done to raise personal allowances and raise the old age pension to a level that will eradicate the need to have a bureaucratic system of means tested top up payments. These have potential to be enduring achievements. Why is it that a Tory/Liberal Democrat Coalition can seriously consider socialist economic measures to protect the less well off and Labour cannot? Truly, the political world as we once understood it has been inverted.

As has been indicated above, stealth taxes were part of New Labour DNA in government. Pension funds were simply the worst example. The word stealthy means creeping or insidious, hoping not to be noticed until it is too late. National Insurance contributions (employers and employees) have been familiar targets for My Generation in office. If NI contributions were ring fenced it would not matter, except of course that they would be lower. As NI contributions go into the general exchequer it is simply income tax by any other name. An income tax reduction from 22% to 20% coupled with NI increasing from 10% to 12% is not a reduction in direct taxation. New Labour in office was every bit as happy as their Tory predecessors to expand the scope of taxes on spending, VAT being the exception, as the headline figure is almost as emotionally loaded as the headline figure for income tax. For fiscal conservatives the switch from direct to indirect taxation is part of their core philosophy, that individuals make better decisions than the state about how to spend their money, that choice enhances freedom, and lower direct taxation creates employment. For New Labour, indirect taxes, charges and the withdrawal of subsidies which taken together are taxes by any other name, are simply discreet (or not so discreet) means of raising revenue to fund the politically correct society. As ever, these taxes are cloaked in pseudo morality. Yvette Cooper defended the indefensible when claiming that Home Improvement Packs (HIPS) which added further costs to house purchase benefitted the environment. It is one thing to know the environmental rating of the home you wish to buy or sell, it is another thing entirely to have the will or the means to do anything about it. This was simple grandstanding. Council bin fines, air passenger duty and levies on our already huge fuel and energy bills are part of the same tax family and are covered in more detail in the chapter on environmental policy. Even the taxes on tobacco and alcohol, which are far easier to justify in terms of a moral purpose, raise around three times more than the cost to the welfare state of tobacco and alcohol abuse.

Let me make it clear that I do not take the view that the state is congenitally incapable of spending wisely. However, the sad truth is that New Labour in office squandered the money it had squirreled away in its first term on an orgy of public spending that made little difference to the quality of our lives as citizens. Equally, the private sector can be just as sclerotic and bureaucratic, and just as likely to act in its own interest rather than that of the public, not least because there is another stakeholder, i.e. the shareholder. Privatisation of energy and water has been little short of a disaster for the consumer. I accept that re-nationalisation was not a realistic option, but My Generation in power could have regulated these industries properly and prevented them from being taken over by foreign companies with no interest in the British consumer except for what they can screw out of them. The private sector is not the repository of all virtue. You only have to read Adam Smith, the original free market guru, in "The Wealth of Nations" (1776), to find cautionary notes about the ability of business to thwart the public interest,

The state sector has the key advantage of not having shareholders who demand their dividend. However, My Generation has created a whole swathe of scavenging bureaucrats with a direct vested interest in expansion of their power heedless of cost. New Labour has created massive bureaucracies in the Ministry of Defence ,where there are more civil servants than armed forces personnel, in the Health Service, where a massive swathe of pen pushers administer the ludicrous internal market, and in the Police and Prison Services, where armies of glorified clerks attached to senior staff set, measure and monitor contradictory performance targets. In the NHS administration, costs jumped from 5% to 12% as a result of the introduction of commissioning, the fancy name for an internal market. Under John Birt, the BBC spent 25% of its income on management costs. Has the public got a better NHS or BBC as a consequence? Of course it hasn't. Why has it taken a Conservative Home Secretary to abolish performance targets for the police? And, of course, right across the public sector are armies of diversity managers and monitors measuring compliance with bogus equality legislation and dreaming up ever more bureaucratic hurdles to jump to justify their existence. After all this money has been spent, you will still wait 4 hours to be seen in Casualty, the time spent waiting in the ambulance on the car park not counting towards the target. It is seen as acceptable for highly skilled paramedics to be kicking their heels on a car park when people could be dying so that managers can claim to have hit their targets and claim the bonuses that accompany "success". This is simply obscene. And if you are admitted to hospital, it will cost you to watch the television. It will also cost you an arm and a leg to use the telephone and, to ensure that you use only the hospital payphones, bureaucrats will tell you, untruthfully, that you cannot use a mobile phone because it may interfere with the working of NHS equipment. Added to that, expect your visitors to be fleeced at the hospital car park. This is what New Labour calls "co-charging" i.e. you pay again for that which you have already paid for in your NI contribution and which used to be free. In case New Labour has forgotten, who is most likely to be sick? Well of course it is old people. Who is likely to have the least disposable income? You've guessed it – old people. Someone tell me, how is this socialism?

New Labour has also presided over a public sector bonus culture which in its own way mirrors that of the dysfunctional banking sector it so admires. The largest bonuses as ever go to the highest paid. Michael Spurr, Director General of the Prison Service, received a bonus in 2009 that exceeded the annual salary of the lowest paid full time staff, including people who have direct prisoner contact. Having worked as a prison governor, and being acquainted with Mr Spurr, I can vouch for the fact that he earns every penny of his six figure salary. Most workers accept that their boss should be paid more than them and accept that the greater the responsibility and accountability, the greater the pay differential. However, bonuses are different. The public sector does not sell goods or services and does not compete for the most part in a market place. It cannot go bankrupt. Senior managers do not make investment decisions that affect the employment prospects of tens of thousands of workers. Senior public sector managers are at risk of dismissal only for disciplinary infractions. Unless mistakes result from gross negligence (and not always then) being less than competent in a post carries no risk of dismissal or demotion, just a sideways move to a desk job out of harm's way. For these reasons fat bonuses which go to public sector bosses who are credited with achievements that are in reality delivered much lower down the unrewarded food chain, are not merited and should form no part of the culture of a Labour government in office.

New Labour will happily boast of the millions it spent on health, on education, on criminal justice, on public transport, on improving the environment and on the welfare state. These are things that we have paid for in taxes and the government has purchased on our behalf. The only proper way in which to audit the value of the spending is against the improvement in service to the public. The story is one of abject failure. Can you see a doctor more easily than in 2001? No, you cannot. Has the standard of nursing care improved? No, it is has not. Witness the scandal in Stafford where 1200 patients are believed to have died because of poor care. Instead, we now employ graduate nurses whose real aim is to secure a well paid management job, of which there are now many in the NHS. Two thirds of senior management jobs in the NHS are now held by women, most of whom are former nurses. Why are there not proper financial incentives to keep the best nurses on the wards? Pardon me for asking a silly question. Emptying bed pans and providing empathy for distressed patients is devolved to much lower paid health care assistants who sometimes have only the most rudimentary grip on the English language.

Are our streets safer? Are there more police on the streets? No, there are not. Indeed, like the Health Service, routine policing has been devolved, in this case to Community Support Officers who command the confidence of no-one, and command the contempt of the criminal classes. The streets of our sink estates have been surrendered to feral children and our city centres at weekends surrendered to binge drinkers. Have educational opportunities improved? Again, the answer is firmly in the negative. New Labour has presided over rampant indiscipline and has actually penalised schools financially that exclude anti-social elements. Where parents seek to beat the system by using either financial muscle or making real sacrifices to move into the catchment area of a good school, My Generation's response has been to pillory them and bring in random balloting for places, regardless of whether a five year old is prevented from attending the same school as older siblings, regardless of the distance, and regardless of the environmental impact of a state sponsored school run. All the while of course, the children of our rulers get places in the very best schools. George Orwell would have been impressed. Equality legislation does not apply to the political class. As for public transport, try commuting to London. Year on year the trains have become more overcrowded and fares have exceeded inflation. House building has dropped to 1930s levels, despite unprecedented demand. Combined with excessive immigration, the effect has been to push up prices for those who can still afford to buy, and push up rents for those who cannot. Of course, if you are in receipt of housing benefit, this does not matter. The welfare state, of which more in the next few paragraphs is now dysfunctional, the thrifty are penalised and the feckless featherbedded. This is a litany of failure, but not a failure of socialism as conservative critics would no doubt say. There is not a shred of anything recognisable as a socialist commitment in this long list of wasteful spending and abject policy failure. What happened to the idealism of My Generation?

Of all the things that make me angry, highest on the list is the treatment of the most elderly in our society. No one disputes that social care is expensive and that an ageing population imposes significant burdens on the working population. It is very difficult to argue now that the duty of looking after the very elderly is properly that of the family. Some elderly people have no family and others are estranged. Social change has broken down the old ties of kinship where younger generations married locally and settled a few streets away. Divorce has fractured families. In many cases there is simply not room for multi-generational occupation of homes. Even where there is room, the demands of work may make it impossible for care to be provided. In the final analysis, most of us have no real ability to cope with geriatric conditions such as advanced dementia and double incontinence. Added to that, many carers are themselves pensioners with the diminution of physical strength that entails. Lifting one's spouse or parent may require huge effort. These are not excuses, these are real practical problems. In so far as Labour had a solution, it just continued with previous government policy. Those with nil or minimal resources got free social care, those with assets were and still are forced to liquidate them. In most cases where charges are levied, elderly people are asset rich and cash poor, the only realisable asset being the family home. The only way a sale can be prevented is if a spouse or close relative over 60 still lives there. Thus, if you are over 60 and have a parent still alive, you are recommended to move back to your childhood home.

The inequity is simple. Ordinary people, who have scrimped and saved to buy a modest home, are being treated in the same way that the aristocracy were treated when death duties were introduced. The taboo on inherited wealth has now passed down to the working classes. What sort of message does this send to those who aspire and those who believe that an individual should take personal responsibility for their own maintenance and the welfare of their children? In the South East, if you are lucky enough to die at a great age and simultaneously avoid the need to go into residential care, then the inheritance tax threshold of 325K will slash your children's inheritance. The fact of the matter is, that in certain parts of the country what were once considered modest family homes have become absurdly inflated in price because of the failure of housing policy, the skewing of the economy to the South East, and more recently mass immigration, yet they are treated as though they are wealthy and their families are expropriated. Furthermore, if you look at the houses of the elderly you will notice something else. Many of these asset rich homeowners are otherwise desperately poor with nothing left over for maintenance or the provision of double glazing. The same people cannot afford to heat their homes in winter because of the outrageous behaviour of the virtually unregulated oligarchy of foreign owned ex public sector energy companies. As a country, because of New Labour's conscious decision to ape the Tories and allow key industries to fall into the hands of foreign owned companies, we are now as a nation no longer in control of our own energy supply, and the elderly are absolutely at the mercy of their predatory pricing policies. I have come to the conclusion that My Generation hates the old, and punishes them for their defiance of the political class. If you don't believe me, remember how Gordon Brown described Gillian Duffy, a Rochdale pensioner who owned her own modest home as a "bigot" for daring to raise immigration during the 2010 election campaign. Pensioners' votes cannot be bought, so they must be taught a lesson with winter as a weapon and expropriation the penalty for daring to be both thrifty and frail. How is any of this socialism?

Compounding this catalogue of failure is the fact that things are different in Scotland, Wales and Northern Ireland all of which have devolved administrations. In Scotland, social care for the elderly is free, there are no prescription charges, and no university tuition fees for Scottish students studying at Scottish universities. The reason for this; the outdated Barnett formula which goes back to 1978 and was the brainchild of Labour Minister Joel (now Lord) Barnett who devised it in order to ensure that public spending was equitable between England and the other component countries of the UK. At the time it was a perfectly logical thing to do. However, the formula was based on percentage share of the UK population. In the intervening 30 years or so, the population of England as a proportion of the UK has increased and therefore the proportional share of population of the UK by Scotland, Wales and Northern Ireland has decreased. Unfortunately for the English taxpayer, the share of public spending allocated to the component parts of the UK has not changed. The main beneficiaries of this situation are the Scots where public spending per head is now 20% greater than in England, which readily explains why the Scots can have free social care for the elderly, free prescriptions and no tuition fees. I have no problem with the Scots having such progressive policies, indeed I applaud them. The problem is that someone else pays for them, which is palpably unfair. However, the political arithmetic is a huge problem for Labour and an impossible one for a party without a moral compass. The landslide Labour victory of 1997 eliminated the Tories from the Scottish electoral landscape. Four years later in another Labour landslide the Tories won one Scottish seat. Even now with the Tories in office they still only hold one seat north of the border.

Interestingly, the two landslide victories actually delivered Labour a majority in just English seats for the first time since 1945. However, this made reform harder than easier. New Labour was committed to Scottish dissolution and intended to be the senior partner in the first devolved

Scottish Parliament. This was not time to dispense with the pork barrel. The senior ranks of New Labour included influential Scottish MPs such as Gordon Brown, Robin Cook and Donald Dewar, the man who duly became Scotland's First Minister in 1999. The back benchers were more Old Labour, but retention of their Westminster seats depended on the continuation of the subsidy. There is simply no rational case for subsidising Scotland any more than there is a case for subsidising French peasant farmers, but My Generation in power chose to connive at a basically immoral proposition at the expense of the English taxpayer who deep down they regarded with contempt. We are the cash cow that exists only to be milked. Needless to say the law of unintended consequences did its work and the Scottish Nationalist Party achieved an overall majority at the 2011 Scottish parliamentary election.

So in England if you want to become a nurse you have to pay for the privilege, because nurses now have to be graduates, but in Scotland your education and training will be free. And if siren voices ever have their way, police officers and prison officers will also have to be graduates, which means that they too will have to pay around 55k plus compound interest for the privilege of holding down a vital role in the service of the public. Like teaching, these are jobs that are aspired to by the sons and daughters of ordinary working people. This in a society in which bankers pay themselves huge bonuses, dodge their taxes and bring the country to the brink of bankruptcy.

There is a theory that the better off were the main beneficiaries of the welfare state. It is certainly true that the middle classes benefitted from the 1944 Education Act and from the establishment of the NHS. However, as we have become a nation of heavily taxed home owners, quite properly the welfare state has extended to the payment of mortgage interest as a welfare benefit to these citizens, albeit after a qualifying period which ensures they exhaust any redundancy pay. Pre Second World War, the middle class tax burden was so light that they could afford servants, as well as school fees and medical bills. During and after the war the great increase in taxation needed to finance the war and reconstruction ensured that only the upper and upper middle classes could finance their pre-war life style. In return for their increased taxes, they gained access to free grammar schools and to a free at the point of use health service. Both the grammar schools and the health service were equally available to the working classes, which was not the case pre-war. Academic ability is not distributed by class, unlike attitudes to the value of education. The abolition of an independent system of selection by competitive examination led only to self-selection and a weakening of social mobility, as it has proved beyond the wit of government to achieve universal provision of a good education. A similar situation exists in the health service where a post code lottery for drug provision emphatically negates the universal principle.

Thus, in politically correct Britain fertility treatment for women with no means of supporting a child i.e. no husband, no partner, no job, cannot be denied or the poor dear will go to court at our expense to claim her human rights have been breached. Yet the self-same Primary Care Trust will happily refuse life prolonging cancer treatments to desperate patients. This is an utterly perverse situation. Back in 1999, a health authority in Cambridgeshire went to the Court of Appeal to seek the overturning of a judgement that they must continue to treat 11 year old Leukaemia victim Jaymee Bowen. In other words representatives of a health service, which was once the pride and joy of Labour Britain, went to court with a Labour government in power to seek an order that would hasten the death of a child. As Jaymee put it when asked by the press of her understanding of the situation, "they're trying to kill me". I still cannot comprehend how a health authority was allowed to spend taxpayers' money to seek a reversal of this judgement. Yet again, I can only point to the total absence of a moral compass and basic human empathy. The welfare state treats our troops with equal disdain. Homes for heroes were called for by Labour as long ago as 1918, and delivered after 1945. That policy has been abandoned in favour of people who have made little contribution and know that breeding to excess is the way forward in terms of exploiting the welfare state. New Labour, despite its foreign adventures, does not really like the armed forces as they are perceived to have male values. Chapter 13 covers in detail the betrayal of the working class, from whom the bulk of our troops emanate.

At this point, I need to be clear about my understanding of the nature and purpose of the welfare state. Prior to the election of the Attlee government in 1945, the UK had a welfare system as opposed to a welfare state. The provision of alms to the poor was part of the Christian tradition and in medieval times relief was distributed from the great abbeys. The sons of the poor would receive free education from the monks. The state got involved in poor relief as early as 1601 when the Poor Law was formally enacted. What was known as outdoor relief lasted until Puritan values triumphed in the early days of the industrial revolution when the Poor Law Amendment Act of 1834 introduced the Workhouse test. This dramatically sharpened up the distinction between the deserving and the undeserving poor to the extent that only those who successfully evaded the workhouse (or prison) could have been considered as deserving. The workhouse system gradually broke down and foundered completely when mass unemployment struck with a vengeance from 1921 onwards. Outdoor relief paid out of the rates returned and Neville Chamberlain intervened to prevent some local authorities raising the rates to pay more generous relief. By standardising rates, the Poor Law was effectively nationalised. Unemployment insurance, like old age pensions introduced by the pre-war Liberal government, had broken down under the strain of mass unemployment and the authorities could do little more than introduce euphemistically named transitional allowances, dole by any other name, to prevent the unemployed and their families from falling into total destitution. It would be hard to say that they succeeded, given the sufferings of the unemployed in this era. The policy was combined with a means test which saw even the smallest piece of income such as a boy's paper round, deducted from the payment. Thus adult men were reduced to dependence on their children. In reality, the state continued to treat the unemployed poor as one undeserving block. The memory of the means test has effectively shut down debate on what is actually a legitimate distinction between the deserving and the undeserving poor.

The wartime coalition commissioned William Beveridge to report on post war reconstruction of a system of social security. It is impossible to understate the impact of this report and its influence on all subsequent governments. Beveridge identified five giants to be slain; want, idleness, ignorance, disease and squalor. Out of this report was enacted the modern welfare state which introduced a comprehensive insurance principle for health and unemployment, secondary education for all via the 1944 Education Act, a public housing programme adopted with equal enthusiasm by the Conservatives in the 1950s and of course the jewel in Old Labour's crown, the National Health Service. Behind this ambitious programme there were firm principles. The insurance system, although compulsory, placed responsibility on the individual to make provision for bad times. There was no question of something for nothing. The amount paid in was earnings related so that the better off paid according to their means. The overriding assumption was that working people provided for their own families and the state stepped in when that was not practical or possible. Ordinary working people clearly did not have the means to pay for curative drugs or education. While they could afford rents or mortgages if in work, clearly they could not build their own homes. Homes for heroes required planning and allocation of scarce resources. Crucially, after 1945, there was a consensus that government had a responsibility to secure full employment, which for a generation was largely achieved. This consensus only broke down with the accession of Mrs Thatcher, when once again the unemployed were demonised. The other side of the bargain, as has been said, was that individuals were expected to take the work that was available. Thus, in working class communities, those who did not work when it was available were considered to be the feckless undeserving poor. Indeed, failing to maintain one's self was a criminal offence punishable by imprisonment. If anyone knows the date of the last prosecution, please let me know.

The charge laid against My Generation in power is its abject failure to deal with the breakdown of the bargain between the state and the individual. The embedding of a culture of unemployment, which so afflicted the heavy industrial areas of this country in the 1930s, was partly offset by the tradition of respectability, greater respect for authority and the influence of religion, but it was the outbreak of war which demanded a supreme national effort simply to survive that was the real antidote. When mass unemployment returned 50 years later, deference was dead and the nuclear age had altered the rules about national survival in the event of conflict. Although unemployment had dropped to 1979 levels by 1997, 1.5 million people unemployed plus those hidden away on disability benefits and early retirement still represented a hard core problem. If the jobs are not there, then people cannot work. If the social housing is not there or the price of family housing is prohibitive, then people cannot move to areas where there is work. If the population grows faster than the availability of employment, then clearly unemployment will not fall. If the education system is lousy, then employers will look for better qualified employees abroad. If parental and school discipline are lacking, then young people will struggle to acquire the necessary work ethic. Finally, if it pays to subvert the benefit system rather than work, then the Jeremy Kyle show will have queues of chavs desperate for their 15 minutes of fame for years to come.

All these things are interlinked and all susceptible to a greater or lesser extent to action by a competent and committed administration. Governments cannot create productive jobs, but they can provide a climate in which what is legitimately the domain of private enterprise can thrive and thus create employment. This is not to say that the private sector should have the right to pay as little as it likes, dismiss workers with impunity, and treat safety with contempt. The worst American style employment practices have no place in this country but at the same time My Generation in power has allowed the development of a bureaucratic, sclerotic, form filling culture to blunt the cutting edge of innovation and enterprise, a process not absent under the Tories because of the baleful effect of EEC membership. Restrictive practices are now the domain of the state rather than trade unions. My Generation stands accused of presiding over a slowdown in housing construction which has only served to push up rents and prices of existing stock, thus hindering essential mobility of labour. This would not matter if the population were static, but it has instead presided over record immigration which quite naturally increased the pressure on house prices and rents, increased the competition for jobs and depressed wages to the extent that pay at or close to the minimum wage is the norm in areas where there is a high concentration of immigrants. Despite its much vaunted drive to improve education standards, in reality New Labour has inflated qualifications to the point where a grade C at GCE has all the value of the German Mark in 1923. Employers are faced with school leavers who, despite their clutch of certificates in leisure and tourism, are functionally illiterate and thanks to indulgence and lack of discipline in the home and school, are ill fitted for the world of work. Mass immigration has given employers a choice that they have exercised. Governments do suffer from the lack of democratic accountability of global capitalism. Nevertheless, it is not beyond the wit of government to tackle school and social discipline and provide incentives for employers to employ those who currently live at the margins of our society, and if necessary to use sanctions, the most effective of which would be to cut off the supply of migrant labour. My Generation in power simply didn't bother, although it is fair to say that many of these problems were inherited from the outgoing administration. New Labour's only significant reform in favour of working people was the minimum wage, but praise for this has to be tempered by the relatively ungenerous level at which it was set and the absence of a London weighting.

The fundamental purposes of a state benefits system are to provide for those temporarily out of work through no fault of their own, to provide for those who medically cannot work and support themselves, and to top up the wages of the low paid so that they can feed, clothe, warm and house themselves to an acceptable standard. The first of these does not work properly as claimants can wait for weeks for benefit payments. This administrative inefficiency is a massive deterrent to taking short term temporary work. As housing benefit can take even longer to process, claimants could lose their homes. Thus, we have a situation where those willing to work risk being punished, whereas those not willing to work will plead their human rights if their benefits are stopped. In itself the second of these, that benefits are paid to those medically unable to work, is a hallmark of a civilised society. However, New Labour in power preferred like their Tory predecessors to use receipt of Incapacity Benefit to disguise the problem of long term unemployment. With regard to the third of these purposes it is often forgotten that 80% of benefits paid to people of working age are paid to people in employment. Every penny of that is testament to government failure to build sufficient houses, failure to regulate the energy market, and of course to our membership of the EU which since 1973 has cut us off from cheaper food from Commonwealth countries. It is undeniably the case that you cannot have market rents in a low wage economy and total self- sufficiency at the same time. In London the private sector rent on a modest family home can be significantly more than a month's take home pay for a full time minimum wage earner. The lower paid also spend a much greater proportion of their income on essentials such as food, energy and public transport and thus are the most vulnerable to sudden price hikes. New Labour has presided like its predecessor over a low wage, low skill, low tech economy for the majority of workers. Like its predecessor, it consigned manufacturing to history when in fact there is a market for high quality manufacture which of course requires high skill levels and investment in vocational training. Instead our youngsters get a B.Tech in Leisure and Tourism or a degree in Media Studies, depending on their position in the intellectual food chain. New Labour preferred to use complex tax and pension credit systems to tackle poverty and income inequality, rather than use the tax system effectively by raising personal allowances and providing decent state pensions to the old as of right. Effectively, New Labour imposed high taxation and high prices on the working poor and then recycled some of it back as a means tested dole. Since when was this socialism?

Leaving out the obvious anomaly of housing benefit, the level of which is a product of failed public housing policy, it is clearly unacceptable that life on benefits should be more lucrative than work. Life on benefits reinforces marginality, reinforces inequality, and reinforces feelings of worthlessness and resentment towards authority. It is corrosive of the character. Having appointed Frank Field to think the unthinkable about welfare reform, Tony Blair made him subordinate to Harriet Harman, who had no intention whatsoever of permitting a reform of benefits that would threaten the dependence of the underclass on state largesse, which in 1997 given Labour's huge majority seemed a limitless horizon. There is no feminist or socialist justification for encouraging young women of low intelligence to have large broods of bastard children by multiple fathers of equally low intelligence who cannot support them. Equally, there is no socialist justification for permitting married or stable co-habiting couples to have large broods of children at the expense of the taxpayer. These families obviously make major claims on social housing. Indeed, another child can be the key to a larger house. For a generation now we have had the ability to control fertility almost entirely, yet as a society we persist in encouraging the very people who can least afford to have large families to do so at the expense of the taxpayer. There is evidence now that members of the generally law abiding Muslim community have picked up on the racket. As our laws do not, rightly, recognise polygamy, second and subsequent wives are treated as single parents and receive housing, child and welfare benefits accordingly. This was exposed by an Asian peer, so it is not a racist fantasy. Finally, of course, there is the welfare largesse paid out to foreign nationals. Britain is a magnet for health tourists and economic migrants from all over the world who know that the land of milk and honey exists on these shores in the form of free handouts from the generous British taxpayer. Thanks to My Generation in power giving up previous wider veto powers in the EEC, we are now faced with migrants from EU countries being able to claim certain benefits from Day One in the UK rather than after three months. It remains to be seen if Coalition plans to reintroduce the qualifying period are ruled unlawful by the European Court of Justice. EU workers have been a boon to Britain's employers, who have been able to choose them instead of our own who they regard as dross. Now the dross of Europe will have another incentive to come to Britain, in addition to those already here to take advantage of our liberal penal code.

All the while any attempt to suggest that these individuals and groups constitute the undeserving poor exist is rudely silenced by the nation's political elite. Sir William Beveridge would be turning in his grave if he could see the perversion of his great vision, and what has befallen the Liberal party of which he was a member, and what has befallen the Labour party which in 1945 had the drive and ability to create the New Jerusalem. The money changers are not the only people to have desecrated the temple.

PART THREE:

POWER TO THE PEOPLE

CHAPTER 20

POWER TO THE PEOPLE: ADDRESSING THE DEMOCRATIC DEFECIT

In my lifetime (I am 61 at the time of writing) there have been fifteen general elections. I have been eligible to vote in ten of them and my ballot has been cast in nine different constituencies. These are - Darwen (which until 1983 when the constituency was merged with Rossendale included the part of Blackburn where I lived), Newcastle-under-Lyme, West Norfolk and Kings Lynn, Stoke-on-Trent Central, Bedford, Milton Keynes South West, Dover and Deal, Worthing West and Lewes. Additionally, I have cast my vote in two referenda, on EU (then Common Market) membership in 1975 and on the Alternative Vote in 2011. I would have to admit to being a little less punctilious with regard to council elections but even so have voted on the great majority of occasions. I have been represented by MPs from all three major parties. Until 2005, I never voted anything other than Labour in a general election. It is fair to say that some of those candidates have been more worthy of my vote than others. From 2005 onwards I abandoned knee jerk tribal voting. As I have said, the Labour party left me and many more like me. Freed from my self-imposed obligation of loyalty, I have since taken a broader view looking at the quality of candidates and local issues. Thus, I felt able to vote Liberal Democrat in Worthing West on a key local issue regarding the building of a new ASDA superstore near existing local shops that would have become boarded up glue sniffing dens (the Liberal Democrats were opposed), but not able to vote Liberal Democrat in Lewes in 2010 because of what I saw as blatant political opportunism by the sitting Liberal democrat MP Norman Baker, when he criticised HMP Lewes over the self -inflicted death of a remand prisoner facing a locally high profile murder charge. If I had been living in Buckingham I would have voted UKIP against the Speaker, if I had been living in Haltemprice I would have voted for David Davis who genuinely stands for civil liberties, if I had been registered to vote in Ross and Cromarty I would have voted for Charles Kennedy who one day his party will regret ditching, and if I had been registered to vote in Middlesbrough I would have happily voted for Labour's Sir Stuart Bell, who more than 20 years ago stood up for wronged parents in the Cleveland sex abuse scandal that never was.

The point I am making is that I have always regarded the suffrage as precious and that not to use it without good reason is a sign of moral dereliction. In my short teaching career I taught pupils about the sequence of Reform Acts that eventually led to the abolition of the iniquitous property qualification in 1918, through to universal adult suffrage in 1928 which ended the discrimination against women, and the lowering of the age of eligibility for the suffrage to 18 in 1968. I taught it with relish and never failed to emphasise just how hard won the vote had been, and never failed to emphasise how that compared with the many countries where there were no elections, or if there were, they were totally corrupt. I taught about gerrymandering in Ireland, which was one of the key issues for the Northern Ireland Civil Rights movement in 1968-69. My faith in representative democracy was total and I saw the franchise as the ultimate symbol of democracy. As such, it never occurred to me to write "none of these useless fuckers" across a ballot slip. I could not do that. However, I have now moved to a position whereby I believe that the Returning Officer should be compelled to give a breakdown of spoilt papers, in which expletives are deleted only in the interests of public decorum. Ballot spoilers have at least taken the trouble to attend the polling station. Indeed, if we were to adopt compulsory voting, spoiled ballot papers would have a great deal to say about the extent to which, or more likely not, politicians command our esteem. If the Bradford West by-election won by George Galloway is anything to go by, we know the answer. I had always held to the view that by not voting you had no grounds for complaint about the deeds and omissions of the government.

I have a particular memory of two witty aphorisms from Ken Livingstone, one of the more interesting political figures of my lifetime. Mr Livingstone once said, "If voting changed anything, they'd abolish it." More amusingly, also attributed to him is this line, "It doesn't matter who you vote for; the government always gets in." Many a true word is spoken in jest. Ken Livingstone did indeed suffer from being abolished when voting changed something. In 1981, Mr Livingstone became Labour leader of the Greater London Council after the local elections of that year sufficiently strengthened the left wing of the Labour group on the Council to allow him to depose Andrew McIntosh, who had actually led the party during the election campaign. He caught the national imagination by slashing tube fares through levying a special rate, which was later struck down as unlawful in the courts when contested by Bromley Council, which had no underground stations. He was a thorn in the side of Mrs Thatcher, with stunts like posting huge banners at the GLC building showing the mounting employment figures. Mr Livingstone also attracted national notoriety by his open support for the IRA, which caused The Sun to label him "the most odious man in Britain". The Conservative government was determined to neuter him and abolished the Greater London Council in 1984, although the legislation did not take effect until 1986. Its powers were returned to the boroughs.

Ken Livingstone was no doubt describing his own experience, as our history over the last 180 years has been about extending the franchise rather than abolishing it. The real questions are whether or not our collective and individual freedoms have advanced as a consequence and whether or not meaningful and beneficial social change has been achieved as a consequence of possession of the franchise and representative democracy. I used to believe that they had.

There have been three hugely significant reforming governments in the 20th century; the Liberal government of 1906-1916 led firstly by Henry Campbell-Bannerman and from 1908 by H.H. Asquith, the Labour government of 1945-1951 led by Clement Attlee, and the Conservative government of 1979-1997 led first by Margaret Thatcher and from 1990 by John Major. In practical terms, the outbreak of war in 1914 finished the Liberals as a reforming administration, Attlee's government was an exhausted and embattled force between the elections of February 1950 and November 1951 when its tiny majority made life very difficult indeed, and the Conservatives were rendered a lame duck government in September 1992 by "Black Wednesday", which wrecked their overrated reputation for financial competence. Mired in sleaze, they limped on until 1997. Whether or not I approve of the reforms is not the point. I do not deny my admiration for the Attlee government or indeed my admiration for the imaginative, innovative and combative Liberal administration elected in 1906. With regards to Mrs Thatcher's government, Chapter 4, The Long Dark Night, details at length my criticisms of and reservations about the true merit of that administration and the radical social change that it brought about. Nevertheless it cannot be argued that Mrs Thatcher was anything other than a strong, visionary and decisive leader who restored Britain's prestige in the world. Furthermore, she made it on merit without any assistance from quotas or all women shortlists in the face of the kind of bias against women that the hatchet faced feminists of My Generation have never had to endure. For Mrs Thatcher's admirers, and there are many, this was the government that set the economy free and restored Britain's faith in itself, and on that basis it was worth the cost. No war is won without casualties. However, what I think about the Thatcher government is not evidence of the failure of representative democracy as an institution. By tearing itself apart and allowing what we would have then called the centre left of politics to be split, Labour permitted the Tories to govern the country twice with majorities in excess of a hundred, despite the Conservative share of the vote at each of those elections being lower than in 1966 when they were handsomely defeated. It was Labour that denied the majority of voters a choice and a voice.

Liberal Democrats have vociferously argued the opposite, that in fact Mrs Thatcher's victories of 1983 and 1987 were and are evidence of a dysfunctional system. Indeed, no party has achieved in excess of 50% of the vote at any general election since the exceptional circumstances of 1931. The only other occasion this occurred in the 20th century was in 1900, the first of the century's twenty-six general elections. For Liberal Democrat politicians (not necessarily voters) this is evidence only that on every occasion since when there has been single party government, by definition it lacks legitimacy since it does not represent a majority of voters. This is an oversimplified argument based firmly on an assumption that coalition is actually what voters want. On the occasions that hung parliaments have occurred, 1923, 1929, February 1974 and 2010, these have been the result of individual decisions by the electorate not collective ones. It should be noted that opinion polls were not available in 1923 and 1929 to potentially influence outcomes and in February 1974 they predicted a Tory majority. The British voter is largely tribal. The decisive outcome of the AV referendum provided the proof, were it needed, that the electorate do not want a system that makes coalition governments more likely. They do not wish to write a blank cheque for post-election deals. The Liberals and their successors, the Liberal Democrats, have not since the unique circumstances of 1931 campaigned for a coalition government, not least because they know full well how that would resonate in the polling booths. At every election since 1974 they have dodged the question, "In the event of a hung parliament, will you support Labour or the Conservatives?" for exactly that reason. The electorate is largely suspicious of electoral pacts other than in exceptional circumstances. Pre-election pacts such as those put to voters in 1918 and 1931 had wholly in the case of 1918 and partially in the case of 1931, broken down by the time the next election was due.

The first formal coalition to face the electorate as such was the First World War government led by David Lloyd George, in what is known to history as the "coupon election" of 1918. Interestingly, although it had a massive parliamentary majority, the coalition actually polled less than 47% of the popular vote. Unfortunately for the Liberal Party it was split at the 1918 election between those who wanted to continue the coalition and those that did not. Broadly, coalition Liberals accepted the leadership of Prime Minister David Lloyd George and opposition Liberals accepted the leadership of former Prime Minister H.H. Asquith. The gestation of the split came two years earlier when Conservative members of the coalition were vocally unhappy with the prosecution of the war under Prime Minister Asquith. The Conservatives were supporters of conscription, whereas the Liberals were split between those who opposed conscription and those who supported it. David Lloyd George supported conscription and supplanted Asquith as prime minister. The Conservatives, who were the majority party in the coalition elected in 1918, called time on the coalition in 1922, but the Liberals went into the election still split between the Asquith and Lloyd George factions. In terms of seats, the Conservatives won comfortably but with only 38.5% of the popular vote. However, the real significance of the result lies in the fact that the Labour party which had elected its first members only in 1900, moved narrowly into second place in both the number of seats and the number of votes cast. In the 1923 election, despite that fact that Liberals were united again under Asquith and increased both their vote and seats (115 to 158), they were still behind the Labour Party which formed a minority government. The following year, the Liberal vote slumped from 29.5% of the vote to under 18% and the number of seats plummeted to 40. Asquith lost his seat and died before the next general election where under Lloyd George's leadership, and standing on a radical platform of Keynesian economic reform, they polled just over 23% of the popular vote, but won only 59 seats.

The potent Liberal myth of an unfair system has its earliest manifestation here but the truth is that the 1929 election confirmed their third party status. Labour, the largest single party, had over 37% of the vote and the outgoing Conservatives actually polled 38.1%, a figure which included the Ulster Unionists. In October 1931 the emergency "National" government that had replaced the minority Labour government in August of that year went to the polls for a "Doctor's Mandate". The Conservatives, who dominated the coalition, polled 55% of the vote. The Liberal party split into three factions, one formally allied to the government as Liberal Nationals elected without Tory opposition, the Liberal party itself which informally supported the National government, and a rump of four members who were effectively Lloyd George's family party. There were 71 Liberals of various hues in the House of Commons, but by no stretch of the imagination was there a meaningful Liberal presence or voice. At the next election, in 1935, the total number of Liberals fell to 54 but only 21 of these were what could be termed the official Liberal Party. The number of Liberal Nationals aligned to the Conservative party continued to outnumber official Liberals in the House of Commons until 1964. Not until 1983 would more than 21 official Liberals secure election to the House of Commons and not until 2005 would the 1929 total of 59 MPs be exceeded.

After World War II the Liberals swiftly ceased to be a national party. At only one election between 1945 and 1974 did the Liberal party contest more than 50% of parliamentary constituencies. The nadir was reached in 1951 and 1955 when only 109 and 110 Liberals respectively sought election. Their share of the national vote fell to barely 2.5%. Prior to Jo Grimond taking over the leadership of the Liberals in 1956 and re-positioning the party to the non-socialist left of centre, assimilation into the Conservative party in the same way as Liberal Nationals was seriously discussed. After the 1955 and 1959 elections they held precisely six seats, and two of these were as a result of electoral pacts with the Conservatives to give each other a free run in the two seats up for election in each of the northern towns of Huddersfield and Bolton. Other than that, only North Devon, Montgomery, Cardigan, and Orkney and Shetland returned Liberal members to the House of Commons.

Electorally, they were a party of the Celtic fringe. In this period they were scarcely more visible in local authority elections. The usual dating for the liberal revival is 1962 when Eric Lubbock sensationally snatched Orpington. This seat was held in the 1964 General Election but the five other Liberal gains were in Scotland and Cornwall. Only at the 1966 election would they gain two mainstream English constituencies. From the early '70s onwards disillusion with the failure of the Labour and Conservative parties to address Britain's decline saw growing support not only for the Liberals, but also for Nationalist parties in Scotland and Wales. The Labour split of 1981 gave birth first to the Social Democrats and then to the alliance of Liberals and Social Democrats that contested the 1983 and 1987 elections, before merging to form what we now know as the Liberal Democrats. The Liberals had already adopted proportional representation as a key manifesto plank before the 1983 General Election at which the alliance won a quarter of the popular vote, but only 4% of House of Commons seats. Instead of a breakthrough there was a massive sense of let down and a growing sense of grievance.

The campaign for electoral reform has a longer history than is commonly known. As long ago as 1910, when there was a minority Liberal administration maintained in power by Labour and the Irish Nationalists, a Speaker's Conference reported in favour of a change to the Alternative Vote system. In 1923 the Liberals proposed the adoption of AV in the House of Commons but it was defeated. In 1931 the minority Labour government informally propped up by the Liberals succeeded in piloting a bill to introduce AV through all its stages in the House of Commons and it was through to the final stage in the House of Lords when the government fell in August. This is the closest the system for Westminster elections has ever come to change, although we have seen proportional representation using the Single Transferable Vote (STV) introduced for elections in Northern Ireland (1973) and the European Parliament (1999) and we have seen the Additional Member system (a hybrid of first past the post and STV) used in the devolved Scottish and Welsh parliaments since 1999. G.R. Dangerfield identifies the death of Liberal England as taking place between 1910 and 1914 and ascribes it to the bitter political battles that were being fought over the Parliament Act and female suffrage, the industrial battle being fought with organised Labour and the virtual insurrection in Ulster that was taking place as the House of Lords could no longer block Irish Home Rule. However, only one of these, industrial militancy, had the power to destroy the Liberal party as an alternative party of government.

The period 1918-26 was a period of bitter industrial relations and trade union militancy as workers fought to hold on to jobs and where jobs were retained to hold on to hard won pay and conditions. The Liberal Party, which had taken the fledgling Labour party under its wing before the war, now found it had a cuckoo in its nest. However, instead of seeking to find answers to the nation's problems and taking on board legitimate popular aspirations, the Liberals preferred to tear themselves apart, rather as Labour did between 1979 and 1983. By the time the Liberals had something to offer the nation at the 1929 General Election the train had left with Labour in the driving seat. Instead of taking advantage of the Labour split in 1931, the Liberals split into three instead. The point of the extended history lesson is that the Liberal Party has only itself to blame for its wilderness years. Whatever the faults in the system of representative democracy from 1867 to 1970, it cannot be argued that a defective electoral system was hindering it from working. Until 1928, when universal adult suffrage finally arrived, the real democratic deficit lay in the right to vote. Nor is it fair to argue that the Conservatives, who were in government either alone or in coalition for all but three of the twenty one inter war years, were undeserving benefactors of a system strained by the presence of a third party. When the crunch came in 1924 and 1931, the bulk of Liberals happily co-operated with the Conservatives first in ousting Labour, and then in 1931 engaging in an electoral pact with the Conservatives. The Liberal Party was not left wing in this era, and as the 1931 election results demonstrate, neither was the country.

The real breakdown of representative democracy begins with the government of Edward Heath (1970-74) breaking its promise not to join the Common Market, (now EU) without "the full hearted consent of the people." Under Mrs Thatcher, although she would eventually realise her mistake, we got further locked into an undemocratic Europe via the Single European Act of 1986 which updated the original Treaty of Rome. Her successor John Major signed the Treaty of Maastricht in 1992 which further reduced our sovereignty as a nation. Between 1992 and 1997 the UK suffered the long, lingering disintegration of his government under the weight of its own arrogance, hubris and sleaze, inflicting a level of discredit not seen on our system of government since Lloyd George was found to be selling knighthoods and peerages back in 1922. After 1997, instead of arresting the breakdown of our democracy, My Generation in power accelerated it, which is the central thesis of this book. As we have seen, for Liberal Democrats the cure lies in radical electoral reform, i.e. the introduction of proportional representation. The New Labour analysis is different. The system has broken down because of social exclusion. The disproportionately low number of women, gays, and ethnic minorities mean that parliament does not mirror the nation and the same applies to key institutions such as the BBC, the armed forces, the police and the civil service. Additionally, Labour Prime Minister Gordon Brown was content to join the Liberal democrats in embracing PR, as it would insure against defeat and protect the victories of Britain's cultural revolutionaries and recreate the broad left alliance from the student days of My Generation. Until recent years, the Conservatives did not worry unduly about the failings of our system of representative democracy. Tory democracy has always had a patrician flavour and it is natural enough not to worry about the demerits of a system that brings you success and the spoils of office. Tories have always emphasised the sovereignty of parliament, which we have learned to our cost over the last forty years is not the same beast as sovereignty of the people. From 1918 to 1997 the Conservatives had been in office either on their own or in coalition for 59 of the 79 years between periods in the wilderness. However, when the Conservatives were finally deserted by the electorate they were hammered, losing three consecutive general elections, 1997, 2001 and 2005, and returning less than 200 MPs on each occasion. Not since 1906 had less than 200 Tories been returned. The Conservative analysis was that the system was now weighted against them, in that the percentage of Tories elected was less than the percentage share of the vote, not as blatantly as against the Liberals, but weighted nevertheless. Their superficial solution is a reduction in the number of MPs from 650 to 600 and equalising the size of the constituencies, so that, theoretically, every vote has the same weight.

Minority party voting had been growing since 1974. In 1951, over 96% of voters who turned out voted Labour or Conservative, although it must be said that this was skewed by the fact that the Liberals contested only 17% of the constituencies. In 1983 the combined Labour and Conservative vote was just over 70% in the face of the largest third party vote in 50 years. By 2010 the combined vote for the "big two" had dropped to a record low of just over 65%. The outcome of that election was telegraphed in the opinion polls. The Liberal Democrats shouted ever louder for proportional representation. As has been said, the Labour Prime Minister, Gordon Brown, announced himself as a convert. The Conservatives contemplated the fact that 36% of the vote gave Labour a comfortable working majority of 64 in 2005, but left them 20 seats short of an overall majority in 2010.

In truth, all of the prescriptions put forward by the three main parties are flawed as none address the real problem, the disconnection between the population and the politicians who claim to represent us. This is why the doctrine of the sovereignty of parliament between elections is no longer working. In 2001 turn out nationally dropped to 60%, the lowest since 1918. At the previous election it had been over 70%. In 2010 the Conservatives "won" the election with 36.1% of the vote. However, when abstentions are taken into account this represents barely 23% of those eligible to vote. It is a truly terrifying figure. The current coalition is composed of parties for whom 60% of those who turned out voted for, but less than 40% of those eligible to vote. Proportional representation has many weaknesses, but the fact is that it does not address mass opting out by the electorate. As such, a majority in the House of Commons would no more be a majority in the country than in the first past the post system. It is not unlikely that opting out by voters would increase as no-one could hope to get their first choice of government. There is nothing fair (Nick Clegg's favourite word) to the electorate about permanent coalition, institutionalised post electoral horse trading, and third parties becoming permanent parties of government. At least under the current system around two thirds of voters can go into the ballot box with the hope that their party might win and deliver a programme that they broadly support. Supporters of PR point out the benefits of parties working together. Few would argue against its value during two world wars. However, in peacetime the fact is that with the exceptions of 1918 and 1931, political parties do not go to the country offering coalition and history tells us we should be very afraid when they do.

PR would institutionalise coalition without us voting for it and the Liberal Democrats would be a permanent party of government without ever having to aspire above third party status. I can think of few things more profoundly anti-democratic. PR in the form it is used for the Euro elections, with its giant multi member constituencies, would be an even greater conspiracy against the electorate by the political elite. Local democracy already suffers considerably from the penchant of both the Labour and Conservative parties to either rig local shortlists or parachute in preferred candidates. Large multi member constituencies simply disconnect the voter from the candidates. How are you supposed to know who is your MP, the one who represents you? How do these MPs identify with the voter? The answers in short are you don't and they won't. The PR system favoured by the Liberal Democrats is STV, Single Transferable Vote. In this system, once candidates have achieved the quota to be elected, for example in a ten member constituency 10% plus one, surplus votes are then transferred. Someone needs to explain to me how votes being transferred without the voter's permission is remotely democratic. This is something I normally associate with the regime of Robert Mugabe. The worst form of PR is the list system. Under this form of PR, the pretence of voting for an individual candidate is abandoned. You vote simply for the party and you get the MPs your party hierarchy wishes to give you. Party favourites are top of the list. Those who lack patronage and those who have offended the party leadership will find themselves on the cold list, permanently. In the unique circumstances of Northern Ireland, PR (using the STV system) works well, but in Italy it has institutionalised both instability and corruption and in Israel it has made progress to peace in the Middle East impossible, as no government can command a majority in the Knesset without having to accommodate religious extremists. PR opens up the spectre of the BNP gaining representation in the House of Commons and having to be appeased so that a government can function. I readily concede that the Additional Member system (a combination of single member constituencies and a party list system) works for Germany, but it has to be remembered that German democracy, re-established in 1949 after the horrors of the Hitler dictatorship, is deliberately skewed against single party government. The question is not what is good for Germany, or for devolved governments in Ulster and Scotland with limited powers, but what is good for us.

It is no surprise that influential figures in the Labour party are prepared to embrace electoral reform. The calls for 50% of the cabinet/shadow cabinet to be female, 50% of candidates in winnable seats to be female, and for ethnic minority representation in the House of Commons to reflect ethnic minority representation in the community are in effect calls for PR on the basis of identity. Stretching this argument only a little, one presumes that there would need to be an all gay shortlist in one of three constituencies in the city of Brighton and Hove. No one would pretend that there has not been a history of discrimination. Within living memory, women in the Labour party were expected to make the tea and Conservative women serve the coffee. After meetings in Labour clubs men and women drank in separate areas and likewise at Conservative gatherings men and women would retire to separate rooms. Feminists do not regard Mrs Thatcher as an icon, but it cannot remotely be denied that her success in smashing through the ultimate political glass ceiling has benefitted women seeking political careers.

Openly gay candidates had to wait longer for acceptance. Margaret Colquhoun, MP for Northampton North 1974-79, broke new ground when she came out as a lesbian in 1976 and the press had a field day. Her own local party was no less prejudiced and de-selected her, although she was reinstated by the party hierarchy. She was defeated at the 1979 election on a swing of around 8%, significantly larger than the national swing of 5.2%. In 1983, at the Bermondsey by-election, Peter Tatchell, the known to be gay Labour candidate, was crucified in the press and subject to the kind of campaign by some of his opponents that made the gutter look like the moral high ground. The Labour vote dropped from 63% to 26% and the Liberal victor and the still MP, Simon Hughes romped home on a 44.2% swing. In 1997, things were very different. The candidacies of Stephen Twigg, who stunned the nation by defeating Michael Portillo, Ben Bradshaw and Chris Bryant, all of whom were openly gay, barely registered as being anything out of the ordinary. The country had largely moved on. At the time of writing, I would confidently venture the view that only the odd Conservative association would be unduly concerned with a candidate's sexuality. Even the National Front, forerunner of the BNP, put forward a candidate that the party knew to be gay, even if the electorate did not. Ethnic minority candidates are now also run of the mill. In 1987, as one of three black Labour MPs, Diane Abbott became the first black female member of the House of Commons. In 1992 (the Conservatives have tended to run behind Labour in eliminating irrational discrimination), John Taylor was selected by the Cheltenham Conservatives to fight the seat, but sadly a rump of the local party refused to accept him on blatantly racial grounds. Mr Taylor was defeated at the election in what was believed to be a safe seat. He was later the first black Tory peer. Thirteen years later, things were much different. One good example will suffice. Adam Afriyie, was selected by the Conservative Party for the true blue constituency of Windsor, something that would have been inconceivable twenty years earlier. Mr Afriyie increased the Conservative majority at the expense of the Liberal Democrats.

New Labour, and for that matter the Conservatives under David Cameron, are fighting battles that apart from a few last outposts, are largely won. Sadly the Labour leadership in particular, but also the current Conservative Prime Minister have not caught up with the way the world has changed and remain obsessed with a politically correct ideology of social engineering based on identity, rather than on the merits of the candidate. The most practical demonstration of this sloppy thinking is the fate of the "Blair Babes" elected in 1997, which is dealt with in Chapter 2. In its own way the all women shortlists were every bit as iniquitous as the unofficial all public school shortlists that pertained in some local Tory parties, and the all third rate trade union hack shortlists that were not uncommon in some Labour industrial backwaters. Eliminating merit as a criterion for selection diminishes parliament and cheats the public. Patronage and favouritism, whether under the guise of the old boy network or dressed up as positive action or positive discrimination, effectively recreate the rotten boroughs that existed prior to the 1832 Reform Act. It is deeply shameful, but it is how corrupt ruling elites full of their own sense of entitlement behave. As for the Conservatives, their preference is to indulge in dangerous tinkering. Quite what a reduction from 650 to 600 constituencies is supposed to achieve is unclear. The saving to the public purse is peanuts. Over the course of the ten to fifteen years between boundary reviews, constituency sizes will become distinctly unequal again with the normal demographic changes that occur over time. Historically, boundary changes have always benefitted the Conservatives as Labour voting inner city constituencies shrink. In the end, the Conservatives are engaging in petty gerrymandering. The other big concern is that there will be more sitting MPs than available seats, which will allow party big wigs to arrange for the non-adoption of MPs who the leadership have found difficult. This is another example of abuse of power by the elite and another abuse of democracy.

To go forward we need to abandon the doctrine of the sovereignty of parliament and instead embrace the sovereignty of the people. There is no other theoretical model that will mitigate and dissipate the power of the political elite to ignore the electorate. They may not realise it at the moment, but the political class would actually gain in credibility as a result. Representative democracy will always trump participatory democracy as most citizens are content to let others govern on the basis that they do not themselves have the time, inclination or ambition to do so. Unfortunately, the political elite interprets this as a form of popular deference given to the elite on the basis that they are the experts who can be trusted to act in good faith on their behalf. The reality is that the political technocracy which runs our country is simply a new and malign establishment replacing the old establishment which was so memorably described by Anthony Sampson (1926-2004) in his seminal work published in 1962, "The Anatomy of Britain".

However, it is important to remember that the sovereignty of parliament itself has been massively eroded. We are ruled by the European Commission and the European Court of Human Rights. Brussels and Strasbourg trump the British parliament. A House of Commons full of politicians with the courage to renegotiate the relationship with the EU, and preferably to leave it, is urgently needed. Similarly, with the European Convention on Human Rights, sovereignty can only be regained by the repeal of the Human Rights Act which incorporated European human rights law into our legal system. These changes are non- negotiable if we are to regain our status as a fully functioning democracy. Although it is not wholly consistent with my stance that there are no such creatures as intrinsic human rights, I have no particular objection to a return to the position pre 1966 where the UK was a signatory to the convention, but opted out of the jurisdiction of the court in Strasbourg as this does not compromise our sovereignty. At the time of writing this paragraph (July 2014), there is a little less than 12 months to run of this parliament. The kind of revolution that we need is not one that can be triggered by the usual suspects going on strike or by a repeat of the orgy of rioting and looting by the nation's criminal classes that took place in August 2011. In May 2014 UKIP won the European elections breaking the century long tradition of either the Labour or Conservative parties topping the poll. This was a stunning victory and the cross party ruling class must continue to be challenged at the ballot box. Breakthroughs by UKIP and independent candidates at by-elections, which if part of a consistent pattern, have the capacity to start a bandwagon that will roll into the next general election, thus putting them on notice that the end is nigh and that the British people have woken from their slumbers and intend to reclaim their democracy.

I accept that a new political class would replace the old. That is the nature of representative democracy. It will need to be kept in check by fully functioning democratic institutions. It will need to be more representative of the community. Labour's tired answer is politically correct quotas. There is a key intellectual flaw in basing representation on identity in that it assumes homogeneity where it may and indeed very likely, not exist. We already know that class identity does not necessarily dictate party allegiance. Working class conservatism is a well understood political phenomenon without which the Conservatives would never be able to govern. Women comprise over 50% of the population and if they voted as a bloc then virtually all MPs and ministers would be women. The truth is that women do not vote as a bloc any more than men do. Bill Clinton memorably coined the phrase "It's the economy, stupid" in his successful 1992 American presidential election campaign. If one takes an economic issue, that of child benefit which is paid directly to the mother and which the coalition legislated to means test from 2013, there is no sisterhood on the issue. Opinion polls quite clearly show that another issue, old fashioned class politics, comes into play. The question why should higher rate taxpayers receive universal benefits is a fair one and is argued over hotly. The question why people should have the right to have very large families at public expense is equally fair and equally divisive. It is not necessary to rehearse those arguments here, but it is necessary to point out that voters assume a variety of identities as rich or poor, employed or unemployed, public sector or private sector, homeowner or tenant, single or in a committed relationship. These are merely a few examples. It is also ludicrous to pretend that child benefit levels are not an issue for men. After all, it is still part of the family income.

The same arguments apply to ethnicity. Traditionally, Labour has benefitted from the immigrant vote. Although there is some truth in the view that Labour benefits on the basis that it is traditionally more immigrant friendly, particularly where skin colour is concerned, it is also the case that, typically, immigrants begin at the bottom of the social structure and therefore there is a class affinity in voting patterns. It also needs to be remembered that many members of established migrant communities are vigorously opposed to large scale immigration, not because they wish to prevent others having the same privileges, but because they understand the risks to social cohesion and their own hard won acceptance by the host community. Homosexuality only became a party political issue after the infamous clause 28 forbidding the promotion of homosexuality in schools was enacted in 1988. It is certainly the case that there were above average pro Labour swings in the three Brighton and Hove constituencies in 1992 and 1997, but they were not sufficiently above average as to be remarkable. In 2010, the Tories admittedly detoxified of the earlier anti-gay stance, regained both Brighton Kemptown and Hove, but the Green Party seized Brighton Pavilion, electing its first ever Westminster MP. It suggests that the good burghers of Brighton and Hove have other more pressing concerns than their sexuality.

I tend to have very mixed views about the USA and about some of our European neighbours. Nevertheless, both can teach us something about the weapons they deploy to enhance the will of the people at the expense of the will of the elite. For American politicians life can be an electoral treadmill. Congressmen face re-election every two years. The President is elected every four years and is permitted a maximum of two terms. The exhausting race for the White House begins in January with the Republican caucuses in Iowa and ends only in November, when the final candidates face the voters. Senators are more fortunate in that they are elected for a six year term. However, before Presidents, Senators, Members of the House of Representatives (usually known as Congressmen or women), Members of State Assemblies and State Governors can face their opponents at the ballot box they must also face members of their own party in primary elections. This system works either through caucuses, which are broadly similar to selection by party activists which is the norm in the UK, but crucially without shortlisting and, much more commonly, via full scale elections in which real voters registered as party supporters cast their ballots. For more minor offices there is only one primary but at the top end of the spectrum, presidential hopefuls face a primary in every state unless or until they withdraw. Critics will no doubt argue that the system allows all kinds of fruit cakes to not only have their fifteen minutes of fame, but in some cases get elected. However, this is democracy at work. If the local population wants a State Assembly man who is an evangelical Christian with all that implies, then that is what they get. If the local population wants a hard line district attorney (state prosecutor, an office which is elective in some states), then that is what they get. The American system isn't perfect as the recent standoff between President Obama and the House of Representatives over healthcare insurance reforms for which the President has a clear mandate, amply demonstrates. Equally I can't pretend that some of the American politicians who get elected don't make me uneasy, but they make me far less uneasy than the patrician liberal elite that constantly conspire to frustrate popular will. John Stuart Mill warned about the tyranny of the majority and indeed this is often quoted as the definitive authority for limiting democracy. However, this confuses the mob with the majority. Mill was simply expressing the fear of eminent well to do Victorians of the great unwashed after the 1867 Reform Act enfranchised male members of the working classes for the first time and it should be seen in that context. Voting in secret is mature political behaviour, not mob rule. Returning to the USA, as the offices being contested become more important and as the process advances, then the fruit bats, the bigots and the rampant homophobes tend to be eliminated. Unfortunately, the vice presidential candidates which are picked by the presidential nominees at the party conventions escape this process, a weakness which permitted Sarah Palin to be on the Republican ticket. However, this is not a weakness of the primary system.

The biggest weakness of the American political system is that candidates for major political office are almost uniformly wealthy. Political independence has to be bought and paid for before the candidate can face the electors. There is no equivalent of a trade union funded nationwide Labour party. I have become a reluctant convert to at least some state funding of political parties for the purpose of contesting elections. If we are to have primary elections, they will need not only to be compulsory for parties which have polled a specific minimum percentage of votes in the previous contest, but they will also have to be paid for. It is perfectly possible to restrict candidates in terms of what is permitted to be spent on leaflets, TV broadcasts and the staging of public debates in the locality at public expense, and to forbid private expense in the interests of a level playing field. If we want our democracy to be sound it may not be cheap, and the current system of leaving the political process to be paid for by wealthy individuals and trade unions does not empower the voter. Getting representative candidates through to the final electoral stage, via a primary process will reduce the number of party hacks who enter parliament, it will reduce significantly the influence of unrepresentative local activists, and it will eliminate parachute candidates. The clear positive outcomes are enhanced local democracy and representatives who because of the local credibility they command will be empowered in parliament. The power of a party Chief Whip to threaten or even procure the de-selection of an MP will disappear. Political parties will be healthier and dissent will not be the province of self-appointed martyrs. None of this would inhibit the ability of independents to stand in elections after primaries have been completed. I would advocate that the primary system is adopted for the election of mayors and, potentially, also for county and city council elections. I don't believe that this kind of institutional change would succeed overnight as there is a huge decline in political participation to reverse. However, doing nothing is not an option.

A further plank of reform, making more offices subject to election, has already been tentatively explored by the political parties. The electing of mayors, long the norm in France as well as in the USA, has proved to be a success, not least because independent candidates have been elected in a number of towns and cities in preference to party hacks. The election of former Police Superintendent Ray Mallon in Middlesbrough and more interestingly of Stuart Drummond, alias H'Angus the Monkey, in Hartlepool, a gentleman who on Saturdays acted as mascot of the local football club, were viewed derisively by critics. Predictably, they missed the point. The citizens of Hartlepool were expressing their independence at the ballot box and revelling in their new found freedom. If that involved contempt for conventional politics, then politicians should ask themselves honestly why the voters preferred a man dressed in a monkey suit wearing a Hartlepool United football kit. As it turned out H'Angus the Monkey was sufficiently effective as mayor to be re-elected on two further occasions, as indeed was Mr Mallon. Both men are still in post, though Mr Drummond no longer acts as the Hartlepool mascot. It seems that the voters' contempt for existing local politicians was not misplaced. Like the Freedom of Information Act, elected mayors were part of a brief Prague Spring of democratic scrutiny that New Labour in office would regret but dare not reverse.

In London, the Metropolitan Police Authority has been scrapped and its powers handed over to the Mayor. In the summer of 2011 the unelected and unaccountable MPA suspended Assistant Commissioner John Yates and in doing so effectively forced his resignation. A subsequent inquiry cleared him of any wrongdoing, but no one under that system can be held accountable for the premature loss of a fine police officer. The resignation of Mr Yates and subsequently that of the Commissioner,

Sir Paul Stephenson, were procured by politicians with their own agenda against the Metropolitan Police. The Home Secretary has acted to create the office of Police and Crime Commissioner for each of England's 43 police forces, a measure opposed by Labour and a cadre of politically correct Chief Constables who are now part of the political class. These replaced the unelected police and, as has been said, unaccountable police committees which were filled to the brim with political appointees. Unfortunately, the first elections held in November 2012 were something of a disaster with only 15% of voters going to the polls. Part of the explanation lies in the almost complete lack of promotional publicity for the elections, but also in the selection of discredited political figures in some areas as party candidates. Teresa May should reflect and consider very swiftly the introduction of primary elections for these important posts or perhaps, more radically, banning organised political parties from contesting the elections for Police and Crime Commissioners for a period of ten years. Only then will local people get action on things they care passionately about, such as anti -social behaviour by problem families and domestic burglary, which all too frequently are where our police forces fail.

The principal of elected officials can be taken much further. Elected District Judges to replace lay magistrates with wider sentencing powers is an obvious starting point to complement elected Police Commissioners. The election of local heads of the local Crown Prosecution Service to mirror the American system of District Attorneys is not without merit, not least because of the incompetence, malice and partiality that has characterised some of the recent celebrity sex abuse prosecutions. Going further, what about elected adoption panels tasked with finding homes for those who languish in care and graduate in disproportionate numbers into the penal system, because politically correct Social Services actively hinder finding loving homes for desperate children. Indeed why not elect Heads of Social Services? I also think there should be elections for those who head up quangos, such as the Commission for Equality and Human Rights, pending the adoption of a written constitution and the setting up of a permanent constitutional commission that would render such bodies redundant. Quangos are amongst the worst examples of the abuse of patronage by the ruling elite. Finally, if we are to retain a public service broadcaster funded by a compulsory licence fee, then it is not unreasonable either for the BBC Board of Governors to face election. The imaginative reader could doubtless find other areas in which to introduce democratic competition and thus improve public participation. Like the sale of council houses and the privatisation of state industry, this is an idea for which time has come, and unlike privatisation does not replace one vested interest with another.

An utterly crucial plank of reform is the use of referenda. These are common in a number of continental countries, most notably Switzerland. It is pure constitutional snobbery to believe that as a consequence our continental neighbours are in some way inferior. To argue that it is not part of the British tradition, or that they cut across the traditional sovereignty of parliament and are therefore unconstitutional is no more than vested interests defending their own privileges. As we do not have a written constitution and a referendum has never been struck down by a court the unconstitutional argument is simply nonsense. Our politicians cite the fact that as a policy was in the manifesto and they have been elected, the voters must have given their consent. This of course is arrant nonsense as election manifestos are a packaged bundle that we are expected to swallow whole. The truth is that voters would sometimes like table a la carte. Politicians harp on constantly about choice, but in reality seek to restrict us to set menus so they can stuff the voter with the inedible and the allergenic.

National referenda are relatively new to Britain, but our politicians have had no difficulty authorising them when it has suited their own designs. Most famously we were magnanimously granted a referendum by Harold Wilson's Labour government in 1975 when we were invited to decide whether to stay in or leave the European Community on the basis of the renegotiated terms, such as they were. The reality is that this was a political fix by the wily Wilson to resolve the problem of a cabinet split down the middle. Since then we have had one other national referendum on changing to the Alternative Vote system for Westminster elections, which took place in 2011. We have also had referenda on devolution in Scotland and Wales in 1979 and 1997. A referendum on Scottish independence will take place late in 2014. In 1973, Edward Heath held a rather meaningless referendum in Northern Ireland, asking voters whether or not they wished to remain in the UK. The result was predictable and the referendum was boycotted by Nationalist voters. A more meaningful referendum was held in the province in 1998, when its citizens approved the Good Friday agreement.

The Good Friday agreement was also put to citizens in the Republic of Ireland by its government.

Below that level, there used to be local option at county level in Wales regarding whether or not public houses could open on Sundays. This system lasted from 1961 to 2003, when local option was repealed. So there is no shortage of precedents, and it cannot be disputed that apart from the obvious exception of local option, they have all involved constitutional change. Yet, we have been denied referenda, systematically, by governments on the Maastricht and Lisbon treaties which have diminished our national sovereignty and changed significantly our relationship with Europe. Equally, there was no referendum on incorporating the European Convention on Human Rights into British law, which has de facto ceded power to unelected foreign judges. I have already demolished the argument that its presence in the 1997 Labour manifesto was sufficient authority. In reality, the referenda we have had are actually plebiscites, whereby the government seeks approval for its plans rather than acting on popular concerns that transcend party politics. As a people, we need referenda to regain our sovereignty as a nation.

The current government has engaged in a lazy con trick regarding electronic petitions, whereby 100,000 signatures will force the Backbench Business Committee to consider scheduling a debate. Even if a debate takes place it is in no way binding on the government. The chances of such a vote triggering a successful no confidence motion against a recalcitrant government are zero. What faint glimmer there might have been has been extinguished by an entirely novel law enacted by the coalition government which brings in fixed term parliaments. So if our government loses a motion of confidence tomorrow, we still cannot have a general election until May 2015, unless the motion is carried by a two thirds majority. Unless the party system falls apart totally, this is physically impossible. There is more chance of spotting flying pigs. Fixed term parliaments are just another part of the conspiracy against the voter, and are particularly unacceptable when we are ruled by a coalition for which no-one voted. The Conservatives, shamefully, cannot even claim that it was in their manifesto. We need referenda to enfranchise the voter against the political elite and to compensate for the failings of the party system. It is crucial that all major constitutional changes are the subject of referenda. It is inconceivable that the monarchy would be abolished without a referendum. Why can't we have one on the proposed change to the rules of succession which previously gave precedence to the male line? Again, the government had no mandate for this change. We should have been asked. My own belief is that the country would have endorsed the change. It would have been democratic to put it to the test before putting it to Commonwealth heads of government. The same applies to House of Lords reform. The current situation is a mess that can be traced back to the well intentioned creation of non-hereditary peerages created by the Life Peerages Act of 1958. We need a Royal Commission on reform, composition and role of the House of Lords followed by a referendum.

Referenda should not be limited simply to internal constitutional matters. I offer three more examples, the power to declare war in certain circumstances, the imposition of the death penalty, and the funding of church schools. The first two are linked since both are about state sponsored killing. I readily accept that if our country is physically attacked or a friendly country is attacked and its survival is at risk, a good example being Kuwait in 1991, then a referendum is a non -starter for all the reasons that are obvious. However, in the case of premeditated decisions such as those to invade Afghanistan and later Iraq after 9/11, there was ample time to consult the electorate without endangering national security and without risking the survival of the lawful government of an ally. Foreign conflicts of necessity put at risk the lives of our young men, and increasingly young women. How much better it would be if Mr Blair had had the real support of the country for the invasion of Iraq, rather than relying on doctored intelligence, corrupted legal advice and deliberately deceiving the opposition leader under Privy Council conditions. Instead, our troops left some years later, our tails between our legs and only our reputation as America's poodle enhanced. The nightmare in Afghanistan goes on. If our leaders intend to behave as though we are the 51st State of America, then maybe the American Alliance should also be a matter for referendum. I have only a little doubt that the American Alliance and concomitant NATO membership, along with the possession of nuclear weapons would be approved in a referendum, much to my regret, but again the ability of our leaders to deal with our allies from a position of strength would be enhanced. A small majority would put America on notice regarding its behaviour.

As for the death penalty at home, I am personally opposed and would campaign against its reintroduction. However, as a democrat, I believe that it is time this particular boil was lanced and the people given a say. Pleased as I am that no executions have been carried out since 1964, I take no pleasure from the fact that the electorate has never been consulted about what is not a party political issue. I do not link corporal punishment and capital punishment as they serve different functions. A referendum on birching might horrify the Guardian reading elite, but the law abiding citizens forced to live on crime ridden estates who suffer on a daily basis, might have a different view and deserve to be heard. This is where the silenced majority lives, and lives in fear.

I have no personal objection to the existence of church schools and do not believe that their admission criteria are a matter for the state. However, there is one very obvious reason why the politically correct state is able to attack church schools with impunity. That is because for historic reasons they are funded almost entirely by the taxpayer rather than the faithful. A wealthy established church and a wealthy papacy are particular beneficiaries. There are no rational grounds, in my view, for taxpayer subsidy of religious proselytising and it is time we were asked whether we wish to continue with a system that has long been a historical anachronism. France and the USA are no less Christian countries for the absence of church schools. French Muslims are perfectly able to follow their faith without a state subsidy. If it follows logically that there is a referendum on whether or not we need an established church, a very major constitutional issue, then so be it. If my views put me in a minority, then so be it. It's called democracy and I want more of it.

However, it is essential to be clear where referenda should not apply. I do not think it is appropriate that the individual personal freedom of consenting adults is a matter for referenda. It is no more the legitimate right of single issue busybodies than it is of the state to abolish historic freedoms. There must be no power anywhere in a free society to prohibit as opposed to regulate alcohol consumption, no power to abolish sporting events such as the Grand National since intrinsic animal rights are as bogus a concept as intrinsic human rights, and no power to impose censorship on grounds of taste or sensibility, other than to protect children and those otherwise vulnerable. I have mentioned earlier in the text the situation in Wales whereby public houses could be closed by what was known as local option between 1961 and 2003. This is not democracy, but unrepresentative minorities enforcing their will regarding an activity that is lawful in the rest of the country in small areas where they predominate. It is only a question of time before some local government areas have Muslim majorities. It is not acceptable that people who constitute just less than 5% (2011 census figures) of the population of England and Wales as a whole could have the power to close down community facilities on the basis of verses in the Koran that are in any case open to interpretation. This would be an example of the tyranny of the minority, which we already experience at the hands of the political elite. I am not singling out Islam, merely pointing out the potential for intolerance to take hold where democracy is not both libertarian and vigilant. Local option is a dangerous and illiberal weapon. Thus, if brothels were to be legalised, it should apply nationwide. It is unlikely that one would be set up in the Outer Hebrides, the last bastion of strict Scottish Presbyterianism and if it were, one imagines it would soon close for lack of interest. However, the point is that there should be one law for all so that it protects the freedoms of all, rather than protecting those who wish to restrict freedom. That, of course, means there is no more room for Sharia law than there is for European law.

Another controversial subject is smoking. As a reformed smoker, I gave up in 1980, I regard it as a noxious habit and am glad that I no longer have to run the gauntlet of smokers at a public bar and walk away with a clean suit stinking of tobacco. However, smoking behind one's front door is a matter for the individual and not a matter for me and the majority like me who do not smoke. Smoking is regulated and taxed, and the taxes raised are far in excess of what is necessary to tackle tobacco related health problems. Gambling is likewise regulated and taxed. Referenda should never be available to use for campaigns to re-criminalise abortion and homosexuality, or to copy certain American states which still have criminal sanctions for adultery. Matters of faith and sexual morality are a matter for individual believers and religious communities. I respect individual piety, but religious totalitarianism is not compatible with a free and democratic society. Sexual behaviour can be regulated in other ways. Shame has never appeared on the statute book but community disapproval, as expressed by shunning those whose lawful sexual behaviour has shattered families, has always been an effective weapon. The government can also regulate sexual incontinence by remodelling the welfare state and tightening divorce laws so that it does not reward those who believe that they can bring into the world unlimited children with no visible means of support, and those who see marriage as a contract well worth abrogating in order to obtain a free house at the expense of a blameless spouse.

I have advocated regaining sovereignty from Europe and thence replacing the Sovereignty of Parliament with the Sovereignty of the People. To achieve this, I have proposed the use of primary elections, the expansion of offices that are held by election rather than appointment, and the wider use of referenda for constitutional matters, and matters of life and death such as war and the power to execute murderers. Underpinning this, there needs to be the written constitution alluded to earlier in this chapter. It must guarantee our independence as a nation and free us from the tyranny of foreign courts such as ECHR and other foreign jurisdictions such as the European Commission. It follows that there is one legal code for all, in front of which we are all equal. The freedom to police our own borders is an essential component. It must enshrine free speech, freedom of association and a free press. It must elevate the rights of the law abiding above those of the lawless. It is vital that any such constitution focuses on responsibilities as well as rights. No one should be eligible for compensation as a consequence of an injury sustained during the commission of a criminal act. It must guarantee the rights of property not just against squatters but against the state in all but limited circumstances. It must prescribe and circumscribe the power of the police, and when the government can deploy emergency powers. It must impose responsibilities on parents to discipline their children and empower individual teachers to impose moderate and reasonable discipline where parents cannot or will not. It goes without saying that it should outlaw discrimination based on irrational and irrelevant grounds such as race, gender or sexuality, but not grant privileges. The place of referenda and electoral procedures must be specified. A threshold of 250,000 signatures sounds about right. Procedures to change the constitution must be specified. Here we can learn from the Americans. It will be a British document that represents our people and our culture, not an unrepresentative elite and its revolutionary agenda. Finally, it will need to be interpreted where disputes occur and where referenda are sought by a permanent constitutional commission able to rule decisively about what is and what is not constitutional. The sacrifice of sovereignty should never be possible without a three quarters majority in a referendum, so that never again can unrepresentative elites deliver our freedoms to European institutions to do with as they see fit.

It may be that the reader can add to this list. At the very least, it should be thought provoking. With every passing day the hi-jacking of our history and cultural identity, our freedoms and our sovereignty by an unrepresentative revolutionary elite marches on relentlessly in its mission, which is to make the process irreversible and complete a conquest from within as complete as that achieved by William the Conqueror after the Battle of Hastings.

Lightning Source UK Ltd.
Milton Keynes UK
UKOW04f1359101014

239926UK00001B/2/P